The Fort in Fort Worth

The Fort in Fort Worth

by

Clay Perkins, M.D.

Cross-Timbers Heritage Publishing Company
Keller, Texas

Cross-Timbers Heritage Publishing Company
(an affiliate of Cross-Timbers Area Heritage Promotion Corporation)
1520 Scot Lane
Keller TX 76248
Metro (817) 498-5150
FAX (817) 581-7663
Email wytclt1@airmail.net
www.cross-timbers.org

Printed in the United States of America

05 04 03 02 01 5 4 3 2 1

Library of Congress Cataloging-in-Publication Data

Perkins, Clay, 1963-
The fort in Fort Worth / by Clay Perkins
p. cm.
Includes bibliographical references.
ISBN 1-930566-09-3 (Hard cover : alk. paper) — ISBN 1-930566-10-7 (Trade paper : alk. paper)
1. Fort Worth (Tex.)—History. 2. Fort Worth (Tex.)—History, Military. 3. Fortification—Texas—Fort Worth—History. 4. Frontier and pioneer life—Texas—Fort Worth Region. 5. Indians of North America—Wars—Texas—Fort Worth Region. 6. United States. Army—History—19th century. I. Title.
F394.F7 P47 2001
976.4'5315—dc21

2001004763

Cover and book design and layout by D. & F. Scott Publishing, Inc.,
North Richland Hills, Texas

This book is dedicated to
all of those who encouraged and helped me
and to the men and women who,
despite the hardships and hard work,
built the foundation for our city.

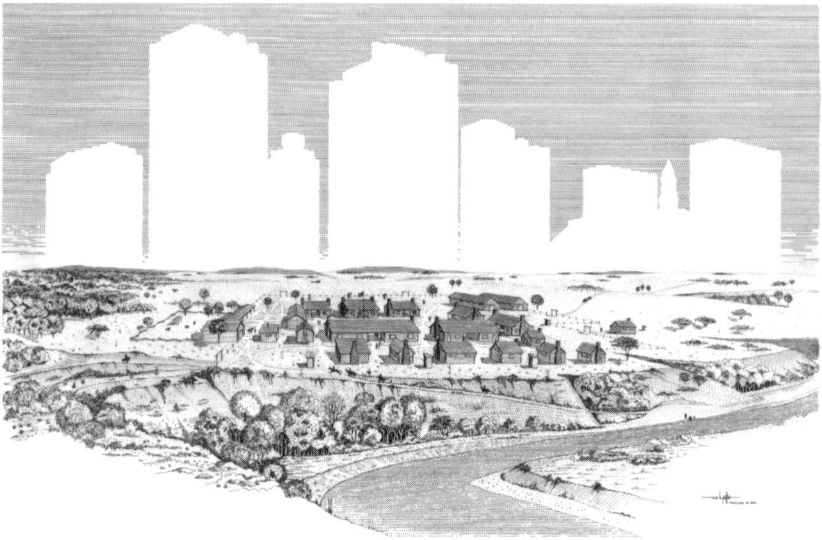

Fort Worth: The Seed for the City

This sketch shows the fort with the skyline of the modern city silhouetted in the background. This graphically shows that the fort was the seed for the city. The artist shows the river bending a bit too soon, but it highlights the river. The road going down the slope to the river was a street that existed until the 1949 flood. If you look up the head of the road, you will see a road heading south. This either became Main or Houston. The road in front of the barracks was Bluff Street, and this area too, has been eroded somewhat. We think the road through the middle of the parade group was Belknap, and the one in front of the officers quarters was Weatherford, but we have no definite proof. It seems like the modern streets would be built on the original ones, but we can't be sure. We know that Belknap was the road to Belknap and crossed the river somewhere below the fort. Weatherford was the road to that city, and crossed the river near the seventh street bridge. (Copyright William Potter.)

Contents

Contents

Preface

When I was growing up in Fort Worth, we learned in school that Maj. Ripley Allen Arnold founded the city in 1849. Later, as a cadet at West Point, I found that Ripley Arnold had also been a cadet at the academy, and that he may have written a famous song still sung there. I was curious to know more about Maj. Arnold and the old army post in Fort Worth.

I left the army in 1991 to start a career in medicine. When I came home during school breaks and my residency, I began looking for information about the frontier fort, and found that very little had been written about it. I decided to research the history of the fort and write a book.

My goal was to include as much information about the fort in Fort Worth as possible. I had to describe the military situation in Texas at the time to put the story in context. What happened here was affected by events throughout the state and the country. I hope this book will be useful to historians and those who want to know what happened here more than 150 years ago.

Many people helped me in this work. My parents, Brian and Larue Perkins, encouraged me and paid for much of my research. My wife, Cassandra, read each chapter several times and made valuable suggestions. Local historian, Mary Curtis, donated her research files. Carolyn Selzer and Alex Troup of Dallas gave me important information about Gouhenant and Icaria. Stan Hoig gave me the newspaper story about the "Battle of Fort Worth." Christoph Nguyen, M.D., helped me with the French translation. Jim Marrs and Dink Starnes encouraged my interest in the subject, and Michael Meier at the National Archives patiently showed me where to find the original documents concerning the fort. I wish to thank them and the many others who were kind enough to help me with my research, including Dr. Donald Worchester, a well-known author who helped edit the final manuscript. Finally, I want to thank Willard and Cinda Thomas for their hard work and dedication in publishing this book.

Dr. Claude Clayton (Clay) Perkins
The Fort in Fort Worth, 2001

Publisher's Prologue

Go back with me more than 150 years in time to a bluff above a junction where the Clear Fork and the West Fork of the Trinity River flow together and become one.

The riverbeds are lush with tall trees and would, from above, look like three wide, green ribbons tied in a bow. Between these river ribbons is a broad expanse of prairie stretching eighty miles north to the Red River and three hundred miles south to the Gulf of Mexico. Where we are standing, this prairie is framed a few miles to the east and a few more to the west by dense forests varying in width from five to fifty miles and so thick with trees and thorny vines that they form an almost impenetrable barrier. They are the Upper and Lower, or Eastern and Western, Cross-Timbers. They give this area one of its names—"The Cross-Timbers."

East of the eastern forest another river, the Elm Fork, joins the east flowing ribbon, and from these rivers the area gets its other name—"The Three Forks of the Trinity."

Out on the prairie, we see buffalo and deer grazing. Beside the timbered creek beds near the rivers, with an abundance of wildlife, we see people living in villages of thatched houses that look like large haystacks or beehives. We also see a few teepees and cabins. Along the creeks, we see narrow fields planted with corn, yams, and other vegetables.

Altogether it is a serene scene, but the bluff is about to become the epicenter of a tornado of change that will temporarily alter that peace. The prevailing wind of migration from the east-southeast is going to become a tornado when four gale forces crash together here and change this prairie and this forest from a wilderness to a metropolis. The change will be far more sweeping and destructive than the tornado that swept through this same place in the spring of the year 2000.

The prevailing wind is the constant push of "Native Americans," or "Indians," westward from the Atlantic and northward from the Gulf of Mexico. They are being pushed into a few tribes who have lived in The Three Forks Area for years. Those doing the pushing are the "Euro-Americans," or "Whites." The Indian War, the longest war in American history, did not start in Texas: it started on the Atlantic Coast and the Gulf Coast in the early 1500s. It is now coming to this bluff.

Churning up this constant breeze of movement are four gale forces. Let's call these forces the *greeners*, the *hawks*, the *doves* and the *misers*. These forces exist on the sides of both the Native (Asian) Americans and Euro-Americans. In other words, both have them.

Greeners see the grass on the other side of the fence as greener, or better. The land, the water, the women, the game, the shelter, etc. are always more desirable on the other side. Hawks use or advocate the use of force to aid the greeners on their side and protect them from greeners on the other side. Doves want to talk, bargain, or buy the things their greeners want. Misers don't want to spend money in the process.

Keeping these four gales balanced is another force. Let's call this force *knights*. They are public servants who take on the job of calming conflicts. If the conflict is with those of a different government or society we use the word "soldiers" or the phrase "armed forces" although, in this area, they are sometimes called "rangers." If the conflict is within our own government or society, we call them "police." These are the people about whom you will read in this book. Sometimes the only way to fight fire is with fire.

Before 1836, when Texas became a Republic, only a few people of Wichita and Caddo origin lived around this bluff. It is on the boundary of Comancheria, a vast area that includes the western parts of Texas, Oklahoma, and Kansas, and the eastern parts of New Mexico and Colorado. Comancheria is bounded on the east by the Cross-Timbers and on the west by the Rocky Mountains. The Comanche tribes and their allies, the Kiowas, who roam this area on horseback, kill or capture anyone who dares move onto the Great Plains. If not for the Comanches and their allies, Texas would probably still be part of Mexico. The Spanish, and then the Mexicans, could not stop the mounted raiders from the plains. They let the Americans settle south and west of the Red River only to provide a "white" buffer between themselves and the Comanches.

The eastern tribes being pushed here—the Iroquois, Delawares, Cherokees, Choctaws, Chickasaws, Creeks, Kickapoos and Seminoles—are farmers who depend on planting and reaping. Like the whites, they supplement their produce by hunting the abundant game, and many own slaves—both black and native. However, they are in the way of the constant westward advance of whites.

There were variations in culture between the western tribes like the Comanches, Kiowas, Apaches, Sioux, etc., but their distinguishing trait is that they were hunters who depended on the bison or buffalo for their food, clothing, and shelter. They gathered some produce, berries, and roots on the plains, but their primary occupation was following buffalo herds from the south to the north and back again. They also owned or captured slaves, some of whom were white.

Prior to 1836, the Spanish and Mexicans visited this area, but the Comanches did not let them linger. The eastern natives were being pushed into the area, and they survived by staying out of sight. The Cross-Timbers and the edges of the prairie between them provided a place to hide and survive. Now Texans are coming from both east and south. They see the wood and fertile land in the Cross-Timbers and the forage on the prairie. The aggressive Comanches as well as the farming tribes living in the Three Forks area push back by raiding whites along the Red River and in east Texas. Something has to be done to protect settlers from the raiders of the Three Forks.

The first president of the Republic of Texas, Sam Houston, is a dove. He and Indian Agent Robert Simpson Neighbors want to draw a line across Texas from northeast to southwest and keep greeners on both sides back of the line. They hope to reserve more than three-fourths of the new Republic of Texas for Indians.

His successor, Mirabeau B. Lamar, is a hawk. He wants to drive the Indians and Mexicans out of the republic, which then included all of eastern New Mexico and parts of Kansas, Oklahoma, and Colorado. He sends the Texas Army and Texas Rangers to drive the Indians to Oklahoma. This opens the Three Forks area for an increasing and accelerating foray of white men.

Houston returns in 1842 to reverse the expulsion and try again to establish a boundary line. In 1843, the eastern natives and some of the Caddos and Wichitas sign a treaty and a line is drawn. However, no one consults the Comanches, Apaches, Kickapoos, Kiowas, and others.

The line runs through the bluff on which we are standing. Trading houses are to be built on the line to trade the green from one side to the other. A trading house is built near here on the Clear Fork in 1843, but Indians close it by capturing the traders and seizing their goods. Unfortunately, only doves pay any attention to the line. Hawks demand that rangers be stationed along the line to keep the Indian greeners on their side. However, the misers in the Texas Congress erase funds for patrolling the line.

In December 1845, the greener problem passes to the hawks, doves, misers and knights in the United States of America—Texas is admitted as the twenty-eighth state of the union. The U.S. hawks have just finished having their knights drive the Seminoles down into the Everglades or out to Indian Territory.

However, first they will have to deal with the Mexicans, who have not given up their claim to the Nueces strip, which includes all of south Texas and much of southwest Texas. During the next two and a half years, the American army, including volunteers from Texas, will focus to the south on the Mexicans. Only a few Texas Rangers would protect the frontier line, and greeners, hawks, doves, and misers on both sides will die.

In 1848 and 1849, the soldiers who fought the Mexicans return to Texas and begin stringing out along the line drawn five years before by Houston and Neighbors. Many eastern Americans and many of the military leaders in Texas want to establish the reservations that Houston wanted ten years ago. He is in Washington as a United States Senator from Texas, and he pushes his viewpoint. There is a problem though: when Texas was admitted to the United States—the only independent nation to voluntarily join the union— he public lands remain the property of the state. The misers in the U.S. Congress will not pay the state for land for the reservations, and the misers in the Texas Legislature are not going to give it to the Indians.

The army begins building a series of forts along the Houston-Neighbors line and on June 6, 1849, a fort arises on the bluff on which we are standing. It is named Fort Worth. When it opens, the gales begin to calm down on our bluff and by 1853 blow the Indians farther west and north. Once again the Mexicans are threatening war, and to meet this threat, the fort is closed. With that, our story will close.

You see, each person dealing with the fort is a greener, a hawk, a dove, a miser, or a knight, and how they interact will make the story of the life and times of this fort. One can compare the situation on the bluff from 1849–1853 to the situation in Israel and Palestine in current times—two cultures fighting for the right to live in the same space.

We owe a debt of respect to the men who built the fort. Eleven of them died while serving here, and their physical remains are buried on the bluff. A few of the children and a number of the men who served here and died later are buried in the same cemetery, including Gen. Edward Tarrant and Maj. Ripley Arnold. Most of them were not "native born," but came from Ireland, England, Germany, and other European countries. The most important aspect of paying our debt is letting the younger generation know the truth about war and the way the west, and every other direction, has been won. If we teach them that the hawks are evil and that war is unnecessary and that knights are to blame, they will become doves who will be dominated by hawks from the other side.

The book you are about to read is the story of that storm as it revolved on and around this bluff. It was researched and written by Claude Clayton (Clay) Perkins, M.D. Clay was born and raised near the bluff, graduating from Paschal High School and, like many of the officers who served at the Fort in Fort Worth, was appointed to the U.S. Military Academy. Dropping out after two years, he went to Israel to live and work on a kibbutz, but returned to West Point and received a commission as an infantry officer. After finishing his military service, he went to Baylor Medical School and earned his M.D. He wants, like the publisher, to let the younger generation know about the fort and what it did, and to help them see that it took a war to win the west. We would not be here today if we had not been blessed with men and women who would fight for the right to live here in peace. He also wanted the story to be factual, and spent years researching it as a recreational break from his medical studies. Many of the stories about the fort he had heard growing up here turned out to be incomplete or just plain incorrect, but the real story is more interesting than the "war stories" told years later.

William B. Potter created the drawings of the fort included in the book as part of a project to recreate the fort. They are based on detailed research and descriptions, especially the quartermaster's report of Col. William G. Freeman in September 1853. Freeman's sketch, Figure Q, along with other descriptions and comparisons gives us a good view of what the fort looked like. It was a small fort, originally built to house fewer than seventy-five people. It would be cramped and disappointing in both size and appearance to modern eyes. However, to settlers here at the time, it was big and beautiful. It still is to those who appreciate its function rather than the appearance. Most importantly, the fort brought about the city of Fort Worth.

To help make the story more readable, we have moved some of the details to footnotes and some detailed quotes to an appendix. The book is based as much as possible on primary sources of information. Serious students will want to read the footnotes and appendix as they read each chapter to get the best feeling for what those who were there said and felt about the situation.

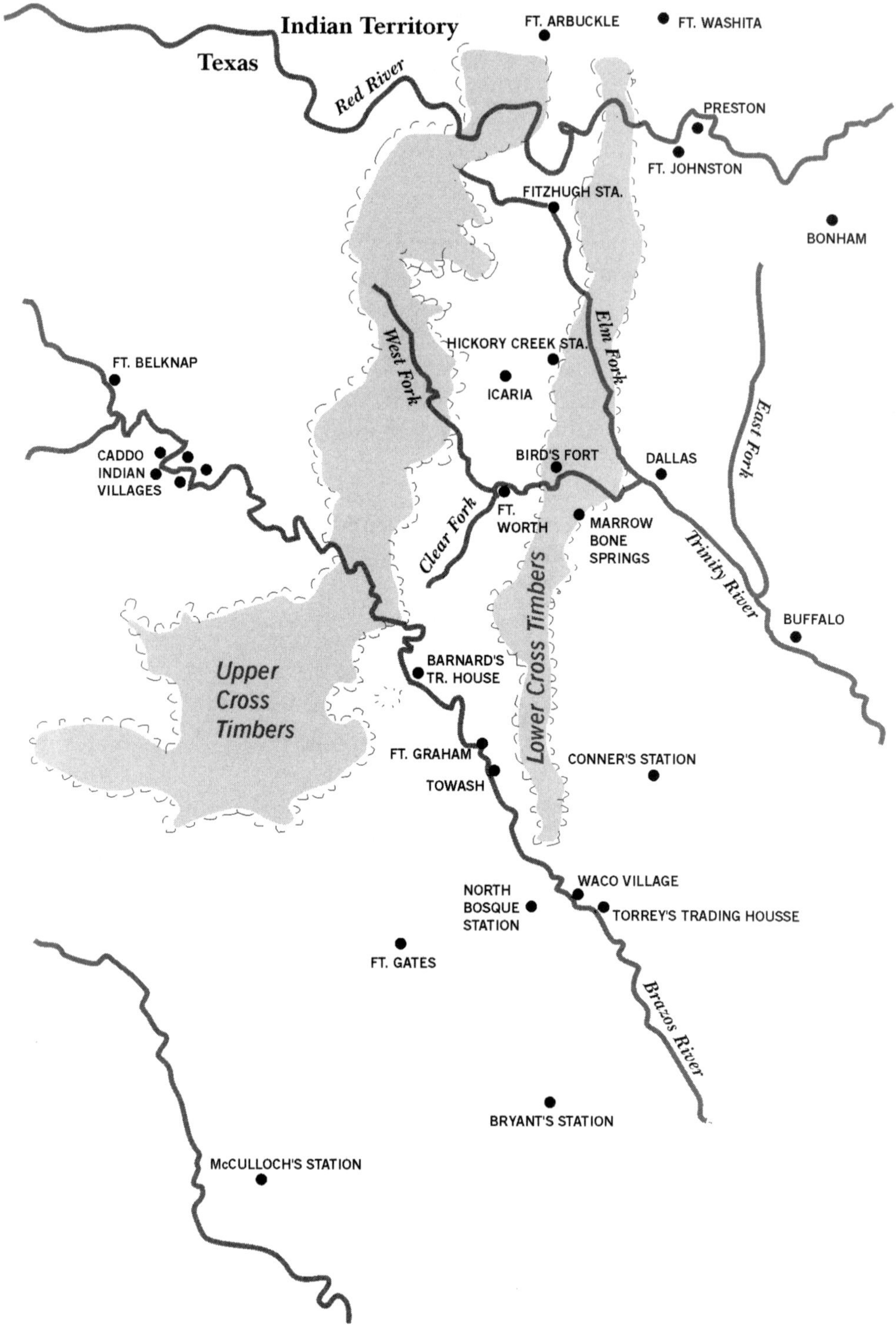

Indian Territory
Texas
Red River
FT. ARBUCKLE
FT. WASHITA
PRESTON
FT. JOHNSTON
FITZHUGH STA.
BONHAM
West Fork
Elm Fork
HICKORY CREEK STA.
ICARIA
FT. BELKNAP
East Fork
CADDO
INDIAN
VILLAGES
BIRD'S FORT
DALLAS
FT.
WORTH
Clear Fork
MARROW
BONE
SPRINGS
Trinity River
Lower Cross Timbers
BUFFALO
BARNARD'S
TR. HOUSE
Upper
Cross
Timbers
FT. GRAHAM
TOWASH
CONNER'S STATION
NORTH
BOSQUE
STATION
WACO VILLAGE
TORREY'S TRADING HOUSSE
FT. GATES
Brazos River
BRYANT'S STATION
McCULLOCH'S STATION

1

Before the Fort

Let's begin the story of Fort Worth in 1837, the year after the Republic of Texas won its independence from the Republic of Mexico.

We could start millions of years ago with the geologic formations that produced the soil and environment on which the Cross-Timbers will grow and through which the Trinity River flows. The Cross-Timbers are the dominant geographical feature. They consist of dense forests of post oak and blackjack oak trees made almost impenetrable by thorny vines and bushes. It was, and still is in some places, so thick it was called the "Cast Iron Forest." On a map, the Cross-Timbers is shaped like a giant rugged cross with the body stretching about seven hundred miles from central Texas to southern Kansas and two cross arms stretching about four hundred miles through central Oklahoma. It is like a dense garden in the middle of a vast prairie.

At the Red River, the body splits into two legs stretching south. The western leg is known as the Western or Upper Cross-Timbers because it is on higher ground. The eastern leg is known conversely as the Eastern, or Lower Cross-Timbers. Between these two legs is a sea of grass known as the Grand Prairie. The Trinity River drains this area. Fort Worth is located on the Trinity between the two legs. The Trinity and the Cross-Timbers would dictate the location of the fort; however, it was only a geographic feature and not an active part of our story.

We could start hundreds of years ago with the Spanish, French, and American expeditions into Texas. Or we could start with the white settlements to the south, the east, and the northeast along the

Red River because they pushed the Indians from the areas they were occupying into the lands of tribes that had been here for years.

We could start our story with the Indians who occupied this bluff above the Three Forks in the Cross-Timbers. Most of the tribes in the area were part of the Caddo Confederacy, which included a number of groups speaking a similar language. They had occupied eastern Texas and the adjoining regions for at least a thousand years.[1] They lived in villages of thatched conical huts which, to white visitors, resembled beehives or haystacks. They raised corn and other vegetables and supplemented their diet by hunting.

The Kichai tribe had lived on the Upper Trinity since the early 1700s.[2] The Wichitas lived along the Red River to the west of them. The Wacos also roamed across much of north and central Texas. One of their villages then stood on the Brazos River where Waco is located.[3] The Anadarkos and Ionis, both Caddo tribes, were refugees from Louisiana and East Texas. Their villages were strung along the Trinity and Brazos River valley.

Other tribes, not related to the Caddos, also lived in the area. The Kickapoos, Delawares, and Shawnees were recent immigrants from the East Coast of the United States.[4] They had been escaping west for more than two hundred years, and many of the Delawares were guides, interpreters, and scouts for the whites.

The Comanches, Kiowas, and Apaches roamed the Great Plains to the west. They were stronger, more mobile, and more aggressive than the Caddos and other agriculturally-based tribes because they lived by hunting, supplemented with trading and raiding. However, they preferred to raid the Texans and Mexicans to the south, who had more, but didn't have the Cross-Timbers for protection.

However, we will start in 1837, with the first documented events that would lead to the fort. The upper Trinity River Valley was still a safe haven for the Indians living here. All of these tribes were raiding into Texas and Mexico, taking anything and anyone they could carry, and destroying or killing the rest. It was a need to stop the Indian raids that brought the first Texans into the area.

Sam Houston, the first elected president of the Republic of Texas, took office in October 1836. During his first two-year term, he sought accommodation for and coexistence with the Indians. He hoped to establish reservations in both east and north Texas and let them stay where, or near where, they were living. However, his efforts failed—the reservations never materialized, and Indian attacks were a constant danger.

One settler who came to North Texas in 1836 recalled the period from 1836 through 1841 as "five years of constant warfare."[5] To fight the war and to protect citizens near the frontier, the republic raised volunteer companies of mounted men. Known as rangers, they enlisted for short terms, usually six months or a year, and provided their own horses, arms, clothing, and equipment.[6] They were among the first whites to visit the upper Brazos and Trinity River valleys.

In 1837, Texas Ranger Lt. A. B. Benthuysen described a patrol through this region. This is the first specific documentation about events in or near the area. He and seventeen rangers left their station on the Little River (near today's Temple) on October 13, 1837, and followed a trail of stolen horses to the northwest. On November 4, the rangers crossed the forks of the Brazos, possibly about seventy-five miles west of where the Fort in Fort Worth would be built. The men followed "shod horse tracks going in a northeasterly direction." Benthuysen's report of the patrol continues as follows:

> On the 10th on the headwaters of the Trinity, I fell in with a large body of Indians in a moving position towards the southwest. I first supposed them to be Kechies, but was afterwards informed that they were Toweash, Whacos & a few Kechies & Caddoes; I got this information from the Shawnees and Delawares. I judged the Indians to be about one hundred & fifty strong. About fifty or sixty of them were armed with rifles, and the balance had bows & arrows.
>
> I stationed my men in a point of timber to defend ourselves. About three o'clock the Indians made a charge upon us and completely surrounded our position when they commenced firing from their Rifles upon us. They had fired eight or ten shots before we returned their fire. There was a continual firing kept up on both sides until about half past four at not more than pistol shot apart, when we had the good fortune to kill their principal Chief, when they retreated a short distance and ceased firing. I flattered myself that the action was done. Up to this time we had four men and six horses killed.
>
> In about fifteen minutes the savages again advanced and fired the woods on three sides of us. The fourth side was prairie, where their horsemen with bows & arrows were stationed. Our only alternative was to charge through those Indians who were armed with Rifles, in preference to those who were armed with bows and arrows. As we could not move our horses through the fire we left them.
>
> Sixteen [sic] of us charged about fifty Indians and drove them before us. Six more of my party fell dead in making the charge. Eight came through alive but three out of the eight were wounded . . .

> Mr. Bostwick, after being shot through the body, loaded & fired his Rifle three times & had the fourth load in his gun when he expired in the act of drawing his ramrod from his Rifle. Young Cooper insisted that we should help him up and let him fight after securing a death shot.
>
> After breaking through the Indians we commenced our retreat on foot. We had just crossed the skirt of timber when we again came in sight of the Indians. They did not attempt to pursue us but stood and looked at us. They had enough of the fight for we had killed about fifty of their warriors.
>
> Nov. 20th ten days after the fight we arrived at the Eye & Caddo village or camp. We first discovered an Indian on the prairie. We followed him to his village. When we arrived there, we found the warriors drawn up to receive us in a hostile manner. They were all armed with Rifles & the Squaws had Bows & Arrows. I expected nothing else but we should have to fight them, but after a good deal of parleying, they said that our little party might stay there that night. We then dressed the wounds of the men and camped in the midst of the hostile camp. On the 21st we crossed the River Trinity at three Forks. That evening we arrived at the Kickapoo village, who were very friendly and treated us with the utmost hospitality.[7]

Benthuysen wrote his report from Houston on December 8, 1837. He mentioned few landmarks, but his account suggests that the fight took place in the country northwest of Fort Worth. A historical marker located just north of Decatur, Texas, in Wise County, asserts that the battle took place on two nearby hills known as the Knobs. Another marker in Young County claims that the battle took place north of Graham.

One year after Benthuysen's patrol, Jonathan Dyer, a general of the Red River County militia, led an expedition from the northeast against the Indian villages on the upper Trinity and killed a few Indians. However, Dyer found that little rain had fallen, and consequently, there was not enough grass to support his men's horses:

> I sent most of my men home and went with eighty men within two miles of the Caddo Village, but could not make much discovery, being on the most westerly fork of the Trinity, and destitute of provisions, we were obliged to return. I could find but very few Indians. We had a skirmish with some Caddoes. We killed six and we had two men wounded.[8]

While Dyer and his militia were on the upper Trinity, three hundred Indians attacked a party of surveyors about fifty miles to the south, in what is now western Navarro County. On October 8, 1838, twenty-five surveyors were ambushed and driven into a ravine. About eighteen surveyors were killed. The survivors returned to the battlefield later, and buried the dead near the site of today's Dawson.[9]

Later in October, Texas Brig. Gen. Thomas Jefferson Rusk began planning a three-pronged attack into the Three Forks for December. He would lead a force from the east, Dyer would come from the north, and Brig. Gen. Mosley Baker would come up from the south. The expedition was weakened by diversions to other areas and lack of food for men and horse.[10]

Mirabeau B. Lamar succeeded Sam Houston as president of the Republic of Texas on December 10, 1838. He wanted to drive the Indians out of Texas, and he authorized a series of expeditions to clear all the Indians from the republic. In the summer of 1839, Texas militia drove the Cherokee Indians from east Texas.[11] As the Indians were pushed out of east Texas, whites began to move into the Three Forks region. Surveyors were working in the area by 1839. However, they were liable to being attacked and killed at any time.[12]

To protect whites advancing from the east, the Texas Congress voted to establish a line of forts to defend what was then the western frontier. The line would stretch from the Nueces River in the south to the Red River in the north. To connect the frontier forts, a military road would be needed. Construction of the "Military Road" began in August 1840, when about two hundred infantrymen under Col. William Cooke marched north from Austin. The expedition crossed the Brazos at the Waco village and continued north to the Trinity, following the approximate route of today's Interstate Highway 35 and 35 East.

They crossed the Trinity near Dallas, and made their way to the Red River. Cooke and his men established outposts at the Cedar Springs crossing (in today's Dallas) and on the Red River. The Red River post (a few miles west of today's Denison) was named Fort Johnston, probably in honor of Albert Sidney Johnston, Lamar's Secretary of War.[13]

President Lamar's campaigns made east Texas safe for settlers, but bankrupted the treasury. In the spring of 1841, the Texas Congress disbanded the army. Cooke's soldiers returned to Austin for discharge. Although the forts were abandoned, the road became an important route for pioneers. Settlers could travel directly from Austin to the Red River for the first time.[14] The fight would now be left up to the local settlers.

Texas Militia Brig. Gen. Edward Hamilton Tarrant, the man for whom the county would later be named, had served in the Texas Congress and had been involved in the two Dyer campaigns. His men called him "Old Hurricane." In May 1841, he assembled sixty-nine settlers at the abandoned Fort Johnston for another attempt to drive the Indians from the upper Trinity. Tarrant believed there was a large Indian village somewhere in the area. Indians from this village were believed to be attacking and stealing from the settlers to the northeast and east.

On May 24, 1841, they discovered more than two hundred Indian lodges along Village Creek, which now forms part of the boundary between Fort Worth and Arlington. The settlers attacked, and in a running fight along the banks of the creek, Tarrant's men killed about a dozen Indians. The Texans halted their attack after Indians shot and killed Capt. John Denton, and the Texans realized that the village stretched for miles—they were outnumbered.[15]

In July, Tarrant returned to Village Creek with four hundred men, but the village had been abandoned. He ordered Maj. Jonathan Bird and a hundred volunteers to construct a fort and secure the area. Bird began building an outpost on the Trinity in the late summer of 1841 near the south end of Main Street in present-day Euless, east of Fort Worth. Bird's volunteers expected to claim the open land near the fort. They did not realize that Congress had recently granted the area to the Texas Land and Emigration Company, known as the Peters Colony. When the volunteers discovered that they could not claim the land, they abandoned the fort.[16]

The Texas Emigration and Land Company was established to encourage settlement. The company was to provide colonists with supplies and homes; in return, the company would receive title to one half of the land in the grant, which included most of north central Texas. The company succeeded in bringing several hundred settlers to north Texas. However, it lacked the funds to fulfill its basic obligations, such as surveying and assigning tracts. Non-colony settlers moved into the area, and created a tangle of claims that was not resolved until 1853.[17]

After Bird's men left their fort, a few settlers moved into the buildings. They stayed on through the spring of 1842, but Indian attacks, supply problems, and other hardships led them to abandon the site. They retreated about fifteen miles to the east, to where John Neely Bryan, Dallas's first settler, had been living for a few months. Bryan married the daughter of one of the Bird's Fort pioneers.[18]

Sam Houston was reelected to a second term as president of Texas, and succeeded Lamar in December 1841. He immediately reversed Lamar's policy of fighting the Indians and sought peace. Meeting the leaders of ten tribes at the site of Bird's Fort, he signed a new peace treaty on September 29, 1843.[19] This treaty provided most of the information known about the Indian situation in the area at that time. Among the signers was Jose Maria, chief of the Anadarko. He was a respected leader among the Indians, and he came to represent many bands in their dealings with whites.[20]

The key provision of the treaty was a boundary between Indian lands and lands open to white settlement. This "line" idea formed the basis for Indian policy in Texas for years. Indians would be forbidden to go below the boundary line, and whites were forbidden to go above it. The line would be marked by a series of licensed trading houses. Indians would be able to live in peace on their side of the boundary and could exchange furs for manufactured goods with the traders. The trading houses would be augmented with Texas Ranger stations in 1846, and replaced by U.S. Army posts, such as Fort Worth, in 1848 and 1849.

Houston licensed Norman Chatfield and A. G. Kimbell to open Trading House #1 on the Trinity. Two employees, Edward Terrell and John P. Lusk, opened for business on the Clear Fork near its junction with the West Fork. They trapped and traded for about a year, but the venture died when hostile Indians took the two men captive. They escaped from their captors, fled the area, and did not return for years.[21]*

In 1845, Mathias Travis and Isaac Spence obtained permission to reestablish the trading house on the Trinity. On September 9, 1845, Spence wrote to officials in Austin that he was setting up the business at Marrow Bone Springs, about fifteen miles east of where Terrell and Lusk had stayed. A Texas Ranger officer, Thomas I. Smith, had guided him to the springs:

> I have stopped at what is called the Marrow Bone Spring in the Lower Cross Timbers about two or three miles from the West Fork of the Trinity river the same place where a council was held with Indians some two or three years ago. Col. T. I. Smith went with me to the spot in company with two Indian Chiefs and pointed it out as the most suitable place for the Trading House and the one where all the Indians wish it to be placed. I have put up a House 36 feet long by 16 feet wide with a frame roof, covered with two foot boards nailed and enclosed with half logs as pickets fastened together in a substantial manner, I am putting up some other necessary outbuildings for our convenience com-

*Their cabin was probably southwest of downtown Fort Worth. Different accounts give conflicting information concerning the site. In a 1905 interview, the reporter states that it stood on the western edge of today's hospital district. Timmons and Knox quote sources that seem to place it closer to the Tanglewood subdivision, others place it in the botanical gardens.

> fort and security all of which I am having enclosed with strong and substantial pickets.[22]

Travis's and Spence's trading house was evidently no more successful than the first venture. After October 1845, it disappeared from the historical record. The site, and perhaps the buildings, became a ranger station the following year.*

Houston also licensed Torrey and Company to operate Trading House #2 on the Brazos. John Torrey and his brothers, David and Thomas, had operated stores and trading houses in Texas since 1838. They built the new business about eight miles down river from the abandoned Waco Village in early 1844. Their business flourished, became a center of commerce and government, and developed into the city of Waco.[23]

Three months after Spence wrote his letter from Marrow Bone Springs, the U.S. Congress gave final approval to the annexation of Texas. Texas became the twenty-eighth state of the Union on December 29, 1845. President Anson Jones lowered the Texas flag in Austin on February 19, 1846, and transferred power to a state government. Mexico, however, had never recognized Texas's independence, and annexation quickly sparked a war with Mexico.

When Texas became part of the U.S., the federal government in Washington assumed responsibility for the defense of the frontier. The U.S. Army sent three companies of dragoons to Texas in September 1845. Dragoons were mounted soldiers trained to fight on horseback.†

Companies A, G, & I of the 2nd Dragoons left Fort Washita, Oklahoma on September 13, 1845, in accordance with General Order 37.[24] The command reached Austin on October 10. Companies A and G rode on to San Antonio, arriving October 28.[25] When the Mexican War began, the dragoons were ordered south to become the mounted force of Gen. Zachary Taylor's army. This left the frontier with neither rangers nor soldiers for protection.

Lietenant Colonel William S. Harney, the executive officer of the 2nd Dragoons, was the senior U.S. Army officer in Texas, and he took steps to remedy this situation. On June 26, 1846, Harney asked the governor to raise five companies of mounted volunteers to defend the frontier.[26] Texans hurried to enlist in the new ranger companies and they were ready for duty by August.

---

* This site, which would soon be called Johnson Station, is along Johnson Creek in Founders Park in south central Arlington.

† The name *dragoon* would be replaced by the name *cavalry* in 1855 and the 2nd Dragoons would become the 2nd Cavalry in 1861.

Lieutenant Governor A. C. Horton positioned ranger companies at Castroville, San Antonio, and Bryant's Station (about eighteen miles southeast of today's Temple). A fourth ranger company went to Torrey's Trading House on the Brazos. The fifth company was stationed in the trading house at Marrow Bone Springs.[27]

The rangers arrived at their stations in about August 1846.[28] Captain Andrew Stapp's company of Collin County men provided their own horses, guns, and supplies.[29] John Neely Bryan organized a ranger company around the new village of Dallas but since the governor already had five companies, he could not accept Bryan's men for service.[30]

Stapp was free to position his men as he thought best.[31] He decided to establish an outpost on the Elm Fork of the Trinity, about ten miles south of the Red River.* It was set up about September 18, 1846.[32] William Fitzhugh was commander.[33]

The governor wanted Stapp to divide his men into two squads, so it seems likely that the command continued to use the camp at Marrow Bone springs.[34] In any case, the Trinity River trading house remained his official station.[35] The rangers at the Brazos Station apparently set up an outpost on Richland Creek and called it Smith's Station, for their commander, Thomas I. Smith.[36] The Brazos River Station remained his official position.[37]

Lieutenant Governor Horton ordered his rangers to send a messenger or patrol to adjacent stations at least twice each month. Since Capt. Stapp's men were at the northern end of the line, they would maintain contact with Fort Washita,[38] a U.S. Army post in the Indian Territory, located near Durant, Oklahoma about forty-five miles northeast of the Elm Fork Station.[39] Preston, a settlement on the Texas side of the Red River, was an important crossing for military traffic between Texas and the Indian Territory at that time.[40] Stapp's company was discharged at the Elm Fork Station on February 2, 1847, having served from July 24, 1846 to February 2, 1847.[41]

Local settlers immediately wrote to Governor J. P. Henderson demanding that the rangers stay on in the area. Consequently, he agreed to reenlist the company for twelve months.[42] Twenty-three of Stapp's men reenlisted. Fifty-seven new men brought the company's strength up to eighty.[43] Governor Henderson, dissatisfied with Capt. Stapp, replaced him as captain with his former lieutenant, William

---

*The 1852 Peters Colony Map shows a ranger station about three miles southeast of today's Gainesville, off FM 372.

Fitzhugh.[44] The camp on the Elm Fork became known as Fitzhugh's Station, or Fort Fitzhugh.[45]

To extend his line, Fitzhugh sent half of his men to Hickory Creek, about a day's ride, or thirty miles south of the Elm Fork Station.[46] The Hickory Creek Station was located on the western edge of the Lower Cross-Timbers just outside today's Denton.*

Fitzhugh's men patrolled the Grand Prairie and the Cross-Timbers for two years, until February 1849. After his ranger service, Fitzhugh helped found the town of Gainesville near his old ranger headquarters.

Torrey's Trading House #2 continued to grow during this period. George Barnard, the manager at Torrey's, sold supplies to rangers, settlers, and Indians alike. In April 1847, Robert S. Neighbors accepted an appointment as U. S. Indian agent,[47] and began working from Torrey's by June.[48]

Neighbors believed that the boundary line between whites and Indians should be strictly enforced. He felt that, if the military kept the whites off the Indians' lands, peace could be preserved until some sort of permanent solution was reached. Governor Henderson agreed with Neighbors and ordered his ranger captains to keep whites from settling above the line.[49] Neighbors and others expected that, ultimately, the government would establish reservations for the Indians and teach them to farm and raise livestock.

Neighbors held a council with Jose Maria and other Indian leaders at Torrey's in September 1847. The Indians realized that they were again in danger of losing their homes to the whites and asked Neighbors where they might settle permanently. Jose Maria's Anadarkos and other bands were at that time, living on the Brazos about forty miles above Torrey's Trading House. Neighbors advised them to gather near the Kichai village which was about 150 miles above Torrey's, near today's Possum Kingdom Lake.[50]†

About August 1847, a second company of rangers commanded by Middleton Tate Johnson was stationed near Torrey's. Johnson County is named in his honor and he was also the individual most

*The 1852 Peters Colony Map shows the Hickory Creek station about one mile northeast of Pilot Knob. The station was probably a few hundred yards southwest of where I.H. 35-W crosses Hickory Creek. The Peters Colony map refers to Pilot Knob as "Smith's Mountain," suggesting that T. I. Smith's rangers may have used the Hickory Creek Station before Fitzhugh.

†Over the next two years, the Anadarkos, Ionis, Caddos, Tawakonis, and others built villages near the Kichais. They would live there until 1854, when they would be moved to a federal reservation near Fort Belknap.

responsible for the establishment of Fort Worth. Johnson was born in South Carolina in 1810, and served two terms in the Alabama legislature while still in his twenties. He then emigrated to the Republic of Texas and settled in Shelby County, near the border with Louisiana.[51] There he became involved in the feud known as the War of the Regulators and the Moderators. The origins of the feud are obscure, but they seem to have involved crooked land deals, personal enmities, and vigilante justice. The county became the scene of ambushes, lynchings, and murders.[52]

Johnson, a man of considerable means, was a leader of the Regulator faction. President Sam Houston called out the militia and arrested the leaders on both sides in 1844. He directed a committee of neutral citizens to write a peace treaty; two leaders from each side signed the document. Johnson signed for the Regulators.[53]

He was elected to the Texas Congress in 1845. When the Mexican War broke out, he raised a company of volunteer cavalry. His first lieutenant was Ephraim N. Daggett, another Regulator leader.* Johnson and his men fought in the Battle of Monterrey in September 1846. After the battle, they were discharged and returned home.[54] Back in Shelby County, he recruited a new company of mounted volunteers.[55] His new company was mustered into federal service as Texas Rangers, issued flintlock rifles and cavalry pistols, and assigned to frontier duty.[56]

Ranger companies on the frontier were commanded by Lt. Col. Peter H. Bell, and were known as Bell's Regiment.

Johnson's men rode to the old Waco village, where they joined Capt. Shapley Ross's company.[57] Records of the trading house show that George Barnard sold the rangers such supplies as clothing, ammunition, saddles, bridles, and pack mules.[58] In some cases, he advanced their pay.[59] This was a good business decision because Torrey's was probably the only place the rangers could spend their wages.

Captain Johnson enforced Neighbors's policies up to a point. When a lawyer named Spencer settled above the frontier line, Neighbors asked the rangers to remove him. Johnson wrote Spencer a letter in which he ordered him to return to the settlements. When Spencer ignored the letter, Johnson made no move to evict him.[60]

Neighbors was dismayed to learn that Lt. Col. Bell had ordered the rangers not to interfere with whites who settled above the frontier. Bell even ordered Shapley Ross to move to a new station on the

* (Daggett would later be known as the "Father of Fort Worth" for his role in bringing the county seat to Fort Worth.)

North Bosque, fifteen miles above Torrey's and beyond the line, to protect the new settlers. George Wood, the new governor of Texas, sided with Bell. Neighbors predicted that the Indians would respond with violence.[61] Bell ordered Johnson's company to move from the Brazos to the West Fork of the Trinity.[62] He left the Brazos in January 1848, and was at Marrow Bone Springs by February 1.[63] The rangers named their new home Kaufman Station. David S. Kaufman, one of Texas's new representatives in the U.S. Congress, had helped write the truce that ended the Regulator-Moderator feud. However, the name did not stick—most people called the place Johnson's Station.

As Neighbors predicted, the policy of allowing settlers to go above the line led to violence. Charles Barnard reported that Indians had killed three surveyors, and that Capt. Johnson's men had killed a Caddo boy on April 14, 1848:

> This evening by the arrival of Mr. Rolfe from Captain Johnson's Station, I have received the following information—viz—that on the 9th inst. April three surveyors engaged in running the line of the Peters Colony were killed and scalped by some Indians supposed to be Witchitas. The balance of the party, who had just returned from the settlements, having been gone about two days, found them. It is supposed that the act was committed by the Witchitas out of revenge for the killing of their people by Highsmith's Ranger company. I also learned the particulars concerning the killing of the Caddo boy. He states, that the surveyors sent to Captain Johnson for assistance in burying those killed, and accordingly a party was sent up for that purpose. They returned to camp on Thursday evening. One of the wagons had just arrived and the driver reported having seen a party of six Indians on the road, and on inquiry what tribe they belonged to, could obtain no satisfactory answer. The next morning a scout commanded by Lieut. Joseph Smith was started in search of these Indians to ascertain their intentions. They did not find the party, but discovered the boy at a short distance from camp. On sight the party immediately started in pursuit, and on coming up called to him to stop. The boy being frightened took no notice and kept on running. They then ran ahead and across his way for some time, but he still kept on, when one of the men, thinking to stop him, made an attempt to secure his rifle, and caught hold of it. The boy drew his knife to defend himself, and was immediately shot through the hand, which was followed by a volley from the party. Mr. R. reports great excitement among the whites in the vicinity of the station, on account of the murders of the surveyors, and does not think it safe for any Indian to be about unless he should go directly to the post.[64]

Neighbors believed that the rangers had killed the Caddo without provocation. Jose Maria, the Anadarko chief, warned him that the Caddos might seek revenge. Neighbors arranged a council at Torrey's the following autumn, where he, Bell, Johnson, Ross, and Smith met with Jose Maria, Chief Towash of the Ioni, and Chief Haddebar of the Caddos. The Indians agreed not to seek revenge for the incident, in exchange for a payment of $500 to the boy's family, and a promise to put two of the rangers on trial.[65]*

In May 1848, Governor Wood ordered a new ranger company, led by Capt. John Conner, to protect Limestone and Navarro Counties.[66] Conner's men were mustered in at Austin on May 5, 1848.[67] Conner occupied Smith's old station on Richland Creek (about four miles west of today's Milford).[68] Bell's Regiment now comprised ten companies, and was authorized both a colonel and a lieutenant colonel. Peter H. Bell was elected colonel. Middleton Johnson was elected lieutenant colonel in July 1848. Johnson left for regimental headquarters, and Lt. Smith took over the company at Johnson Station.[69]

The Mexican War ended in May 1848. Under the terms of the Treaty of Guadalupe Hidalgo, Mexico gave up the territory, which now includes Texas, California, New Mexico, Arizona, Colorado, Nevada, and Utah. The U.S. Army returned from Mexico in the fall of 1848. Regular army troops became available to defend the frontier again.

Most of the companies of Bell's Regiment were mustered out in December 1848. The rangers at Marrow Bone Springs were discharged on December 15, 1848.[70] Captain Fitzhugh's company rode from Elm Fork to Conner's Station, where they were discharged on February 2, 1849. Fitzhugh's two lieutenants had been on duty for two and a half years.[71] Lieutenant Colonel Johnson was discharged at the same place the following day.[72] Soon afterwards, he began preparing to settle permanently at Kaufman Station. The last Peters Colony contract had expired the previous summer, and Johnson claimed Marrow Bone Springs and the surrounding land.

To replace the rangers, one company of U.S. dragoons occupied the Brazos Station, and a second occupied Conner's Station. Governor Wood and "Colonel" Johnson were unhappy with this arrangement: the entire frontier between Richland Creek and the Red River would be without troops.

Governor Wood and Johnson would have to persuade the army to build a fort on the upper Trinity.

---

*There is no record that any rangers were ever tried for the killing.

Blue Mound Vista from Old Fort Worth. (Copyright William Potter.)

2

The U.S. Dragoons Occupy the Bluff

Before the Mexican War, much of the U.S. Army, which now had responsibility for the western frontier of Texas, was stationed in a line of forts just west of the Mississippi River stretching from Minnesota to Louisiana. Few whites ventured beyond this line onto the Great Plains because they were dominated by the fierce and territorial plains Indians. The Indians along the frontier were generally peaceful, as the land was owned by the federal government and was therefore under military control. Three regiments of mounted troops were able to keep the peace—the 1st Dragoons, the 2nd Dragoons, and the Regiment of Mounted Riflemen.

This frontier drastically changed when the Mexican War ended on May 30, 1848.[1] The territory the army had to defend expanded by almost two thousand miles. Gold was discovered in California and more Americans poured into the new western territories. Settlers and traders traveled to California, Oregon, and New Mexico. And Texans settled on their western frontier in increasing numbers. All of them not only wanted, but expected and demanded, army protection from Indians.[2]

The U.S. Congress, struggling to pay for the recent war, decided to reduce the army to its prewar strength of about ten thousand men.[3] The same three mounted regiments with a combined strength of about 1,500 men, would patrol all the territory west of the Mississippi. It would soon be apparent that this force was too small for the job. In Texas, the shortage was acute. A handful of dragoons had to cover over eight hundred miles of frontier wilderness. Texans demanded that Washington do more to defend them: if not, they would take matters into their own hands and drive the Indians from the frontier. They had done this in 1841.

The army began deploying to Texas in October 1848. Brevet Major General David Twiggs, the first colonel of the 2nd Dragoons, had been promoted and was assigned the problem. He was the commanding general of the 8th Military Department, then headquartered in Galveston, but he didn't want the job. Nevertheless, he developed a plan that followed the frontier plan of the Republic of Texas, while guarding against anticipated further problems with Mexico. He divided his department into two districts: the Rio Grande District to protect south Texas from Mexicans, Indians, and rustlers; and the Frontier District to protect the area from the Rio Grande to the Red River.

At that time he had about 1500 soldiers—six companies of the 2nd Dragoons, ten companies of the First Infantry and three companies of the 4th Artillery. He assigned his artillery and most of his infantry to San Antonio and to posts along the Rio Grande. He ordered two companies of the 1st Infantry to Austin and one to Fredericksburg. Four companies of dragoons, A, B, F, and I, were ready to sail for Texas, and they would be stationed on the Indian frontier.[4] He was following guidance given him by Maj. Gen. Zachary Taylor in a letter dated October 30, 1848. Two additional companies of dragoons, G and C, were en route from Carlisle Barracks, the Dragoon School of Instruction in Pennsylvania.[5]

On November 5, 1848, the steamships *New Orleans*, *Alabama,* and *Colonel Stanton* sailed into Galveston Bay, carrying two hundred of the men and horses of the 2nd Dragoons. In Galveston, they boarded two steamboats, the *Reliance* and the *Billow*, and steamed up Buffalo Bayou to Houston. The four companies along with the regimental headquarters arrived at Houston on November 6, and set up camp near the city.[6] They spent several days preparing for their march to the Indian frontier. On November 9, 2nd Lt. Samuel Starr and a party of new recruits arrived from Carlisle Barracks. When all was ready, the dragoons rode west, towards Austin.[7]

A cold rain fell as the dragoons rode west. Since the army did not yet issue raincoats or ponchos, the men had only their wool overcoats to protect them from the rain. The overcoats, of course, soaked through after a short time. Private Matthew Patterson, a new recruit with Company F, remembered the journey nearly forty years afterward, and claimed that it had ruined his health.[8] Lieutenant Starr described the march in a letter to his wife, Eliza:

> One and one half miles from Houston was the Dragoon Camp to which I proceeded. The Dragoons, consisting of four companies, left that camp for this place, Austin, on the 11th instant, and arrived there on the 24th. Thirteen days spent in traveling 200 miles. Think of that, Dragoons, too. But we passed over the very worst road in the world and our train of some thirty wagons buried themselves—up to the hubs is a common expression—up to the bodies is no exaggeration in the mud. It began to rain the morning we marched from Houston, and continued to rain for about five days. A moist time we had of it.[9]

The dragoons camped outside Austin, but remained only a few days. Regimental headquarters moved into the Austin Arsenal. The companies moved out to relieve the rangers of Bell's Regiment. Company A headed south to establish a post on the Medina River, about ten miles upstream from Castroville. Company B rode to McCulloch's Station, about forty miles northwest of Austin (near today's Burnet). Company F rode north, to relieve Shapley Ross's men at the North Bosque Station. Company I set out for Conner's Station, on Richland Creek. The stations were to be taken over by the military and the rangers mustered out.[10]

Twiggs had no desire to command the troops in Texas, and had requested another assignment months before.[11] A new commander, Bvt. Maj. Gen. William Jenkins Worth, was assigned to replace him. Worth took command in San Antonio on December 26, 1848.

General Worth was a distinguished officer. He had enlisted in the army during the War of 1812, had become an officer, and had built a fine reputation during three decades of service. He ended the six-year long Second Seminole War in Florida in 1842. He served as a division commander during the campaign to capture Mexico City in 1847, and emerged from the war a national hero. The title "hero" meant he should be regarded as a potential candidate for president.[12]

Worth played an important role in shaping the United States Military Academy at West Point. He was commandant of the Corps of Cadets from 1820 until 1828. With Col. Sylvanus Thayer, the Superintendent of the Academy, he brought high standards of discipline and professionalism to the school. His Battalion Orders, a statement on the nature of duty, is still memorized by incoming cadets at the academy.

Company F, 2nd Dragoons, commanded by Capt. Ripley Allen Arnold, left Austin for Shapley Ross's Station on the North Bosque River, arriving on December 8, 1848.[13] A snowstorm covered the countryside with several inches. A pioneer recalled that the Brazos

River froze over, and people crossed on the ice at Waco.[14]* Arnold renamed the station Camp Inge, in honor of Lt. Zebulon M. P. Inge, a West Point classmate and fellow officer in the 2nd Dragoons who had been killed at the Battle of Resaca de la Palma in May 1846.

Arnold's second in command, Lt. William Saunders, mustered out Capt. Ross's men.[15] Ross returned to the area a few weeks later and, in the spring of 1849, opened a ferry over the Brazos and built the first house in Waco. His son, Lawrence Sullivan "Sul" Ross, would later become a Texas Ranger captain, governor of Texas and the namesake of a university.[16]

The Indians who lived in the area above Torrey's Trading House #2 realized that it was time to move west again to escape the tide of white settlers. The Anadarkos, led by Chief Jose Maria, and the Ionis, led by Chief Towash, abandoned their villages on the Brazos. Following Neighbors's advice, they built new villages near the Kichais, about 150 miles up the river.

George Barnard had bought Torrey's Trading House in July 1848 for $9,697.[17] He and his brother, Charles, moved, in order to stay close to their Indian customers. The new business was relocated on a bend of the Brazos opposite Comanche Peak, within sight of today's Granbury.[18] Barnard transferred the first stock of goods to the new trading house on May 10, 1849.

Charles Barnard and his wife, Juana, lived at the new trading house. Comanche Indians on the Rio Grande had captured Juana Cavazos Barnard in 1844. Mrs. Barnard remained at or near Barnard's Trading House until her death in 1906.[19] See appendix #2–1 for her story of the capture as told to her daughter in 1903.

Indian raids had been a fact of life in Texas for generations. Nevertheless, Worth and other army leaders hoped to win over the Comanches and others through friendly persuasion. In February 1849, Gen. Worth ordered his soldiers:

> . . . by kindness, and all proper forbearance, to conciliate the Indian tribes protect them from violence and injustice, and make

---

*Ross's Station was probably just west of today's Lake Waco, in or near Speegleville Park. The site was probably flooded when the lake was built. George B. Erath recalled in 1876 that Ross established a fort on the Bosque in late 1847, "where L. P. Standifer now lives."[20] McLennan County deed records show that Standifer's homestead was on the west bank of the North Bosque, on the G. H. Roberts Survey. Today's North Speegleville Road follows much of the western boundary of the Roberts Survey. The southern boundary of that survey was about one mile south of Tennant Creek, which crosses today's Speegleville Park.

> them understand their true interests and their obligations. In the fulfillment of these duties, the intelligence of officers and the zeal of soldiers will supply deficiency in numbers.[21]

To help Indian Agent Neighbors promote good relations, Worth ordered Arnold to provide him with a dragoon escort when he visited the Indian tribes.[22]

Reports from the field initially confirmed Worth's viewpoint. For example, the post commander at Fredericksburg reported "that the Indians in this vicinity are sincerely disposed to be friendly, and that the preservation of such relations depends entirely on the white inhabitants." German settlers, he warned, incited the Indians by selling them liquor and cheating them.[23]

In February, as more soldiers and supplies arrived in Texas, Worth ordered his men to establish a new line of forts on the Indian frontier west of the ranger stations. Bvt. Brig. Gen. William S. Harney, the commander of the 2nd Dragoons, would be in charge of the new line of forts in his role as colonel of the 2nd Dragoon Regiment, and commander of the Frontier District.[24]

In designating these new posts, Worth faced a dilemma. He had only six companies of dragoons and a handful of mounted infantrymen with which to patrol the Frontier District, from the Red River to the Rio Grande. If he created a new outpost with each company, the garrisons would be able to send out only one or two dozen men in a crisis. The rest of the men would have to stay behind to guard the fort.[25] On the other hand, if he stationed two companies per post, then thirty or forty men might be available in an emergency. But he could only establish a few such posts, and they would be far apart.[26] He chose the latter option, and decided to abandon both Camp Inge and Conner's Station, and combine the garrisons at a single post. Company F, from Camp Inge, and Company I, from Conner's Station, would establish a new fort on the Brazos, at the abandoned Ioni village thirty miles above Waco. Together, these two companies would guard the territory between the Brazos River and Fort Washita, about 150 miles to the north.[27]

Company F's new station was Camp Thornton, near the Towash Indian Village. Towash was the chief of the Hainai, or "Ioni" tribe. The Hainais were Caddo Indians who had migrated to Texas from Louisiana in about 1835. The Hainais had abandoned Towash Village a short time earlier, on advice from Indian Agent Neighbors. Captain Arnold named the new post Camp Thornton, in memory of Capt. Seth Thornton, who had commanded Company F during the Mexican War, and had been killed in the fighting before Mexico City.

The site of Camp Thornton was probably flooded when Lake Whitney was constructed in the 1940s. Thornton had commanded Company F during the Mexican War, and had been killed in the fighting before Mexico City. He had been in on the incident that ignited the Mexican War. A number of his men were killed or captured by Mexican dragoons in May 1846. Thornton was returned in a prisoner exchange after the Battle of Resaca de la Palma.*

Texas Governor George Wood followed the movements of Company F and the other dragoons with keen interest. Like many Texans, Wood believed that Washington was not doing enough to defend the frontier. When he learned that Worth did not plan to station any troops between Camp Thornton and the Red River, he became concerned. He wrote to Worth on February 12, 1849. He reminded the general that the area between the Brazos and Red Rivers was home to many settlers, and that "some of the most refractory and insubordinate tribes within the limits of the state" lived just west of the settlements.[28] The Indians were restless and the frontier was on the brink of war. He urged stationing troops somewhere between the Towash Village and the Red River.

Wood chose Middleton Johnson to deliver his letter to Worth in San Antonio. Johnson had been discharged from the ranger service at Conner's Station just nine days before, and intended to settle at Marrow Bone Springs. He, of course, was anxious to have troops stationed on the Trinity, west of where he planned to live. When he delivered the governor's letter, Johnson apparently warned Worth that the settlers were about to attack the Indians and start an Indian war.[29]

Despite the lobbying of Wood and Johnson, Worth did not want to build a fort on the Trinity. He acknowledged that, at some time, it might become necessary to build such a fort. Unfortunately, there were no mounted troops available to do so. For the present, he would send Bvt. Brig Gen. Harney, to visit North Texas and study the matter. He also urged the governor to persuade the settlers of north Texas not to attack the Indians. If the settlers started an Indian war, they would regret it, for the army was too weak to protect them all.[30]

In a separate message to Harney, Worth emphasized that he had no wish to build a new post on the Trinity. Company I of the 2nd

---

*The precise location of Camp Thornton is not clear. A marker in Lake Whitney State Park overlooks the site of Towash, a community that grew up near the Towash Indian Village. Towash survived into the twentieth century, and appears on many old maps of the area.

Dragoons, at Conner's Station, was under orders to join Arnold's men at Towash Village. If absolutely necessary, Harney could temporarily divert Company I to the Trinity.[31] Johnson may have called on Harney in Austin. In any case, he agreed that there should be dragoons on the Trinity.

Company I, under Lt. J. Y. Bicknell, left Conner's Station on the first of March. Instead of joining Arnold's men at Towash Village, they rode to Marrow Bone Springs. Five days later, they returned to Conner's Station, and made preparations to move to Camp Thornton.[32] Johnson, waiting for Harney to make his tour of north Texas, was puzzled by this reversal. He described the tense situation on the frontier to a friend on March 22:

> We have no very particular news only that Bicknell's company of dragoons has been ordered from this place back to the Brassos [sic]; . . . they only remained here five days. I do not know the cause, but the order emanated from General Worth. I learn that General Harney is anxious to have troops here, but is overruled in it . . . General Harney has visited the Brassos Station, and I have just received a message from him that he will be up to my place in a few days, to examine the situation of the country. When he comes, I hope he will do something in the way of giving protection—our portion of the frontier is now in the worst condition it has been in since 1839. The Indians are stealing continually, and the citizens are (some of them) killing the Indians whenever they are seen and under any sort of suspicious circumstances. This must soon lead to general hostility, and the only thing that can prevent it is the introduction or employment of some kind of troops on our settlements . . . Arrangements are now in progress to organizing a party to go and attack the Wishita Village and recover the stolen property—I look on this movement as the beginning of *hostilities* carried out, and of this there can be no doubt, unless the government takes it in hand . . .[33]

When the dragoons returned to Conner's Station, they learned that six of the horses they had left behind in camp had strayed or been stolen. They hurriedly packed their equipment and supplies, and left for Fort Thornton the next day. When they arrived on the Brazos, Lt. Fowler Hamilton sent Lt. Samuel Starr with twenty-nine men and the post guide in the direction of Comanche Peak, with orders to recover the horses. Hamilton ordered Starr to capture the perpetrators but, if capture was not possible, he could "punish them in any manner you deem fit."[34] Arnold later denied that any horses had been stolen from Company I, suggesting that the horses had probably strayed.[35]

Harney visited the dragoons at Towash Village in March. He inspected the area and found that the surrounding land was swampy, and offered poor grazing and timber. He selected a site for a new post to replace Camp Thornton. The new site was about six miles up the Brazos, near a village where the Anadarko tribe, led by Jose Maria, had lived until recently. He established Fort Graham there on March 27, 1849. Company I moved to the new post on March 31st and Lt. Saunders brought Company F from Camp Thornton a few days later.*

On April 6, 1849, Lt. Samuel Starr wrote to his wife from the newly established Fort Graham:

> Dear Eliza, we left our camp on Towash Village on the 4th of April for this place, which is 8 miles from Towash. Here will be established a permanent military Dragoon Post. The scenery here is really beautiful. You must not suppose because a place is termed *village* that it has red and white houses all in a row, a meeting house, a school house, and tavern. No, no. Towash is an old Indian Village abandoned some time ago. The Wigwams, built of prairie grass, are in the form of cones, resembling exactly a hay stack, if you chance ever to have seen such a thing, you know exactly how an Indian's lodge in Texas looks. These lodges are scattered over a considerable piece of ground. Fort Graham is, or rather *was* a counterpart of Towash, but nearly all the lodges were burnt when the prairie was set on fire 6 weeks ago, and there are now left a few only, scattered here and there, over an extremely beautiful valley.
>
> I have time for no more of this at present. An express leaves tomorrow morning early for Austin. I am in the daily expectation of the arrival of Capt. Arnold, who will relieve me in the command of the company, when I shall start for Austin. Yours Truly,
> S. H. Starr[36]

Shortly after Starr's arrival, Maj. Arnold was ordered to Austin to testify in a court-martial in which he charged Lt. Saunders with drinking on duty. Details of his charges and the results are in appendix #2–3. Arnold returned to take command of Fort Graham on April 16.[37] His wife, Catherine Bryant Arnold, probably joined him at about this time, bringing their young children. Lieutenants Starr and Saunders left for other assignments, leaving Arnold as the only officer.[38]

In May, Arnold received word that he had been promoted to brevet major.[39] "Brevet" promotions were honorary promotions, given to officers in much the same way that medals are awarded today. Arnold's brevet promotion to major was conferred in recognition of his gallant conduct in the battles of Palo Alto and Resaca de

---

*The fort was probably named for Lt. Col. William M. Graham of the 11th Infantry who was killed at Molino del Rey on September 8, 1847.

la Palma in the Mexican War. The brevet promotion entitled him to wear the insignia and uniform of a major, and to be addressed as such on most occasions.

Civilians also moved to the new post on the Brazos. At least four merchants sought to be appointed the sutler at Fort Graham.[40] The post sutler was a merchant whom the post commander authorized to do business on post.*

Harney traveled across north Texas in March and April, explored the countryside, and formed a plan for its defense. He returned to Austin and wrote his report to Worth on May 1. He agreed with "Colonel" Johnson: there should be a dragoon post on the Trinity, about where the West Fork enters the Lower Cross Timbers. He also wanted to build a new post below Fort Graham, near today's Gatesville. He wanted more men to garrison these new posts. Four companies of the 2nd Dragoons were stationed in New Mexico, out of his immediate control, and he hoped that the War Department would transfer them to Texas. He also wanted Congress to increase the size of each company to a hundred men, as it had been during the Mexican War. And he wanted every man to carry a Colt revolver. He was confident that, with such a force at his command, there would be no Indian troubles in his district.[43]

Brevet Major General Worth died unexpectedly of cholera just one week after Harney made his recommendations. For more on cholera and Bvt. Maj. Gen. William Jenkins Worth's death and burial see appendix #2–2.

After Worth's death, command of the 8th Military Department passed temporarily to Harney. He lost no time in establishing the new post on the West Fork of the Trinity. On May 10, he ordered Maj. Arnold to establish the new fort. Arnold received Harney's order on May 15, and rode out from Fort Graham with a detachment of dragoons that same day.[44]

Arnold and his dragoons rode to Johnson Station. Johnson was the best person to guide Arnold in choosing a site for the new post.

*According to muster rolls, D. B. Mosby, a former steamboat captain from New Orleans, is named as the post sutler at Fort Graham at the end of June 1849. Mosby followed Company F to Fort Worth, and became the post sutler there for about two years. Each company of soldiers was authorized four laundresses, who cleaned and mended uniforms. Muster rolls also indicate that Mary Horan, a 33-year old Irish immigrant with two young children was one of the laundresses.[41] The Horans, too, followed Company F to Fort Worth, and remained there until at least November 1850.[42]

He was the most influential citizen in the area and knew the countryside well. He had recently returned from Shelby County, where he had disposed of his property. Four friends from his old home returned with him to Marrow Bone Springs.

One of these men, Joseph R. Parker, had been a member of Johnson's frontier rangers.[45] Another, Simon Farrar, was a former Regulator, and had served in Johnson's company at Monterrey.[46] When Arnold, Johnson and the dragoons set out to locate a site for the new fort, the Shelby County men came along. In 1893, Simon Farrar recalled the trip:

> Col. Johnson, Dr. Echols, Charles Turner, Joseph Parker and myself came out with Col. Johnson from Shelby County and after staying about a week at Johnson's Station, we started in company with Major Arnold's command up the Trinity River in search of a place to locate the regular U.S. troops. We passed through the Cross Timbers, crossing the different creeks as best we could, through a wild and beautiful country inhabited only by Indians, wild Mustang horses, innumerable quantities of deer, wolves, and wild turkey.
>
> About two or three o'clock in the evening we halted in the valley east of where Fort Worth now stands and killed a deer for supper, though we might have killed many more but we did not wish to be encumbered with them. We passed our first night near Terry Springs, east of Fort Worth known as cold spring where we enjoyed ourselves hugely with jokes, etc., indifferent to Indians, wolves, and all the wild enemies of the white man.
>
> Next morning Col. Johnson, Major Arnold, Dr. Echols, Charles Turner, Jos. Parker and myself started to locate the barracks. We went west until we reached the point where the courthouse now stands, there halted and reviewed the scenery from all points and I thought it the most beautiful and grand country that the sun ever shown on, and while at that place, and in view of all advantages of a natural point of defense, and our late experience at Monterrey, wherein the strategic action of General Worth had so terribly defeated the Mexicans, we there, in honor of that grand old hero, named the point Fort Worth.[47]

One of the dragoons was Pvt. Alphonso Freeman. In 1902, while in his eighties, Freeman told a newspaper reporter that Fort Worth was established on May 8, 1849.[48] This date is clearly incorrect. Freeman may have meant to say May 18. Since Arnold's men left Fort Graham on May 15, they could have reached Johnson's Station by the evening of May 16, and camped at Terry Springs the following night.

Arnold left fifteen men behind at the new post, and returned to Fort Graham. On May 31, he reported from Fort Graham that the fifteen men were "on detached service at Camp Worth, on the West Fork of the Trinity River."[49] On June 4, he left Fort Graham with the rest of Company F.[50] Company I remained behind under the command of Lt. Fowler Hamilton.

Arnold arrived at the new post on June 6.[51] Major Arnold referred to his new station as "Fort Worth" in all subsequent correspondence and documents. Arnold moved the post to the bluff overlooking the Trinity on about August 1, 1849.* Much of the command was suffering from malaria in the summer of 1849, and it was thought that the higher ground was healthier.[52]

Major Arnold and his men began to build a frontier post for the fourth time in six months. Kate Arnold and the children moved from Fort Graham to Johnson's Station, where they waited until quarters were ready at the new post. The small garrison began to settle into a routine of guard duty, cutting timber, and scouting the countryside to the north.

The army had come to the bluff, but many of the Texans still wanted to get rid of the Indians. With dragoons at Fort Worth some settlers wanted to send a new expedition against the Indians. R. S. Neighbors warned of the plan in a letter from Fort Graham, written on June 23:

> General Tarrant with from one hundred to one hundred and fifty men is about to start from captain Johnson's old station on the trinity river on a campaign against the Indians. I learned that he intends to visit the neighborhood of the Wichita Mountains and attack any Indian villages he may fall in with, destroy their cornfields, and capture their horses, etc.[53]

Despite popular perceptions to the contrary, the army took their job of protecting the Indians as seriously as their job of protecting settlers. At Fort Worth, Maj. Arnold learned that settlers planned to gather on July 14 on Hickory Creek. Arnold reported the matter to headquarters in San Antonio:

---

*Although Farrar recalled visiting the bluff where the courthouse now stands, the first location of Fort Worth was about one mile to the northeast of the courthouse, at a place called Live Oak Point. The precise location of the encampment is not certain, but it was probably in or near today's Trader's Oak Park on Samuels Avenue.

> Information has reached me, that one Mr. Maloney of Denton is about raising a company to proceed to the Indian nation for the (avowed) purpose of recovering stolen horses. This Mr. Maloney, Contends (I am Told) that the party that lately came in and delivered up the stolen horses (Which they captured from the Wichitas,) had many other horses in their possession which had been stolen from the poor citizens. All this I know to be false. The company were to rendezvous at Hickory Creek tomorrow (distance about 23 miles). I shall be upon the ground and represent to them their suicidal course. For if they intend to protect themselves (no complaints since I have been here) the regulars may be withdrawn for other service and that *no rangers will be required.* I persuaded General Tarrant out of his trip, but I beg the general [Brooke] to give me some Directions how far may I go, when I see that the object is to get up an Indian war. Beed-eye one of the old and principal chiefs of the Ionis is here with his family on a friendly visit, and is satisfied with the frontier line pointed out to him.[54]

Major Arnold may have talked the settlers out of their expedition. In any case, we hear no more of it in official records. The episode raised an important question: What could the army do to prevent white settlers from crossing the frontier and making trouble? The War Department eventually concluded that the army had no authority whatever over the settlers, and added to the problems of the officers and men serving at the forts in Texas.

U.S. Dragoons in the Mexican War. (Copyright www.arttoday.com)

First Fort

The fort was begun in the river bottom near the modern-day Samuels Avenue Crossing, probably close to Traders Oak Park and the Cold Springs. To try to avoid a malaria ("bad air") epidemic, the fort was soon moved to the bluff to get out of the bad air. However, the soldiers still had to go into the river bottom to gather wood for their buildings and fences. So they were still mosquito food. This scene depicts the early fort location, but we have no idea exactly where it was. Indians often came to the fort during the day to ask for food, and at night to take what they could steal. Major Arnold was proud of the fact that, unlike other forts, his command never lost a horse to the Indians. (Copyright William Potter.)

Dawn on the Trinity Bluff

This drawing is looking east-northeast and shows the fort at dawns early light.
This is often used to represent the beginning of the fort. (Copyright William Potter.)

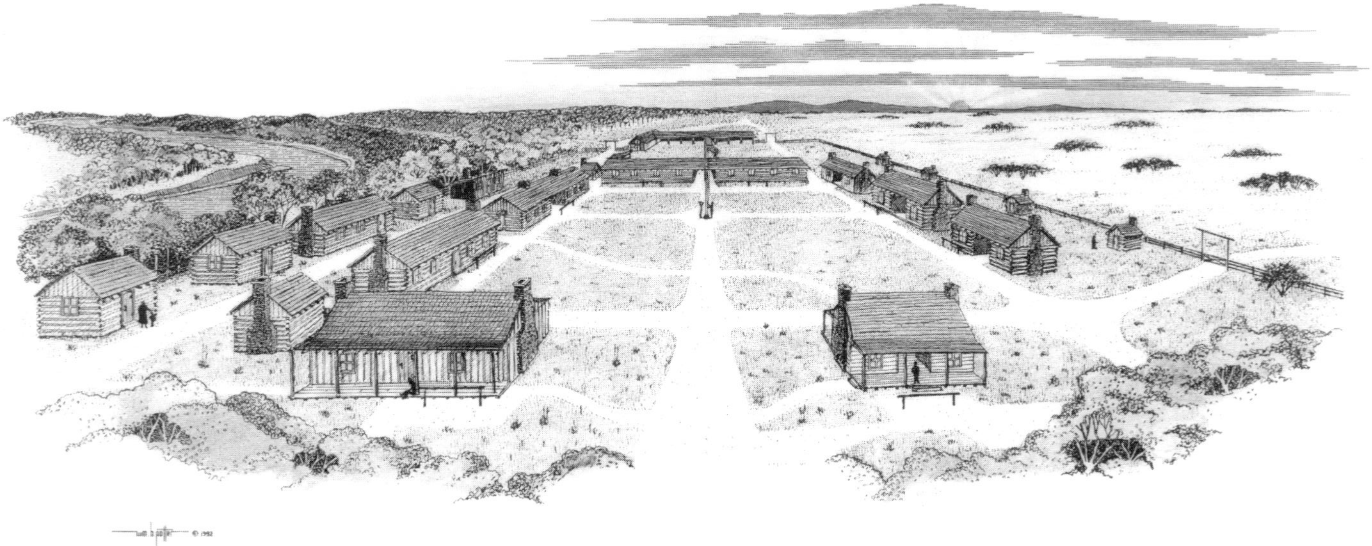

3

Brevet Major Ripley Allen Arnold

The man who founded and named Fort Worth, Bvt. Maj. Ripley Allen Arnold, was a warrior, a dedicated and competent professional soldier, a devoted family man, and a gregarious, good-natured, and hospitable southern gentleman. As the first leading citizen of the city, he set an example that still sets a standard for dedication and leadership. In many respects, the city of Fort Worth is his legacy.

As a warrior, he fought in three wars—the Second Seminole War, the Mexican War and the Cross-Timbers War. He was awarded brevet promotions for his daring leadership in the first two. His leadership and actions in the third resulted in making the area safe to live in, and pushed the fight to the west. Not one of his men were killed or wounded in their work of patrolling and clearing the area.

As a dedicated, competent professional soldier, he took care of the men he commanded and tried to get them better food and equipment. He was a stickler on keeping the fort clean and sanitary. He knew how to maintain discipline and respect.

As a family man, he doted on his wife and children. He always strove to provide them the best housing and education.

As a gregarious, good-natured, hospitable southern gentleman, he placed great value on his personal honor. This often got him into trouble. He became irate if someone accused him of less than honorable actions or intentions. He loved to have fun, partying with his fellow officers. He entertained guests visiting the area in his home.

Few records of Arnold's life have survived. His descendants believed that he kept a diary, but that it and other family papers were destroyed in a fire. The records that do survive are fragmentary, and most deal with minor episodes in his life. Men who knew Arnold said that he was a tall, handsome young man with auburn hair.

He was born in Pearlington, Mississippi on January 17, 1817. His father, Willis H. Arnold, was the principal of the Pearlington Academy and was active in local politics. He was elected to serve as clerk of the county courts. He educated his son at his academy and when Ripley was old enough, assisted his father at the school.[1]

In November 1833, Ripley applied for admission to the United States Military Academy at West Point. After applying, he left Pearlington for Ohio to study at the Oxford Academy. Mississippi's congressmen selected him as one of their nominees for the class of 1838. He entered West Point on July 1, 1834, at the age of seventeen. Nominations were political patronage at that time, and the nominees were usually the sons of men who supported a congressman in some manner.

Willis Arnold supported Henry Clay and the Whig party. Ripley Arnold later wrote that he "had been born and raised a Whig," and that his father had been "the only man in Hancock County, Miss. who dared to vote against General Jackson."[2]

His West Point career was rocky, and he stood in the bottom one-third of the class in academics. In January of his freshman year, he was involved in a fistfight with two sophomores and was court-martialed. According to the charges, Arnold struck a sophomore with a chair and threatened the other with a knife. Arnold was found not guilty. The two sophomores were convicted of fighting and other violations, and were expelled.[3]

He is associated with a familiar West Point tradition. A tavern run by Mr. Benny Havens stood just outside the military reservation. During his last year at the academy, Arnold is supposed to have slipped off there to meet an old friend, Lt. Lucius O'Brien. That night, O'Brien began writing the lyrics for a song—"Benny Havens, Oh!"[4] Arnold added to the lyrics. Freshmen cadets are still required to learn the verses. Today, when the Corps of Cadets marches in public reviews, the West Point Band often plays the old drinking song; Arnold is announced as the composer.

His senior year was particularly difficult. One Sunday in October 1837, he and two friends left the academy grounds to visit a nearby village. A staff officer saw them there. They were court-martialed and sentenced to three months of room confinement.[5]

On January 17, 1838, just three days before the end of his room arrest, he slipped out of his room and left the grounds. He said that he left to attend "a party given me on my birthday-night by some young ladies of my acquaintance." According to Arnold, he returned to find that his roommate and other cadets were drinking liquor in his room. To avoid further trouble, Arnold left his room to sleep in that of a friend, Cadet Wardwell.[6]

An inspecting officer discovered the gathering in Arnold's room and noted his absence. He was court-martialed for the third time on January 19. Believing that he could only be punished for visiting another room after Taps, Arnold did not take the matter very seriously. His statement to the court gives the impression that he saw this as an opportunity to give a good speech and impress his classmates. His years at West Point had probably taken the edge off his rural southern accent, and it is not difficult to imagine him smiling a bit as he spoke to the officers of the jury:

> It does appear from the testimony of every witness that I neither saw the fatal jug in question, nor tasted of its still more fatal contents. It is, indeed, gratifying to me to have satisfactorily proven to this court, that I have for once (at least) withstood temptation, and, instead of joining in "the revels, the sports and the wiles" of my more lively companions and roommates, I have sought a refuge from temptation and danger by ensconcing myself in the bed of my taciturn and studious friend, Cadet Wardwell. And here let me take the occasion to express the coincidence of my belief with that of the celebrated moralist and philosopher, Paley, who, with as much wisdom as justice, conceives that virtue consists in the resistance to temptation . . . I left the peaceful dormitory of my friend Wardwell to seek with rapid strides, my own room and a calm night's rest. While traversing the opening which separates the North from the South Barracks, a light broke upon my vision, a light glimmering from the dark lantern of Lieutenant Burbank as he was descending the winding stairway. And the appearance of this faint luminary was immediately followed by the exclamation, in the words of him of Santillane—"En voulant eviter Scylla je suis tombe dans Charybde. [In seeking to avoid Scylla, I have fallen into Charybdis" This is a reference to Greek mythology: In attempting to avoid Scylla (a dangerous rock), I have fallen into Charbydis (a whirlpool); meaning—caught between two evils or, dangers.] And having my conclusion confirmed by meeting with several disconsolate and lonely looking individuals on the stairs, I immediately reported my return to the inspector.[7]

Arnold was in more trouble than he realized. Arnold believed that another cadet, Henry Wallen, had stolen some uniform trousers and drafting instruments from a storeroom, and the young southern gentleman, would have nothing to do with him. Wallen, who bore a grudge against him, testified that Arnold had gone off post to buy the jug of liquor. As a result, the court found Arnold guilty of violating his room arrest, and voted to expel him from the academy. They recommended the sentence be commuted to two weeks of confinement in the academy prison.[8]

On January 30, Arnold was on trial again. Cadet Wallen accused Arnold of refusing to speak to him and of circulating false reports that Wallen was a thief. Academy officials added charges that Arnold had gone off post to the birthday party. This time, Arnold's defense was sober, factual, and, in light of his earlier statements, completely hopeless. The court found him guilty of leaving the post, and voted a second time to expel him.[9]

His sentence allowed him to resign, thus avoiding the humiliation of public dismissal. He submitted a letter of resignation, which was accepted March 17, 1838.[10] In the meantime, he appealed his expulsion to Maj. Gen. Alexander Macomb, the commanding general of the army. He stated that his offense was "a youthful 'indiscretion,' for which I have suffered the most grievous remorse." He appealed to Macomb's "generosity."[11] Macomb was generous—he reduced Arnold's sentence to two weeks' confinement.[12]

He graduated on July 1, 1838 with his classmates. He finished the year with 199 demerits; he was lucky—200 meant expulsion. His class numbered forty-four graduates. Second Lieutenant Ripley Allen Arnold and twenty-five of his classmates were sent to fight in the Second Seminole War.

After graduation, he took several months leave. During this time, he married Catherine Bryant, the daughter of a former army surgeon from Bay Saint Louis, Mississippi. A family legend holds that he met her in Kentucky while he was recruiting for the army. Kate's father opposed the marriage because he thought that his daughter was too young. Census records show that she was fourteen years old.[13] He eloped with Kate one night in August 1838. He borrowed a boat, rowed his fiancée across the mouth of Bay St. Louis to Pass Christian, and married her there the next day.[14]

Arnold's bride, Catherine Bryant, was the daughter of Thomas Bryant, a former army doctor who had been the post surgeon at Fort Leavenworth, Kansas. Catherine had spent her earliest years there. Her father left the army in 1835, but he returned in 1836 as a dragoon lieutenant in the new second regiment. Bryant probably moved his family to Bay St. Louis while he served in Florida. Bryant left the army again in 1838 and was evidently living in Bay St. Louis with his family when Ripley Arnold graduated from West Point.*

He joined the 2nd Dragoon Regiment in Florida in January 1839. The Second Seminole War was in its fourth year when he arrived. The conflict began when the U. S. government attempted to deport the Seminole Indians to Indian Territory. The Indians fled into the swamps and forests of Florida, from where they waged war on the army and the white settlers. The war dragged on until 1842, when Col. William J. Worth defeated the last bands of Seminoles in a battle in which Arnold would participate and be breveted captain.

When Arnold reported for duty, the 2nd Dragoons were divided among small outposts in northern Florida. His first assignment was with Company F, stationed at Fort Shannon. He became the third in command of a company of fifty men. One of his first duties was to command a detachment of dragoons escorting a supply train from Palatka to Fort King in February 1839. The following month, Arnold was reassigned to Company K with whom he would serve for many years.

The 2nd Dragoons left Florida in June 1839 to recruit and retrain. The regiment spent the summer and fall of 1839 encamped near Trenton, New Jersey. Arnold left his company to work at regimental recruiting stations in New York and Baltimore. The regiment returned to Florida in November 1839.[15]

Colonel David Twiggs was the first colonel of the regiment, and led the 2nd Dragoons in Florida. In the spring of 1840, the army imported a number of bloodhounds from Cuba. Twiggs hoped to use the dogs to trail the Seminoles through the Everglades. In March 1840, Twiggs took about sixty dragoons and 140 foot soldiers on a ten-day scout, along with Indian guides and the bloodhounds. Lieutenants Ripley Arnold, Hamilton Merrill, and William J. Hardee led the dragoons. All three had been classmates at West Point. Twiggs set out on March 21, 1840. He kept his infantry close to the main roads and sent Arnold, Merrill, and Hardee to explore the countryside. The column carried an inflatable pontoon bridge for river crossings. As the column marched and scouted, more and more men fell ill. Twiggs had to be evacuated by steamboat after only one week and command of the dragoons passed to Lt. Col. William S. Harney, the executive officer of the 2nd Dragoons. Then a soldier died in camp after he accidentally shot himself, and to compound their problems, the dogs refused to follow the Indians' trails.

---

*Bryant's service is outlined in his consolidated correspondence file, records of the Office of the Surgeon General. His dragoon service is outlined in Rodenbough.

On about the eighth day of the patrol, the column surprised three Seminoles walking on a trail. The dragoons charged the Indians, killing one and taking another prisoner. The prisoner, after being threatened with death, agreed to lead the soldiers to a point on the Weekiwa River. Wild Cat, a Seminole chief, was encamped on the opposite bank.

Lieutenants Arnold and Merrill crossed the river with fourteen dragoons about one mile below Wild Cat's camp. They were to cut off Wild Cat's retreat if he fled in that direction. Hardee and the rest of the dragoons first sent an Indian guide across the river to demand Wild Cat's surrender. Wild Cat refused and threatened to kill the guide. The river was only about a hundred yards wide. The dragoons swam across the river, but on the far bank, discovered that their ammunition was wet and their firearms were useless. So they retreated across the Weekiwa. Arnold and Merrill searched the opposite shore. They captured a few of the enemy's horses, but Wild Cat and his band escaped.

The expedition came to an end on April 1, 1840, when the column marched into Volusia. Lt. Merrill noted that although they had only been out ten days, many of the soldiers were barefoot and others had thrown away their blankets and overcoats. Merrill pronounced the bloodhounds "the great humbug of the day."[16]

Arnold spent the next two years serving at a succession of small posts in Florida. At some point, Kate came to join him in Florida. Their first child, a daughter, was born there in about 1840. Ripley and Kate named her Florida Belle. He was promoted to first lieutenant in February 1841.

An anecdote in the regimental history mentions Arnold in Florida. Alcohol is again at the center of the story. Arnold's commander instructed him to pack a mess chest for an expedition. The senior officer inspected the chest later and found that it contained no food, but several gallons of whiskey. Arnold explained himself as follows: "Now, Captain, I have been in a good many camps and have always found plenty to eat; but confound me, if in any one, I ever found plenty to drink."[17] His commander guessed that he would go far in the army.

In the spring of 1842, he became one of the few army officers to win distinction in the Seminole War. Colonel Worth, commanding U. S. forces in Florida, was determined to bring the war to an end. In April 1842, Worth led about two hundred infantrymen into the Pilaklikahai swamp to search for a Seminole band led by Halleck-Tustenuggee. Arnold and Company K accompanied Worth.[18] On

April 19, the infantry's guides found the Indians' trail, about forty miles west of present-day Orlando. The trail led into a hummock, a low island covered with trees and brush. The infantry fixed bayonets, formed a skirmish line, and charged forward through mud and water. Captain Richard McCall led the infantry charge. He later wrote:

> I gave the word, "forward!—double quick!" and in an instant we were breaking through the thicket at them, while the rat-a-tat-tat of their rifles was answered by a hearty shout from our men. It was Halleck-Tustenuggee and Octe-Archy with their warriors. The principal part of them were opposite our center, (the twenty-eight men of my company,) and they exchanged two successive shots with us, they retiring as they fired . . . It was a running fight in pretty thick cover and we charged them too hotly for deliberate aim on either side.[19]

Worth and the Company K charged the Indians on McCall's left. In the course of the attack, Arnold and eight dragoons came under fire from a large party of Seminoles. He rallied his men and fought bravely. The Seminoles killed one dragoon and wounded two others before McCall's infantry came to Arnold's assistance.[20] Captain McCall continued his account:

> I was ordered with my twenty-eight men to the left and got on to the pine ridge just in time to relieve Lieutenant Arnold of the Dragoons from an uncomfortable position. He and nine men had been separated from his company, advancing to this point, and they were attacked in the open woods by the party we had just driven from the other hummock . . . I again charged with my detachment, but they would not stand another shot. I pursued about a mile, and losing all traces of them, returned to the battle ground.[21]

Arnold's bravery and leadership impressed Worth, and he made Arnold a company commander for the rest of the operation, and awarded him a two-month leave when it was over.[22] Worth also recommended him for promotion to brevet captain. Brevet ranks were a rare honor in Florida. A review of the West Point Classes of 1837, 1838, and 1839 shows that eighty-two of the graduates served in Florida, but only Arnold and three others won brevet promotions.

Halleck-Tustenuggee surrendered to Worth shortly after the fight at Pilaklikaha. With only a handful of Seminoles still at large, the government in Washington decided to withdraw the army from Florida. The dragoons stayed in Florida through the summer of 1842 and then rode to new stations in Louisiana and Indian Territory.

Lieutenant Arnold rode with Company K to the U.S. arsenal at Baton Rouge where they spent the winter of 1842–1843.* Kate Arnold traveled to Louisiana to be with her husband. She gave birth to a second daughter, also named Kate, in Baton Rouge in January 1843.

In the spring, the company marched northwest to Fort Jesup, Louisiana. Most of the 2nd Dragoon Regiment was already in garrison there. Fort Jesup stood on the old Spanish road that connected Natchitoches, Louisiana with Nacogdoches, Texas. The fort was positioned to guard America's border with the new Republic of Texas.

Arnold served at Fort Jesup for two years. For most of this period, he served under Seth Thornton, as second in command of Company F. This seems to have been a relatively uneventful time for him, his wife, and their two little girls. However, on December 2, 1844, he faced a court-martial again. This time, the trouble arose from an argument with a fellow lieutenant. Arnold and Lt. Stephen Dobbins, a Pennsylvanian, were standing on the porch of the adjutant's office at Fort Jesup. Arnold and Dobbins had once been at odds at West Point. Dobbins angered Arnold by reporting him for a violation of regulations and it seems that Arnold still bore a grudge. A witness described the incident:

> Dobbins said that the Spaniards about here had voted the Whig ticket, and that they were, a degenerate, ignorant set, and if he had been correctly informed, they were somewhat tinctured with Negro blood, and were the meanest of God's creation.
>
> Capt. Arnold remarked that he was mistaken, that some of them were respectable men, that he knew them, that they had been a long time in the country. He said, "look at the voters in Pennsylvania, one half of them are a damned sight meaner class of people than our blacks in the South." Mr. Dobbins then approached him and said, with some emphasis, "I distinctly and positively say it is not so—it is not so, sir," repeating it. Capt. Arnold then said "I don't care a damn what you say, sir, it is my opinion and I don't care for yours."
>
> Capt. Arnold turned off at the same time, and walked towards the north end of the porch. In a few moments after he turned and approached rapidly towards Mr. Dobbins in a very excited manner, when, as near as he could possibly get to him, he said to him, "God damn you, sir . . . you have frequently attempted before in conversation to insult me, and God damn you (or God damn me) sir, if you ever attempt it again, I'll slap your face—I'll slap your face, sir.'[23]

*The barracks building where the garrison lived is still standing, just a few hundred feet from the state capitol.

Dobbins pressed charges of "conduct unbecoming an officer" against Arnold claiming that Arnold had lied about the incident in a conversation with other officers. Arnold denied it. He characterized Dobbins's charge as a feeble attempt to maintain his reputation. A gentleman, Arnold hinted, would have "demanded instant satisfaction." In other words, a gentleman would have challenged Arnold to a duel.[24] The court found Arnold not guilty and Col. Zachary Taylor, the post commander, approved the verdict. He noted that the matter had been a great waste of time, and he urged his junior officers to get along with one another.

Conflict with Mexico brought an end to the Arnolds' settled life at Fort Jesup. In 1845, Mexico threatened to go to war over the pending U. S. annexation of Texas. President Polk responded by sending Zachary Taylor to Corpus Christi, Texas, with a small army. The 2nd Dragoon Regiment rode away from Fort Jesup in July 1845 to join Taylor's army on the Texas coast—a journey of more than five hundred miles. Arnold served as the regimental chief of staff during the march.[25]

General Taylor's army established a camp where the downtown area of Corpus Christi now stands. They remained there during the fall and winter, waiting for the Mexicans' next move.

Arnold left Corpus Christi for New Orleans in December 1845, to recruit for his regiment. While he was recruiting, Gen. Taylor marched his army south to the Rio Grande. Taylor's men constructed Fort Brown on the site of today's Brownsville. He returned from recruiting duty in April 1846.

At about the time he returned, Companies F and C of the 2nd Dragoons were ambushed while scouting along the Rio Grande. Every man in the patrol was either killed, wounded or captured. This was the event that officially opened the Mexican War.

Captain Arnold served as Bvt. Brig. Gen. David Twiggs's aide during the battles of Palo Alto and Resaca de la Palma, fought north of Fort Brown on May 8 and 9, 1846. General Taylor defeated the Mexicans in both battles. Arnold described his part in the battles in a letter to Henry Foote, the U.S. Senator from Mississippi.

> I do not hesitate to say that as Twiggs's chief staff officer, that I communicated almost every order given in those battles, and that from the nature of my duties, I saw more of the battles, and was longer under fire, than any other one engaged . . . My share in the Battle of Resaca did not end when the enemy retreated, for General Taylor desired to send instantly to Fort Brown (a distance of four miles, and in the direction, which the enemy had taken) for additional physicians. I immediately volunteered for the service; he gave me six men from his bodyguard, and with

> these I started at full speed. As I passed Capt. Ker, who was the advance of our pursuing force, he advised me to halt, as I was upon the rear of the Mexican Army. I simply replied (without halting) that I was ordered to Fort Brown, and went on. I reached the Rio Grande with the rear of the Mexican Army, so mixed up with them that our own fort opened upon me, and I had absolutely to seek safety under the wall of a house, until I could hoist a white handkerchief on a sabre and capitulate with our own fort. I was at this time exposed not only to our own fire, but also to that from Matamoras, which was brisker than it had been during the entire bombardment. Soon as my white flag was seen, the fire ceased from our fort, and I rushed into Fort Brown, the first man who had reached it from General Taylor's Army (after leaving Point Isabel). Soon as I gave them the glorious news, nine cheers went up 'long and loud,' and the firing from Matamoras ceased for the war. I returned to the battlefield with two doctors within two hours from the time I left it.[26]

After the victories at Palo Alto and Resaca de la Palma, Taylor made plans to invade northern Mexico. He spent the summer of 1846 preparing for a campaign to capture Monterrey, which lay 180 miles west of Brownsville.

Arnold was made a quartermaster officer in Taylor's force. Monterrey fell to the U. S. Army on September 28, 1846.[27] Arnold made no mention of having taken part in the battle for the city. Despite the loss of Monterrey, the Mexican government would not consider peace negotiations.

President James Polk then directed Maj. Gen. Winfield Scott to take the regular army troops serving in northern Mexico and use them to capture the Mexican port of Veracruz. From Veracruz, Scott would march inland to capture Mexico City. Taylor would continue to occupy the Monterrey area, but his force would consist of state volunteer regiments. To bolster these state troops, three companies of the 2nd Dragoons would remain in Monterrey with Taylor.

Captain Arnold stayed at Monterrey with Company H, therefore missing the battles of Scott's Mexico City campaign. However, he and his men played an important role in protecting Taylor's supply lines. Mexican guerrillas and bandits, known as *rancheros*, began attacking Americans on the roads. The dragoons stationed in Monterrey were constantly in the saddle, serving as escorts, messengers, and scouts.

Most of these duties went unrecorded, but a few details of his life in Mexico turn up in various records. A pay voucher shows that he bought a slave named Carter as a servant.[28] An Ohio officer's diary notes that when Arnold's company rode into the U. S. supply base at Camargo on March 5, 1847, the Ohio volunteers mistook them for Mexicans, and prepared to repel their attack.[29] Eight days later, while riding to Monterrey with the Ohio regiment, Arnold led a squad in searching a Mexican farmhouse. The dragoons discovered a few *rancheros* hiding nearby. The Mexicans escaped, leaving behind some of their guns, cartridge boxes, and rations.[30]

From March 28 until April 28, Arnold commanded four companies of Jefferson Davis's Mississippi Rifle Regiment as they escorted a supply train between Monterrey and Camargo.[31] In May, he led an unsuccessful patrol in search of three dragoon deserters.[32]

His Mexican War service ended in October 1847, when news arrived that Capt. Seth Thornton had been killed near Mexico City. Arnold was promoted to the permanent rank of captain and made commander of Thornton's Company F.

However, instead of joining Company F in Mexico City, he returned to the United States for another tour of recruiting duty.[33] This time, he enlisted new soldiers in Kentucky and Ohio; Kate joined him in the Midwest where she gave birth to a third daughter, Sophia, in Indiana. He continued to recruit new men until November 1848.

Arnold then joined his company in East Pascagoula, Mississippi, for the movement to Texas. Most of the other men in the company had alsos proven themselves in the Mexican War.

Low Water Crossing

This scene shows a supply wagon heading north from the fort across the river. Escorting wagons was one of the missions of the soldiers at the fort. (Copyright William Potter.)

4

Company F, 2nd U.S. Dragoons

Ripley Allen Arnold and other regular army officers left behind a few official documents and records that tell us something about their lives. However, it was the enlisted men of Company F, 2nd Dragoons, who built the post that grew into the city of Fort Worth. The fort could have neither functioned nor survived without them. However, we know far less about them, although their lives were no less eventful than those of the officers who led them.

A total of forty-seven men were in Company F on June 6, 1849 when they came to the Trinity. Of those, twelve were relatively new to the army. They had enlisted in the summer of 1848, undergone brief training at Carlisle Barracks, and joined the company at Houston in November 1848.[1]

The rest of the men were veterans of the Mexican War. With a few exceptions, they had enlisted in New York City in May and June of 1846 and had fought together in the campaign to capture Mexico City. At Fort Worth, the combat veterans held the noncommissioned officer positions, and they defined the collective personality that every military unit develops.[2]

Both the veterans and the new recruits were chiefly immigrants. Only eleven of the forty-seven soldiers were born in the United States. Fort Worth's founders included seventeen Germans and eight Irishmen. Company F also included three Englishmen, a Swiss, a Dane, a Pole, and a Scot. Three others, whose records were not easily found, probably included two Germans and an Irishman.[3]

Company F, 2nd Dragoons, under the command of Capt. Seth Thornton, was involved in the incident that ignited the Mexican

War. The company was ambushed by Mexican troops on the Rio Grande on April 26, 1846. Nearly all the men of the company were killed or captured. After the Battle of Resaca de la Palma on May 9, Thornton and his remaining men were exchanged for captured Mexican troops. Company F was dissolved, and its men assigned to other companies.[4]

News of the incident reached the East Coast in May. Lieutenant Henry H. Sibley, recruiting officer for the 2nd Dragoons in New York City, had enlisted only nine men in March and April. With the news of the start of the Mexican War, he decided to try a new approach:

> Taking advantage of the impetus thus naturally given to the recruiting service, and the consequent excitement in the city, I immediately advertised in several papers for recruits, and had large hand bills printed and profusely distributed throughout the city.[5]

Sibley's advertisements worked, and by May 31, he had enlisted more than a hundred men for his regiment. Among these recruits were many of the men who established Fort Worth. The recruits, mostly German and Irish, were of "the very best material." He found that they were "anxious, most anxious, to join their regiment."[6] The recruits spent a few weeks at Fort Columbus, on Governor's Island just south of Manhattan, the army's chief induction center at the time. About the middle of July, the recruits sailed for the mouth of the Rio Grande. They landed in Texas at the end of July and probably spent the summer training and doing fatigue duty.

Company F was reactivated on October 29, 1846, at Camargo, Mexico. Captain Seth Thornton was on leave of absence, so his lieutenant, William Saunders, organized the company. Seventy recruits were on the company roll. Thornton returned from leave and took command of Company F on November 26 1846.[7]

Thornton had been with the 2nd Dragoons since the regiment's creation in 1836. Although slightly built and frequently sick, he was considered brave, even reckless, by his fellow officers. He had a quick temper, which many believed was the result of an unfortunate experience of his youth. He was a passenger on a steamship that caught fire and sank. He saved himself by clinging to floating wreckage, while those around him grew weak and drowned. He was delirious when a boat rescued him.[8]

On December 31, Company F left Camargo for Monterrey, escorting a train of about fifty supply wagons. An American officer noted in his diary that he had seen "Captain Thornton's company of dragoons; fine horses—men dressed in red flannel shirts—presenting a very warlike appearance . . ."[9] Lt. James Hawes, a young West Point graduate, joined the company in January.

At about the same time, Company F was ordered to take part in Maj. Gen. Winfield Scott's landing at Vera Cruz. Major E. V. Sumner put the dragoons through a training program on the Texas coast, near the Rio Grande.[10] A letter written by a dragoon officer describes the training:

> We are in perfect purgatory here, and Major Sumner would be the chief devil anywhere. He keeps us all day marching, running, and drilling as skirmishers (which you know is fatiguing,) through sand knee-deep. Old Sumner has one good effect on us—he has taught some of us to pray who never prayed before, for we all put up daily petitions to get rid of him.[11]

Scott's army landed on the beaches south of Veracruz in March 1847 and laid siege to the city. Company F fought the enemy for the first time on March 25, 1847, a few miles south of Veracruz. Colonel William S. Harney led a mixed force of regulars and state volunteers in an attack on the Moreno Bridge, near the village of Medellin. They lost one man, killed in the attack.[12]

After Vera Cruz surrendered, Scott advanced inland, toward Mexico City. At Cerro Gordo, he found Gen. Santa Anna's army of thirteen thousand men dug in on hills overlooking the road. Scott's infantry attacked on April 18, 1847, and drove the enemy off the hills. Harney's dragoons waited in reserve during the attack. As the Mexican forces withdrew, the dragoons drew their sabers and charged through the retreating army. The Mexican units lost all cohesion and fled.[13]

The U.S. Army did not award medals for bravery until the Civil War. But on March 3, 1847, Congress created the Certificate of Merit as a reward for valor. Ten soldiers in Company F won the Certificate of Merit at Cerro Gordo. Seven of these ten were still with the company when they established Fort Worth two years later.[14]*

On July 30, Company F joined a company of mounted rifles in attacking a Mexican guerrilla force at the hacienda of San Juan de Los Llanos. The Americans attacked on foot, firing their carbines and rifles into the windows of the houses. Lieutenant Hawes was made a brevet first lieutenant for his role in the attack.

Captain Charles Ruff described the fight some years later:

---

*The seven who helped found Fort Worth were Nicholas Beyer, Alphonso Freeman, Augustus Helmerling, Otto Kaas, Francis Knaar, Daniel McCauley, and John Wagner.

There were no special incidents connected with the fight, except the desertion en masse of Dominguez's company of Mexican spies. The fight lasted some three hours, was house-to-house, and brought to a terminus, perhaps, by the terror of the inhabitants, whose houses I found it necessary to direct to be fired, as night was approaching and I had reason to believe, from the long and determined resistance made, that the town contained a body of well-armed troops quite as large as my command."[15]

On August 18, Gen. Worth's division advanced on San Antonio, a fortified hacienda south of Mexico City. Company F escorted Engineer Capt. James Mason and Lt. P. G. T. Beauregard as they rode forward to determine how Worth might attack the hacienda. An infantry officer in Worth's division wrote the following account in a letter home:

> Our troops were moving very slowly. The engineers, with a squadron of dragoons to cover them, were reconnoitering in advance when the battle opened, and the first shot killed Captain Thornton of the dragoons. He was sitting on his horse with his leg thrown over the pommel of his saddle and probably did not know what killed him, for it was an 18-pound shot and it literally tore him to pieces. He was buried immediately beside the road.[16]

A staff officer also witnessed the scene:

> The body was mangled in the most horrid manner. The ball—a sixteen pounder—afterwards struck the road and literally covered me with mud and fragments of stone. A guide was knocked down from his horse within five feet of me, with a shocking wound to his head from a piece of stone . . . The reconnaissance was continued right and left, with some hopes of storming the battery that afternoon, but night and the rain came on, and it was given up.[17]

Worth advanced on San Antonio again on August 20. This time, the garrison retreated as part of a general withdrawal toward the city. Scott's army, in hot pursuit, converged on the fortified Churubusco convent. Harney's dragoons rode to the Churubusco battlefield with Worth's men. Arriving as the battle began, the dragoons were divided into small groups to escort prisoners, and to screen the infantry. Churubusco fell after a fierce struggle.[18]

Among the prisoners captured at Churubusco was Henri Langenhammer, who had served in Company F until August 6, 1846, when he disappeared while on pass in Puebla. At Churubusco, he was found to be serving with the San Patricio Battalion. The San Patricio's were all deserters from the United States Army. Santa Anna had promised money and land to any American soldier who would desert and fight against his comrades, along with a cash payment for any weapons he brought. Many of Scott's soldiers, chiefly German and Irish immigrants, deserted and joined the San Patricio's.[19]

Langenhammer was court-martialed for desertion. At the trial, he claimed that he had gotten drunk, been kidnapped, and forced to serve with the Mexicans. The prosecution countered that he had taken his pistol and carbine with him when he had left camp, indicating an intention to desert. He was found guilty and sentenced to death.[20]

Company F was in combat again on September 8. Worth's division attacked Molino del Rey, a fortified building on the outskirts of Mexico City, where 787 Americans were killed or wounded before the Mexicans retreated.[21] Company F's losses were two dead and six wounded in the battle.

Scott's infantry attacked the last Mexican stronghold, Chapultepec Palace, on September 13. The dragoons waited in reserve during the attack. After Chapultepec fell, the dragoons pursued the retreating Mexicans along the causeway leading to the San Cosmo gate.[22]

When the American flag was raised over Chapultepec, Henri Langenhammer and twenty-nine other San Patricios were hanged for desertion in the village of Mixcoac, two miles away.*

Company F and the rest of Scott's army moved into Mexico City, and established their quarters in the public buildings of the city. This occupation duty would last for seven months, until the Treaty of Guadalupe Hidalgo officially ended the war. There were no more major battles, but bandits and guerrillas still attacked American supply trains and travelers.[23]

On May 12, 1848, Pvt. John Law of Company F was part of a squad escorting a paymaster. The twenty-three-year old Englishman went into the town of Cuernavaca to buy some medicine. Law was attacked on his way back:

> . . . I was set upon by some Mexicans, and stabbed and cut severely under my left arm, and both hands were badly cut in parrying or warding off blows. Also received at same time a severe cut some 3½ inches long in my throat, the instrument striking my leather stock cravat and glancing upward or it would have severed the jugular vein. I then got away and ran to the guard house, where I was rolled in blankets by comrades, and carried to hospital, and immediately cared for.[24]

---

*The San Patricio's are honored as heroes in Mexico today. Two ceremonies are held in their honor each year at the Churubusco Convent, one on September 12, and another on St. Patrick's Day.[25]

Law survived the attack, helped build Fort Worth, and was living in Sonoma, California, at the time of his death in 1908.[26]

Pvt. Alphonso Freeman, one of the Certificate of Merit soldiers from Cerro Gordo, was shot in the left shoulder. The bullet lodged in his collarbone. He made his way off the battlefield to a field hospital, where a surgeon removed the lead ball the next day.[27] He probably fought in more battles than any other member of Company F. He had enlisted in the 4th Artillery in 1840, completed one enlistment, and signed up for a second term. He fought with Taylor's army at Palo Alto and Monterrey, and transferred to Thornton's dragoons shortly before the invasion began. He survived the shoulder wound, helped to establish Fort Worth, and settled in the area when he was discharged.* He lived near Weatherford until his death in 1905, about 92 years old. His descendants are still living in Tarrant County at the time of this writing.[28]

Another Certificate of Merit Winner, Francis Knaar, was also discharged in Fort Worth. He settled here and, in 1860, was one of the men who guaranteed the money for the courthouse to be built in the new county seat. He served in the Tarrant County Hussars during the Civil War and was buried in Pioneers Rest Cemetery in 1867.[29]

When the peace treaty was completed, Company F returned to Veracruz. They sailed for New Orleans on July 22, 1848. The regiment established an encampment at East Pascagola, Mississippi, a few miles from Mobile. Company F had served sixteen months in Mexico, and had fought in nearly every battle of Scott's campaign.[30]

Captain Ripley Arnold joined Company F from recruiting service at East Pascagola in October 1848, just before the dragoons embarked for Texas. Two of the men, Sgt. Jacob Dearing and Bugler Thomas Noland, had served with Arnold at Fort Jesup before the war.† The rest of the men were strangers.

At the beginning of November, Arnold and his men embarked for new stations and new adventures in Texas.

---

* His first wife, Amanda Elliston, died in 1857 and is buried at Pioneers Rest Cemetary.

† Noland enlisted in 1844, at the age of twelve and, after serving throughout the war, was discharged at Fort Worth in November 1849.

Ghosts of the Fort

This drawing shows the rocking chair left at the fort, and now on display in the Cross-Timbers Honorable Military Service Recognition Council Display Room in the Tarrant County Courthouse. It may have been made by Sergeant Abraham Harris, who served in Company F, 8th Infantry, and settled in the city and worked as a carpenter. When the fort closed it was the property of Lt. Jonas P. Holliday. When he left in December 1853, he gave the chair to the wife of Dr. Peak, Florence, who was pregnant with her son, Howard. For years the chair was loaned to citizens when a baby was to be born, or someone was very ill, because it was believed to have lucky and curative powers. (Copyright William Potter.)

The fort on the Bluff
This scene shows the fort and the bluff looking southwest. (Copyright William Potter.)

5

Company F, 8th U.S. Infantry Comes to the Bluff

The prospects for peace in Texas dwindled during the summer of 1849 as Fort Worth was being built and the dragoons were beginning their patrols. More stories of Indian attacks were reported in the newspapers. Brevet Major General George M. Brooke was reluctant to believe these reports, but he was also uneasy about the strength of his forces.

Secretary of War George Crawford wrote to Brooke to discuss President Zachary Taylor's policies regarding Texas. Crawford urged Brooke to continue the defensive strategy that Taylor had outlined one year earlierwhen he was the commanding general in the west. Crawford believed that Brooke's twenty-eight companies of regular troops were adequate for the mission. These twenty-eight companies had an authorized strength of a thousand infantrymen, one hundred artillerymen, and three hundred dragoons and were a larger force than any that the Republic of Texas had put in the field. As a last resort, Brooke could ask Governor George Wood to raise new companies of Texas Rangers for federal service. Crawford advised Brooke to keep this matter a secret, because of "the tendency of a large portion of the American people to seek military employment."[1]

Brooke replied that he intended to make few changes in the basic defense plan, but he believed that he needed more troops. He pointed out that most of his twenty-eight companies of regulars were only half full. He had fewer than a thousand men, including musicians, noncommissioned officers, and the sick. He hoped that

Congress would increase the size of each company to seventy-five or a hundred men. He also urged the Taylor Administration to negotiate a treaty between Texas and the Indians, in order to establish the Indians' right to some part of west Texas. "The Indians being excluded from title to all lands by the statute laws of Texas . . . are at an entire loss to know where are to be their boundaries, and where to be permitted to hunt and cultivate."[2]

Because military officers were often reluctant to believe stories of Indian raids, knowing that whites instigated some, but not all, attacks, there was also a belief that the press was inaccurate and inflammatory. So, if it wasn't reported through channels, there was a tendency to disbelieve it. In a letter to Winfield Scott, general in chief of the army, Brooke noted that:

> No Indian forays have been made for some time prior to my arrival, notwithstanding the constant reports in the newspapers of the state of murder and plunder. Many of these reports, or letters, are said to proceed from very interested motives, such as that additional troops may be called out bringing money into the country and even to the farmers is ascribed a wish for an Indian War, that they may dispose of the great excess of their corn crops (which have never been so abundant, and without some such demand would scarcely repay their labor). These are hard suggestions, but nevertheless, these statements are current.[3]

Brooke seemed more confident in his letter to Scott. He reported that he had six companies of the 2nd Dragoons stationed on the northwest frontier. At Ringgold Barracks on the Rio Grande a battery of light artillery was using its seventy horses to conduct mounted patrols. The army had purchased horses for about a hundred infantrymen earlier in the year, and Secretary Crawford had just authorized him to buy enough horses to put two hundred infantrymen in the saddle. He believed that his mounted force would be able to meet any crisis without calling on state volunteers.[4]

Governor Wood did not wait for Brooke to requisition the Texas Rangers. In the summer of 1849 Wood enrolled about two hundred new rangers, and asked the general to muster them into federal service. Mindful of his instructions from the Taylor administration, Brooke refused. However, he soon changed his views. On August 11, 1849, he asked Governor Wood for three companies of rangers, to serve for six months. He explained his decision to the War Department:

> By dispatches received this morning from Corpus Christi, I have been informed that, within four or five miles of that point, several persons have been wounded, some killed, and a German boy, with

> a large number of horses, & other property, had been carried off by a party of Comanche Indians. They were pursued and overtaken by a party of mounted rangers, lately ordered out by Governor Wood, killing four of the Indians, recaptured the boy, all the horses except three or four, with the baggage and provisions of the Indians. This is the first reliable information which has been received by me, of Indians (real Indians) being in that part of the country . . . Under these circumstances, I have not hesitated to make a requisition for three mounted companies.[5]

Other reports confirmed that the Indians were hostile. Indians stole a number of horses from Bvt. Lt. Col. William J. Hardee's dragoon company at Camp Leona.[6]

Brevet Brigadier General William Harney reported that forty or fifty mounted Caddo warriors were visiting farms north of Georgetown, and stealing corn, hogs, and cattle. He had sent troops to order them back to their side of the frontier, but the Indians returned later. He, at this time, also recommended the establishment of a new fort to the south of Fort Graham.[7]

Lieutenant Vielé of the 1st Infantry described an Indian raid near Laredo at that time. Vielé's soldiers were serving as mounted infantry. His account confirms Gen. Worth's fear that small outposts would not be able to dispatch an effective fighting force in an emergency. On July 21, his soldiers and some Mexican laborers were cutting hay on the Rio Grand River above the fort. Some Indians cut their boat loose, and set up an ambush. When it was foiled, the Indians escaped into Mexico. Also, on August 12, a raiding party of Indians again avoided pursuit by crossing the border.[8] Quotes from Vielé's report are in appendix #5–1.

By the end of August 1849, Brooke was thinking of adopting a more aggressive strategy against the Indians. He considered sending his soldiers to attack them in their villages. In the end, he decided that he would need more mounted troops for such an attack to be successful.[9] At the time, it was believed that several thousand Comanche warriors were living in Texas. The actual number was probably in the hundreds.

For the time being, Brooke decided to endorse Harney's recommendation and build a new fort in the Frontier District. The 8th Infantry established the new post, named Fort Gates, on October 26, 1849, on the Leon River.[10] He believed that regulars should man Fort Gates. He feared that the Texas Rangers might attack the Indians living in the area, and start an Indian war. Brooke believed that the rangers were equal to any of his regular troops, but he did not plan to call for any more, because: "the calling out of the three companies already seems to have greatly increased the desire of the people of this state for the raising of more."[11]

Meanwhile Brooke and the army had supply problems. Fort Worth and the other northern posts were difficult and expensive to supply. Most army supplies were transported via the Gulf Coast. Hauling provisions and supplies to the upper Trinity and Brazos by wagon was expensive, and many routes were tried at various times.

Harney thought that supplies for Fort Worth and Fort Graham could be shipped up the Trinity River. The highest point on the Trinity that steamboats could reach was Buffalo, about sixteen miles northeast of Corsicana, and seventy miles from Fort Worth.[12] In order to establish a supply depot there Companies F and H of the 8th Infantry occupied Buffalo in the summer of 1849.

A letter, written on July 21, 1849, from Porter's Bluff, Texas, mentions the army's preparations to supply the northern posts via the Trinity. Porter's Bluff was a settlement across the river from Buffalo.[13] The writer of the letter is identified only as "J. T. L."[14] Quotes from this letter are in appendix #5–2.

Buffalo was an unfortunate choice for a depot. The regimental history of the 8th Infantry, written in 1876, noted that "this place proved so very unhealthy that within a short time, there were no men well enough for duty. Ague and fever prevailed to a frightful extent . . ."[15] "Fever and ague" was a colloquial term for malaria. Fortunately, Brooke decided to withdraw the troops from Buffalo.[16] For more on Brooke's rationale see appendix #5–3.

Companies F and H of the 8th Infantry abandoned the encampment at Buffalo in late September. Company H joined the garrison at Fort Graham.[17] Company F, commanded by Capt. Robert P. Maclay, marched into Fort Worth on October 6, 1849.[18]

Maclay belonged to a distinguished Pennsylvania family. His great-grandfather had been a delegate to the First Continental Congress, and his great-uncle had been one of the first two United States senators from Pennsylvania. Maclay graduated from West Point in 1840, joined the 8th Infantry Regiment, and served in Florida and Mexico. He was wounded at the Battle of Resaca de la Palma, and suffered for years from chronic dysentery, which he contracted in Mexico.[19]

Maclay's second in command was 2nd Lt. John Bold. During the Mexican War, he enlisted in South Carolina's Palmetto Regiment, along with his brother, Charles. John served as a corporal in the battles for Mexico City in 1847. After the war, he successfully applied for a regular army commission, and joined the 8th Infantry in 1848.[20]

Maclay's company included forty-five enlisted men. The first sergeant of Company F from 1848 until 1853 was Edward F. Brenner. Sgt. Brenner had been promoted from private to sergeant for showing exceptional "bravery and good conduct" during the attacks on Molino del Rey and Churubusco, in Mexico. At the time that Company F arrived at Fort Worth, Capt. Maclay had demoted Sergeant Brenner to private, and Sergeant Abraham Harris, another Mexican War veteran, held the top enlisted position. However, higher headquarters reversed Sergeant Brenner's demotion, and he became first sergeant again in January 1850.[21]

Every infantry company was allotted one drummer and one fifer. Company F's drummer and fifer were brothers. John McCann, the fifer, and Henry McCann, the drummer, were both born in New York, and both enlisted in New York City in July 1846. John was twelve years old when he enlisted, and Henry was fourteen. Both boys were assigned to the 8th Infantry, and both served throughout the campaign to capture Mexico City.[22] The two transferred to Company F in the spring of 1849.[23] A third boy, Owen McCann, served in Company C of the same regiment.*

Captain Maclay's infantry company had a background much different from Bvt. Maj. Ripley Arnold's company. Company F of the 8th U.S. Infantry had served throughout the Mexican War, and had been in the thick of the fighting along the Rio Grande and in the Mexico City campaign. However, most of the men were discharged at the end of the war. New recruits filled the ranks of Worth's regiment.

Company F's journey to the Texas frontier was marked by one of the worst army disasters of the era. The 8th Infantry left Jefferson Barracks, Missouri on November 23, 1848, and traveled by riverboat to New Orleans. The troops reached New Orleans about two weeks after cholera broke out in that city. The regiment sailed for Port Lavaca, Texas, on December 15. On December 17, 1848, about 350 soldiers and civilians encamped outside Port Lavaca, waiting for baggage wagons to arrive from San Antonio. A cold front moved in during the early morning hours, bringing wind and rain. At the same time, many soldiers and their families began to fall ill from cholera. A severe cholera epidemic was in progress by dawn.[26]

---

*Henry McCann served in Company K during the Mexican War, and John served in Company I.[24] Owen McCann, also born in New York, enlisted in October 1845, in New York, at the age of thirteen. He served in Mexico and was discharged at Ft. Croghan in October 1850.[25]

The epidemic lasted seven or eight days. 114 soldiers, one officer, and perhaps 35 women and children died in the tragedy. In Company F, twenty-one men died in three days, leaving only thirty men alive.[27] Since people believed that many illnesses were caused by environmental factors, such as weather, it was thought that the storm had caused the sickness. Major Pitcairn Morrison, commanding the troops at Port Lavaca, found the epidemic inexplicable, because his men were well fed, well clothed, and sleeping in new tents. Morris described the epidemic as "one of those mysterious visitations that cannot be accounted for."[28]

The soldiers who survived the epidemic marched inland to Victoria, rested a few days, and then marched to San Antonio. There they stayed at Camp Worth, outside the city, until April 1849. During this period, the companies received new recruits, and exchanged their obsolete flintlocks for new, percussion muskets.[29]* Many children had lost both their parents in the cholera epidemic and were adopted by other soldiers. Worth allowed the quartermaster to issue rations to the orphans.[30] Company F was sent first to Fredericksburg, and then to Austin, Buffalo, and finally Fort Worth.[31]

The arrival of Capt. Maclay's company brought the strength of Fort Worth's garrison up to about ninety men.[32] The infantry could not pursue mounted Indians, but Maj. Arnold certainly needed more men at his post. Infantrymen could cut timber, construct buildings, and guard the post. In an emergency, all able-bodied dragoons would be able to scout and fight.

Brooke's plan made sense, but many infantry officers felt that it made their men into "hewers of wood and drawers of water for more favored corps."[33] And Texas politicians and editors never tired of complaining that the infantry were of no use in Indian warfare. Despite the criticism, Brooke's plan increased the effectiveness of the mounted troops that were available to him.

Now there were two companies in a fort laid out and built for one. It would be a tight squeeze.

---

*The new muskets were almost certainly Model 1842 muskets; conversion of flintlocks to percussion did not get under way until after June, 1849. See the annual reports of the chief of ordnance for 1848 and 1849.

6

How the Fort and the Area Were Described

There are a number of descriptions of the Fort in Fort Worth, the site on which it was located, and the area around the fort. Some of the descriptions were written down at the time they were made, and some were made by people who were there, but recorded some years later.

First Sergeant Abraham Harris recalled, in 1901, how the new post looked when he and the other members of F Company, 8th U.S. Infantry, came to the bluff on October 6, 1849, four months after Bvt. Maj. Ripley Arnold's arrival:

> Major Arnold's headquarters were a tent, pitched on the block just west of the courthouse square; and his command camped around him, according to army regulations. When we arrived, that is Co. F 8th Infantry of which I was a member, we were assigned quarters near the bluff, and my individual quarters were near the clump of live oaks, now standing behind the public wagon shed. In fact those venerable trees were direct at my tent door . . .[1]*

---

*For more information on army tents at this time period, see appendix #6-1. According to the 1898 Sanborn Insurance Co. map, the public wagon shed stood about where the Criminal Courts Building stands today, on the northwest corner of Houston and Belknap streets. According to an undated letter by Mrs. Florence Peak, the officer's quarters were built along Belknap Street, and Dr. Thomas H. William's house stood near the corner of Belknap. These trees may be the ones between the county parking garage and Heritage Park near the corner of Houston and Belknap Streets.

The infantry joined in building the post. Fort Worth, like all U.S. Army posts at the time, was built around an open parade ground with a flagpole near the center. On the north side of the parade ground, closest to the river, the men built two barracks out of logs. Behind the barracks stood cook houses, and cabins for the laundresses. On the south side of the parade ground, the soldiers built three sets of officers' houses. Each house had two rooms, with a covered passageway, or dog trot, separating the two rooms. On the west side of the parade ground, the soldiers constructed a cabin that served as the post adjutant's office. A hospital stood next to the adjutant's office. On the east side, the men constructed stables, a guard house, and storehouses.

Most of the buildings at Fort Worth were constructed of logs, with dirt floors. Some buildings, such as the stable, were "palisade works," a type of construction common on the frontier, in which walls were made of logs placed vertically in the ground. Others, such as Maj. Arnold's quarters, were built of hewn logs—logs cut flat on two sides to make a smooth, finished appearance. The army provided broad axes and adzes for hewing timber at frontier posts. As the fort grew, the Quartermaster Department provided a horse-powered sawmill and some lumber was purchased from civilians. Thus, some buildings, such as the hospital, were of frame construction.

However, the results were not satisfactory. Lieutenant John Bold described one set of officers' quarters in 1851: "Timber for frame, got out by enlisted men, and put up green. The weather-boarding has shrunk so much, as to admit winds and rain on all sides. Roof admits rain freely."[2] The other buildings at the post, according to Bold, were just as bad.

Part of the problem may have been that the infantry, like the dragoons, began to fall ill with malaria. The ninety or so men of the garrison suffered 247 cases of malaria during October, November, and December 1849.[3] According to Lt. Bold, "The buildings were put up under a burning sun, with little or no aid from the government, by a weak and sickly command, unacclimated, and breathing the infectious malaria of the bottom-lands, where alone timber suitable for building can be obtained. They were erected hastily, and are of a very temporary character."[4]

One of the first descriptions of Fort Worth was written towards the end of 1849. Brevet Major General George M. Brooke ordered Lt. W. H. C. Whiting of the Corps of Engineers to travel to all the forts in the Frontier District to make a report on their condition and usefulness. The following is an excerpt from his report on Fort Worth:.

Fifty-four miles above Fort Graham, in nearly a north direction, at the junction of the Clear and West Forks of the Trinity River is Fort Worth. An excellent road skirting the western edge of the lower Cross Timbers is already made between the posts. The latter is the most northerly of the chain of forts and is the most objectionable in its position. The Trinity, a rapid stream to which belong many tributaries, is subject to very sudden rises. Unlike the rivers to the SW, its valley is a level flat between which and the great prairie there is but one descent. Between two and three miles wide and covered by a heavy growth of trees and underwood, this valley is by the freshets converted into soft mud and when the water subsides it leaves to the sun a great mass of half-rotted vegetable matter and half-dried mud, whence the constant sickness in the region is engendered. Fever and ague prevail through the whole year and the troops have suffered from it very much.

The timber which exists at all westward of the Cross Timbers is only found in the valleys of the streams and there it is impossible to live. The troops are therefore forced to the high plains, exposed all winter to the northers and sleets of the country and in summer to the scorching heats.

The fort has been laid out on a scale rather contracted, probably as designed originally but for one company, and the arrangement of the stables I cannot commend. They are much too near the quarters of both officers and men, and however thorough their police may be, in summer cannot but be offensive. The question of security is readily settled. A picketing with a guard is ample, particularly considering the nature and mode of warfare of the public enemy. To place the stable within shot from the barracks and in such wise that its approach in event of a coup-de-main is commanded, I think is all that is required.[5]

Lieutenant Whiting thought that the stables were too close to the barracks, but Maj. Arnold knew better. The horses were safer that way. A letter from Bvt. Lt. Col. William J. Hardee, written from Camp Leona on August 26, 1849, illustrates why:

My own tent and the tents of my men are about a hundred yards from the stable; two trusty non-commissioned officers sleep within the enclosure; a sentinel guards the horses, who cries the hours regularly; the horses are all fastened with chain halters, which cannot be broken off without noise, and yet, I regret to say, horses have been stolen in spite of these precautions.[6]

Hardee was a graduate of West Point, had studied cavalry tactics in France, and was a rising star in the regiment. One can imagine how painful it was to report to Brooke that a handful of savages had stolen the horses from his own stable.

Lieutenant Whiting's report continues:

> A mill worked by horse-power hard by the post and the thickly wooded bottom of the Trinity furnished cheap and ample supplies of lumber and fuel. A coarse grained marble making excellent building material and plenty of lime and sand are abundant. No post is so plentifully supplied as to forage and subsistence. Within 40 miles are the little villages of Dallas and Alton and numerous hamlets are found through the Cross Timbers which afford nearly all that is required for consumption by the troops.
>
> The route between Fort Worth and the Red River is already practicable for about 80 miles touching the western edge of the Cross Timbers. After crossing Hickory Creek, 30 miles north from the post, the houses of squatters are found every ten or twelve miles, until the village of Preston is found in Coffee's Bend of the Red River.
>
> The distance between Fort Washita and Fort Worth is 120 miles and entirely too great for the garrisons to scout over effectively. An extensive line of country is exposed to the depredations of Wichita's, a wild tribe with whom as yet no relations have been established. They live upon the Red River some 50 miles west of the line and are particularly hostile. Should it be deemed sufficiently important to establish another post between Forts Washita and Worth, I would recommend the position at the Elm Fork of the Trinity, formerly a ranger station and about midway on the road, as satisfying all the requisite conditions.[7]

Whiting offered an explanation for a puzzling phenomenon. Most of the Indians known to live in Texas made their homes in the north, not far from Forts Worth and Graham. But, apart from the occasional theft of a horse or a few heads of cattle, the Indian attacks all took place in south Texas. Whiting believed that the Indians were afraid of retribution from Fort Graham.

> Fort Graham is regarded by them as a council spot, a place where they will make their treaties and receive their presents. To see and feel the power of the country directly at their homes has upon them a great effect. Its proof is that while hundreds, perhaps thousands of them are ranging through the woods and up the creeks it seems perfectly safe to travel, and the numerous animals of the post graze on the broad valley of the Brazos mouth in and out without disturbance or theft. The relations which exist at this post satisfy me that the nearer to them garrisons of force are established the better the results.[8]

A historical sketch in the 1877 City Directory describes the general appearance of Fort Worth when the buildings were finished:

> The quarters for the soldiers, with shops for the smiths and other artisans in a double row of buildings, made of logs or of pickets, and all neatly whitewashed, composed the North line of a parallelogram, and were immediately on the bluff. Facing these, and distant some two hundred and fifty feet South, were the officers' quarters. The eastern boundary of the parallelogram consisted of long lines of stables, while the hospital building, quartermaster and commissary offices completed the enclosure on the West. The enclosed space made an ample parade, and was decorated East of center with the tall flagstaff.
>
> The larger warehouses containing Quartermaster and Commissary stores, were on a line with, and West of, the officers' quarters, while the sutler's store still West and North of these, occupied the ground where is now the family residence of our late fellow-citizen G. W. Newman.
>
> The buildings were comfortable, and with their ever freshly whitened walls in regular lines, presented quite an agreeable appearance.[9]

Almost a year later, on June 17, 1851 Col. Samuel Cooper inspected the post and described the fort in his report:

> The buildings of the post were formed chiefly of logs by the labor of the troops. They were arranged in a square and consisted of three sets of officers quarters; six blocks of company quarters, for two companies, with kitchens and mess rooms; a small commissary store-house, in which the commissary & qur. masters stores were carefully arranged and preserved; bake-house; company store-rooms; hospital with kitchen; adjutant & quartermasters office; carpenter & blacksmith's shop; laundress quarters; and a range of stables for horses of one company, with corn crib and forage lot. I was unable to obtain an estimate of the cost of these buildings, but suppose it could not fall short of $4,000, including the price for materials.[10]

The final inspection, and the one which gives us the clearest picture of what the fort looked like was made by Col. William G. Freeman on September 7, 1853, ten days before the fort closed. His description of the fort was:

> The post is on a disputed tract of land, and nothing has been paid for rent of for the timber and fuel cut. The buildings (Figure Q) are of logs and were constructed by the troops. A dragoon express is sent weekly to Fort Graham for the mail, which is brought there by the same conveyance from Waco, the post officer for both stations.

> The nearest towns or villages are Dallas, with 350 inhabitants, 38 miles East, and Birdville and Alton, with a population of 50 each, distant 9 and 35 miles, respectively.[11]

It is figure Q from his report that allowed Mr. William B. Potter to make drawings in the early 1990s of the fort, the buildings, and life at the fort, which show in great detail the exact dimensions of the buildings. He began the project to try to convince the citizens and government of

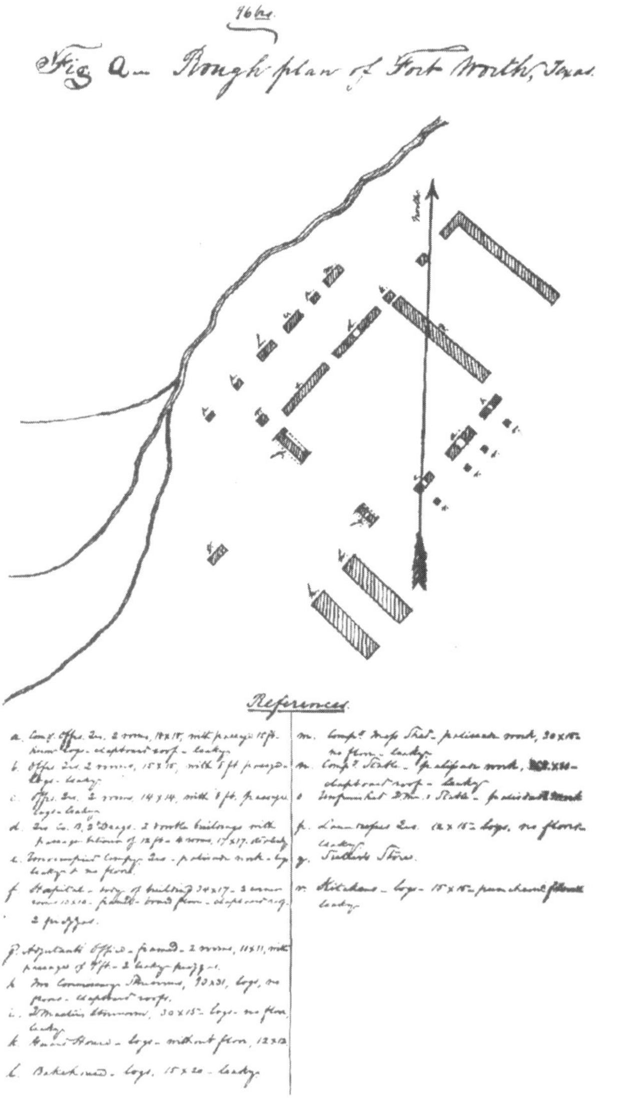

Fort Worth, that the fort should be reconstructed as a historical site in order to honor the history of the founding of Fort Worth.

Dr. Williams, the post surgeon who arrived in late 1849 provided future generations with a description of the native plants and animals of the area. Williams's report on the geography and climate of Fort Worth, submitted to the surgeon general in 1852, reads:

> It is built upon the northern extremity of an extensive high prairie, with a southern exposure, and at an elevation of one hundred

Fig. Q
Rough Plan of Fort Worth, Texas

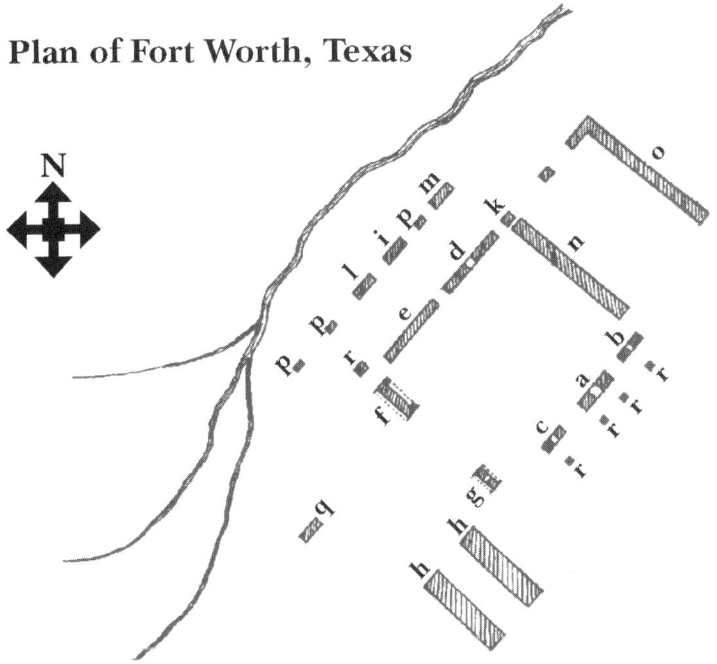

- a. Comp. Offrs. Qrs. 2 rooms, 18 x 18, with passages 15 ft — hewn logs. Clapboard roof – leaky.
- b. Offrs. Qrs. 2 rooms, 15 x 15, with 8 ft. passage. Logs – leaky.
- c. Offrs. Qrs. 2 rooms, 14 x 14, with 8 ft. passage. Logs – leaky.
- d. Qrs. Co. B, 2 Drags. – 2 double buildings with passage between of 12 ft – 4 rooms, 17 x 17, roof leaky..
- e. Unoccupied Compy. Qrs. – palisade work – logs. Leaky & no floor.
- f. Hospital – body of building 34 x 17 – 2 corner rooms 10 x 10 –painted-board floor – clapboard roof —- 2 piazzas.
- g. Adjutant's Office – framed – 2 rooms, 11 x 11, with passage of 7 ft. – 2 leaky piazzas.
- h. QMs. Commissary Storerooms, 40 x 31, logs, no floor – clapboard roofs.
- i. Q. Master's Storerooms, 30 x 15 – logs – no floor, leaky.
- k. Guard House – logs – without floor, 12 x 12.
- l. Bakehouse – logs, 15 x 20 – leaky.
- m. Comp's. Mess Shed – palissade work, 30 x 10 – no floor – leaky.
- n. Comp's. Stable – palissade work, 40 x 30 – clapboard roof – leaky.
- o. Unfinished Q. M's Stable – palissade work.
- p. Laundresses Qrs. 12 x 15 – logs, no floors, leaky.
- q. Sutler's Store.
- r. Kitchens – log – 15 x 15 – puncheon floor. leaky.

and fifty feet above the ordinary low-water mark of the Trinity. Immediately above the fort, the "Clear Fork" of the Trinity empties into the "West Fork;" the former running west by south, and the latter northwest by west. These streams form at their junction an expansive bottom, covered with a dense growth of trees and underwood. This bottom, following the course of "West Fork," extends from west to north, and from thence to east of the post.

Southeast of the fort lies "Sycamore Creek," a small tributary of the Trinity. On the South and southwest there is an extended prairie.

The general character of the country is high, undulating prairie, alternating with the rich and fertile bottoms along the water-courses . . . The most remarkable features of this portion of the country are the two great belts of forest, known as the Cross Timbers. The upper is about thirty-five miles north, and the lower, five miles south of Fort Worth, and are composed entirely of post-oak. They extend from the Brazos across Red River, and are separated by a prairie, which, with the exception of clumps of mesquite trees, is entirely destitute of wood.

Settlements are rapidly increasing along the borders of the lower Cross Timbers, below the fort, on account of the convenience of timber for building, fencing, &c., and the abundant supply of water.

. . . The animals that inhabit this section of country are: the antelope, red deer, black wolf, gray wolf, prairie wolf, foxes (gray and red), black bear, panther, tiger-cat, wild cat, lynx, polecat, opossum, squirrels (gray and red,) hare, and Mexican hog. The buffalo have entirely disappeared, and but a few droves of wild horses are now to be found near the post. Among the birds, we have the wild turkey, pinnated grouse, quail, turtle-dove, meadow-lark, mocking-bird, red bird, blue-jay, blackbird, red-headed woodpecker, flicker, prairie bird of Paradise, sparrow, turkey-buzzard, raven, crow, hawks, and owls, of different varieties.

The fish that are afforded by the streams are: catfish, buffalo, trout, perch, and sunfish.

The trees that appertain to the country are: red oak, burr oak, post oak, live oak, black-jack oak, elm, ash, pecan, sycamore, black walnut, box-elder, hackberry, cottonwood, and mulberry. Of the plants growing in the vicinity, I have noticed the red bud, buckeye, flowering dogwood, woodbine, stag-horn sumac, smooth sumac, sweet-brier, blackberry, common elder, milkweed, wild morning glory, Indian turnip, black snakeroot, yellow ladies-slipper, red mulberry, wild plum, honey-locust, red root, two-leafed Solomon's seal, common sunflower, and dandelion.[12]

There was always some question about who owned the land on which the fort was built. Colonel Middleton Tate Johnson had told Arnold that he had claimed the land, and the army could use it as long as they needed it.[13] The confusion on titles for land resulted in a lawsuit against Maj. Arnold. In May 1852, Maj. Arnold returned to defend himself in the District County of Birdville. A man named Louis Cohen sued Arnold for cutting trees on land which Cohen clamed to own. Arnold described the case in a letter to the adjutant general:

> When I built Fort Worth, No owner could be found to and land in the vicinity, and I cut indiscriminately. About one year after, this man Ca-heen settled near the post, and commenced selling liquor to the soldiers & Indians. I forbid him to enter the limits of the garrison upon penalty of being confined to the guard house. He then sent me notice forbidding me to cut any timber or wood upon a certain section of land in the vicinity.[14]

Arnold ordered his men to stop cutting on Cohen's claim, but Cohen sued Arnold for the loss of fifty thousand oak, ash, elm, pecan, and hickory trees, valued at $2000. Arnold's lawyers, McCoy and Reagan, countered that Cohen had no valid title to the land. The jury voted in favor of Arnold.

Site Plan

The drawing on the following page shows the location and size of each building. We don't know exactly how far apart the buildings were, but can estimate from the locations and separation of similar buildings at other forts that still exist, or from those for which we have information. (Copyright William Potter.)

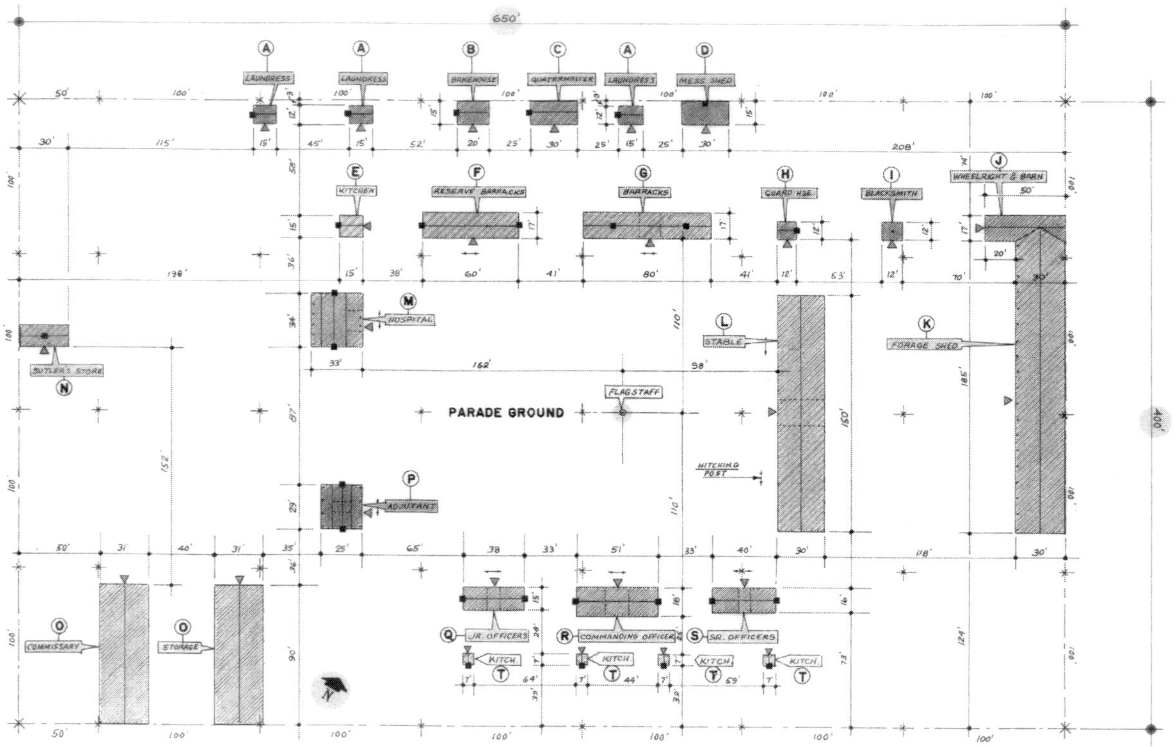

SPECIAL NOTES TO BUILDER: THE BUILDING DRAWINGS IN THIS PRESENTATION HAVE BEEN MADE AS A GUIDE UPON WHICH ACTUAL CONSTRUCTION CAN BE BASED. IT SHOULD BE NOTED THAT ALL THE BUILDINGS WERE SHODDILY DONE, HAVING BEEN BUILT BY INEXPERIENCED SOLDIERS. POSSIBLE EXCEPTIONS WERE THE COMMANDING OFFICER'S QUARTERS AND THE HOSPITAL. ALL BUILDINGS, HOWEVER, WERE FRESHLY WHITEWASHED INCLUDING THOSE WITH "BARK-ON" LOGS AND WERE SAID TO PRESENT A VERY PLEASING LOOK.

SYMBOLS:
- ▼ DENOTES BLDG FRONT
- HITCHING POSTS
- BUILDINGS
- FLAGSTAFF
- 100 FOOT MARKS
- CHIMNEYS

wm.b.potter © 1990

SCALE: $\frac{3}{4}'' = 40'$

OLD FORT WORTH

SITE PLAN

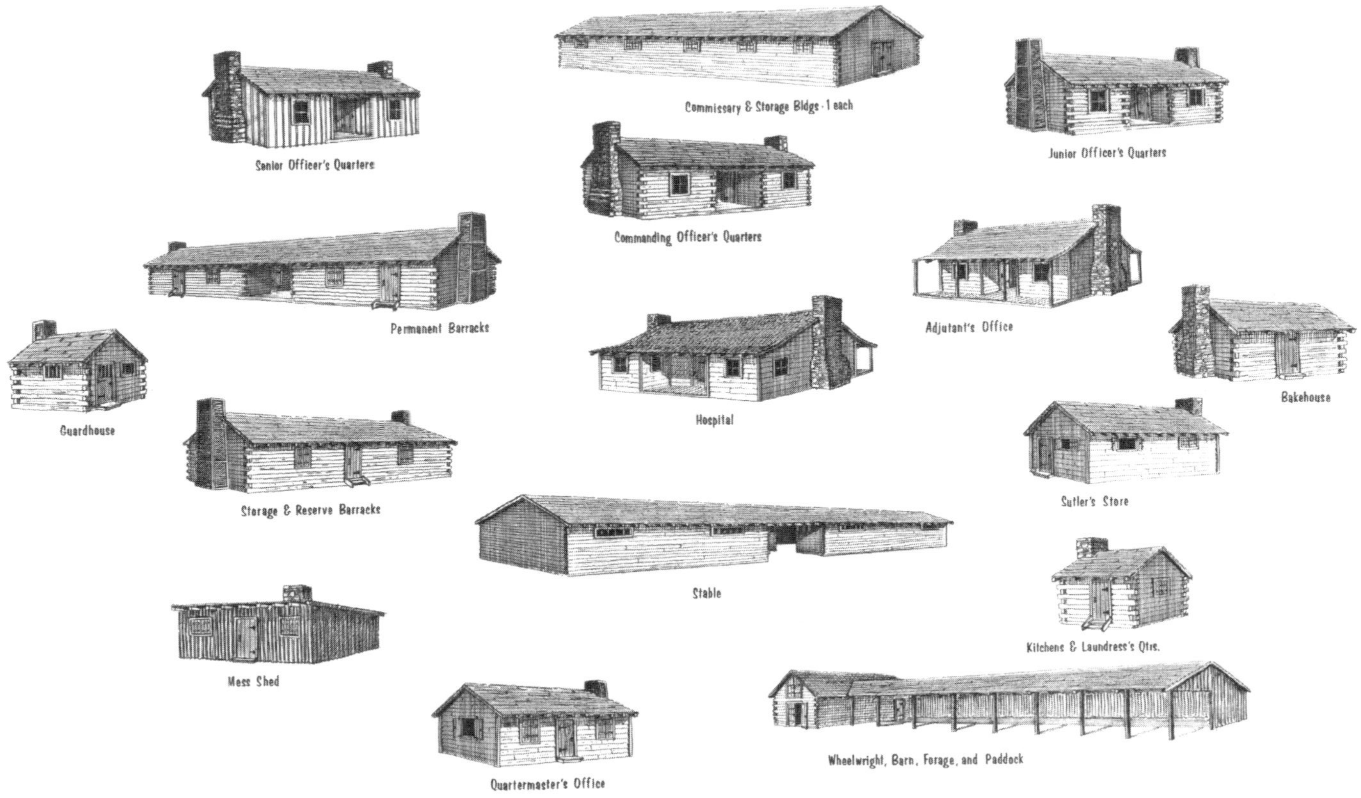

Buildings

This sketch shows each of the buildings at the fort. (Copyright William Potter.)

Old Fort Worth
U.S. Army Outpost on the Trinity

This drawing shows the fort from a bird's-eye view, and depicts each structure and area in detail. Beginning in the upper left corner and moving clockwise, the first area is the stable area with the forage shed in the rear and the stables in the front. The tree shown in the stable area may be the one still standing back of the old criminal courts building at the corner of Houston and Belknap. The next area is the garden where the soldiers were supposed to grow their own fresh food. Then comes the officers' quarters with the commanding officer's house in the center of the three. In the upper right corner are the two quartermaster warehouses, where food and equipment were stored until it was issued to the troops. Below is another garden area and the sutter's store. The suttler was a civilian authorized to do business on the post. In front of them are the post headquarters and the post hospital. Along the bottom of the drawing are the two barracks for the enlisted men, with the kitchens and bakehouses for the troops behind them, and storage sheds for saddles and horse equipment. (Copyright William Potter.)

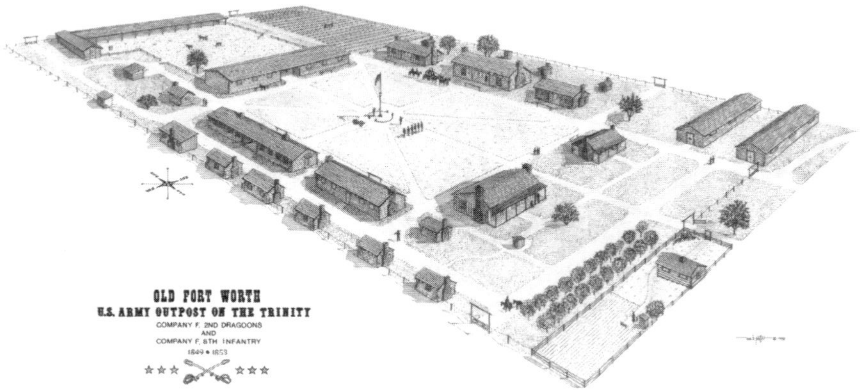

7

The Military Situation In Late 1849

By the end 1849, the line of forts that Bvt. Maj. Gen. Worth had planned was complete. The Frontier District in which Fort Worth was the northernmost post included eight forts. The southernmost fort in the line was Fort Duncan, at Eagle Pass on the Rio Grande. Then came Fort Inge, on the Leona River near today's Uvalde.[1] Next was Fort Lincoln, established at D'Hanis;[2] Fort Martin Scott about two miles east of Fredericksburg;[3] Fort Croghan, located three miles south of Burnet;[4] Fort Gates, on the Leon River south of Gatesville; Fort Graham on the upper Brazos; and then Fort Worth. Fort Merrill, on the Nuedes River near George West, would be added on March 1, 1850.

A similar chain of forts, manned by artillery and infantry, guarded the lower gulf coast and the Rio Grande. Fort Polk was at Port Isabel, guarding Brazos Santiago Pass, the entrance to Laguna Madre.[5] Fort Brown, near Brownsville, served as the headquarters and supply depot for the Rio Grande District.[6] Ringgold Barracks, near Rio Grande City, lay about a hundred miles west of the coast,[7] and Camp Crawford, later known as Fort McIntosh, at Laredo.[8]

Military forces in the state of Texas were administered by the 8th Military Department, with headquarters in San Antonio. The army rented the Alamo, repaired its chapel, and used it as a quartermaster depot. Brevet Brigadier General Harney, the commander of the Frontier District and colonel of the 2nd Dragoons, made his headquarters in Austin. Between twenty and thirty dragoons were usually stationed there, including the musicians of the regimental band.[9]

The mission of the Frontier District was to keep the whites south and east, and the Indians to the north and west of the line of forts. To insure this, they mounted regular patrols. On March 20, 1849, three months before soldiers came to the Trinity. Worth issued orders directing how his dragoons should conduct their patrols. Each fort would send out a patrol, or "scout," on the second day of each month. The scout would include at least twelve enlisted men, under the command of an officer or noncommissioned officer, and would ride north and east until it reached the next fort in the line. For example, the scout from Fort Graham would ride to Fort Worth and back. The scout from Fort Worth rode to Fitzhugh's old ranger station, following a route much the same as that of today's IH-35. The scouts were to stay out for two to three weeks, and return to their home base by the twentieth or twenty-fifth of the month.[10]

The patrols' first priority was to protect white settlers from the Indians. Their second was to stop Indian war parties from crossing into Mexico, as the United States had agreed to do in the peace treaty of Guadalupe Hidalgo. Their third was to protect the Indians from the whites, and to promote good relations with the tribes.[11] Worth's scouting orders, with some modifications, remained in effect for about two years.

When Company F came to Texas, the dragoons were armed with sabers, Hall carbines, and single shot pistols. The Hall carbine, in use since 1833, was an innovative weapon, which loaded at the breech rather than the muzzle. The Hall fired a paper cartridge and had to be reloaded for every shot.[12] The dragoons' muzzle-loading percussion pistol, carried in a holster over the pommel of the saddle, was reliable, but slow to reload. Around the end of June 1849, the dragoons were issued six-shot Colt "Walker" revolvers for the first time. These weapons, along with all their equipment, clothing, food, and water were carried on their saddles.

In December 1848, the Ordnance Department had five hundred Colt "Walker" revolvers stored at the Baton Rouge Arsenal. These pistols, produced for the Mexican War but never issued, were reserved for the 8th Military Department.[13] On May 1, Harney wrote that he expected the pistols to arrive any day.[14] They were issued to the dragoons in Fort Worth sometime in late May or early June.*

*On June 15, Harney notified Lt. Samuel Starr that two of Starr's men had pawned their Colt pistols.[15]

Ordnance officers in San Antonio issued instructions on the care and use of Colt pistols on June 25, 1849.[16] The new Colt revolvers gave the dragoons a significant advantage in combat with the Indians. The Indians, aware that their bows and arrows were no match for the dragoons' carbines and revolvers, avoided fighting the soldiers. Indian fighting in Texas became an exercise in chasing the Indians until the soldiers' horses and supplies were exhausted.

When Bvt. Brig. Gen. Harney took temporary command of the 8th Military Department after Worth's death on May 7, 1849, he took a less conciliatory approach than Worth had. He directed his post commanders to inform the Indians that they were forbidden to go below the line of the forts. If Indians were thought to be on a raiding expedition, they would "be pursued and treated as open enemies,"[17] and he suspected that there was a major leak in the line through the two trading houses. He wanted to shut down the Indian trading houses. He was convinced that the trading houses encouraged Indian raids: "The most notorious are Torrey's, situated on the Brazos, and Warren's in the Upper Cross-Timbers, on the Red River. So long as these people are permitted to carry on trade with the Indians, at a distance from military control, and to receive from them, property which has evidently been stolen, we may strive in vain to prevent the depredations . . ."[18]

He asked the commander of the Western Division either to close the trading houses or force them to move to a military post where they could be properly supervised. His frustrations highlight a new problem for the army. In the past, they had fought Indians in territories that had not yet achieved statehood. Law enforcement was a federal responsibility, and the soldiers had authority over both whites and Indians. In Texas, only the state legislature could regulate the conduct of white citizens. The legislature declined to close the trading houses. On August 20, 1849, the adjutant general of the army acknowledged that U.S. troops had no authority over white Texans. The army therefore had no authority to keep whites on their side of the frontier line.[19]*

*The federal and state governments had different goals in mind. Washington wanted the state legislature to set aside reservations in Texas, where the Indians could be settled, monitored, and taught to farm. The state government wanted Washington to remove the Indians to reservations on federal lands in the Indian Territory. The stalemate continued until 1854, when the legislature relented and created two small reservations west of

By June 1849, Harney realized that Indian war parties from north Texas were traveling to the unsettled wilderness south of San Antonio and attacking whites. Once the Indians were in south Texas, they could live off of wild game, and attack settlers and travelers from Eagle Pass to Corpus Christi. He learned that many of these war parties traveled through the Bandera Pass, northwest of San Antonio. To interdict these war parties, he stepped up patrols there.[20]

Worth's permanent replacement, Bvt. Maj. Gen. George M. Brooke, took command of the 8th Military Department on July 7, 1849.[21] Brooke had served competently since 1808. Despite reports of trouble with the Indians, Secretary of War George Crawford ordered Brooke to avoid conflict if possible. He had Crawford's instructions copied and sent to Fort Worth and the other posts. Crawford's guidance read in part:

> The red man is usually alive to a sense of justice, as he is quick in the resentment of injury. To the extent of your authority, you will redress his wrongs and thereby furnish the practical proof that your acts are in keeping with your intent in doing justice. At the same time . . . if they are to be taught by punishment alone, let them have their first lesson, with such repetitions as may be efficacious.
>
> Our aim should be, to act toward the Indians with firmness and truth, and, at the same time, avoid a course of conduct with them, which might tend to destroy their confidence. No severe measures should be adopted against them, without clear and undoubted evidence of their guilt. Such a course might involve the government in a border war, without our having justice on our side, to sustain us.[22]

Brooke issued more instructions to his junior officers concerning scouts. If a patrol discovered an Indian war party, the patrol leader should send a messenger to the nearest post, so that a second detachment could join in the pursuit. It was apparent that the real challenge was not fighting Indians, but catching them.[23]

Patrol leaders often reported that, when their supplies ran out, they had to abandon the trails of Indian war parties. To increase the range of his mounted troops, Brooke ordered the patrols to take one pack mule for every two soldiers. The mules would carry equipment, ammunition, rations for the men, and forage for the animals. To lighten the load, rations were limited to hard bread and coffee.

Fort Worth on two different forks of the Brazos. Many Texas tribes moved onto the reservations in 1855. Local whites treated them so badly that, in 1859, the federal government moved them to reservations in the Indian Territory for their own safety.

Post commanders were to hire four civilian muleteers to manage the animals. Commanders were also to hire one man to serve as a guide and interpreter. Guides should be "men of intelligence," who knew the countryside and the Indian languages.[24]*

Brooke ordered a mountain howitzer to be stationed at Fort Worth.[26] The mountain howitzer was a small cannon, able to fire a twelve-pound exploding shell up to one thousand yards. In rough terrain, it could be disassembled and carried on mules. It was usually kept at the fort, and was not taken on routine scouts. Fort Worth's howitzer arrived at some time in the last three months of 1849.[27]†

A few of Maj. Arnold's official letters from Fort Worth are preserved in the National Archives. They describe life at the new post in the summer of 1849. On June 18, just twelve days after he established Fort Worth, Maj. Arnold wrote to the adjutant general to refute a newspaper report that the Indians had stolen some of his horses:

> Having seen a paragraph going the rounds of the newspapers, stating that the Dragoons above Waco village have lost many horses by the Indians, I have the honor to contradict such a report and to state that the two companies of Dragoons which have been under my command since their arrival in Texas Companies F and I have not had a single horse stolen since their arrival in Texas in November last nor have I heard of any Indian depredations committed in this part of the country for several months.
>
> About one hundred Indians of the different wild tribes are now visiting me. They brought down and delivered up some thirty-five horses, which they had taken from the Wichitas, horses stolen within the last year from citizens. Three Wichita chiefs are here and promise everything for the future. All is peace and quiet on this frontier.[28]

After the Indians left, Arnold received word that some settlers believed that the Indians still had a number of stolen horses. A rumor circulated that the settlers would gather on July 14 to attack the Indians. He had no authority to stop the settlers, but he reported the news to Brooke. On July 23, Brooke urged Governor Wood to use his authority to prevent the attack. He wrote:

> . . . official information has been received from the officer commanding the military post on the West Fork of the Trinity, of a

---

*An 1851 document named John Lewis, a Delaware Indian, as Fort Worth's guide and interpreter.[25]

†It was this howitzer that Maj. Arnold was supposed to have used to drive off a band of hostile Indians in April 1851.

> contemplated expedition against the Indians in that quarter, under the command of a Mr. Maloney of Denton County, Texas, for the (avowed) purpose of recovering stolen horses. It is contended by Mr. Maloney that a party which lately came in, and delivered up some stolen horses (which they had captured from the Wichitas) had many others in their possession which had been stolen from our citizens. The officer in command above mentioned [Brevet Maj. Arnold] states that he knows this to be false. The company of Mr. Maloney was to have rendezvoused at Hickory Creek, about 23 miles from the post, on the 14th inst.[29]*

One of Arnold's chief concerns was a lack of soldiers. A dragoon company was authorized one captain, two lieutenants, and sixty-one enlisted men.[30†] On June19, only forty-six enlisted men were actually assigned to Company F. Of the thirty-seven privates, seven were on some sort of special duty, such as clerk, wagon driver, saddler, or hospital steward. Five were too sick to work. Arnold reported that Private Matthew Patterson, who had suffered so much on the rainy march from Houston to Austin, was "perfectly worthless—can't trust him with horse or equipment."[31] Arnold decided to plead his case with the adjutant general in Washington. He sent him a copy of the company roll call together with the following message:

> General: I have the honor to ask that you look over the enclosed roll of my company and to request that if there are any drilled recruits at the Cavalry Depot at Carlisle Barracks, Pennsylvania that my company be filled up. (Those assigned me from detachment brought out by Lieutenant Smith in November last with one exception had not even been drilled at the Carbine Manual or Saber Exercises or at least knew nothing of either).
>
> I am building a new post at this place (the extreme Northern Frontier yet occupied) and my company is so small that I cannot keep up my scouting parties. I have represented this matter to the Col. of the Regiment i.e., Harney and have asked that I might at least have a subaltern officer. I require a bugler. The boy that I have is sickly and his time will expire in November next.[32]

---

*Maloney's expedition appears to have been a rumor or a threat. In any case, there is no subsequent mention of the matter in official records. (Vigilante attacks of this type would force the federal government to close the Brazos River Indian Reservations in 1859.)

†Companies of dragoons, infantry, and mounted riflemen were each allowed 1 captain, 1 first lieutenant, 1 second lieutenant, 4 sergeants, and 4 corporals. A dragoon company was authorized 1 farrier/blacksmith, 2 buglers, and 50 privates. A company of mounted riflemen included 2 farrier/blacksmiths, 2 buglers, and 64 privates. An infantry company included 2 musicians and 42 privates.

Arnold's manpower shortage grew worse as the summer went on. The dragoons of Company F were victims of malaria in increasing numbers. At times, as much as half of the garrison was sick.

Malaria was endemic to the Trinity River Valley. July, August, and September seem to have been the worst months. The first Texas Rangers to be stationed in the area suffered a high rate of illness. Governor J. P. Henderson reported in November 1846 that Capt. Andrew Stapp's company "have been so severely afflicted with sickness during the latter part of the summer and fall that they have not been able to give the required protection. They will be able however to do so as soon as they recover their health."[33] Detailed medical reports are not available, but malaria seems a likely culprit. In 1848, four of Fitzhugh's rangers died of "fever" at the Hickory Creek Station.[34] In the summer of 1848, a group of French socialists tried to establish a commune a few miles from the Hickory Creek Station. The settlement was abandoned after the group fell ill with fever and seven men died.

Anopheles mosquitoes, which breed in standing water, transmit malaria. To construct buildings for the new post, the men had to go into the forests that grew on the floodplain of the Trinity to cut timber. These woods were a breeding ground for the mosquitoes. On June 30, twelve men were sick.[35] In July, the forty-seven soldiers at Fort Worth suffered forty-five cases of malaria.[36] On July 31, twenty-three men, half the garrison, were sick.[37]

There was no army doctor available to serve at Fort Worth, so Maj. Arnold hired a civilian physician named Jesse M. Standifer. Dr. Standifer, formerly of Shelby County, had been the contract surgeon for Middleton Johnson's frontier ranger company.[38] His family lived at Johnson's Station while he worked at the fort. He named his first son Ripley Arnold Standifer.[39]

People had recognized a connection between fevers and standing water since ancient times.[40] In 1849, doctors believed that when dead plants decayed in water, they gave off invisible vapors. These vapors were believed to cause the disease which we call malaria, and which they knew as intermittent fever. Nineteenth-century physicians recognized that a hilltop was a healthier place to live than a river bottom. On higher ground, the wind would disperse the vapors, and fewer people would get sick. Escaping malaria was the reason the fort was moved from Live Oak Point to a bluff overlooking the Trinity River. With half of his men sick, he hoped that the hilltop would prove a healthier site.[41]

The move provided little relief. Dr. Standifer reported thirty-four cases of malaria in August and forty four cases in September, with twenty-one men sick on the last day of the month.[42] The soldiers continued to cut timber in the river bottom, where they were bitten and infected. Quinine was an effective treatment for the illness, but it did not prevent reinfection. The sickness rate did not improve until November brought cooler weather.[43]

The harsh grips of malaria and a lack of soldiers made Maj. Arnold's assignment a difficult one. However, such conditions were common at frontier army posts. Arnold was well prepared for the task. At age thirty-two, he had worn the uniform of a dragoon officer for eleven years. He had already faced similar challenges in Florida, Louisiana, and Mexico.

One of his Christmas presents in 1849 would be not only some additional troops, but an officer who could help him with the myriad of additional duties officers have to perform when they are at a fort.

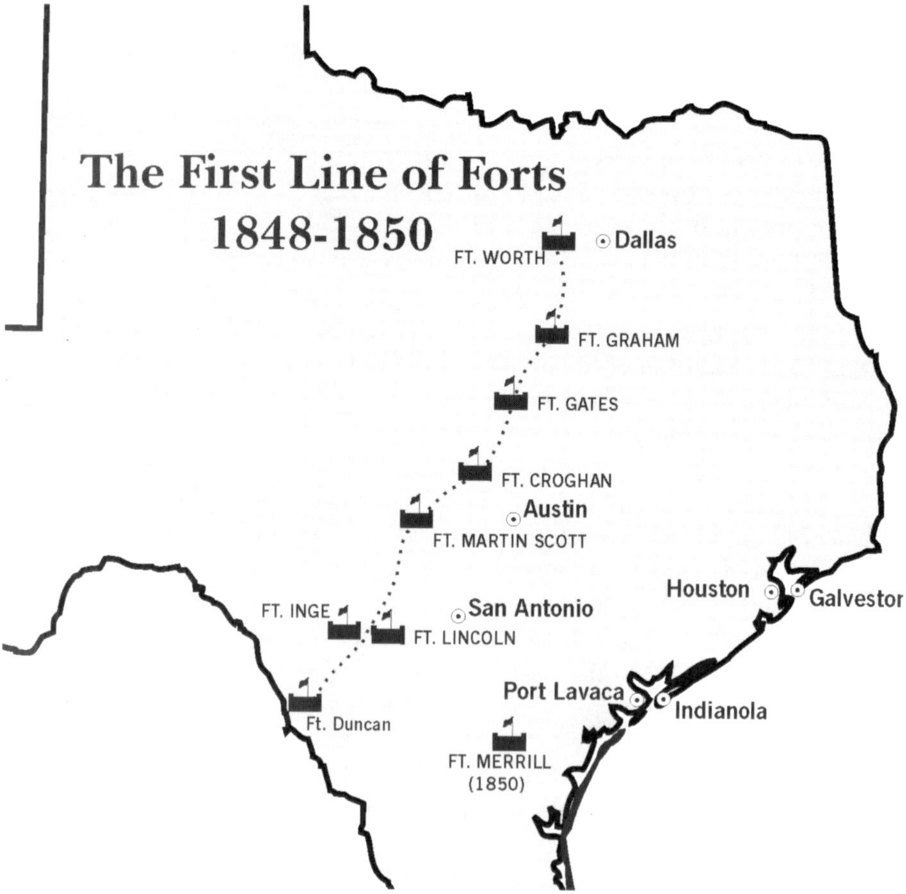

8

Lieutenant Samuel Starr

Eighteen dragoon recruits and one officer joined the garrison at Fort Worth on Christmas Day 1849.[1] The officer was 2nd Lt. Samuel Starr, newly reassigned to Company F. He had served in the company the previous spring at Towash Village and Fort Graham. This time, he was permanently assigned to Company F and would remain for two years.

He had had an extraordinary career in the army. He was born in Leyden, New York, on July 31, 1810. His father moved the family to Rome, New York, a short time later and began operating a hotel.[2] His letters indicate that he received a good education, but after working as a carpenter, he enlisted in the 4th United States Artillery on October 27, 1832.

His enlistment records show that he was five feet seven inches tall and had fair skin, blue eyes, and brown hair.[3] He soon became a sergeant in Company G, 4th U.S. Artillery, served in Florida, and was in at least one skirmish with the Seminoles.[4] He left the service when his enlistment expired in October 1837.[5]

He married Miss Eliza Kurtz, a fellow New Yorker, in 1841. They had a son and a daughter; the daughter they named Achsah Kate.[6] It is not clear what trade Starr pursued between 1837 and 1846. At the time the Mexican War broke out, he was unemployed and having difficulty finding work.[7]

Before the Mexican War, the Corps of Engineers included only officers. When the war began, Congress created a company of engineer troops. It was organized and trained at West Point.* Samuel Starr enlisted in Company A, Corps of Engineers, in New York City on June 23, 1846. The recruiters were looking for young men in excellent health, so Starr said that he was thirty-two years old, although he was actually a few weeks short of his thirty-sixth birthday.[9] He was promoted to corporal soon after he enlisted.[10]

The engineers sailed to the mouth of the Rio Grande where they joined Gen. Taylor's forces. Also known as sappers and miners, they were issued muskets and began learning the standard infantry drill. Starr was promoted to sergeant on November 1.[11] When the men had been drilled into shape, the company marched 350 miles across northern Mexico to Tampico on the Gulf coast.[12]

Sergeant Starr was determined to make a name for himself in combat. He wrote to Eliza from Matamoras, Mexico on October 23, 1846, and told her, "I expect soon to win a sword at the storming of some one or more of the enemy's batteries."[13] Eliza was less preoccupied with martial glory. She laughed at his determination to win a sword, and complained about his prolonged absence. She told him that their daughter, Kate, had said that, since her Papa had been gone for so long, her mother should find a new one.[14]

First Lieutenant Gustavus W. Smith and 2nd Lt. George B. McClellan led Company A through the war. A third officer, Lt. John G. Foster, was attached to the company for Scott's Mexico City campaign.[15] These officers were chosen from the top graduates of the military academy. The engineers landed with Scott's army at Vera Cruz, and, after a skirmish with the Mexicans, began constructing roads around the beachhead.[16]

Sergeant Starr hoped that he could win a promotion to lieutenant. By all accounts, he was a natural leader in battle. He was also proud and stubborn. When he was convinced that he was in the right, he was prepared to argue with his superior officers. He got into just such an argument at Vera Cruz and was reprimanded. He wrote to

*The history of this unique unit is recorded by its wartime commander, Lieutenant Gustavus W. Smith, in *Company A, Corps of Engineers, 1846-'48 in the Mexican War* (Battalion Press, 1896). A copy is in the Jenkins Garrett Collection at U.T. Arlington. The letters of Hiram B. Yeager, an enlisted engineer, are found in the Daughters of the Republic of Texas Library at the Alamo. Yeager describes their training in engineering tasks at West Point and he mentions that the men went to Mexico in fatigue uniforms "a roundabout such as regular soldiers wear"—and would receive uniform coats on their return.[8]

Eliza that she could probably understand how this had come about: "You who know me so well know that injustice or wrong of any description chafes me exceedingly, and that I can never, let the consequences be what they may, forbear to express my indignation."[17]

Incidents such as this one became a recurring feature of Starr's military career. He wrote to Eliza soon afterward that he had given up hope of being promoted since he was not a West Point graduate.[18] Perhaps he realized that he had hurt his chances by being insubordinate. In any case, he disliked West Pointers and took care to insult them when he had the opportunity.[19]

He redeemed himself at the Battle of Cerro Gordo. He volunteered to join the infantry's main attack, and, leading a detachment of nine other sappers, showing himself to be a brave and aggressive leader. He first led his men into a bayonet fight with the defenders. H. B. Yeager notes that in the fight, one man's bayonet broke, and another was severely bent.[20] As the Mexicans retreated, Starr helped turn a Mexican cannon on the retreating enemy. He was, after all, a former artillery sergeant.

After the battle, he wrote to Eliza that he had captured Mexican Gen. La Vega's aide and taken his sword. "I have in fact won that sword at last, notwithstanding you laughed so much about it, so let us drop the subject."[21] Starr was struck above the knee by a musket ball that had ricocheted, but it left only a painful bruise. Yeager confirms that a man in his company captured La Vega's aide at Cerro Gordo.[22]

His commander, Lt. Smith, mentioned him in his official report: "Sgt. Starr attracted my particular attention by his gallant and efficient conduct. Sgt. Starr was the ranking non-commissioned officer with the detachment of the engineer company which accompanied Col. Harney's command at the Battle of Cerro Gordo. I would recommend him for promotion."[23]

After the Battle of Cerro Gordo, the American forces occupied the city of Puebla. There, Starr received word from Eliza that his son had died. Samuel fell ill and was admitted to a makeshift hospital, and managed to get into trouble again. Lying on the stone floor of the hospital, he wrapped himself in an old tent for warmth. Starr's first sergeant, David Hastings, came to the hospital and demanded that he give up the tent. Starr refused. Hastings seized the tent and yanked it away, leaving Starr to lie on the stones. Starr's letter says: "I was very weak, but I managed lying on my back to kick his shins."[24] He was arrested, but, when his officers heard the story, they reprimanded Hastings. Samuel told Eliza that he was "in daily danger of knocking my superior officer down."[25]*

At the Battle of Contreras, his company again attacked alongside the infantry. The next day, he and his company took part in the pursuit of the retreating Mexican army. He described the route as strewn with "arms of every kind, lances, muskets, carbines, pistols, sabers, belts, cartridge boxes, quantities of ammunition, dead and wounded Mexicans, Americans, too, broken wagons, gun carriages, et cetera, et cetera."[27]

The Mexicans made a stand at the fortified convent of Churubusco. When the engineers arrived at Churubusco, they found themselves under fire from both Mexican and American artillery batteries, and they took cover in a cornfield. Samuel described their predicament to Eliza:

> Grape, canister, howitzer shells, and a terrible tornado of musket balls passing on, around, between, and through some of us . . . I took advantage of a lull in the storm and made for the ruin of a mud cabin on our right.
>
> . . . I found our company commander, Lt. G. W. Smith, and three or four of our men already there . . . when the proper time arrived the charge was sounded by the attacking columns, and our fellows, numbering six or seven (the rest being scattered throughout the cornfield) plunged from behind the mud wall and were the first to enter the fort, being some fifty yards in advance of the other forces.[28†]

General Scott's forces attacked the Mexican fortress of Molino del Rey on September 8, 1847. The night before the attack, Starr's company

---

*Hastings transferred to the engineers from Co. K, 4th Artillery in April, 1847. He served through the war as first sergeant.[26] He appears in Percival Lowe's *Five Years a Dragoon* as Lowe's lieutenant and, in Lowe's opinion, was a superb officer.

†Lieutenant G. W. Smith's report of the battle differs slightly from Starr's. Smith confirms on p. 46 of *Company A Corps of Engineers U.S.A.* that his company was under fire from an American battery for at least ninety minutes in the cornfield. Smith, however, states that he withdrew his company until after Churubusco fell. Starr and his five or six comrades probably either did not receive Smith's order, or else ignored it. His company commander met with him on August 24, 1847. Smith told him that he had recommended him for a commission in recognition of his bravery at the Battles of Cerro Gordo, Contreras, and Churubusco. He wrote home that he was pleased, but that he was skeptical that the promotion would materialize.[29]

commander issued him a gimlet, some nails, and a leather satchel containing forty pounds of gunpowder. Smith told him that a storming party of six hundred men would assault the Mexican fortress before dawn. The Americans would advance to within fifty yards of the main gate, and then halt. He was to creep forward with his satchel of powder, bore holes in the gate with the gimlet, and attach the charge with the nails. He would light a sixty-second fuse, return to his men, and take cover. After the gate was destroyed, he would lead twenty engineers back to the gate, to clear away any remaining obstacles. The six-hundred man storming party would follow the engineers through the gate.[30]

He wrote to Eliza that "the powder part of the plan, as well as the surprise, for some reason unknown to me, was abandoned . . . and not much to my regret, I assure you."[31] The attack on Molino del Rey was a conventional infantry assault. He led twenty men in the charge on the fortress, against heavy fire from the defenders. Lieutenant John Foster was severely wounded, and nine of Starr's men were either killed or wounded.[32] The Americans retreated after taking hundreds of casualties. He refused to retreat, and kept his detachment at an angle in the wall of the fort, protecting Lt. Foster, until another assault force drove the Mexicans out.[33]

Starr and his men fought again at the San Cosme Gate, where they helped force an entry into Mexico City itself. He wrote to Eliza that by this time he and his men were ragged, dirty, and half- naked.[34] After the fighting ended, his company moved into the Post Office building and settled into the routine of occupation duty in Mexico City.[35]

As the months went by, Eliza Starr grew more and more unhappy. Her son had recently died, and she missed her husband. She had to move in with her father in New York City, where her relatives criticized Samuel for running away to join the army. It appears that some of Eliza's relatives could have found a job for Samuel, but he was too proud to ask for help. The in-laws suggested that he had enlisted because he was too lazy to work.[36] Samuel was incensed when Eliza told him all this:

> I would sooner have laid down my right arm and had it sawn at the shoulder, could I by that means have got what I was in search of, than to have been compelled to ask employ. This is a feeling I cannot overcome. It has been with me from earliest childhood. I can remember instances of it when I could not have been more than five years old. It was born with me.[37]*

---

*Starr's intense dislike of asking a favor of anyone would get him into trouble with Col. Charles May in later years, and would result in his spending nine months under arrest in 1853 and 1854.

His in-laws had such a low opinion of soldiers that Eliza was reluctant to tell them that Samuel was only a sergeant. He wrote Eliza that:

> I have no desire to have my rank in the Army concealed from anyone. My rank and situation are, in every way, respectable. Publish it therefore to them all. Were I near them, I would shout it in their ears. I, even I, Samuel H. Starr, am a sergeant in the Corps of Engineers! Dare you whisper aught against me, or the rank I hold? Your sister Almira is to be pitied that she could so forget herself as to throw scurrilities at me through her sister. She, no doubt, only repeats the observations of her gambler husband.[38]

Many of the noncommissioned officers in his company were tired of the service, and began writing their congressmen for discharges. Hiram Yeager's letters from Mexico City in the spring of 1848 mention these efforts and discuss his attempts to be either discharged or commissioned as an officer.[39] Eliza may have asked Samuel to seek an early discharge as well. He wrote her that he was determined to serve until a peace treaty was signed, even if the occupation lasted for years:

> . . . I have seen blood flow in rivers, almost; arms, legs, heads, and dead bodies scattered everywhere in the greatest profusion, yet I wish to see the war out. I have been jostled more than once by my dead comrades falling, shot through the head or heart, against me; have seen my wounded countrymen basely murdered by the dastardly foe after having begged for quarter, and have fought to protect others from a like fate, therefore I want to see it out. True, at times a yearning to be with you and Kate seizes me with almost irresistible power, and at such times I would give the world almost to be by your side, but, on second thoughts, it is my interest to stay—and yours—so I must see it out.[40]

In this same letter, Samuel also responded to Eliza's charge that war was "foolish, useless, wicked, unjust, unholy, simple and sinful"[41]: Samuel replied that:

> I consider this war wise, useful, pious, just, holy, and by no means wicked, notwithstanding the Tribune, Cousin Powers, Aunt Eliza, and your opinion to the contrary my dear Eliza. It is wise, because it is the surest and most inevitable method of extending the benefit, the influence, and the power of our free institutions over the continent of America . . .[42]

His company returned to West Point, New York on June 23, 1848. On July 13, he wrote to Eliza: "I have this day received a commission in the 2nd Regt. U. S. Dragoons, and have accepted the appointment . . .

Remember now that you are an officer's lady."[43] He had set out to win honors in Mexico and had succeeded. Tens of thousands of men served in the regular army during the war. Only a few dozen were rewarded with commissions. Only ninety-eight such commissions were awarded between 1815 and 1860.[44]

He was ordered to the Cavalry School of Instruction at Carlisle Barracks. Like Governor's Island, it was a major induction center for the regular army. He went to work teaching foot drill to the new recruits. On October 13, he learned that he had been promoted from brevet second lieutenant to the permanent rank of second lieutenant. He was pleased; he planned to make a career of the army, and this promotion would give him seniority over the new West Point graduates joining his regiment.[45]

Samuel, Eliza, and Kate sailed from Philadelphia to New Orleans in November 1848. He was in charge of a detachment for the 2nd Dragoons. He left Eliza in New Orleans and joined his regiment in Houston. She remained in New Orleans for six months, while he was transferred from one frontier outpost to another.[46]

He rode from Houston to Austin with the dragoons. He first served a few weeks with Company B at McCulloch's Station. In March and April, he served with Company F at Towash Village and Fort Graham. In May, he joined Company C in San Antonio and rode with them to a new post on the Leona River. He helped build the new post, later to be named Fort Inge.[47]*

As he prepared to move to the Leona, he told Eliza that she and Kate should at last come to Texas. His company commander, Bvt. Lt. Col. William J. Hardee, was leaving to bring his wife from New Orleans, and Eliza could travel with them. He wrote that she should take a boat from New Orleans to Port Lavaca, on the Texas coast. The fare would be about $22 for Eliza. From Lavaca, she should take a stage to San Antonio.[48]

He was somewhat concerned about how Eliza would fit in. In this era, there was virtually no social interaction between officers and enlisted men. Officers' wives and enlisted men's wives likewise kept apart. The few enlisted men who were promoted to officer rank were not always fully accepted by their new peers.[49] Starr mentioned to Eliza that he was worried that her New Orleans hotel was not

*This was the second time a post was named Fort Inge. Brevet Major Arnold named his first station in Texas, Shapley Ross's Ranger Station, Fort Inge.

"genteel" enough, and that Hardee and his wife "might think the less of you" as a result.[50]*

Samuel advised Eliza to buy some household items before she left New Orleans:

> You had better bring a few articles of house "fixins" which perhaps will be more than your funds can pay for. I will mention the most necessary articles first, in their order of utility, viz: A carpet for a pair of wall tents, 3 yards wide by 6 yards long—A Mosquito bar for a double bed.—Something suitable for a curtain to hang across a tent to divide it into partitions, a neat or *genteel* pattern of some worsted stuff, is the most suitable purchase. ½ a doz. table knives, with good German silver, and plated forks—½ doz. table spoons—½ dozen tea do. These things cannot be had here at all, or at very exorbitant rates . . . If you can engage a good female servant (black or white, black preferable,) in Orleans, at a reasonable rate, do so. Engage her by the year if you can, but do not pay more than 8 dollars per month.[51]

He expected that he and Eliza would live in a tent. It was common, as his letter suggests, for married officers to receive two wall tents.[52] An officer who visited Fort Duncan in 1854 found the married officers still quartered in tents: "Individual taste dictates the interior arrangements. Some of the ladies drape their canvas wall with red and white. The floors are carpeted. The furniture is convenient. There are books, musical instruments, etc."[53]

Eliza arrived at Port Lavaca on about June 15, 1849. On June 29, Samuel wrote from the Leona River that he was about to go on a scout. Eliza proceeded to San Antonio. She later wrote: "I arrived at San Antonio while he was away on the scout and was greeted by the report that he had shot a soldier."[54]

The details of the incident appear in the report of a board of inquiry, held at Starr's request at Camp Worth, near San Antonio, on July 21, 1849. He had left the Leona on about June 30, 1849, commanding a detachment of fourteen dragoons. He and his men were part of a larger patrol, which also included twenty-nine mounted infantrymen. Lieutenant George Pickett and Lt. Daniel Hustin were leading the infantry. Pickett, the senior officer present, was in command.[55] The patrol rode to the headwaters of the Rio Frio. On the evening of July 1, as the cook made dinner and the men prepared their camp, Starr ordered two men to tend to their horses, which were grazing near the camp. One of the men cursed aloud that he didn't

* Later letters suggest that his fears were unfounded. Eliza Starr became good friends with Mrs. Arnold and their children became playmates.

think they were going to be allowed any dinner. Starr immediately ordered the man tied to a tree near the camp, a common punishment for insubordination and other offenses.

He left the area to tend to other matters. Private Foggerty and seven or eight dragoons approached Lt. Pickett at the officers' tent. They asked to see Starr. When Pickett asked what Foggerty wanted, he began to argue about the punishment Starr had ordered. Pickett and Hustin ordered Foggerty and his companions back to their part of the camp. Starr returned a few minutes later, and Lt. Pickett told him what had happened. Pickett warned him that Foggerty had his Colt revolver in his saber belt, and that he meant trouble. Starr seized his saber and his Colt pistol and strode down the hill to the enlisted men's area, shouting, "Where are those men who wanted to see me?" Foggerty approached him, and called for his companions to help him out. Pickett reported that Starr reached to grab Foggerty's pistol from his belt, at which point Foggerty jumped backward, drew and cocked the revolver, and pointed it at Starr. Starr cocked his revolver, aimed, and both men fired at the same time. Foggerty fell dead; Starr was unhurt.

Pickett ordered his infantrymen to disarm and arrest the mutinous dragoons. They were later tried by court-martial for mutiny. The enlisted men all swore that Foggerty had acted alone. They also testified that, when Starr had confronted Foggerty, he had seized him by the collar and had begun beating him with the saber. All the mutinous dragoons were acquitted. Pvt. Dennis Oates was found guilty of unsoldierlike conduct, and sentenced to one year of hard labor.[56]

Starr requested a board of inquiry to investigate his conduct in the incident. His fellow officers found that he acted in self-defense.[57] The War Department issued a mild reprimand, pointing out that tying up soldiers was strictly forbidden, even if it was common practice.

About two weeks after the board of inquiry, he received a letter from Maj. George Deas, Gen. Brooke's adjutant. At the end of May, Starr had taken some wagons from the Leona to San Antonio in order to pick up corn for the post's horses. He found only a small amount of corn in the depot at San Antonio, and took the opportunity to haul three wagon loads of lumber back to the Leona. Starr's commander, Bvt. Lt. Col. Hardee, had asked him to bring all the lumber he could find.[58]*

---

*Among the records of the trial is Hardee's requisition for supplies with which to build the post on the Leona. Hardee asked for the following

When Col. Harney heard about Starr and the lumber, he got mad. Harney had run into Starr in San Antonio, and had told him that he must saw his own lumber. General Brooke heard of the matter, and, through his adjutant, asked Starr to explain himself.[59] True to form, Starr sent a sarcastic and insubordinate reply to Maj. Deas. He told his side of the story, and concluded by apologizing for having distracted Gen. Brooke: "I grieve the more, sir, when I reflect on the weighty responsibility which I have incurred (though by no voluntary act of mine) in diverting the general's mind from the important command of a hostile frontier overrun by Indians who were almost daily murdering American citizens."[60]

Starr and Harney seem to have had similar personalities. Both men were stubborn, opinionated, defiant of authority, and unwilling to tolerate the slightest dissent from their subordinates. It is not surprising that they collided. Harney charged Starr with insubordination, falsehood, and disobeying orders. Starr spent the summer in arrest, and was tried on November 17 at Fort Gates. He was found guilty only of insubordination, and was reprimanded in published orders.[61]

After the court-martial, Starr did not return to Company C and the Post on the Leona. Instead, he was ordered to join Maj. Arnold and Company F at Fort Worth. Eliza remained in Austin when Samuel set out for Fort Worth. Starr and eighteen dragoon recruits reached the West Fork of the Trinity on Christmas Day 1849. Starr wrote to Eliza on January 6:

> Dear Eliza,
>
> I arrived here at 11 o'clock, A.M. Christmas day. The weather has been so cold snow and ice on the ground, and in the air, alternating with cold rain, that, as I am living in a tent, I found it quite impossible to write. I am still living in the same way, though the weather is milder today, but rainy. I see but little prospect of getting into quarters for the present.
>
> I like this post better than I expected I should; though it is situated on a very high prairie and exposed to all the winds that please to blow. This will be an advantage in the summer, but then there are no trees for shade, and I am told that mosquitoes are plenty. The prospect is extensive and rather pretty. There are many settlements around, and a small town, Dallas by name, thirty-five miles down the Trinity. The consequence is that the

---

supplies: 2 kegs 8d nails, 1 keg 10d nails, 1 pit saw, 1 cross-cut saw, 1 cross-cut file, 1 pit saw file, ½ doz. hand saw files, 5 tarpaulins, 1 grindstone and crank, 2 scythes and hafts, 100 lbs. iron, 6 felling axes and halves.

market affords plenty of milk, butter, fowls, eggs, but no vegetables. The latter, perhaps, may not be ordinarily styled a consequence, but it may be regarded as such in Texas.

I have not seen as good a table, as Mrs. Arnold spreads, since I have been in Texas. Mrs. A. is quite a firm little lady, with four children. I have joined the Bachelors' mess, which is composed of three officers, including the doctor, besides myself. Living is cheap. Major Arnold, although he has four or five servants, and is in the daily habit of entertaining strangers and other guests, paid but 29 dollars for his house keeping in one month. I have some hope of getting a house suitable for my family by March. Hardly before then, as things progress but slowly here. I like Major A., so far, well; and the officers are pleasant and gentlemanly fellows, all. Had a very merry time from the 25th Dec. to the 1st Jan. Mrs. Fowler Hamilton was a guest, with her Husband, of the Major's. I got sick from the effects of the merry making and was compelled to take medicine. Am well now. I shall leave in company with Major A. and Lt. Bold for Dallas tomorrow, if fair. I have relieved Major Arnold in the duties of Q. Master, and Mr. Bold in the duties of Comsy. and Post Treasurer.

There is a French Gentleman here teaching all the officers, Mrs. A. and her two daughters (one 11, the other 6 years old) the French language. I shall begin to take lessons on my return from Dallas. I wish you and Kate were here to join in the study. He teaches the language after a plan very simple, requiring very little effort of the memory. He is a [illegible] genius, teaches music, drawing, dancing, everything.*

I forget to mention that we had all the country girls at a dance in Christmas week. One, six feet high. When the officers called for them they were shoeless, so they purchased a lot of Boy's Brogans and shod the girls. They had no strings for their shoes, so they even danced in their stiff cowhide shoes without.—Clatter, clatter.—Affectionately, Samuel H. Starr.[62]

Starr wrote to Eliza again on January 15:

I went to Dallas, as I told you was my intention, and have returned. While at Dallas the Sons of Temperance had a celebration (of something) which we attended. In the evening the

*The Frenchman whom Starr mentioned was Adolphe Gouhenant. He and about thirty other Frenchmen had come to Denton County in 1848, and had attempted to establish a utopian colony on Oliver Creek. The colony had failed, and most of the settlers returned to Shreveport, Louisiana. Gouhenant stayed on in north Texas and became a well-known figure in both Dallas and Fort Worth. More details are in chapter 20.

> citizens gave us a ball in honor, as they informed us, of the U. S. officers then present. In the morning we were presented with the bill of expenses—including all the expenses—which we paid. I suppose this was to illustrate the principle that "he who dances must pay the fiddler."
>
> I have moved into one end of the building which is to be our house when the doctor gets his done; and am comfortable enough. I have purchased a horse. Nothing else to say, only my love to yourself and Kate.[63]

This is only the start of Samuel Starr's story. His actions and his antics will continue through the book until the time the Fort in Fort Worth closes.

9

The Military Situation in Texas In 1850

Texas Governor George Wood completed his two-year term in December 1849. His successor was Peter H. Bell, the former commander of the Texas Rangers on the frontier. Before Wood left office, he made a final appeal to the War Department to station more mounted troops in Texas. His letter sums up the arguments that were prevalent in Texas at the time.

Wood argued that for twelve months the army's defense of Texas had been a failure. The infantry and artillery were no use against Indians. The distance between the frontier forts was too great, and Indians could slip through at will. The peace treaty, which the War Department advocated, would never work. It was futile to negotiate with the Indians, "into whose social system the right to steal and kill is incorporated as fully as their right to breathe the common air." He insisted that the situation demanded "a military force adapted to, and adequate for, the purpose."[1] In other words, the army should either station more mounted troops in the state, or muster more Texas Rangers into federal service.

Secretary of War George Crawford rejected Wood's recommendations. Crawford pointed out that Texas already had more army protection than any other state in the Union—there were more troops in the state than there had been at any time during the days of the republic. Crawford asserted that the state government was to blame for its Indian problems. The Texans were driving the Indians from their homes, and refused to set aside reservations where the Indians could live in peace.[2]

While the governments in Washington and Austin argued, the Indians continued to raid the frontier. On December 27, 1849 Indians killed four people near Castroville and made off with a number of horses.[3] Dragoons from Fort Lincoln and Fort Martin Scott pursued the killers. For a detailed report by Bvt. Capt. William Steele of this pursuit, see appendix #9–1.

After the attacks near Castroville, Gen. Brooke asked the War Department for permission "to authorize the most severe measures of retaliation. I cannot perceive the avoidance of a general war."[4] Brooke now conceded that he did not have enough men to police the frontier.[5] He saw only two ways to end the attacks. One way was for the government to make a peace treaty with the Indians, settle them on reservations, and give them food until they learned to farm. The other way was for the War Department to send more mounted troops to Texas, and allow Brooke to attack the Indians' villages.[6] The federal government did neither.

On December 31, Indians killed a 1st Infantry soldier within half a mile of Fort Duncan. A traveler named Maj. Bryan was killed on January 11, 1850, about thirty-five miles from Goliad. A party of Tonkawas stole some horses near Fort Gates. Other livestock thefts were reported on the Brazos and on Willis Creek. At the end of January, Gen. Brooke authorized the three ranger companies to serve a second six-month term.[7]

In February 1850, an army ambulance was attacked near Fort Inge. Private Kellogg of the 8th Infantry was killed near Fort Duncan on February 22. Lieutenant Hudson of the 1st Infantry reported a Tawakoni war party on the Rio Grande at about the same time.[8] On March 6, 1850, Gen. Brooke requested that Governor Bell raise a fourth company of rangers for federal service.[9]* Brooke reported to the War Department that his call for more rangers was regrettable, but necessary: "In fact, the road between this point San

*The ranger company was to be organized as follows: 1 captain, 1 first lieutenant, 1 second lieutenant, 4 sergeants, 4 corporals, 2 musicians, 2 farrier/blacksmiths, 64 privates. Volunteers would provide their own horse, saddle, bridle, and lariat. The government would provide a percussion rifle, pistol, and ammunition. William A. A. Wallace's rangers were mustered in at Austin on March 23, 1850, and served for eighteen months. Wallace's company reenlisted at Ft. Inge on September 24, 1850, and again on March 23, 1851.[10]

Antonio and Ft. Duncan cannot be traveled with safety, unless the public trains and private parties going through the country, on their own highway, are protected by strong escorts."[11]

He repositioned his troops in order to put more mounted troops in the field. The garrison at Fort Polk, at the mouth of the Brazos, was too far in the rear to scout for Indians. He abandoned Fort Polk on February 9, 1850, and transferred two companies of the 1st Infantry away from the Rio Grande.[12]

These two companies established a new post, Fort Merrill, on March 1 about 60 miles northeast of Corpus Christi, near the point where the road from Corpus Christi to San Antonio crossed the Nueces River. This area had been the scene of many Indian raids.[13]*

While the Indians raised havoc in south Texas, the garrison at Fort Worth continued the routine of scouting the country to the north. One of Lt. Starr's first duties was to lead the monthly scout. Post Order #3 for 1850, dictated by Maj. Arnold on January 9, gave Starr his marching orders:

> Lt. S. H. Starr in command of a sergeant and ten men of F Co. 2nd Drg. will proceed tomorrow morning on a scout—he will keep below the line or direct road hence to Preston (Coffee's Bend.) He will go as far as Fitzhugh's Old Station on Elm Fork of the Trinity—and farther if he should hear of any Indians below the line.[14]

Arnold's order suggests that the garrison at Fort Worth was using Fitzhugh's Station as a regular stop on their monthly scout. Since the Hickory Creek Station was about a day's ride from Fort Worth, it seems possible that it, too, became a camping ground for the dragoons.

Lieutenant Starr also took over as acting assistant quartermaster and assistant commissary of subsistence at the fort. These two positions made him responsible for supplying the garrison, and accounting for government property at the post. Most supplies came from New Orleans, but Starr purchased a few items locally.[15]

Captain Maclay of the infantry went on sick leave on April 21, 1850, probably due to the chronic dysentery he suffered. He remained on leave for a year. Lieutenant Bold took charge of the infantry until November, at which time a new officer, 1st Lt.

---

*It was probably named for Capt. Moses E. Merrill, 5th Infantry, who was killed at Molino del Rey on September 8, 1847. Brevet Major Hamilton Merrill, post commander at Fort Worth in 1852 and 1853, had no apparent connection with the1st Infantry, and, in 1849 and 1850, it was customary to name forts in Texas for deceased officers.

Washington Street, joined the company. Street became the second highest ranking officer at the post and, when Maj. Arnold was away, served as post commander.[16]

Unlike most army officers, Lt. Street had grown up on the frontier. His father, Gen. Joseph M. Street, had been a frontier lawyer, editor, and militia officer in Kentucky and Illinois. He graduated from West Point in 1847 and began his service in the war with Mexico, coming to Texas with the 8th Infantry in 1848.[17] He served at Fort Graham in 1849 and 1850.[18]

Washington, one of Gen. Street's fourteen children, was born in Shawneetown, Illinois on January 2, 1825, where his father served as the county clerk. In 1827, Gen. Street became the U.S. Indian Agent to the Winnebago tribe. He moved his family to the agency at Fort Crawford, near today's Prairie du Chien, Wisconsin. Eight years later, Gen. Street became the agent to the Sac and Fox tribes, and moved his family to an agency near today's Ottawa, Iowa. Hundreds of Indians came to the agency at various times. Washington and his brothers worked on the family farm.[19]

Slavery was prohibited in Street's home state of Illinois, but the Street family had several black servants. While Lt. Street served at Fort Worth, his servant was a black man named London Triplett.[20] Triplett was apparently a family servant from Illinois who accompanied Street to Texas.[21]

On April 30, the dragoons were ordered to turn in their Mexican War vintage Colt revolvers for a newer model.[22] The new pistols were shorter and lighter, and of higher quality.* Colt's revolvers were so prized on the frontier that thefts became a problem.[25] A deserter from Company B, 2nd Dragoons, made off with five of the guns in November 1850. Each pistol had cost the government twenty-five dollars.[26] 8th Department Headquarters finally ordered that all revolvers be locked up when not in use.

In the summer of 1850, Gen. Brooke launched a large, coordinated scouting operation in south Texas. In May, a detachment of Texas Rangers attacked a Comanche war party south of San Antonio, and captured a wounded Indian. The prisoner told them that the Comanches were preparing to slip into South Texas and begin raiding. Brooke decided to send troops to intercept the Comanches. In

*Colonel Harney received about one thousand new Colt revolvers in late 1849 or early 1851. This group of pistols was of the type known to modern collectors as the "First Model Dragoon."[23] Mounted infantry continued to carry the old Walker revolvers.[24]

the past, the army scouts had conducted their patrols with little coordination between posts. This time, Brooke put his troops under the command of a single dragoon officer. He hoped that the operation would "operate as a complete checkmate" to the Comanche raids.[27]

On June 4, 1850, Brooke ordered Bvt. Lt. Col. William J. Hardee, at Fort Inge, to search South Texas for Comanches. Hardee's operation commenced on June 23, 1850. Two companies of dragoons, one company of Texas Rangers, and one company of mounted infantry searched the trails and waterholes between San Antonio, Corpus Christi, and the Rio Grande. The rangers and the dragoons converged at Fort Merrill. None of the patrols discovered any signs of Indians.

On July 8, Hardee received word at Fort Merrill that Indians had been spotted around Corpus Christi. He sent Wallace's Texas Rangers and Capt. Oakes's dragoons to search for the raiders. Captain Oakes found an Indian trail, followed it for two days, and attacked a small party of Indians on July 11. Oakes's men killed two Indians and captured twenty-two horses and mules.

On July 18, Hardee ordered his men into the field again. This time, they were to head towards the Rio Grande, and meet up at Fort McIntosh, in Laredo. Hardee sent out his companies so that ten columns, each column pursuing a different direction, were moving simultaneously between the Nueces and the Rio Grande. Wallace's rangers found a large body of Indians on the Nueces. The rangers killed seven Indians and wounded nine. Three rangers were wounded. Hardee's men assembled at Laredo by July 27.

In August, Hardee ordered his men to return to their original stations, searching the countryside along the way. Captain Oakes's dragoons fought the Indians a second time. The dragoons killed three of the enemy, but Oakes was severely wounded in the skirmish. Texas Rangers attacked a party of thirty Indians and killed two. Hardee returned to Fort Inge on September 6, 1850, and reported the results of his campaign to Gen. Brooke.[28]

> The Indians disperse themselves over the country in small bands, prowl around the settlements, awaiting a favorable moment to murder and rob, and having accomplished their objective, they speedily cross the Rio Grande and elude pursuit, or fly with speed to their homes in the upper country. It is difficult, nay, impossible to overtake and punish any of the parties, when they become aware of pursuit. If in danger of being overtaken, they scatter, and, each pursuing a different route to some remote point, they effectually baffle the skill of the most experienced trailers. My object has been, as far as circumstances would permit, to push my scouts through

> unfrequented parts of the country, to take up the trails where Indians least expect to be pursued, to follow these trails cautiously and quietly, and in this way take them by surprise.[29]

Hardee praised the performance of the Texas Rangers, but noted that "in irregular cavalry, where the horses are owned by the volunteers, it must be expected that they will consider the preservation of their animals as paramount to all other considerations."[30] Brooke decided in August to retain the ranger companies for another six months.[31]

While Hardee's command was searching for Indians in south Texas, another army patrol was also pursuing Indians along the northern frontier. Captain George Blake and Bvt. Maj. Hamilton Merrill followed an Indian trail from Fort Martin Scott to the Caddo Village on the Upper Brazos, accompanied by Lt. Washington Street and twelve mounted infantrymen. They arrived at the village on August 8, 1850. Lieutenant Washington P. Street and twelve mounted infantrymen rode with Merrill and Blake. [32] For a detailed report by Capt. Blake, see appendix #9–2.

In a bill dated June 17, 1850, Congress allowed the president to increase the strength of all companies serving in the West to seventy-four men. The increase had little effect at first, but eventually the companies stationed at Fort Worth grew from about forty-five men to about sixty-five men each. The same legislation also allowed the army to purchase more horses for the infantry.

Shortly after Blake and Merrill's patrol to the Caddo Village, rumors of a new and more dangerous Indian attack began to circulate. In September 1850, Governor Bell notified Brooke that the Comanches were believed to be gathering on the Upper Brazos, and preparing to attack the northern frontier. Rumor held that George Barnard had abandoned the trading house opposite Comanche Peak out of fear of the Comanches.

Brooke passed the information on to Indian Agent John H. Rollins, a lawyer from Mississippi who had replaced Robert Neighbors in late 1849. Rollins had considerable sympathy for the Indians, but he was in poor health, and he was not an effective advocate. He suspected that the Barnard brothers were up to no good. He reported that they may have been stirring up trouble in an effort to sabotage a peace council that he was trying to organize. He believed that the Comanche were peaceful, but that they had been provoked by the military:

> That some portion of the Comanches are hostile there is no doubt, but that the body of the nation is so or wishes to become so I do not believe. Those who have lost relatives or friends upon

> the Rio Grande wish to be revenged and the Chief cannot govern them. They went to the Rio Grande for food, not blood—they would not have gone could a subsistence have been obtained otherwise. They were met & punished—some times wrongfully—and they are deeply incensed, for it seems to them that the government, by denying them the only country where food can be procured, intends to starve them. The alternative had been painfully presented to them, *starve or steal*. Choosing the latter they have been caught & punished and they wish revenge.[33]

The Comanche uprising never materialized. Brooke urged Bell to close down the trading houses, without success.[34] Rollins continued his efforts to convene a treaty council. There is no record of how the rumored Comanche uprising affected the garrison at Fort Worth. The post returns show that Maj. Arnold took the unusual step of personally leading the monthly scout in September; perhaps he wanted to be in command in case there was trouble.[35]

At about the end of 1850, the dragoons in Texas were issued a new weapon. The Ordnance Department had concluded that the Hall carbine was too fragile; one ordnance officer complained in 1845 that "the stocks of Hall's carbine that we now have in use are continually splitting and flying in all directions." [36] The Hall was replaced with a cavalry musketoon. The musketoon, a single-shot gun that loaded at the muzzle, resembled a musket with a shortened barrel. Like the musket, it fired a .69 caliber bullet with three small buckshot. However, within months, dragoon officers would begin to complain that the musketoon was completely worthless.

Also near the end of the year, headquarters directed company commanders to report on how the new 1st Dragoon model pistols, which had been issued in the spring performed.[37] Brevet Major W. J. Hardee praised the new weapons: "My company has been using Colt's repeating pistols for more than a year, during which time they have been fully tested . . . Two issues of pistols have been made to my company the last received are the shorter, lighter, and more durable . . . Of my last issue of pistols, not one has burst and not one is out of repair." [38] The powder flasks that came with the revolvers were less than ideal, and were gradually replaced with cartridges.[39] The ordnance return of Company A, 2nd Dragoons, dated 3/31/51 lists powder flasks but no cartridges.

Starr's wife, Eliza, and his seven-year old daughter, Kate, stayed in Austin. Eliza was pregnant. Samuel wrote to her on April 19, 1850 that he hoped to come and get her in May. Samuel left Fort Worth on May 11, and returned on June 8, but Eliza seems to have remained in Austin.[40] Samuel wrote to her again on July 4th, 1850.

> Dear Eliza, I am rejoiced to hear through Dr. Roberson, that you have a young daughter, and that you are both doing well. I spoke to the Dr. before I left about a servant, a nurse, for you, and he told me he put you in the way of getting one—I hope he did so. I have just risen from a 'Fourth of July dinner' and my ideas are not the clearest, so excuse my short epistle. Tell Kate that I have a beautiful fawn for her. It follows me wherever I go, and is wonderfully tame—the little rascal, though, chews everything it can get at. He has eaten one summer coat up for me, has spoilt, in a measure, your mosquito bar, &c. I shall have to send him/her, properly, with the kitchen. Affectionately yours, Sam. H. Starr. [41]

Eliza named the girl Anne. Samuel wrote to Eliza again on July 20th.

> Dear Eliza, I have made arrangements to come for you again the 5th or 6th of August so, I shall probably be in Austin the 10th or 11th of that month. I postponed it till that time for two reasons. 1st, By not leaving this post till after the 31st inst. I shall avoid being reported in the monthly Post Return as "absent without leave," and 2nd. By putting off my visit till the latest moment will give you more time to recover your health and strength. Another reason I have Col. Middleton Johnson starts for Austin at that time and by waiting I shall have the pleasure of his company I have made a bargain with Col. J. for two servants, one as a nurse which I shall take down with me, and the other as a cook and house servant. Write me and tell me the state of your health and the children's'. Affectionately yours S. H. Starr.[42]

Eliza Starr came to Fort Worth after Anne's birth. She became a good friend with Catherine Arnold, and their children became playmates. Sadly, two of the Arnolds' children, Sophie and Willis, died that year. The two were buried about half a mile northeast of the post, near the road to Live Oak Point and Daggett's Store. Stone slabs, five feet long and three feet wide, were laid over the graves. The burial ground grew into Fort Worth's first cemetery. The stone markers are dated 1850 on one end, and still mark the graves in Pioneer's Rest Cemetery.

Paymaster Albert Sidney Johnston came to pay off the garrison at the end of October 1850. The correspondence files in the A. S. Johnston Papers contain a two-hundred-dollar check to Maj. Arnold drawn on the Bank of Louisiana, dated November 1, 1850.[43]

Johnston, who had once served as Secretary of War for the Republic of Texas, was a graduate of West Point. He served as an officer of state volunteers during the Mexican War and, after the war, secured a commission as a paymaster in the regular army.[44]

Johnston began serving in the late summer of 1850. Johnson signed for about $3,000 in gold and $1,000 in silver from Paymaster J.

Y. Dashiellon, August 7, 1850.[45] He had a difficult job. Based in Austin, he paid troops at Forts Martin Scott, Croghan, Gates, Graham, and Worth. The round trip was 621 miles. Johnson and a small escort made the trip six times every year. Johnston, whose health was poor, spent six months of the year in transit, camping out on the open prairie.[46]

Johnston paid the men in gold and silver coin. Officers were sometimes paid with checks. John Bold, a second lieutenant of infantry, earned $25.11 each month in base pay. Dragoon lieutenants, such as Samuel Starr, earned $33.11. Officers with the permanent rank of captain earned $40.00 monthly. Additional allowances for food, horses, servants, time in service, command status, and brevet rank raised the officers' total earnings by another fifty to one hundred dollars. Thus Maj. Arnold earned $188.00 in October, 1850, to provide for himself, his family, two servants, and three horses. Officers received no extra allowances for being married.[47]

Lieutenants and captains were authorized to keep one servant, while majors were allowed two servants.[48] Paymaster Johnston's records show that most officers either bought or hired Negro slaves as servants, and were reimbursed by the government. Major Arnold owned two slaves, Rebecca and Henry, in 1850.[49] The army reimbursed officers $15.70 per month for each servant's food, clothing, and wages.[50] Some officers dealt in slaves.[51]

The army pay scale for enlisted men changed little between 1838 and 1854. Privates received $7.00 each month. To discourage desertions, $1.00 of every private's pay was withheld each month, and paid in a lump sum when he was honorably discharged. Corporals received $9.00 with none held back. Sergeants earned $13.00 monthly, and first sergeants, $17.00. The seven men in Maj. Arnold's company who had won the Certificate of Merit during the Mexican War received an extra $2.00 every month. Dragoons received an extra $1.00 per month for mounted service. If a man reenlisted, he received a bonus of three months' pay.[52]

The Quartermaster Department paid men for nonmilitary labor. A soldier assigned for ten consecutive days as a laborer, blacksmith and farrier, muleteer, artificer, hospital steward, or saddler, received an additional fifteen cents and one gill of whiskey per day.[53] The extra fifteen cents, together with the food, shelter, clothing, and medical care which the soldiers received, made the soldiers' pay comparable to that of unskilled laborers.[54]

Soldiers might be broke between paydays, but they often left the army with a considerable sum of money. A discharged private would receive the sixty dollars that had been withheld during his enlistment.

Mexican War veterans received a cash bonus of three months' pay, and were eligible for grants of federal land. A travel allowance, based on the distance to the soldier's place of enlistment, could add the cash equivalent of another two months' pay. Most soldiers did not receive all of the uniforms which regulations allowed them; the men received a cash payment for the uniforms not issued. Thus, the Mexican War veterans in Maj. Arnold's company typically left Fort Worth with over $200 in cash. Private Nicholas Beyer, who enlisted in New York City on May 18, 1846, and was discharged at Fort Worth five years later, received $223.26 upon discharge.[55] Private Frederick Burlage, who enlisted in New York on May 13, 1846, received $234.02 when he completed his enlistment.[56] It would be difficult for a laborer to save that amount of money, even in New York or Baltimore.[57]

Paymaster Johnston was usually absent on the day that a man completed his term of enlistment. In those cases, the post sutler could pay off the soldier and collect the money from Johnston later.[58]

Contemporary accounts describe paydays as occasions of widespread drunkenness, gambling, and discipline problems. Private Richard Bennett, serving with the 1st Dragoons in New Mexico in 1850, described a payday there:

> Paymaster arrived yesterday. Paid off the troops. Night came. The long rows of beds in our quarters were occupied. Benches were all full. Money changed hands as fast as possible . . . All much engaged. Morning found many still gambling. Lost their sleep and their money. This is a practice followed very much by soldiers.[59]

Henry C. Daggett, who had served in Middleton Johnson's ranger company in Mexico, operated a store on Live Oak Point, on the original site of Fort Worth. County courts were held there in 1850 and 1851. While Maj. Arnold could prohibit the post sutler from selling alcohol to soldiers, he had no authority over civilian merchants such as Daggett. Nevertheless, Arnold did what he could to suppress drunkenness at the post. He wrote Maj. Johnston the following note on October 31:

> Major Johnston having experienced great annoyance & having the health of my command impaired by citizens selling liquor in the vicinity of my Post I have determined to deprive my men of the means of encouraging this despicable traffic, and have therefore the honor to request you will not pay them again until March 1851.[60]

Major Arnold's strictness may have backfired. On November 6 and 7, 1850, three men took their wages and deserted. Major Arnold sent Lt. Starr after the deserters, with the following instructions:

> Lieutenant Samuel H. Starr 2nd Drg with a detachment of 4 men will proceed immediately in pursuit of deserters, Pvts. Anderson, Reardon, 2nd Drg, and Pvt. Biggins, 8th Inf. He will proceed in the direction of Fort Washita until he learns from inquiry of the settlers, whether they have taken that route if not he will turn east until he strikes the main road leading from Dallas to Shreveport, where he will again inquire should he hear of the Deserters, he will pursue them until he overtakes them. [61]

The army offered a $30.00 reward to anyone who apprehended a deserter. Despite the reward and the best efforts of Lt. Starr, the three men escaped. Nine men deserted from Fort Worth in 1850, out of a garrison that rarely exceeded a hundred troops.[62]

As 1850 drew to a close, Secretary of War Conrad prepared his annual report to the Congress.[63] The record of events in Texas contained little in which the War Department could take pride. His gloomy report sounds much like the letter that he had received from Governor Wood one year before. Conrad admitted that the frontier was too large to defend with the number of troops available. The companies stationed on the frontier were under strength. He did not endorse an expanded role for the rangers, but he did ask Congress to create an additional mounted regiment. He also called once again for the state government to establish Indian reservations.[64]

Although Conrad was gravely concerned about the situation in Texas, there was some cause for optimism. In December 1850, Indian Agent Rollins made a peace agreement with the Comanches, Lipan Apaches, Tonkawas, and Caddo Indians. The agreement was signed at a council held on Spring Creek, near the San Saba River. The Indians agreed to stop raiding, return all white captives, and stay west of the line of forts. The United States government agreed to turn over a captured Comanche boy, as well as a large amount of manufactured goods. The government promised that, in the future, it would provide the Indians with food, seeds, and tools for farming, schools, and missionaries. Brooke would finally get the peace treaty he had sought since coming to Texas in July 1849.

The Spring Creek agreement did not have the full force of law, but Rollins made the agreement in good faith, and Gen. Brooke ordered his troops to honor the agreement.[65] He hoped that President Fillmore would send instructions to negotiate another treaty, which, with Senate ratification, would become law. His optimism is apparent in his message to the War Department.

> I have great satisfaction in forwarding the enclosed articles of agreement entered into between John H. Rollins, Special Indian

> Agent for Texas, and the Comanche Indians, and other tribes of the state. It is to be hoped that peace may be, for some time, restored to the border, and I believe that if proper advantage be taken of the friendly disposition of the Indians, by holding at once a treaty with them, with full instructions from the Government, a firm and lasting peace may be established.[66]

He sent a copy of the agreement to Governor P. H. Bell urging the governor to support the treaty:

> . . . You will perceive by my order that I have directed the different stipulations to be carried into effect by the troops under my command with a hope, that the citizens of the State may take a corresponding action.
>
> This treaty, incomplete as it is, being without instructions from the General Government is yet of great importance, as it is expressive of friendship towards the whites and the strong desire of the Indians for peace. This feeling should be taken advantage of by the proper authorities, by holding a more general council in which all difficulties can be explained, a proper understanding come to, and the future intentions of the President made known.[67]

Brooke's optimism was short-lived, however. The Spring Creek agreement collapsed almost as soon as the ink had dried. Within weeks he would be planning an expedition to attack the Indians' villages.

Finding Shade

This drawing shows soldiers resting under a tree. The view is to the southeast. Depending on your view, they could be cleaning their weapons or shooting dice, a favorite pastime in the frontier army. (Copyright William Potter.)

Sunset on the Trinity Bluff

This drawing, looking west, shows the fort at end of the day. Note the horses coming in, and the flag detail at the flagpole. This drawing gives an indication of the location of Bluff, Belknap and Weatherford Streets. (Copyright William Potter.)

10

The Big Scout

When Bvt. Maj. Gen. George M. Brooke came to Texas in June 1849, he had hoped to keep the peace by treating the Indian tribes fairly, and by punishing individual Indians who came below the line of forts on raids. For eighteen months, his approach had failed. The Indians attacked at will, and his small force could do little to stop them. The Spring Creek Treaty had been his last hope for securing peace on the frontier.[1] However, the hope for peace dissipated quickly and within weeks the dragoons were preparing to go to war against the Indians.

At his headquarters in San Antonio, the new year brought reports of more Indian raids in South Texas. On January 7, 1851, he reported that Texas Ranger Capt. H. E. McCullough had fought a skirmish with a Lipan Apache war party.[2] Eight days later, he wrote that a ranger patrol had spotted a Comanche war party carrying blankets and knives that Indian Agent Rollins had distributed at Spring Creek.[3]

When the Indians failed to turn over their white captives and stop raiding the settlements, he concluded that he had been tricked. He believed that the treaty had been a ruse meant to secure the release of a Comanche boy whom the Texas Rangers had captured.[4] His frustration turned to anger. On February 5, 1851, he notified the Secretary of War that he had decided to attack the Indians' villages with six companies of dragoons. Brevet Lieutenant Colonel William J. Hardee would lead two dragoon companies through the countryside west of the Colorado River. Brevet Brigadier General William S. Harney would lead four companies east of the Colorado. The dragoons at Fort Worth would join Harney. All six companies would link up on the Clear Fork of the Brazos, and continue the expedition through the hunting grounds of the Comanche.[5]

Brooke's decision to attack meant that the army would abandon the policy of conciliation that it had followed for the last two years. In early 1849, Bvt. Maj. Gen. William J. Worth had instructed his officers to treat the Indians with kindness and forbearance, and to protect them from violence and injustice.[6] After Worth died, Brooke's orders were to treat the Indians with firmness and truth, in the interest of doing justice.[7] Now, he ordered Harney to attack. He sent him the following instructions:

> My present plan is, that you take the four companies of your regiment on the line from Fort Martin Scott to Fort Worth, and that you visit all the Indian lands from the eastern border of Texas to the Clear Fork of the Brazos. That, whenever you may be convinced that any band of Indians has been engaged in hostilities, below the line of frontier posts (and particularly since the pretended treaty), you will punish them severely, destroy their villages and other property, take their cattle, horses, and mules, and make as many captives as possible, to be held in confinement as hostages for the good conduct of their bands . . . When positive murder can be proven against any Indian or Indians, they should be put to death on the spot. Should, however, any of the tribes come forward and deliver up any murderers or stolen property—you may pass them by—but with a good strong talk as to what they may expect at some future day in the event of any complaint being made against them.[8]

Brooke intended to begin the campaign in April 1851, when the prairie grass would provide grazing for the dragoons' horses.[9] On February 8, dragoon company commanders were ordered to report how many horses they would need to bring their companies to full strength.[10] On February 12, Harney sent a warning order to his company commanders, instructing them to prepare for the expedition. In the order, he wrote that he expected all six dragoon companies to bring at least seventy men to the field. Officers were to train their new recruits in horsemanship, and to practice firing the musketoon and revolver. Commanders were also to designate and train a crew for the mountain howitzer that each company would bring to the campaign.[11]

Harney, who was to lead four companies, gave detailed instructions concerning how his troops should be equipped. His order is included here because it is one of the few surviving documents that describe how the dragoons prepared for field service:

The following will be the allowance of transportation, tools, stores, etc., to each company, and you will make your requisitions accordingly.

Twenty pack mules and four muleteers—the mules to be assigned as follows—one for the company officers, one for the company tools and ammunition, one for the salt designated for the company horses, and one for horse shoes and nails. Sixteen mules will then be left for the transportation of subsistence, which should, allowing 200 pounds to each mule, enable each company to carry at least thirty days' rations.

Five axes and two augers, one 1 inch, and one 1½ inch, will be taken for the use of each company. Two hundred pounds of salt, to be taken for the company horses. The subsistence stores will comprise, bacon, meat-biscuit if it can be obtained, flour, sugar, coffee and salt.

Two camp kettles and one Dutch oven will be allowed to each company, and no other cooking utensils will be taken into the field.*

Each company will take into the field a mountain howitzer, with an allowance of 20 rounds of ammunition, which will be carried in the limber box. (Companies C, G, & F, will use the howitzers they now have, and if necessary make requisitions on the Ordnance Department for ammunition. Companies A, B, & I will be furnished with howitzers and ammunition from these headquarters, and company commanders will take immediate measures to get them to their companies.)

A large allowance of horse shoes and nails, adjusted for use, and the tools to put them on; must be provided for each company. Saddles, Bridles, Saddle Blankets, and Halters, must be put into complete order. To each set of Horse appointments there must be added a grazing rope of 1 inch thickness and 20 feet long, and a picket pin 12 inches long, and one inch square at top, surmounted by a ring of proportionate strength.

The allowance to each man will be one complete suit of clothing, which he will transport on his person, with an addition of 1 pair of pants, 2 shirts, 1 blanket, 1 pair of shoes, and 1 great coat—the additional allowance of clothing, except the great coat, which will be fastened to the cantle of the saddle, will be transported in the forage bag; the blanket to be placed over the seat of the saddle. No valises will be allowed. You will see that each soldier is provided with the above allowance of clothing, and no more than the above, and that it is strictly uniform. Neither officers nor men will be

*Camp kettles were cylindrical cooking pots made of sheet metal.

> permitted to wear any article of clothing not strictly in conformity with the army regulations, and any deviation from the prescribed dress will be regarded as a violation of positive orders.
>
> Each man must provide himself with a quart tin cup, and knife. The subsistence used for daily consumption will be carried by each man in his haversack, and hung over his shoulder, and not on the saddle as is sometimes done.
>
> The personal armament of each soldier will be a musketoon and revolver, with an allowance of 100 rounds of ammunition for the former—40 of which will be carried in the cartridge box, and 15 rounds (90 shots) for the latter.
>
> Future instructions will be given in relation to obtaining ammunition for the revolver; no sabres will be worn by either officers or men.
>
> So soon as the pack mules and saddles are received, you will have the latter adjusted to the former, and take such other steps in the way of driving, packing the mules, etc., as you may think most advisable to place the pack train in the most efficient order. The mules should be put into the best state of flesh possible before starting on the campaign.
>
> It is expected that the officers of the regiment, of whatever grade who may engage in the anticipated campaign, will cooperate in the most cordial manner in all the measures whether in the camp or in the field, which may be necessary to secure a useful and honorable result.
>
> The Government requires, the outraged honor of the country demands, and the reputation of the regiment, calls imperatively for such action from all.[12]

It is interesting that Harney insisted that the men wear their regulation army uniforms in the field. The soldiers had taken to wearing broad-brimmed hats, flannel shirts, and other articles of civilian clothing when they went on scouts. Civilian clothes were more comfortable, and saved the soldiers' uniforms from the wear and tear of field service. However, a senior officer was coming from Washington to inspect the 8th Military Department that spring—he may have wanted his men to look good for the inspection.

His order also mentioned that he planned to issue "meat biscuit" to the troops. The meat biscuit was a combination of processed beef and flour, developed by Gail Borden of Galveston in 1850. Borden, an entrepreneur and inventor, thought that his product would provide a light and compact ration for soldiers, sailors and travelers.[13] Dragoon officers hoped that the new ration would help their scouts to travel farther and faster,[14] but the new product proved to be unpalatable, failing "to appease the cravings of hunger, producing nausea, head ache, and great muscular depression."[15]

Brooke never saw his "Big Scout" take the field. On March 9, he died of a hernia in San Antonio.[16] Harney assumed temporary command of the 8th Military Department for the second time and would remain in charge until September.

Harney took a more aggressive approach to policing the frontier. In March, he ordered that any Indian found below the line of forts should be shot on sight.[17] In April, he prohibited army personnel from buying livestock from the Indian trading houses of Barnard, Warren, and others. Harney was certain that the traders bought stolen livestock from the Indians, and thus encouraged raiding. The Texas legislature would not shut down the trading houses, but he could at least deny them government business.[18]

He continued the preparations for the Big Scout, making some changes to Brooke's original plan. He reduced the size of the force from six to four companies, leaving the dragoons at Fort Worth garrisoned to act as a reserve for the expedition.[19] On April 20, 1851, he ordered four companies of dragoons to proceed to Fort Martin Scott, and prepare to take the field against the Indians. The commander of that expedition would be Bvt. Lt. Col. William J. Hardee. Harney again insisted that his men wear the regulation army uniform.[20]

Hardee made good use of the training opportunities that the Big Scout created. In May, Hardee's dragoons gathered in an encampment about two miles from Fort Martin Scott. The bivouac was christened Camp Harney. Hardee, who had run the training program at Fort Jesup before the Mexican War, now set out to train the men in squadron drill.

Harney believed that war was inevitable, but he made one last attempt to settle things peacefully before ordering the attack. He sent Hardee and the dragoons with Indian Agent Rollins to the German settlements on the Llano River to talk to the Indians again.[21] Rollins sent out runners, and succeeded in contacting some of the Indians who had signed the treaty. The Indians, facing attack by over two hundred dragoons, agreed to bring in their captives.[22] They handed over a total of seventeen Mexican citizens to the U.S. Army.[23]

Harney was pleased. The Indians had never before returned captives to the army in Texas. The Indians visited Fort Martin Scott in early May, and assured him that they would stop their raids. He accepted their promises, and canceled the attack he had planned.[24] Hardee led his dragoons into the Indian country at the end of May, but the expedition was a show of force, rather than an attack.[25]

On May 17, 1851, Harney notified Washington of his meeting with the Indians.

> My views in regard to Indian relations in this Dept. have, since my arrival at this post Fort Martin Scott, undergone a complete change. Previous to my coming hither and conferring with the Indians, I regarded a general Indian war as inevitable. But I am now satisfied that the Indians can be in a great measure, if not entirely, prevented from the commission of depredations by suitable activity and perseverance on the part of the troops, and hence the necessity for a general collision with the savages avoided.[26]

Harney's use of force and diplomacy showed that the Indians would yield to a general who would fight. He concluded that his dragoons could keep the Indians in check. On May 15, he issued new standing orders for mounted patrols along the line of forts. The old standing orders, issued by Gen. Worth in March 1849, directed the garrison of each post to conduct a minimum of one scout per month. The monthly scout covered the route between its home station and the next post to the north. Harney now ordered that a scout should set out from each post every week. More scouting patrols meant that Indian trails would be picked up while they were still fresh, and pursuers would have a better chance of success. He also specified that each post was to scout in a sector of territory, rather than merely riding on the road that connected the forts. For example, the garrison at Fort Graham would cover the area between Fort Graham and Fort Worth, but should also visit the Indian villages on the Upper Brazos at least once every month. The garrison at Fort Worth would cover the territory north to the Red River, and as far up the West Fork of the Trinity as Maj. Arnold judged necessary.[27] Harney wrote to Washington that the new system of scouting should discourage raiding:

> For a time, the most lawless of the Indian population will no doubt continue to pillage from the whites whenever an opportunity to do so may occur. If, however, the system of scouts directed in the accompanying order be strictly complied with, the trail of any marauding parties should be discovered in a short time after the transit across the frontier line . . .
>
> When the savages learn that they cannot steal and murder with impunity—when they are properly impressed with the certainty that retributive punishment will follow crime and the violation of treaty obligations, they will soon cease, from the absence of all motive, to prey on the lives and property of our pioneer people.[28]

11

The Indian Incident At Fort Worth

While the dragoons prepared for "the Big Scout,"[1] the infantry prepared for yet another change of station within the line of forts. In 1849, Bvt. Maj. Gen. George M. Brooke had decided to station infantry and dragoons together at most of the posts. This arrangement allowed the dragoons to put more men in the field. The infantry could do the routine chores around the post, and pull guard duty while the dragoons were away.

However, the infantry disliked this arrangement; infantry officers complained that the foot soldiers felt like servants of the dragoons.[2] At Fort Worth, disputes arose concerning which duties were the responsibility of the infantry. Lieutenant Street wrote to head quarters in January 1851, asking to know exactly which tasks his men had to perform.[3] The friction affected the officer corps, as well. Lieutenant Starr pressed charges against Street in early 1851. The nature of the charges is unknown, and Starr later withdrew them, but the incident illustrates the conflicts created by Brooke's policy.[4]

Brooke relented and made plans to move the infantry and dragoons to separate posts. In late March the 8th Infantry began to assemble at Fort Gates and Fort Martin Scott, away from the dragoons.[5] On April 6, 1851, Capt. Maclay's men left Fort Worth for Fort Gates, located about ninety miles south of Fort Worth, the next post below Fort Graham in the line of forts.[6]

However, the garrison at Fort Worth soon might have had reason to wish that the infantry had stayed. A few days after their departure, a force of about one hundred Indians threatened to attack the fort. Major Arnold's report of the incident, if he ever wrote one, has been lost. Surviving details are incomplete, but it appears that the confrontation took place between April 10 and April 20, 1851. Three accounts of the incident have survived. They were recorded fifty to seventy years apart, but they largely agree as to what took place. On May 10, 1851, a newspaper in Henderson, Texas, published the following story:

> Capt. Daggett, of Shelby, who has recently made a tour of the northwestern portion of the frontier settlements, gave us information that a small party of Tonkawas, consisting of five warriors, and one Caddo, who was an outlaw from his own tribe; had a fight with a party of Wacos, in the vicinity of Alton, Denton County, about the 20th April last. That some seven of the Wacos were killed—that the Tonkawas came into the settlements, in a warlike attitude, causing great excitement among the citizens. The District Court, being in session, immediately adjourned, and a runner was sent to Major Arnold, who is in command at Fort Worth.[7]

A messenger brought Maj. Arnold a letter from Judge William J. Todd of the 8th District Court.[8] A copy Todd's letter, dated April 9, 1851 is preserved in Samuel Starr's papers :

> . . . some hundred or more Indian warriors are encamped on the headwaters of Clear Creek within the limits of Denton County. These Indians have driven families from their homes and declared it to be their intention to fight. The citizens are collecting in numbers for the purpose of repelling any assault, which may be made, but by my advice will make no attack, until you are heard from. I would most respectfully suggest to you, the propriety of sending troops enough to remove these Indians out of our limits . . .[9]

On April 10, Arnold ordered Starr to assemble a patrol of one sergeant, one corporal, and twenty privates. The patrol would draw musketoons and Colt pistols and head for "the rendezvous of the Indians." Dr. Williams, the post surgeon, would go as well. Arnold gave Starr verbal orders before the patrol left, but the nature of his instructions is unknown.[10] Therefore, we don't know what the patrol found in Denton County. It is certain, however, that five Tonkawas and one Caddo sought refuge at Fort Worth. Arnold took them in. A newspaper account reports that their enemies followed them to the fort:

> Soon after, 100 warriors, of the Waco tribe, came to the Fort painted, with their bows strung, and demanded the Tonkaways; the Wacoes said the Tonkaways had been subsisting on the flesh of their warriors, who had been killed, and they wanted satisfaction. The Wacoes were desperately enraged and hostile. The

> Tonkaways were not delivered, and the Wacoes left reluctantly, much dissatisfied. General Harney, on hearing this news, issued an order to kill all the Indians who were found below the line, indiscriminately. If such be the fact, a general outbreak is anticipated. We hope that steps will be taken immediately to give protection to our frontier settlers.[11]

A second, more colorful account of the incident was printed in the Fort Worth Register on June 1, 1902. The newspaper was reporting the annual reunion of the Texas Association of Mexican War Veterans. The featured speaker at the reunion was Abraham Harris, who had served as an infantry sergeant at Fort Worth. Also present were Alphonse Freeman and Mrs. Kate Parker. Freeman was the dragoon from Company F who had been shot in the shoulder at Molino del Rey. Mrs. Parker, born Kate Arnold, was Ripley Arnold's daughter.[12]

Abe Harris stated that the Tonkawas had fought a rival band of Indians west of Fort Worth, near the Tannehill homestead. Both Harris and Mrs. Parker recalled that Maj. Arnold sent a patrol to investigate the disturbance. The patrol found human remains showing evidence of cannibalism. After the fight, the Tonkawas fled from their enemies and sought refuge at the fort. Arnold took them in. A short time later, a large number of mounted warriors appeared in the river bottom northwest of the fort. A messenger, bearing a white rag, approached the fort, and demanded that Arnold turn over the Tonkawas to their enemies. Harris clearly enjoyed telling the story:

> They were yellin' out there at the head of Robinson's Branch like red devils. The major he ordered us into line and said if fight was what they wanted, fight it was, and Sergeant McCauly who had charge of the big gun the mountain howitzer brought it out and unlimbered it at the northwest corner of the square at the head of Houston Street. The major he told the rag messenger that he was not in the habit of serving up his guests for breakfast, at least to strangers, and that they might be prepared for a fight.
>
> The Injuns were about three hundred strong, and let me tell you we fellers in blue were but a squad in comparison to them, but we had the gun, and were sure they had never heard her bellow, so while the Injuns were scattered around over the bottom there over the bluff looking northwest, the major said to McCauly, "Sergeant, touch her off and graze the heads of the big bucks over there in the valley if you can without hitting them, but if you should hit one, mind you, there will be no love lost, even if you take his head smooth smack off!"
>
> So the sergeant he pulled the lanyard, and boom! room! doom! rang the shrapnel over the heads of the bucks, and clatter,

> scatter, scatter, clatter went the Injuns hither and thither, scared out of their wits.[13]

Harris concluded his story by saying that the hostile Indians left the fort after Maj. Arnold placated them with a gift of three head of cattle. Sergeant Harris's story generally agrees with Capt. Daggett's. However, it is almost certain that Harris was not being truthful when he claimed that he had stood among Arnold's men. The infantry left Fort Worth on April 6, at least four days before the confrontation, and there is no evidence that Harris did not march out with his company.[14]

Nevertheless, Harris's account is credible. He settled in Fort Worth after his discharge, and had ample time to learn the details of the incident from other soldiers and residents. He may have stretched the truth a bit in telling the story, but he preserved something of the flavor of the event for future generations.

A third account bears considerable resemblance to those of Daggett and Harris. Mrs. N. O. Holloway was a fourteen-year-old girl in 1851 who lived near the post with her parents. She told a newspaper reporter the following story in 1921. Mrs. Holloway would have been about eighty-four at the time of the interview.

> One night about 200 Tonkaway Indians came to the fort and demanded the chief of another tribe. I have forgotten what tribe it was. The soldiers had him locked in the fort and refused to give him up to the warriors.
>
> Finally the Tonkaways asked just to be permitted to talk to him for a minute. The soldiers agreed and the Indian was brought from the stockade. Without a seconds warning the Indians went at him with knives. The soldiers, of course, interfered. And the one way that was safe to get rid of the Indians was to fire the cannon. This the soldiers did, and we never saw anything more of the Indians.[15]

On April 20, 1851, Department Headquarters in San Antonio received a letter from Maj. Arnold asking what he should do with six Indians whom he was holding in his guardhouse. It is reasonable to assume that these were the Indians who had sought refuge.[16] This suggests that the Tonkawas had first sought refuge at the post between April 10 and April 14, 1851. On April 21, headquarters wrote back to say that Arnold should release "certain Tonkaway Indians held at post." The letter took six days to travel between San Antonio and Fort Worth, arriving April 27.[17]

These letters are all that is written in official documents about the Indians. All we know is that something might have happened in Fort Worth, but many historians have serious doubts about the size or importance of the incident.

Another story making the rounds around the turn of the century is a story for which no references or reports have ever been found, and, based on what is known about the army and the Indians, did not happen. It sounds like something that got exaggerated one night and grew from there. However, it is reported here because it is part of the myth of the fort, and even though it probably never happened.

In 1930, a Fort Worth resident named Howard Peak published an account of a battle fought some eighty years before between the Comanche Indians and the garrison of Fort Worth, Texas.[18] Peak stated that his account was based on notes that his father had made concerning the early history of Fort Worth. According to the younger Peak, a band of Comanche Indians led by "Chief Jim Ned," decided to attack Fort Worth. In preparation for the raid, about a hundred warriors made camp to the west of Fort Worth. A passing fur trapper spotted the Indians, and hastened to warn the garrison of the fort. Major Arnold, the commander at Fort Worth, led the troops in an attack on the Comanche camp:

> It was planned to attack from three directions. Major Arnold, Captain Maclay, and Lieutenant Street were to head a detail and at an agreed signal a general charge was to be made. Leaving the wagons behind, the several units set out for position . . . The signal came and our soldiers galloped on the unsuspecting victims in the draw. What follows beggars description. With the aid of the full moon the regulars had every advantage, and as the three detachments made their charge, each unit fired into the surprised and bewildered foe. Jim Ned and the survivors fled to the west. Arnold pursued them and attacked again, this time in a canyon in Palo Pinto County.
>
> From every boulder poured a shower of swift arrows some of which found unerring marks. Seeking such positions of vantage as the situation offered, the regulars pumped such deadly fire from their repeating carbines into the faces of their enemy as to cause woeful destruction of their numbers . . . For several hours the fight waxed fierce, without sign of yielding on the part of the besieged. After hours of fighting, the Indians fled, leaving behind 45 dead. Arnold's command suffered five killed and 15 wounded.[19]

Peak's story goes on to say that Jim Ned returned to Fort Worth for a second raid. This time, the garrison drove the Indians away with a single shot from the post's cannon. This part of the story could be taking a page from the Tonkawa story.

Peak's story makes interesting reading. But when one checks the army's official records, discrepancies emerge. Muster rolls and medical reports show that no soldiers were killed or wounded by

Indians while serving at Fort Worth. The three officers named in the story—Arnold, Maclay, and Street—never served simultaneously at the post. Dragoons at Fort Worth carried single-shot carbines. And, although even small skirmishes were reported to headquarters, no trace of the battle can be found in the state or the national archives.

The Indian chief, Jim Ned, was the chief of a tribe of Delaware Indians that moved around in northwest Texas. Jim Ned was employed as a guide by the Texas Rangers and by the Army at Fort Worth at various times, and is mentioned in the next chapter. There is a creek in Taylor and Coleman County, and an independent school district named for him. It is doubtful that he led a tribe of Comanches anywhere.

Military historians, especially those who have been in combat, know that if such an incident, or anything close to it had happened, there would be glowing official reports recommending medals and awards. They also know that combat actions, like wine, seem to get better with age, and that the liveliest storytellers are those who were not there.

Major Ripley Arnold and his men were competent professional soldiers. The Indians would have known this. Warriors recognize warriors. The real story of what happened in Fort Worth is more interesting than the myths. It was routine, day-to-day hard work and hardships.

12

The Infantry Returns with Horses

While Bvt. Brig. Gen. William S. Harney was meeting with the Comanches at Fort Martin Scott in May 1851, Capt. Robert Maclay's Company F, 8th Infantry was encamped at Fort Gates, living in tents waiting for permanent barracks. They had left Fort Worth on April 6, 1851, in accordance with Bvt. Maj. Gen., George M. Brooke's plan to separate the infantry and the dragoons. Maclay's Company F was joined at Fort Gates by Companies D, H, and I of the 8th Infantry.

After Brooke died on March 9, 1851, Harney assumed temporary command of the department for the second time. In May, he issued his own plan for the frontier. He ordered the establishment of Fort Mason, increased the number of scouts, and, to concentrate his dragoons, transferred Company F from Fort Worth to Fort Graham. He felt that there was no reason to keep four infantry companies at Fort Gates, so he ordered the post commander there to send two companies to Fort Worth.[1]

The post commander at Fort Gates, Bvt. Lt. Col. C. A. Waite, decided to send Maclay's men back to Fort Worth, a reasonable decision considering Company F had served on the Trinity for more than a year and a half, and its leaders knew the countryside well. Waite chose Company H, commanded by Bvt. Lt. Col. James V. Bomford, as the second company since it had served at Fort Graham since October 1849, and its leaders, too, were familiar with north Texas.

As the two companies prepared to leave Fort Gates, Col. Samuel Cooper arrived to inspect the fort and the garrison. On May 28 or 29, 1851, Col. Cooper reviewed the troops. He found that their arms and equipment were in good condition, but their uniforms were almost worn out because a supply of new uniforms had been in storage in Houston since December, awaiting transportation. Their knapsacks were also old and worn. They did fairly well at drill, but the recent move from Fort Worth, together with preparations for going back, had interfered with training.[2]

Bomford and Maclay's companies left Fort Gates on June 6, 1851, and arrived at Fort Worth ten days later. Major Arnold's men left the next day for Fort Graham. Since there were no longer any dragoons at Fort Worth, the infantry now played a role quite different from that of the previous two years. During their first stay at Fort Worth, their main job was to support the dragoons. Some had probably gone out on scouts, using the saddles and cavalry weapons Brooke sent in 1849, but most of the foot soldiers probably spent most of their time working around the post.

The new garrison included about 120 soldiers and four officers.[3] This time, the two companies brought seventy-eight horses with them.[4] About half of each company would be assigned to serve full time as mounted infantry. These men were armed with percussion rifles and pistols, and when possible, they learned the basics of the mounted drill. They kept up the routine of weekly scouts to the Red River just as the dragoons had done.

Bomford became the new commander of Fort Worth. He was a career officer with a strong sense of duty. His father had been the eighth graduate of the U.S. Military Academy. Bomford graduated from West Point in 1832, then served in Florida and Mexico. At the Battle of Monterrey, he commanded his company in street fighting, distinguishing himself when leading a group of soldiers in an attack toward the central plaza of the city. Rather than advancing down the streets, they tunneled their way through the walls of houses using picks and drove the Mexicans back.[5]

Bomford's first lieutenant, Charles D. Jordan, a West Point graduate and also a veteran of Mexico, was transferred away in July. His replacement, 1st Lt. Edward Blake, was also an academy graduate and, like Jordan, served at the post for only a few weeks before being reassigned. Captain Maclay was back in command of Company F, assisted by 1st Lt. Washington Street and 2nd Lt. John Bold. Street led the first scout, leaving for the Red River on June 18, 1851.[6]

The soldiers settled into the same garrison routine that the dragoons had experienced: scouting parties rode to the Red River every week; in late summer, men came down with malaria; Bomford held regimental courts-martial to try minor offenses.[7] In September

1851, Lt. Bold submitted a report on the post's buildings. He reported that the post was in a state of disrepair: all the roofs leaked, and the officers' quarters scarcely kept the rain out. In October, Lt. Bold, as quartermaster, hired five civilians to construct storage sheds. One wheelwright, two muleteers, and one guide and interpreter were also working at the post in the fall.[8]

Brevet Second Lieutenant Frederick Follett joined Company H on October 13, 1851. Follett was a native of Batavia, New York. His father, also named Frederick, was the editor of a Batavia newspaper and a strong Democratic Party supporter. Follett's father had come to Texas in 1836 in order to join the Texas Revolution. The fighting had already ended when he arrived, so he went on a hunting trip to the San Saba mission before returning to New York. Frederick entered West Point in 1846, graduated in 1850, and served with the 3rd Infantry before coming to Texas.[9]

Issuing horses to the infantry was an experiment designed to provide more mounted troops for the Texas frontier. Only Congress could create new mounted regiments or raise the authorized strength of existing units. This left army leaders with two choices—they could call the Texas Rangers into federal service or, they could put infantrymen on horses.

In his first plan for the defense of Texas, Bvt. Maj. Gen. Zachary Taylor had planned to issue horses to two companies of infantry.[10] The mounted infantry began scouting in early 1849, and when a company of mounted infantry accompanied Bvt. Lt. Col. Joseph E. Johnston on his reconnaissance to El Paso in 1849, he praised their conduct.[11] In March, Bvt Maj. Gen. William J. Worth ordered the infantry to make regular patrols along the line of forts.[12] Lieutenant George Pickett of the 8th Infantry led some of these early patrols.

The numbers of mounted infantry grew steadily. In June 1849, President Zachary Taylor's secretary of war, G. W. Crawford, recommended to his generals that they create more mounted infantrymen. He hoped that this would make it unnecessary to call up the rangers.[13] Brevet Major General David Twiggs, commander of the Western Division, authorized Gen. Brooke to buy up to two hundred horses to be used to create a new mounted infantry. He also forwarded three hundred well worn saddles and bridles, "such as are unfit for Dragoons."[14] Brooke issued the new horses to infantry companies. In August, he distributed saddles, pistols, and carbines or rifles to each post, so that the infantry could ride on scouts. Posts such as Fort Worth, where infantry and dragoons were serving together, received arms and equipment for twelve men. At posts where there were no dragoons, the infantry drew arms and saddles for twenty-five men. An officer's wife at Ringgold Barracks on the Rio Grande described an infantry company that had received horses and was learning to ride:

> Without a knowledge of even the first principles of riding, they sat on their horses like a parcel of clothes pins, and it was not an unusual thing to see a dozen dismounted at once, and lie sprawling on the ground; they were instantly up, however, and in their saddles to try it once more. In spite of their mishaps, they seemed to enjoy it very much, and after a few months' perseverance became quite a presentable cavalry company.[15]

Despite the wide use of mounted infantry in Texas, few generals had anything good to say about the practice. General Twiggs reported that, in Florida, mounted infantrymen ruined their horses and could not learn to ride.[16] General in Chief of the Army Winfield Scott endorsed the practice with reluctance, as shown in his statement that "footmen, in the saddle, constitute a mongrel force: inefficient, with great excess in the wear & tear of horses and equipment."[17] Scott wanted another mounted regiment instead. The expenditure for horses would be nearly the same and the men would learn to ride and fight properly.

Scott proposed raising an additional mounted regiment in November 1849.[18] Many members of Congress supported the idea, but Secretary of War Crawford disagreed. He hoped to put an entire regiment of infantry on horseback and send them to attack hostile Indians in their winter villages.[19] On June 17, 1850, Congress authorized President Taylor to provide horses for nine hundred infantrymen. After the bill passed, Secretary Crawford withdrew the War Department's earlier request for a new mounted regiment on the grounds that the additional mounted infantry would suffice.[20]

Taylor died on July 9, 1850, and was succeeded by his vice president, Millard Fillmore. Fillmore made Charles Conrad the new secretary of war. Conrad asked Congress to repeal the mounted infantry law and to authorize another mounted regiment instead.[21] Congress eventually relented and established two new mounted regiments, but mounted infantrymen continued serving in Texas until about November 1853.

The mounted infantry companies had to make do with the worst equipment. General Twiggs's shipment probably included some old Ringgold saddles. As a result, quartermaster officers complained when mounted infantry companies sent their saddles in for repair after just one year of service; apparently, no one had told them that the saddles were unfit to begin with! Brooke, in the spring of 1850, complained that his mounted infantry were "miserable riders, more than one half foreigners, who probably never before bestrode a horse, utterly incapable of using their arms in the saddle."[22]

Despite the difficulties, the mounted infantry improved and they were able to make scouts and patrol. On May 19, 1850, Lt. Charles Merchant of the 8th Infantry was leading a patrol of six dragoons, five mounted infantrymen, and a guide in the countryside near Fort Inge. They encountered a party of eight Indians and attacked; the soldiers killed two Indians and captured four and Lt. Merchant was wounded, but none of his men were hurt.[23] Brooke's opinion began to change and by August 1850, Brooke conceded that Lt. Merchant and others had made "a very favorable impression" on him. He reported that the mounted infantry carried rifles or carbines, Harper's Ferry percussion pistols, and, when possible, Colt revolvers. They were being trained on foot and on horseback and he expected that, in time, they would compare favorably to the dragoons and mounted rifles.[24]

In March 1851, Col. Samuel Cooper inspected Companies A and B of the 8th Infantry at San Antonio. He found that:

> . . . the mounted men (15 in each company) were armed with Hall's Carbines, and Colt's revolver pistols . . . some of the pistols were defective from frequent use, particularly in the rammers, which were loosed from the supporting springs and let down by the jar of the discharge in firing. The horse equipment were in wretched condition, many of the saddles being wholly divested of covering or pads, and the other furniture old & much worn.[25]

On a more positive note, Cooper found that the horses were good cavalry mounts, and that the men and horses were reasonably well trained.

Colonel Cooper's report of his inspection tour provides an interesting snapshot of the mounted infantry in Texas in the first half of 1851. The 1st and 8th Infantry Regiments were stationed in Texas, along with two companies of the 5th Infantry at Corpus Christi. Most infantry garrisons included two infantry companies and could field thirty to forty mounted men. The horses were usually divided between two companies, but for some reason, the commanders at Ringgold Barracks, Fort Duncan, and Fort MacIntosh gave all their horses to a single company. The total number of mounted infantry was in the neighborhood of three hundred.

Cooper found that many of the men were good riders. Some companies carried Hall Carbines, while others carried Mississippi rifles. Most had Colt revolvers, but a few had Harper's Ferry pistols and sabers. Saddles and tack were all old, worn, and unserviceable.

While Cooper was at Fort Martin Scott, a shipment of horses from Ohio arrived for the 8th Infantry. Cooper noted that they had lost considerable weight on the trip to Texas and were the worst looking horses he saw on his visit.

Despite the mounted infantry's successes, the tide of opinion began to turn against such units, although it is not clear why. Even Harney, the old dragoon commander, could see some use for them: in June 1852, he recommended that each infantry company be issued ten or fifteen mules. The infantry could ride the mules until they met the enemy and then dismount to fight on foot.[26]

They were also given many difficult assignments, as proven in a letter from Lt. E. K. Smith. The posts on the Rio Grande were manned by infantry and artillery, both of whom scouted on horseback. On June 1, 1853, Smith wrote from Ringgold Barracks that, in the preceding four months, he had spent sixty days in the saddle, and ridden more than a thousand miles.[27]

The mounted infantry had learned to succeed despite bad equipment, poor horses, and difficult assignments. However, the tide had already turned in favor of the mounted regiments, and on July 18, 1853, Gen. Smith announced that the mounted infantry were to be dismounted. No further cavalry equipment should be given to the infantry, except ammunition.[28] In August, he ordered all mounted infantry companies to bring their horses and equipment to San Antonio to be exchanged for infantry gear.

On October 6, Smith ordered the two companies of the 7th Infantry at Ringgold Barracks to turn in their horses, musketoons, pistols, and Colt revolvers.[29] On October 27, he ordered the mounted company of the 1st Infantry at Fort McIntosh to do the same.[30] Captain Maclay's company was one of the last mounted companies to turn in its horses at Fort McKavett in August 1853.[31]

The mounted infantry experiment was over.

13

Fort Belknap Begins

In late June 1851, as Lt. Washington Street and his mounted infantry patrol made their way north to the Red River, soldiers of the 5th Infantry were establishing a new post in the wilderness to the northwest of Fort Worth. In the spring of 1851, General of the Army Winfield Scott decided to transfer the 5th Infantry Regiment from the Indian Territory to Texas. Scott ordered Bvt. Brig. Gen. William G. Belknap, commanding the 5th Infantry, to deploy the regiment to West Texas, and to construct two or more new posts along the Marcy Trail.

The Marcy Trail, an important route for emigration to California, ran from Fort Smith, Arkansas to the vicinity of El Paso, passing through Fort Washita, Preston, and Northwest Texas.[1] Belknap took two companies of his regiment, led them down the Marcy trail, and explored the countryside around the headwaters of the Brazos. He selected a site on the Red Fork of the Brazos, about ten miles below the spot where the Trail crossed the river.

On June 24, 1851, he established Camp Belknap. He left a captain in charge of the post and returned to Arkansas to send out the rest of his troops. He reported to Washington that it would be impossible to station his men farther west, because there was not enough water or timber to sustain life.[2]

By September, the garrison had grown to six companies and almost two hundred troops.[3] A supply depot was established at Preston,[4] and supplies came from Fort Smith and via the Red River.[5]

Belknap returned to Texas in the fall. Rather than establish new posts along the Marcy Trail, he wished to send his men south, to the headwaters of the Colorado and Concho.

Major Arnold's Company F was detailed to escort Belknap as he explored the countryside.[6] The dragoons left Fort Graham on August 10, 1851, and arrived about a week later at the Caddo Village, near today's Possum Kingdom Lake.[7] Lieutenant Samuel Starr wrote to his daughter from the dragoon camp on September 22:

> My Dear Kate, Your dear, pretty little letter I received the day before yesterday; and the box, too, I have got. I tried and tried to guess what was in it, but I could not so I opened it and found nuts and raisins oh how good they are here, way off from every body and every thing! Thank you dear Kate for such a nice present. I hope you will write me often, I do so like to get letters from you. You must tell me about dear little Annie's health, and Mamma's health, and your health, too. Tell me about how will you learn your book, for I like to hear that above all things.
>
> It is very lonesome out here, papa has to sleep on the ground, live in an old tent, and he has nothing comfortable or good to eat. I expect to go a great deal further away from you before I can come back and see you all. Expect Gen. Belknap to arrive at the camp where the infantry stay, about thirty miles from here, in a very few days, when they all think he will want one company to go with him up the Brazos further, to see that country, where, they say, there is no grass for our horses, nor any water to drink except salt water. This salt water will be bad for my dysentery, dear Kate, but I know that I can kill by hardship a dozen like old General Belknap, so that he will be glad enough to return before I shall care half as much about it.
>
> You must kiss Annie a thousand times for me, and tell me in your next letter if she walks yet—and how big are the leaves on that plant which you water every day, I expect. Very affectionately, dear Kate, your father, Sam. H. Starr.[8]

Before Arnold and Starr could leave Caddo Village with Gen. Belknap, Company F was ordered back to Fort Graham.[9] Arnold and the dragoons were back by October 7.

Every year or two, the army dispatched a senior officer to inspect the troops and report to Washington on their readiness. In 1851, Col. Samuel Cooper inspected the 8th Military Department. He visited Fort Martin Scott between May 18 and May 21, 1851, and reviewed Hardee's dragoons at Camp Harney. He was pleased with what he saw.

Colonel Samuel Cooper made his way north across Texas in the spring of 1851. He inspected Fort Graham on June 4 and 5.[10] After the inspection, he set out with Bvt. Maj. H. H. Sibley and an escort to visit the Indians living along the Brazos River. The party crossed the Brazos near Barnard's Trading House, and reached the Ioni village the next day. In his report to Washington Cooper described the visit:

During this excursion I visited four out of six of the Indian Villages located upon the Brasos within the section of the country over which we passed: to—wit, the Ioni, Keechi, Caddo, & Anandarco. Two other tribes, the Waco & Tawaconis, who have their villages upon the Brasos about six miles beyond the Keechi village are connected with these tribes and of the same general character, but being beyond the limit which I had prescribed for myself, I did not visit them. These six tribes are united in two separate bands, and each band is governed by a head chief, each tribe having its own particular chief who is subordinate to the head chief of the band. Thus, Jose Maria is chief of his own particular tribe, the Anandarco's, Towysh of the Ioni tribe, & Haddebar of the Caddo tribe, and these three tribes are united under Jose Maria as head chief. So also is Acaquash the chief of his own particular tribe, the Waco's, Chacheruck of the Keechi tribe, and Ocherash of the Tawaconis tribe and these three again form a separate band under the head chief Acaquash. These several tribes number in all about two hundred and forty warriors, and including their women and children they amount in the aggregate to about one thousand.

I found these people perfectly peaceable, and in every way disposed to cultivate friendly relations with the whites; they were tilling the earth, raising corn and vegetables extensively, and their crops appeared in a fine state of forwardness and well cared for; but with all this labor and exertion they find it difficult to get along on account of the sparseness of game in the country, which is their chief reliance; at times they are in a starving condition . . .

A few miles from the Keechi village we crossed a broad trail leading a few miles to the North East. I was told by Acaquash that this was the great Comanche trail, which, passing by the Caddo & Keechi villages, led directly across the Red River to the Washita settlements, and was used by the Comanche in driving their stolen horses and mules to those settlements where they were disposed of to traders.

I also found upon the left bank of the Brazos and about two miles below Barnard's trading house, a small band of Delawares & Shawnees, in all about forty warriors and their families. They had recently moved to this place from the neighborhood of Fort Graham on account of the recent department orders which require that Indians found within the line of military posts shall be put to death. They are cultivating corn and are peaceable and well disposed. Some of them are occasionally used as interpreters, guides & hunters.[11]

General Cooper recommended that the government foster relations with the Brazos tribes by providing seed, farming tools, some livestock, and a blacksmith. He also recommended that troops be stationed near the Caddo village, in order to keep an eye on the Comanche trail which he had described. Major Sibley drew a sketch map to illustrate Cooper's report. Sibley drew the Comanche trail leading straight to Warren's Trading House on the Red River.[12]

At Fort Worth, the infantry was going about the same garrison routine. Scouting parties rode to the Red River every week. Many men came down with malaria in the late summer. And as always, they were building and repairing the buildings and getting ready for inspections.

The next post on Col. Cooper's tour of inspection was Fort Worth. Colonel Cooper left Fort Graham on June 15th, and arrived to inspect Fort Worth on June 17. Major Arnold's men had made preparations to move to Fort Graham when Cooper inspected the post. Cooper noted that a total of fifty-six men were present for duty. Major Arnold, Lt. Starr, and Assistant Surgeon Williams were the three officers present. Cooper's inspection report reads as follows:

> This company appeared to be greatly in want of instruction. It was composed chiefly of Germans who were mostly indifferent riders; and the horses, though of sufficient size, strength and activity, and well suited to the service, were not properly trained in the evolutions to any degree of accuracy.
>
> The arms were in a serviceable state, and cleaned & preserved in a proper manner. They consisted of the musketoon, sword, & Colt's pistol. The horse equipment were also fit for service, though much worn. The stables were properly ventilated, and kept in neat order, & the stable duties appeared to be properly attended to.
>
> The quarters of the men were preserved with cleanliness, and their interior arrangements conformed to the requirements of regulations. The messing was properly conducted—provisions abundant & of good quality. The hospital was in neat order & the sick were well attended—medicines & stores sufficient & of good quality.
>
> The company books were regularly & accountably kept, in the form & manner prescribed. The post was in a high state of police and the daily duties were discharged with regularity according to the usages of the service.[13]

After the inspection, the routine continued, and, as always, things were about to change.

14

Smith's Double Line of Forts

In late 1851 and early 1852, the army's attention focused on the Rio Grande. A Mexican named Carvajal, with many American supporters, tried to form a breakaway republic on the south bank of the river. Harney and several companies of dragoons were ordered to the border to prevent Americans from crossing into Mexico.[1] Carvajal's rebellion fizzled after a failed attack on Cerralvo on November 26, 1851, but U.S. troops were on the lookout for him and his supporters until the spring of 1853.[2]

Brevet Major General George M. Brooke's permanent replacement, Bvt. Maj. Gen. Persifor F. Smith, took command of the 8th Military Department from Bvt. Brig. Gen. William S. Harney in September 1851.[3] Smith, a former president of Princeton University, was a hero of the Mexican War. After the war, he served as military commander in California before coming to Texas. Smith intended to overhaul the army's strategy in Texas. The first line of forts had been built to make the best use of a small force. In 1851, the War Department was at last sending reinforcements. The 5th Infantry was already on the Brazos, and the Regiment of Mounted Rifles was scheduled to arrive in the spring.

At his San Antonio headquarters, Smith talked to his officers, read the scouting reports and correspondence of the last two years, and made a plan for a new line of forts.[4] He wanted an advanced line of forts, about 100 miles west. He would keep many of the old forts open, and thus create a double line. If an Indian war party crossed the outer line of forts, the troops there would discover the trail, and alert the garrisons on the inner line. The Indians' retreat would be cut off, and several detachments would pursue them at the same time.[5]

Smith wanted large infantry posts on the outer line. Their chief role would be to intercept and give warning, rather than to pursue war parties. Large posts would give infantry commanders more time to drill and discipline their companies. Dragoons, who would pursue and fight the Indians who crossed the frontier, would man the inner line. It would be cheaper to station dragoons on the inner line, where grass and hay was available and where settlers were already growing corn. To concentrate his forces, Smith planned to shut down the garrisons at Corpus Christi, San Antonio and Austin, and to abandon Forts Merrill, Lincoln, and Gates. He planned to close either Fort Worth or Fort Graham.[6]

In early October 1851, Smith set out to ride the length of the frontier and to visit the areas where he would build his new line.[7] He arrived at Fort Belknap near the end of the month. Brevet Brigadier General. William Belknap, who knew nothing of Smith's plans, was very ill with dysentery when Smith arrived. Belknap wanted to move four companies from Camp Belknap to Pecan Bayou, a tributary of the Colorado. Smith wanted Belknap to station the four companies about fifty miles southwest on the Clear Fork of the Brazos, near the Marcy Trail.[8]*

Belknap had explored the country southwest of his fort, and disagreed strongly with Smith's choice of the site on the Clear Fork of the Brazos. Despite this, Smith insisted and, on November 3, 1851, ordered Belknap to establish the new post.[9] However, Belknap was unable to lead the command. His health had grown worse and, on the post surgeon's advice, he tried to rejoin his family at Fort Gibson, Indian Territory via military ambulance. On November 10, 1851, as the ambulance approached Fort Washita in a cold winter rain, his driver found him dead in the vehicle, and he was buried at Fort Washita.[10]

Fifth Infantry soldiers established Fort Phantom Hill on November 14. It was soon apparent that Belknap had been correct in his assessment of the countryside. There was no timber or drinkable water for miles and hauling them in was an immense labor. Lieutenant Clint Lear described the place in a letter to his wife, written November 14, 1851: "Indeed I cannot imagine that God ever intended white man to occupy such a barren waste."[11]

---

*The actual site ended up about ten miles north of Abilene, and is called Fort Phantom Hill (although this was never the official name of the post).

Smith returned to San Antonio, and lost no time in sending his infantry to build the new line of forts. At Fort Worth, Bvt. Lt. Col. Bomford and Capt. Robert Maclay's men received orders to prepare to change stations. On January 11, 1852, the two companies set off for the San Saba River, where they would begin construction of Fort McKavett, which was to be home to four companies of the 8th Infantry.*

Along the way, Maclay's men joined in the pursuit of an Indian war party. On January 30, 1852, as Company F neared Fort Martin Scott, they received word that an Indian war party was in the neighborhood. They hurried to the fort with forty-two men, forty-two sets of horse tack, and one hundred horses. The post commander there took all the available troops and organized them into two parties, each of thirty men. Captain Maclay and Lt. Cole led one party. Major Longstreet and Lt. Dodge led the other. Since there were no mules, they used their extra horses for pack animals. They set out with ten days rations to search for the Indians' trail.

The next day the post commander issued horses to Bomford's company as well, and sent out two more parties of thirty men.[12] Despite the large pursuing force, the Indians seem to have escaped, and the infantrymen resumed their march to the San Saba, arriving in early March 1852.[13]

At Fort McKavett, the infantrymen began constructing a post on a beautiful hilltop overlooking miles of limestone hills and live oaks.† Lieutenant Street wrote his brother, Joseph, on August 18, 1852, from Fort McKavett:

> The post is quite well situated, enjoying the advantages of good water, air, and an agreeable prospect. Game is abundant, and the country easy to hunt over. I met the Capt. of my company Maclay on his way out, on a sick leave, as I came through San Antonio. This gives me the command of a mounted company, & the only one at the post. Indeed, there is but one other in the regiment. My horses are in good condition, and if there should be any scouting to do, I will be sent.
>
> I keep two excellent horses for my own riding, and exercise every day on horseback, taking my own horses along, and bringing in some birds for the mess. This I find highly conducive to my health . . .

*It was named for Capt. Henry McKavett, 8th Infantry, who was killed on September 21, 1846, in the Battle of Monterrey.

†The stone barracks that they built and lived in are still there. The surrounding countryside, nearly uninhabited, looks much as it must have when the soldiers were there.

> The Indians are daily in the vicinity of our post, and come in very frequently to beg provisions, manifesting the while, unbounded friendship.[14]

Despite the beautiful location, Bomford and Maclay's companies experienced more than their share of tragedy in 1852. Four men died at Fort Croghan. Another man died shortly after arriving at McKavett. Lieutenant John Bold died of unknown causes on May 25, 1852, near Fort Mason. Lieutenant Washington Street survived Bold by only four months. Street committed suicide on September 13, just four weeks after writing to his brother. The post surgeon recorded the date and cause of death "suicidium," and nothing else.[15] Bomford notified Street's family, but his letter said little about why Street killed himself. Street's brother, Joseph, wrote to the post chaplain, to try to learn what had happened:

> Bomford's letter leaves us & his numerous relations entirely in the dark as to the cause of his death and his real & true situation . . . He speaks in his manuscript of difficulties, charges &c, let us know what these all mean if you know. What was the state of his mind when he died? How did he regard the future? The Capt. Bomford says he had been reading his Bible.[16]

The chaplain's reply is not to be found. If Lt. Street was facing some kind of charges, there is no record, and the circumstances of his death remain a mystery.

General Smith's double line of forts would take shape as the year 1852 progressed. In the north, the 5th Infantry was building Forts Belknap and Phantom Hill on the Brazos. The 8th Infantry abandoned Fort Gates in March 1852 and established two new forts in the middle of the outer line: Fort McKavett, on the San Saba, and Camp Joseph E. Johnston, on the North Concho.[17]* In southwest Texas, the 1st Infantry established Fort Terrett on February 2, 1852 and Fort Clark on June 2.[18]†

The War Department had long recognized that the Texas frontier needed more mounted troops. To help remedy matters, the

*It was located about ten miles north of San Angelo, and named for Bvt. Lt. Col. Joseph E. Johnston of the Corps of Topographic Engineers. Johnston would later become a general in the Confederacy.

†Fort Terrett, located on the north fork of the Llano River about twenty-five miles west of Junction, was named for Lt. John C. Terrett, 1st Infantry, killed in the Battle of Monterrey. Fort Clark located on Las Moras creek east of Brackettville, was named for Maj. John B. Clark, who was also killed in the Mexican War. It remained open and active until 1946.

Regiment of Mounted Riflemen was ordered to Texas from the Great Plains. The mounted riflemen began to arrive in the spring of 1852 and were assigned to posts south and west of San Antonio. On May 18, 1852, they established Fort Ewell near the point where the San Antonio-Laredo Road crossed the Nueces River.[19]* Fort Lincoln, the dragoon post at D'Hanis, was abandoned on July 20, 1852.[20]

In north Texas, the Red River proved to be too unreliable to serve as a supply route for Fort Belknap and Fort Phantom Hill; so on September 22, the chief quartermaster officer at the Preston Supply Depot was transferred to Austin. Supplies for Fort Belknap and Fort Phantom Hill were drawn from the depot in Austin until May 1853, when the Preston supply was closed.[21]

All this shifting would bring Maj. Arnold back to the fort he had founded on June 6, 1849. However, he would be coming back without 1st Lt. Samuel Starr, and his family, which now included three daughters; Jo was born in November 1851.[22] Samuel was promoted to first lieutenant and transferred in December. He left for Fort Mason on December 29, 1851 after serving just over two years with Company F.

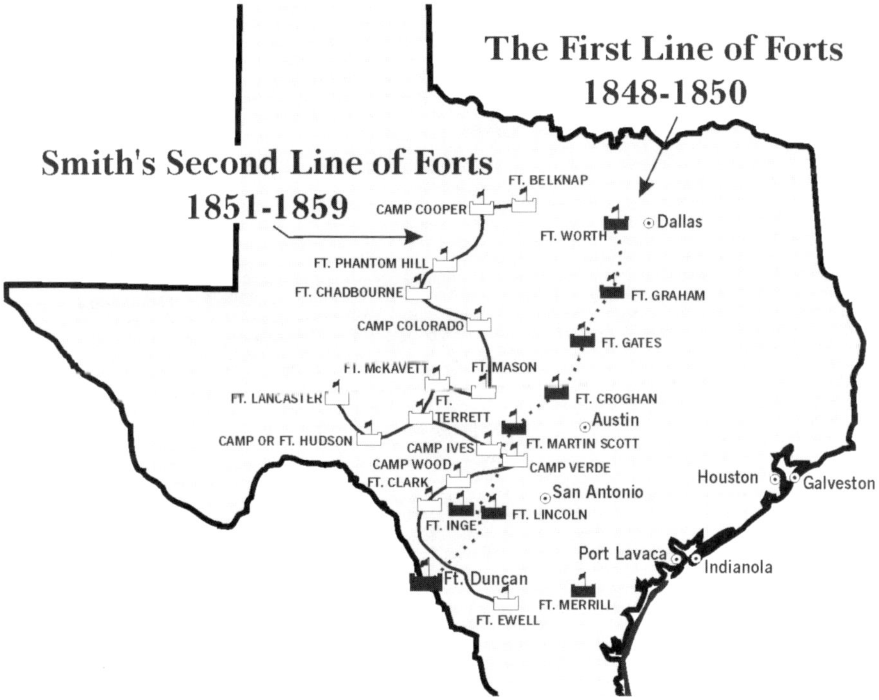

*Fort Ewell was named for Lt. Thomas Ewell of the Mounted Rifles who was killed at Cerro Gordo on April 8, 1847.

The Day Begins

This drawing depicts the start of another day. The flag is going up. The wagon train in the background is pulling out to the west. The view is toward the southwest. The commanding officers cabin is to the left, then another officer's cabin, the warehouses in the upper right and the headquarters cabin to the far right. (Copyright William Potter.)

15

Arnold's Dragoons Come Back For Seven Months

As the two companies of mounted infantry left Fort Worth on January 11, 1852, Bvt. Maj. Ripley Arnold and Company F rode from Fort Graham and took over again.[1] Just as they had been for the first four months the fort existed, they would once more be the only troops stationed there.[2]

Arnold and Assistant Surgeon Thomas Williams were the only officers at Fort Worth. Lieutenant Starr had transferred to Company A, and had left for Fort Mason, while Eliza Starr and the children went to Austin. In Austin, she found that rents were outrageously expensive. She took the children from Austin to Fort Gates, where she found a place to stay.

Samuel wrote to Eliza from Fort Mason on January 18, 1852, one day after arriving. The housing situation there was not encouraging. He wrote, "I had the honor to share Colonel May's bed with him last night."[3] Brevet Lieutenant Colonel Charles May was his new company commander; the post was only six months old, and officers' quarters were evidently in short supply. Eliza and the children would have to wait at Fort Gates.

While Eliza Starr settled in at Fort Gates, Catherine Arnold was at Fort Worth with her husband and children. On February 28, Mrs. Arnold wrote to her friend, Mrs. Starr,

> My Dear Mrs. Starr, I was glad to hear from you through Donnelly but was surprised to learn you had come back to Fort Gates. I had heard of your not remaining at Austin but did not hear

what had become of you. I suppose you are comfortably situated where you are, do you intend going to Fort Mason, or remain there until you go North. Major Arnold expects his leave every Mail but he will not leave until he is tired of Fort Worth it would be pleasant to visit home in the Summer. I am content to stay—if the children were at school I should be better satisfied. The Post is about like it was the same people living near with a few additional families. Mrs. Farmer presented her husband with Twin Boys, but they lived but a few days. Three children in one year that's worse than you. I received the Box of Essence for which I am much obliged we have had many good things made of them. Love to Kate and kisses for the Babies write soon we shall always be pleased to hear from you. Yours truly, Kate.[4]

Florida Arnold, now 12 years old, added a postscript:

Tell Kate she must write to me I would have written to her but it is getting late. I will write next mail give my love to her and Annie and a Kiss for the Baby. Florida Arnold.

Eliza wrote back to Catherine Arnold on March 12, 1852:

Dear Mrs. Arnold, Yours of February 28th was received with much pleasure and I hasten to answer it, notwithstanding, Annie and the baby both have combined to prevent me if possible; "Jo" is crying as hard as her lungs will permit, and Annie is standing by my side saying "up, up" and occasionally, by way of emphasis, gives a pull at my elbow. Donnelly has told you, no doubt, of our journey from Graham to Austin, that we arrived in safety &c. Well, we put up at Hancock's house, (formerly Swisher's) after trying every other in town; and he put us in a little back room up stairs, at the rate of *seven* dollars per day and *fires, extra* with the advantage, every time the door opened, of Annie popping out and getting a tumble down into the yard; indeed, a man fell, or walked off the same gallery and was killed, in consequence of having no banister around it, so you see the propriety of seeking other quarters which we did not find until we brought up at Ft. Gates, the delightful! F. Gates you have heard so much about.

I do wish you could pay me a visit and see the snug little rooms I am occupying, with furniture to match that I have picked up around the garrison: how you would laugh, however, I am quite comfortable, and that is more than I could say when at F. Graham; but my health has not much improved since living here, and the children have all been sick with the chills and fever, or something worse.

Poor Mrs. Farmer is unfortunate with her babies, but I think she would soon have a house full at the rate of three per year.

Who lives in our old house? Does it look the same as of old?

I have given all the kisses to the "babies," you sent, and "Flo's" also, tell Florida Kate often wishes for her and Kitty to play with.[5]

Eliza and the children probably remained at Fort Gates for much of 1852. She and Samuel took leave later in the year and returned to New York. Samuel returned to Texas when his leave expired, but Eliza stayed behind in Cold Spring, a village on the Hudson River opposite the U.S. Military Academy at West Point. The family papers contain an incomplete draft of a letter to Catherine Arnold dated November 27, 1852,

Dear Mrs. Arnold, Here I am once more a *widow* and, although, surrounded by a crowd, I feel, as it were, alone in the world. Mr. Starr left the 20th for "old Texas," (his leave of absence expires the 10th of December,) and it will take him nearly a month to reach his post, we were just twenty nine days coming from Fort Gates to New York and a delightful time we had of it I can assure you, the first and second days of our journey passed without much trouble, but the third day we were overtaken by a thunderstorm and our wagon cover not being waterproof, the rain came through on our devoted heads. O dear! I wish you could have seen us when we arrived at a little house in the middle of a big prairie, with two rooms, each about twelve feet square, and already crowded with travelers, Major Sibley and escort included, well we were glad enough to stop with any odds against us so, in the house we went and there my troubles began. Annie and the Baby were in a terrible state, I leave you to guess, how I felt in being compelled to attend to them before a room full of men, and how we slept that night. That one day was the worst of all our journey.

I have had a good deal of trouble since my arrival at New York with Annie, she has had several spells of sickness, and I have had one serious spell myself, and Jo has an inflammation in one of her eyes that gives me a great deal of anxiety. I am afraid it will not get entirely well as long as she is teething with that exception she is quite well and fat; you remember how very poor she was at Fort Graham? She can say two or three words, and walks about everywhere. I expect your little Nannie could walk long ago, and talk too by this time, do write me a long letter, I shall receive it with so much pleasure and tell me all the news, how Fort Worth looks and what changes have been made since you returned to it, the last thing will be interesting to me. I have heard of the death of poor Mr. Bold, and saw by the papers that Mr. Street committed suicide. How does 'Flo.' and Kitty get along, do you ever see Mr. Ganar? [Gouhenant] Kate is suffering, at present, with a bad cold, she wishes very often to see Flo and Kitty, I am going to send her to Rutgers Institute in N. York City it is one of the best schools in the country.[6]

Mrs. Starr and Mrs. Arnold seem to have lost touch after this; at any rate, the family papers contain no more letters between the two. Eliza remained in New York while her husband served at Fort Mason.

Starr's transfer to Fort Mason left Maj. Arnold with no lieutenant to help run Fort Worth. Arnold again became the quartermaster and commissary officer for the post. His quartermaster records for the first quarter of 1852 show some of the details of daily life at the post.

The Quartermaster Department paid fifteen cents a day to men who performed nonmilitary labor for at least ten consecutive days. Arnold's records show that eight soldiers performed extra duty in the first quarter of 1852.[7] A clerk, a blacksmith, and a teamster each worked full time in their special assignments. An express rider was on duty every day as well. A soldier assigned to tend quartermaster livestock, a second teamster, and a laborer were employed for a few weeks at a time. Arnold paid the men a total of $62.85 for their work. The soldiers paid were: Charles Kinsler, clerk; William Oliver, teamster; John Hannibal, company teamster; James Hanna, attending Q.M. animals; George Siter, blacksmith; Edward Riordan, laborer; John Senn and Michael McNamara, express riders.[8]

Fort Worth was surrounded by good farmland, so the Quartermaster Department bought forage from local civilians. In 1851, Lt. John Bold had made a contract with James Horton to supply grain to the garrison at $1.15 per bushel. Horton delivered the corn and oats to Bold, probably in the fall of 1851. Bold gave Horton a voucher for the grain, to be paid later. On January 20, 1852, Maj. Arnold paid Horton $3,206.05 for 2,787 bushels and 28 quarts of corn. Horton's contract apparently expired on March 15, 1852. On March 31, Arnold paid Horton $1,074.67½ for another 467½ bushels of corn and 700½ bushels of oats.[9]

In March, Company F had fifty-two horses and nine mules at Fort Worth. The Quartermaster Department kept another twenty-two horses and twenty-nine mules, making a total of 112 animals. Each animal was fed eight quarts of grain and fourteen pounds of hay per day.[10] A bushel is thirty-two quarts, or eight gallons. The 3,325 bushels of grain, which Arnold paid for, would feed 100 animals for 133 days. Purchasing forage locally saved the Quartermaster Department a small fortune in transportation costs.

The post quartermaster also paid the civilian employees of the post. Four men were employed as muleteers, at $20.00 per month. John Lewis, the Delaware Indian guide and interpreter, earned $40.00; Maxime Guillot, the carpenter and wheelwright, earned

$40.00. Arnold paid another man, John Pane, $8.00 for catching and returning two stray horses.[11]

Acting as post quartermaster, Arnold paid out a total of $4,889.20 in the first three months of 1852. To procure the cash for these payments, Arnold traveled to Dallas, and made out drafts on Col. T. F. Hunt, a quartermaster officer in New Orleans.[12]

When Arnold became the quartermaster at Fort Worth, he signed for all the property of the Quartermaster Department at the post. Much of the property was important, such as four wagons, an ambulance, and the teams to pull them. Other property, such as unserviceable horses and damaged tents, was of less value. Arnold got the unserviceable property condemned by a board of survey, and he auctioned it off on July 26, 1852. Arnold's auctioneer was 1st Sgt. William Slade. Five government horses sold for between $15.50 and $31.00 each. The sale netted $127.39 for the Quartermaster Department.[13]*

To the west of Fort Worth, Fort Belknap continued to grow in size and importance. The garrison began constructing roads to link it to other forts in the line. On December 19, 1851, Lt. W. N. R. Beall, Lt. Thomas English, and a detail from the 5th Infantry set out to open a road to Fort Graham.[14] The road between Fort Graham and Fort Belknap ran along the north bank of the Brazos.[15] Lieutenant Beall went on to open a road to Fort Worth. The new route branched off of the Fort Graham-Fort Belknap road at a point about seven and one-half miles north of today's Mineral Wells. It ran eastward, across the Grand Prairie, and passed about six miles north of the site of today's Weatherford. It crossed the modern boundary line between Tarrant and Parker Counties about two or three miles south of Silver Creek. It probably followed the ridge now occupied by Camp Bowie Street, crossed the Clear Fork of the Trinity near its junction with the West Fork, and then ran up the hill to the fort.[16] Lieutenant Beall and thirty-one men arrived at Fort Worth on January 30, 1852.[17]

The year 1852 was relatively peaceful. The increased military presence on the frontier may have been responsible for the calm, but deterrence is difficult to prove. At Fort Worth, Maj. Arnold wrote to 8th Military Department Headquarters on only two occa-

---

*The auction disposed of 48 blankets, 6 forage bags, 14 India Rubber canteens, 1 wagon cover, 1 riding saddle, 5 valises, 14 pairs of spurs and straps, 23 curry combs, 15 horse brushes, 1 blind bridle, 1 water bucket, 1 glass lantern, 3 axes, 2 hatchets, 1 spade, 1 shovel, 1 water bucket, 1 water keg, 5 common tents, 1 wall tent and fly, 21 knapsacks, 3 gum elastic bags, 5 horses, and a few pieces of clothing. The buyers were chiefly discharged soldiers.

sions. On April 25, 1852, he requested new recruits for his company, and reported "Indian depredations, etc." Thirty-two new recruits arrived on July 17.[18] On July 27, Arnold reported the return of a scout from the Red River.[19]

In the late summer of 1852, a report reached Gen. Smith that an exploring party led by Capt. Randolph Marcy had been ambushed and murdered by Indians somewhere north of Fort Belknap. Smith reported to Washington that an Indian War was imminent and he ordered additional troops to march from central Texas to the Brazos and Trinity rivers. Within a few days, he learned that the report was false. However, Company B, led by Maj. Hamilton Merrill, was already on its way to Fort Worth, and when they arrived there would be two companies of dragoons there. Probably to rebalance his forces, Smith ordered Company F back to Fort Graham. A new company of dragoons would go to work from the bluff.[20]

16

Merrill's Dragoons Take Over

The new commanding officer of Fort Worth was Bvt. Maj. Hamilton Wilcox Merrill. He and the commanding officer he relieved, Bvt. Maj. Ripley Arnold, had been classmates at West Point, and both had served in the 2nd Dragoons for fifteen years. Many of his letters, diaries, and personal papers have survived, and we therefore know much about him.

Hamilton Merrill was born on February 14, 1814, in Batavia, New York. James, an older brother, was a successful lawyer in Batavia, and was active in the local Whig Party.[1] Hamilton studied law as well, and got a job as a clerk in the office of Whig Congressman George T. Lay. It was Congressman Lay who nominated him for appointment to the U.S. Military Academy class of 1838.[2]

Before joining the 2nd Dragoon Regiment, he was ordered to northern Georgia, where he took part in the Cherokee removal. In October 1838, while traveling to Florida, he wrote that he saw hundreds of alligators, from four to ten feet long, in the St. John's River.

His first duty station was Fort Butler,* and his commander put him to work immediately. On November 18, he led a detachment on a four-day scout. However, they found no sign of Indians and returned to the fort. The day after their return, the command received word that Indians had killed a white couple near Black Creek. He took his men back into the field, pursued the Indians' trail, but lost it. He returned to Black Creek on November 30. The next day, his company received a report of Indians less than three miles away:

*Fort Butler is located in northeast Florida.

> I volunteered on a scout after them, found where they had stayed the night before in a dense hammock so thick that we were obliged to dismount and go on foot. I took from my holsters a pair of pistols, one of which I held in each hand expecting every minute to see the "hell hounds," but they were off. Returned to Fort Butler.[3]

In Florida, Merrill was allowed to choose a horse from a group that had recently been purchased in Tennessee. He selected a fine mount, branded "U.S.D." for United States Dragoons. He named him Black Warrior and rode this horse for ten years—in Florida, on the Great Plains, and in Mexico.[4]

Merrill served in Florida until late 1841. At that time, five companies of the 2nd Dragoons were ordered to Fort Jesup, Louisiana, and Fort Towson, Indian Territory. He kept a journal of the march from Alabama to Fort Towson. The column left Mount Vernon, about thirty miles from Mobile, on November 13, 1841.[5] He started the journey in good spirits—Merrill enjoyed the outdoor life. He wrote in his diary that he would rather sleep on his army blankets than in a hotel in New York City.[6] The officers shot deer and wild turkeys along the way, barbecued wild game in camp, drank egg-nog, and played poker by their campfires.[7] Local citizens turned out to watch the column go by. "We are called 'the great Army' and create great curiosity to the people," Merrill wrote.[8]

Except for a brief stay in Georgia, this was his first trip through the South, and he was not impressed. He thought that the soil was poor, and, as a result of slavery, the people were too proud to do manual labor: ". . . they live a life of indolence and poverty—there are none so poor however but what they have a rifle, which is indeed their [illegible] and one half of their means of obtaining subsistence."[9]

It rained steadily as the dragoons marched through Louisiana. They reached Baton Rouge on January 2, 1842. He saw cotton plantations worked by slaves for the first time. As his men struggled to get their wagons across the muddy roads, he tried to calculate how much money a sizable plantation would make in a year. He was always thinking of a way to make his fortune.[10]

By the second week of January, the cold and rain had left him discouraged and dejected. On January 10, 1842, he wrote that it had rained all night, and he woke with standing water in his tent and that his blankets had been soaked:

> But this is not the worst thing—anything but turning out at 4 in the morning & eating a little ham and hard bread in the rain and then mounting your horse for the day . . . We entered the little city of Alexandria at mid day, wet to our skins and also covered with mud.[11]

Fortunately, a group of Alexandria's residents met the dragoons, and invited the officers to a dinner featuring duck, turkey, and wine. Merrill changed into dry clothes and "felt like another man." The officers and civilians drank and caroused until four AM, at which time the soldiers returned to camp and prepared to resume their march.[12]

In Natchitoches, the dragoons stopped to rest their horses, and the officers attended a ball in town. Merrill was happy to have ladies to talk to, although the women present spoke only French. He remembered enough of his West Point French to hold a pleasant conversation.[13] After leaving Natchitoches, the dragoons struggled onward through cold, mud, and rain for another two weeks. They arrived at Fort Towson on February 5, 1842, nearly three months after setting out from Mount Vernon Arsenal. He reflected that, although the march had been a trial, "nothing would please me more than an order to march over the Rocky Mountains to the Columbia River."[14]

He served at Fort Towson during 1842 and early 1843, taking leave in April 1843, and returning in November to serve at Fort Washita.[15] In garrison at Fort Washita, he served as officer of the day about twice a week, and spent the rest of his time reading and hunting. This was fine with him as he loved to read and hunt. In January 1844, he wrote that the previous twelve months had probably been the happiest of his life.[16] A few entries from Merrill's diary describe his routine at Fort Washita:

> January 23, 1844. Spent the day quite pleasantly in reading, etc.
>
> January 24, 1844. Remained in garrison, made the regular routine of military duty—am again tied up in sword & sash as "officer of the day." . . . Retired at 12 midnight.
>
> January 25, Mounted "Black Warrior" and went a hunting—returned without much success—strengthened the outer man by useful and pleasant exercise. Engaged at "Eucre" in the evening—read a while and went to bed.[17]

Hunting rifles fascinated Merrill. He read about firearms, practiced shooting at targets on the prairie, and tried without success to organize a marksmanship competition. In later years, he became something of an expert on the topic of ballistics. A high point of his sporting career came in December 1844, when he took part in a buffalo hunt with eleven dragoons and ten Indians; he killed five of the animals with his rifle.[18] He enjoyed his life on the frontier, but his diaries show that he was somewhat lonely and he wished that he were married. An entry from 1844 mentions that he was thinking of his sweetheart. The diary does not say who the sweetheart was, but it was probably Miss Louise

Kauffmann of New York City. In 1847, he sent Kauffmann a poem for Valentine's Day. Merrill was preparing to embark for the Vera Cruz landing when he composed the poem, which he called "The Soldier's Farewell." The final verse reads as follows:

> And should fortune bear me o'er the deep,
> And I the howling tempest brave,
> How soon amid the strife might sleep;
> Then who should deck my lonely grave?[19]

As captain of Company B, 2nd Dragoons, he fought in all the major battles of the Mexico City campaign. He captured two Mexican cavalrymen during the attack on the Medellin Bridge. At the Battle of Molino del Rey, Black Warrior was wounded twice, and a bullet passed through Merrill's coat. He was rewarded after the war with a promotion to brevet major.[20] Merrill remained in Mexico City until June 1848.

Occupation duty was pleasant; he had a Mexican sweetheart and learned to speak some Spanish.[21] He pried an obsidian doorknob from a door in the National Palace, and had it made into a walking stick.[22] Major General Winfield Scott detailed him to escort Santa Anna's wife when she left Mexico City to join her husband. He wrote home that she was attractive, and the two got along well.[23] While Company B waited at Vera Cruz to board a transport for home, yellow fever broke out among the soldiers. He and most of his men contracted the disease. When their steamer reached New Orleans, seven men were dead, and forty-one out of sixty-five were hospitalized.[24] He took leave and spent more than a year in recovery.[25]

He returned to his home in Batavia, New York, where a banquet was held in his honor on October 18, 1848.[26] He brought Black Warrior back to Batavia, and showed him at the Genessee County Fair. The crowds loved him. He exhibited the horse on several occasions, and retired him to a stable near New York City where Nelson Merrill, another brother, practiced law.[27]

He returned to duty in January 1850, and resumed command of Company B, stationed at Fort Martin Scott. While he was serving in Texas, Black Warrior's fame and popularity continued to grow. He became a featured attraction of military parades in Manhattan. President Franklin Pierce rode him at a review in 1853. When the animal died in 1857, his obituary in the *New York Herald* was longer than that of Merrill himself, who died in 1892. Merrill donated Black Warrior's bones to the State Medical College at Albany.[28]

He was stationed at Fort Martin Scott from early 1850 until July 1851 and was the subject of a board of inquiry there. The owner of a bar in Fredericksburg stabbed and killed a soldier during an argument. That night, a group of soldiers burned the bar. The owner accused Merrill and two other officers of encouraging the soldiers to set the fire. A discharged soldier testified that the post quartermaster had issued turpentine, rosin, and tar for that purpose. Merrill and the other officers denied involvement. The board of inquiry found them completely innocent.[29]

His older brother, James, left Batavia in 1849 for Wisconsin, and settled in the Milwaukee area.[30] In May 1850, Hamilton bought a 640-acre farm about twenty-eight miles southwest of Milwaukee. Much of the farm was covered with hills, old forests, and a beautiful lake. He planned to keep the land as a country retreat for his later years.[31]

He served at Fort Martin Scott until May 1851. In June, he led Company B on Bvt. Lt. Col. Hardee's scout to the Caddo Indian Village. After drafting the report on the inedible meat biscuit, Merrill established Fort Mason* at the beginning of July 1851. He served at Fort Mason for more than a year.[32]

Like many officers on the frontier, he speculated in land. Six months after he established Fort Mason, he bought five hundred acres adjacent to the post from two German settlers, for $275.00, and sold them in May 1852 for the same price.

His brother, Nelson, acquired a five-hundred-acre tract, which included Fort Mason. Hamilton bought a one-sixth interest in the Post Hill tract in 1857. A county judge seized and auctioned Merrill's land in 1863, on the grounds that he was an enemy of the Confederate States. He reclaimed his land after the war, and collected $26.85 in rent in 1886. His son sold the family's Mason County property around the turn of the century for $3,075.[33]

Merrill seems to have been dissatisfied with his situation at Fort Mason. On May 30, 1852, he asked to be made post commander at Fort Mason. On July 4, he requested that he be transferred to a new post. On July 25, he asked that he and his company be transferred to Fort Graham, so that he could command while Bvt. Lt. Col. Hardee was away.[34] Surviving records do not explain why Merrill wanted to get away from Fort Mason. In any case, his request was granted. He and his company were ordered to march from Fort Mason to Fort Worth. Merrill and his company left Fort Mason on August 5, 1852, and arrived at Fort Worth on August 13.[35]

General Smith's double line of forts was complete by the end of 1852, but Smith made minor changes towards the end of the year. He visited Camp Joseph E. Johnston in October 1852, and decided

*Fort Mason was located in what is now Mason, Texas.

to move the garrison about thirty miles to the north. Companies A and K of the 8th Infantry marched from Camp Johnston, and established Fort Chadbourne* on October 28, 1852.[36]

Camp Johnston was abandoned on November 18 and the ten companies of the 8th Infantry were divided between Fort McKavett and Fort Chadbourne.[37] At about the same time, Gen. Smith decided to move his headquarters and supply depots from San Antonio and Austin to Corpus Christi.[38] His quartermasters protested that the humidity of the coast would ruin their stores, so Smith delayed, and then reversed the order to move the depots.[39] He moved his headquarters to Corpus Christi in 1853.

The peace and quiet at Fort Worth suggested that the post had outlived its usefulness. The Indians visited Fort Belknap when they wanted to meet with army officers, traders, or Indian Agents, or gather information. The area around Fort Worth was drawing more and more settlers. The following year, there would be another crisis on the Rio Grande. When the War Department looked for ways to shift troops to the border, Fort Worth would be deemed expendable.

---

*Ft. Chadbourne was located on Oak Creek about forty miles southwest of Abilene and named for Lt. Theodore L. C. Chadbourne, 8th Infantry, who was killed on May 9, at Resaca de la Palma.

17

The Old Soldiers of Fort Worth Fade Away

Texas was relatively calm during 1853. General Smith's double line of forts seemed, for a while, to keep the Indians out of the settlements. With the Carvajal disturbances subsiding, Smith moved the seven companies of mounted rifles into garrison. On January 13, he ordered four companies to Fort Ewell, two companies to Fort Merrill, and one company to Fort Inge.[1] On April 19, Smith ordered Fort Merrill abandoned, and its garrison transferred to Fort Ewell.[2]

A few violent incidents took place on the northwest frontier. A group of Wacos stole some dragoon horses from Fort Croghan. Brevet Major Henry Sibley overtook them near Fort Belknap, posted guards around their camp, and made them hostages. The Wacos killed a soldier and fled. Fort Belknap, located in the Indian country, was in a better position to deal with such incidents. Fort Worth, nearly one hundred miles east of Fort Belknap, was no longer on the frontier.

The first months of 1853 were uneventful ones at Fort Worth. On January 18, 1853, Maj. Merrill requested that he be granted three months leave.[3] On May 18, he sent in a report of a scout and of new Indian depredations. On May 23, he forwarded copies of letters he had exchanged with a Maj. Henshaw, the commanding officer at Fort Arbuckle, Indian Territory. Merrill recommended that a new fort be built on the Little Wichita River.[4]

On May 15, 1853, Merrill wrote headquarters to ask for authority "to pay Jim Ned (a Delaware Indian) as guide etc. for the time he may actually have occasion to employ him as such."[5] Jim Ned was about fifty years old in 1853, and was remembered in later years by many early pioneers. One settler recalled that Jim Ned was the leader of a band of about sixty-five Delawares. The band lived in huts made from blankets, hunted and fished along the creeks of today's Wise County, and traded furs for manufactured goods with settlers. As more whites moved into the area, the Delawares moved west, to Jim Ned Springs in Jack County, and then onto the Brazos Indian Reservations.[6]

Fort Worth had two unusual visitors in June 1853. One was Albert Brisbane, an American who was active in the socialist movement. The other, Brisbane's companion, Victor Considerant, was an important French socialist. The two men came to north Texas in search of a site for a communal settlement.[7]

They joined a detachment of dragoons for an eleven-day scout through the countryside. Their route passed by a "region where the true mountains rise into peaks"; it is possible that the patrol rode west, toward Fort Belknap and the rocky hills of Palo Pinto County.[8] Considerant recorded that: "Major Merrill . . . said that he was in the habit of making excursions of 15 days, sometimes of a month, into the prairie or forest, without serious inconvenience, and that he and his men did not often give themselves the trouble of erecting tents for the night."[9] Major Merrill, still keenly interested in firearms, asked Considerant to have a number of custom hunting rifles built for him in France.[10]

Considerant visited Dallas, where he found Adolphe Gouhenant. Gouhenant had "begun to gather these wild grapes for the wine press, and last year sold his wine, immediately, at a dollar a bottle."[11] A young French wagon maker, probably Maxime Guillot, Company F's wheelwright, had "arrived two years since [1851] on the upper Trinity with a dollar in his pocket for all his worldly wealth; he is now proprietor of the finest workshop in Dallas, which he has built at his own cost, and has an industrial capital of $1200."[12] He also reported that Luc Bourgeois, a former Icarian, was working as a tailor, raising pigs, and doing well.[13]

Considerant rode south, to Fort Graham, where he noted that the post vegetable garden was in fine condition.[14] He may have met Bvt Maj. and Mrs. Ripley Arnold there; he wrote that "the wife of the commanding officer at Fort Graham told us that, for her part, she would ask nothing better than the assurance of ten more years like this."[15] He examined the medical records at Fort Graham and Fort Worth, and surprisingly, concluded that there was no intermittent fever in north Texas.[16] He claimed in 1854, in Austin, Texas, that "nowhere in the United States is the health of the soldiers so good as in the forts of upper Texas."[17] In fact, twelve soldiers were treated for malaria (intermittent fever) during the month that he visited.[18]

Au Texas, his account of his travels, urged his followers to join him in establishing a socialist commune in Texas. He and about two hundred followers built La Reunion a few miles west of Dallas in 1855. More than five hundred Europeans lived there before the experiment failed and was abandoned in 1859. He moved to San Antonio, took up farming, and returned to France in 1869.[19]

While Considerant and Brisbane dreamed of their socialist utopia, Merrill took care of more practical matters. He made preparations for supplying the post in the coming year. On May 12, he posted the following note:

> Notice—Hay Contracts—Sealed proposals will be received at this office until the 15th day of June next for the delivery in stacks, well put up, and after the order required, (a man from the garrison being furnished to aid and direct in the stacking) of two hundred tons of good and merchantable hay, free from weeds and properly cured, to be delivered between the first day of July and the 25th day of August, 1853.[20]

He got at least three bids. General Edward H. Tarrant, who had led the attack on Village Creek in 1841, offered to supply the hay at $3.25 per ton. H. Blackwell made a bid at $3.99 per ton. George Wilson won the contract with a bid of $2.99 per ton. At fourteen pounds of hay per horse, per day, the two hundred tons of hay would supply a hundred horses for 285 days.[21]

To help the Quartermaster Department plan its budget, Merrill submitted an estimate of how much he would spend in the coming year. Forage for 100 horses and mules would cost $5,280.00. An extra 100 bushels of corn, to be issued to passing supply trains, would cost $45.00. Jim Ned's salary came to $480.00. The extra duty men would earn $600.00. Fuel for the blacksmith's shop, and supplies for the farrier, would each amount to $60.00. He would spend $60.00 on postage, and $300.00 on miscellaneous supplies. He expected to spend a total of $6,861.00 between July 1, 1853, and July 1, 1854.[22]

On August 20, 1853 Merrill submitted a report to the quartermaster general, Thomas Jesup, on the condition of the buildings at Fort Worth. Merrill wrote, "The public buildings at this post are of the most temporary nature, all being log but two covered with green clapboards—mostly leaky—in ordinary condition, though quite unsuitable for the service."[23] A ceiling and covered porch had been added to the hospital at a cost of $75.00. Merrill recommended that no more money be spent on either construction or repairs because the buildings, and the post, were meant for temporary use only.[24]

With the frontier line shifting to the west, Fort Worth's importance diminished, and it became an obvious candidate for closure. The crisis that prompted headquarters to abandon Fort Worth had nothing to do with Indians; instead, it involved a new dispute with Mexico. Santa Anna became president of Mexico again in April 1853. At about this time, the United States and Mexico were attempting to resolve a disputed border survey and other issues. Friction between the two governments grew.

In the summer of 1853, several army officers reported troubling developments along the Rio Grande. Captain E. K. Smith, a mounted infantry officer, described the tensions in a letter to home:

> Trouble seems preparing for us on the other side of the Rio Grande all signs indicate an approaching struggle with Mexico; Santa Anna is concentrating at San Luis Potosi and near this frontier large bodies of troops, & in addition to 26,000 regulars is arming & organizing 9,000 citizen soldiery; the officers opposite us who used to visit & exchange hospitality with us every day or two, have since Santa Anna arrived ceased all intercourse & speak openly & unconcernedly of an approaching campaign . . .[25]

Reports began to come in through official channels as well. On June 18, Maj. G. R. Paul reported the "hostile attitude of Mexico towards U. S." from Ringgold Barracks.[26] On June 30, Col. L. B. Webster reported "hostile demonstrations of Mexico" from Fort Brown.[27] On July 23, there were anti-American riots in the Mexican town of El Paso. Secretary of War Jefferson Davis directed Bvt. Maj. Gen. Persifor Smith to send four companies of the 8th Infantry to that place.[28]

On August 20, 1853, Smith issued an order to change the defense of the entire frontier. The double line of frontier forts would be consolidated, and its troops reduced to a caretaker force. Fifteen companies of infantry, all from the outer line of forts, would be transferred to the Rio Grande, in a show of force.[29]

Teamsters and other extra duty men were ordered to return to the ranks. All mounted infantry would turn in their horses, carbines, and pistols, in exchange for muskets and bayonets. The War Department brought four companies of artillery from posts in the southeastern United States and stationed one each at Fort Brown, Ringgold Barracks, Laredo, and Fort Duncan.[30]

A small force would be left to man the outer line of frontier forts. To provide troops for the outer line, much of the old inner line of forts would be closed. On August 20, 1853, Gen. Smith ordered Forts

Croghan, Graham and Worth to be abandoned.[31] Surgeon Thomas H. Williams was ordered to go to the Rio Grande with the 5th Infantry. Major Merrill's dragoons were first ordered to Fort Mason, but a new order issued August 24, ordered them to Fort Belknap.[32]*

Smith's orders put the whole frontier in motion. At Fort Belknap, Maj. Joseph LaMotte wrote that everyone expected a second war with Mexico.[33] At Fort Worth, Merrill began preparations to abandon the post.

While Gen. Smith was moving his infantrymen to the Rio Grande, Col. William G. Freeman was making an inspection tour of the 8th Military Department. Freeman inspected Fort Belknap on September 3, then took three days to ride to Fort Worth. He inspected Fort Worth on September 7, 1853. His report reads as follows:

> No Indians have visited the post since last autumn except a small party of Caddoes and Ioni's. About 100 of these tribes live with their chief, Jose Maria, on the Brazos, 35 miles above Fort Graham, and 60 miles from Fort Worth. In connection with this subject, Bvt. Maj. Merrill . . . puts down the whole number of Indians living in Texas at 1,570, of whom 250 are warriors, and the other class at 680, making a total of 2,250 men, women and children.
>
> The garrison at Fort Worth consisted of Company B, 2d Dragoons, under Capt. and Bvt. Maj. H. W. Merrill of that regiment. At the time of my visit orders had been received to break up the post and Bvt. Maj. Merrill was only awaiting transportation to remove his company to Fort Belknap. I reviewed and inspected the command, September 7th. There were present on parade Capt. H. W. Merrill, (Bvt. Major), 2d Lt. J. P. Holliday, and 60 men. The only absent officer was the 1st Lieut. (A. D.) Tree who is the Regimental Quartermaster.
>
> The company had only fatigue clothing of the old pattern, but some of the men wore sky blue, instead of the dark blue jackets. They were armed, like the two companies of the same regiment at Fort Mason, with musketoons, sabers, and Colt's revolver pistols. They were reviewed as foot, but inspected and required to exercise both as horse and foot. The clothing, though not new, was in good order and generally well fitted; the arms and accou-

---

*Order #50, 8/20/53, made the following assignments. Ft. Terrett: CO. G. 2nd Drg. and Co. K, 1st Inf. Ft. Chadbourne: Co. C, 2nd Drg. and Co. A, 8th Inf. Ft. Phantom Hill: Co. I, 2nd Drg. and Co. E, 5th Inf. Orders 54, 8/24/53,. made the following assignments. Ft. McKavett: Co. F, 2nd Drg. and Co. H, 8th Inf. Ft. Belknap: Co. B, 2nd Drg. and Co. H, 5th Inf. Ft. Mason. Co. A, Reg. HQ, and Band, 2nd Drg.

trements clean and, except the musketoons, serviceable. Three out of every four of the musketoons had some of the smaller parts broken. The horses (60) are all serviceable, and in finer condition than those of any mounted troops in Texas. Their equipment's were also neat and well preserved.

In the Manual, marching and sword exercises, dismounted, the company showed a fair degree of proficiency. In the saddle, they acquitted themselves very handsomely, marching with accuracy by twos, fours, and with company front, at a walk, trot, and gallop; skirmishing as dragoons on foot, and as mounted foragers; and leaping the bar and ditch with great spirit and perfect mastery of their horses.

I was gratified too to find—it was the solitary exception throughout my tour—the Guard House, that saddest of all places in a garrison, without a single prisoner. Bvt. Maj. Merrill informs me that most of his men belong to the temperance society, and that he has rarely occasion to confine any one of them. Having said this much, it is scarcely necessary to add that I found the discipline and police of the post excellent.

A fine garden of eight acres is cultivated by the command.

QuarterMaster's Department
(2d Lt. J. P. Holliday, Actg. Asst. Q. Master.)
The monthly disbursements average $500, for the purchase of forage, hire of the guide and interpreter (at $40.00 per month) and pay of extra duty men, of whom ten are usually employed. The resources of the neighboring country are very great. Any amount of forage that may be required for the troops can be obtained within 60 miles. Hay is furnished at $2.99 per ton, and corn and oats at 40 and 37½ cents per bushel, respectively. There are 200 tons of hay and 800 bushels of corn on hand. Pine lumber may be had at the mills, 160 miles east, at $15.00 per thousand.

Subsistence Department
(2d Lt. J. P. Holliday, Actg. Asst. Q. Master.)
The provisions, of which the supply on hand was moderate, are stored in rough log buildings, but they appeared to be in good order. The disbursements are about $300.00 per month, principally for the purchase of bacon, flour, and fresh beef. The latter is supplied by contract at 5 cents per pound and issued twice in ten days, two days issue at each time. Bacon, flour and beans can be bought more advantageously in the vicinity than they can be shipped from the North. Thus flour delivered at the post costs the government nearly $15 per barrel while it can be obtained in sacks, on the spot at $8. The cost of the entire ration at the post is 22 cents, 7 cents of amount being added by the expense of transportation.

Medical Department

Just before my arrival Asst. Surgeon T. H. Williams had been transferred to another station and the post was without a medical officer. The doctor had taken with him the hospital records, and the medicines and stores were packed up to be forwarded to Surgeon Turner, the Medical Purveyor. Under these circumstances I could obtain very little information in regard to the hospital department of the post. The building used for the sick is of weather-boards, and consists of one large ward and two small rooms, one of which is the Dispensary and the other the Steward's dormitory. The sick list, I learn, averages daily five men, or about 7 per cent. of the command, intermittence being the most common diseases. Bvt. Maj. Merrill considers the climate temperate and healthful.[34]*

Major Merrill and his men left Fort Worth in two groups, on September 16 and 18. Nine men remained behind under Lt. Jonas. P. Holliday, to guard the public property left at the post. Merrill reported his arrival at Fort Belknap on September 21. Fort Worth's days as an army post were over.[35]

On October 31, Department Headquarters issued orders to transport the stores that Holliday (Asst. Acting Quartermaster) was guarding. Teams from the San Antonio depot retrieved the government property from Forts Worth, Graham, Martin Scott, and Croghan. At about the same time, the supply depot at Austin was broken up, and the contents moved to San Antonio.[36] Holliday and his men remained until about December 6. They reported for duty at Fort Belknap on December 9.[37]

When Holliday left, he gave a rocking chair that had been used at the fort to Florence Peak, wife of Dr. Carroll Peak, who moved into one of the three officers' cabins when the main body left. Sgt. Abraham Harris may have made the chair. He remained in Fort Worth as a carpenter, and built several items of furniture for people in the area. The chair remained in the Peak family, and was loaned to citizens in the city at a time of sickness or birth.[38]

The army continued to build up its forces on the Rio Grande during the fall of 1853. Smith traveled to Fort Brown in September, selected a site for new fortifications, and prepared estimates for permanent barracks.[39] In October, he sent more troops to El Paso, and issued orders to improve the road that followed the lower Rio Grande, in case the river was blocked.[40] The War Department sent

*The portion of Freeman's inspection report concerning the building of the fort are in chapter 5.

Maj. Richard Delafield to construct fortifications at Fort Brown, Ringgold Barracks, Fort McIntosh, and Fort Duncan.[41]

On December 15, Smith ordered the last infantry companies on the frontier to join their regiments on the Rio Grande. Two companies of dragoons would garrison each Forts Belknap, Chadbourne, and McKavett. Forts Mason, Terrett, and Phantom Hill would be abandoned altogether.[42] Fort Terrett was abandoned on January 16, 1854.[43] Fort Mason was closed the same month; the post was occupied briefly in the spring, and reopened in 1856.[44] Fort Phantom Hill did not close until April 6, 1854.[45] Smith ordered Fort Ewell abandoned in December; the order was carried out by October.[46]

The tensions between Mexico and the United States seem to have subsided without incident. On December 30, 1853, Santa Anna agreed to sell the United States a section of northern Mexico for $10,000,000. The sale, now known as the Gadsden Purchase, established the southern border of the modern states of New Mexico and Arizona.

18

Major Ripley Arnold Returns to the Bluff Forever

When Col. William G. Freeman finished his inspection of Fort Worth, he rode next to Fort Graham, arriving on September 9, 1853. He was greeted with shocking news: Assistant Surgeon Josephus Steiner had shot and killed Bvt. Maj. Ripley Arnold three days before. Civilian authorities had arrested Steiner.[1]

Arnold and Steiner had disliked each other since the spring of 1849, when the fort was founded and Steiner reported for duty. With time, the dislike grew into hatred. Arnold left Fort Graham on October 17, 1852, for official business in Washington.[2] At the time he left, he sold a government horse under questionable circumstances. Bvt. Lt. Col. William J. Hardee brought the matter to the attention of Department headquarters in a letter dated February 2, 1853.[3]

Lieutenant Samuel Starr knew Dr. Steiner from the time he had served at Fort Graham. Starr heard about Arnold's problems in a letter from the doctor. Samuel passed the story on to his wife, Eliza, on May 19, 1853:

> The scamp, on going out of the country, sold a government horse and sent 80 dollars by a man of his company to the Q. Master at Ft. Graham, where his company's stationed. The man says he lost the money. Arnold had no authority for selling the horse and is supposed to have sold him for more than $80. Hardee, who commands at Fort Graham, wrote to Arnold in Washington City, D.C., requiring him to return the horse forthwith. It is

> supposed that this letter will bring him back posthaste. Steiner writes me that Arnold's military career is drawing to a close.[4]

Steiner's claim that Arnold's career was over was probably wishful thinking. Court-martial boards were reluctant to convict their fellow officers, and more reluctant still to impose real punishments. Nevertheless, the army sent Lt. James Hawes to Fort Graham to investigate the matter. Arnold was still away when Hawes arrived, but Steiner discussed the matter with Hawes and accused Arnold of misconduct.[5]

The enmity between Arnold and Steiner had existed since the founding of Fort Graham. In May 1849, before Fort Worth was established Steiner wrote in his diary:

> I passed a bad night which I ascribe to A's brutality, who beat his little boy so unmercifully that I became nervous, then angry and sleepless. How I detest to see children harshly treated by those whose duty it is to cherish and love them. Have been reading James's Chivalry and selections from the Edinburgh Review all the afternoon. Went with Brevet 2nd Lt. George Stewart to call on Mrs. Hamilton. Arnold and Lady came in and the redoubtable captain and myself did not speak. We talked gossip all the evening.[6]

Arnold returned to Fort Graham on June 6, 1853.[7] Hawes submitted his report on August 9.[8] The report appears to have been lost. It is known, however, that Arnold was bitter towards Steiner for helping Hawes. Arnold's anger toward Steiner seems quite similar to the grudge he held against Lt. Stephen Dobbins from his West Point days. Both Dobbins and Steiner reported him for breaking regulations. He could not forgive either of them. The mutual hatred turned violent this September. Dr. Steiner got into a drunken quarrel with Lt. Thomas Bingham. Lieutenant Richard H. Anderson reported what happened next:

> . . . There have existed for about a year some causes of disagreement between Dr. Steiner and Major Arnold. On the night of the 5th inst. September, a quarrel between Dr. Steiner and Lieutenant Bingham was the cause of a great deal of noise and disturbance in the garrison. The officer of the day and others were endeavoring to stop the noise when Major Arnold came to the spot and said that such quarrelling and noise could not be allowed and that the officers must retire to their quarters. Dr. Steiner asked Major Arnold whether he intended to arrest him. Major Arnold replied that he did not deem it necessary to do so at the time if he (Dr. Steiner) would retire at once to his quarters. Dr. Steiner replied in an infuriated manner, and amongst other things he said that Major Arnold must not attempt to arrest him, for he would kill him if he did so. No one believed that this threat was made with any deadly intention, but attributed it to the state

of furious excitement into which Dr. Steiner had been thrown by drinking and quarrelling.[9]

The next morning, Arnold asked his first sergeant, William Slade, if he had a pistol he could borrow. Slade replied that he did not, but would borrow one from one of the men. Slade's sworn deposition reads as follows:

> When I gave it to him he said "Slade, I shall have a difficulty with Doctor Steiner so I wish to be in readiness for him and give him the first shot." I told Maj. Arnold that I should be very sorry for the like to happen, and it would be better to take some other measures. He answered "No, damn him, if he comes in my sight I will shoot him. I ought to have done so four years ago, the damn scoundrel."[10]

On the morning of September 6, Arnold sent Lt. Anderson to place both Bingham and Steiner under arrest. Anderson handed Steiner a written order for his arrest. Anderson reported afterward:

> Dr. Steiner read the order for his arrest and threw it on the floor saying that no man should arrest him and that he would see Arnold about it. He left the room in a high state of excitement. I followed him to the door and said to him, Doctor, do not see Major Arnold, you will commit yourself by doing so. It never entered my head that he would commit himself in any other way than by using violent words and in failure to obey the arrest at once.[11]

Corporal Joseph Stewart witnessed the ensuing gunfight. Major Arnold was standing in the passageway of his dog-run quarters, talking to Corporal McCauley. Doctor Steiner, cane in hand, walked across the parade ground from Lt. Tyler's quarters. According to Stewart:

> . . . he walked towards Maj. Arnold and said "I am arrested and should like to know what for." The Maj. replied "for drunkenness and riotousness." Dr. Steiner then told him that he was insulting him. Maj. Arnold then told Dr. Steiner to go to his quarters, throwing his right hand in a very harsh manner to his breast. From the position I occupied I could not tell what he then seized with his hand. Dr. Steiner at the same time was resting his left hand on his cane & his right hand at the time was hanging down by his side. Maj. Arnold brought his left foot back & drew a pistol. It appeared to me that they both drew together but Maj. Arnold fired the first shot at Dr. Steiner . . .[12]

Three other witnesses, James Williams, Edward Folan, and James Donnelly, agreed that Arnold fired first. Donnelley thought that both men drew their guns at the same time. Folan thought that Steiner drew only after Arnold opened fire. Arnold fired twice, but did not hit Steiner. Steiner fired three times, hitting Arnold each time. He died on the porch of his quarters a short time later.[13]

Hill County civil authorities tried Steiner in 1854. The jury acquitted him in one hour.[14] The army tried to capture Steiner and try him for murder, but he fled, and was eventually dropped from army rolls. He continued to live in Texas and became head of the State Lunatic Asylum in Austin in 1860. He died in Marietta, Georgia, in 1873. Steiner's daughter, Ida Mae, married a congressman and became a prominent Washington socialite in the early years of the twentieth century.[15]

Arnold was buried at Fort Graham. In 1854, Adolphe Gouhenant arranged to have the body brought to Fort Worth so that Arnold's remains could be interred in the cemetery northeast of the post next to the graves of his two children, Sophie and Willis.[16] When the U.S. Army gathered the remains of soldiers from the old frontier forts and interred them in a mass grave in San Antonio around 1901, the people of Fort Worth persuaded the army to leave Maj. Arnold's grave undisturbed.[17] Today, a granite boulder marks the burial site. Remaining with Arnold are eleven soldiers who died while serving at the fort. Their names, units and dates of death are:

Isaac Hollyfield	Pvt	F Co. 2nd Reg., U.S. Dragoons	Jun 17, 1851
Michael Farrell	Pvt	F Co. 2nd Reg., U.S. Dragoons	Jun 20, 1851
William McKee	Cpl	F Co. 8th Reg., U.S. Infantry	Jul 24, 1851
Michael Crehan	Pvt	F Co. 8th Reg., U.S. Infantry	Oct 25, 1851
James Ryan	Pvt	F Co. 8th Reg., U.S. Infantry	Nov 27, 1851
Patrick Dolan	Pvt	F Co. 8th Reg., U.S. Infantry	Nov 28, 1851
Peter Riley	Pvt	F Co. 8th Reg., U.S. Infantry	Nov 29, 1851
Thomas Scott	Cpl	F Co. 8th Reg., U.S. Infantry	Dec 16, 1851
John A. Koch	Pvt	F Co. 8th Reg., U.S. Infantry	Dec 28, 1851
William McConnell	Pvt	F Co. 8th Reg., U.S. Infantry	Dec 30, 1851
Jeremiah Long	Pvt	B Co. 2nd Reg. U.S. Dragoons	Dec 2, 1852

19

After the Fort

Life and the Indian Wars did not end when the army abandoned the fort in Fort Worth. The buildings of the fort were immediately occupied by a number of citizens who would begin to build a city. The war with the Indians would last another thirty years.

The Texas Legislature finally bowed to pressure from Washington and, on February 6, 1854, allocated twelve leagues of land—about 55,728 acres—for reservations for the Indians still living in the state. Robert Neighbors, who was again the U.S. Indian Agent, had been arguing for the reservations since 1847 and was selected to help choose a suitable location. In the summer of 1854, he and Capt. Randolph Marcy explored the countryside west of Fort Belknap.[1]

Eight leagues were set aside on the Brazos River, below Fort Belknap, for the tribes that had been living along the Brazos River near today's Graham. Four leagues were set aside for Comanches about forty miles to the west, on the Clear Fork of the Brazos. Jose Maria and the allied bands settled below Fort Belknap. A few Comanches came in to their reservation, as well. However, the presence of the Indians, even in reservations, angered many settlers. They blamed them for any incident in the area. When settlers tried to attack the Brazos reservation, Indian Affairs' officials finally decided to move the Indians to the Wichita Reservation, north of the Red River.[2] Both Texas reservations were closed in the summer of 1859.[3]

Neighbors was shot and killed near Fort Belknap after the Indians were removed, probably in retaliation for his efforts on their behalf. There is some speculation that Doctor Joseph Steiner was involved in the assassination, but nothing could be proven.

Brevet Major General Persifor F. Smith commanded in Texas until 1856.[4] He was succeeded by Maj. Gen. David Twiggs in 1857. When Texas seceded in 1861, Twiggs surrendered all army property to the state government.[5] Federal troops evacuated the state, and the Texas Rangers became responsible for frontier defense again. During the Civil War, the Indians would reclaim dominance over the area between Fort Belknap and Fort Worth, and a number of settlers would lose their lives and their livelihood.

Federal troops returned to the state after the war. By this time, many of the plains tribes had agreed to live on reservations in the Indian Territory. They used the reservations as bases from which to attack the northwest frontier of Texas. The area between Fort Worth and Fort Belknap, which had been quiet in the early 1850s, was especially hard hit. The attacks finally ended after the army defeated the Comanches in the Red River War of 1874–1875.[6] About the same time, hunters killed most of the remaining buffalo, ending the food supply for the Indians on the Great Plains.

Congress granted Arnold's widow, Catherine, a pension of twenty dollars per month. She lived with relatives over the years, and spent the last years of her life in Waco and Marlin, Texas.[7] Family members recalled that she remained devoted to the memory of her husband. Her youngest daughter, Nanny, married Ed Hanrick of Waco, and cared for her mother after 1886. Catherine Arnold died in Marlin in 1892.[8] Florida Belle Arnold married Col. Thomas Manlove in Waco.[9] Kate Arnold married Samuel Parker of Marlin after the Civil War.[10] Samuel Parker is buried in Marlin. Next to Parker's grave is what appears to be an unmarked grave. Catherine Arnold's pension file contains a letter from her daughter, Kate Parker, asking for help in buying a gravestone. It is possible that the unmarked grave is that of Catherine Arnold. At the turn of the century, Kate was a widow, living with relatives in Bay St. Louis, Mississippi.

Captain Robert Maclay served with the 8th Infantry until 1860.[11] He resigned from the army and moved to Louisiana. He became a major in the Confederate Army in 1862, and served as a staff officer with Walker's Texas Division. He served as a brigadier general in 1864, but the promotion was never officially confirmed. He lived in Pointe Coupee Parish, Louisiana, after the war. Despite having spent years at a time on sick leave in the 1850s, Maclay lived to be the oldest surviving member of his West Point class. He died in 1903 at the age of 83.[12]

Brevet Lieutenant Colonel J. V. Bomford served with the 8th Infantry in west Texas, chiefly at Fort Davis, until the Civil War. He was still in Texas when Fort Sumter was fired on. Confederate

Texans asked him to vow not to fight against the South. He refused, and was held as a prisoner of war for a year. He was exchanged for southern prisoners in April 1862. His hometown of Elizabeth, New Jersey gave him a hero's welcome, in recognition of his honor and loyalty. He returned to active duty and was shot and left for dead on the field at the Battle of Perryville, but survived his wounds. He was promoted to colonel of the 8th Infantry in May 1864. He retired from the army in June 1874, after nearly forty-two years of service. He died in Elizabeth in 1892 at the age of 80.[13]

Major Hamilton Merrill served at Fort Belknap and later in Kansas. He survived a steamboat explosion on the Arkansas River in 1854 and resigned from the army in February 1857. On May 20, 1857, he married Louise Kauffman of New York City, after a courtship of about thirteen years. Merrill and his bride did not move to the farm in Wisconsin he bought in 1850. Instead, they settled in New York City, where he practiced law. His obituary in the *New York Times* states that, in later years, his time "was wholly occupied by looking after his large property interests in this city."[14] He never lost interest in hunting and shooting, and wrote articles on firearms for *Field and Stream* magazine. He died in July 1892.[15]

Assistant Surgeon Thomas H. Williams continued to serve in Texas. He was the medical director of the Utah Expedition under Albert Sidney Johnston in 1857 and 1858. He resigned from the U.S. Army to join the Confederacy and served in Virginia during the Civil War. He advanced to the post of assistant surgeon general of the Confederacy. When the war ended, he returned to Maryland and practiced medicine in Cambridge until the turn of the century. He died in Cambridge on September 22, 1904.[16]

Lieutenant Samuel Starr served with the 2nd Dragoons until the Civil War. In 1853, while he was serving at Fort Mason, he was court-martialed again and suspended for nine months. Again his problem was his intolerance of orders he thought limited his authority. Details on the incident and trial are in appendix #19–1. In 1861, he transferred to the state volunteers, and became colonel of the 5th New Jersey Infantry. He served during the Peninsula Campaign in 1862, and commanded a brigade of four regiments of New Jersey infantry. He returned to the regular army in 1863, when he was promoted to major of the 6th Cavalry.[17] His reputation as a fighter earned him the nickname "Old Paddy."[18] He commanded the 6th Cavalry during the Battle of Gettysburg.

On July 3, 1863, he led the regiment to investigate a report of a Confederate supply train in nearby Fairfield, Pennsylvania. Outside

Fairfield, a brigade of Confederate cavalry charged Starr and his four hundred men. Outnumbered by more than three to one, brave and reckless as ever, he ordered his men to charge.[19] This time, his luck ran out. Almost all his men were killed, wounded, or captured.[20] He was shot, and cut by a saber. Army surgeons amputated his right arm. While he was lying wounded in the Blythe home in Fairfield, his old comrade, George Pickett, was leading his famous charge a few miles away.[21]

He served in administrative posts for the rest of the war, while he recuperated and learned to write with his left hand. He returned to the Texas frontier in 1865. The 6th U.S. Cavalry occupied Fort Belknap and Fort Richardson near Jacksboro. H. H. McConnel, who served under him at Fort Richardson, remembered Starr in his memoirs:

> . . . Colonel Starr, universally known as "Old Paddy," had been represented to us as a "terror." A "terror" to evil-doers he was, but a braver, more just, or more honorable officer never wore the uniform, although his particular disposition was such that, like the Irishman, it might be said of him, "he was never at peace only when he was at war."[22]

He retired from the army in 1870, and moved to Philadelphia with Eliza. Their daughter, Kate, married William D. Price, a grandson of a Florida governor. Anne, the daughter born in Austin in 1850, married Samuel Calvin Hayes. Jo Ursula Starr was still alive in 1930, and living in Los Angeles.[23]

Lieutenant Frederick M. Follett went on to serve in the Utah campaign and as an artillery officer in the Civil War. In 1867, he was arrested and cashiered from the service, but was reinstated a few weeks later. On March 9, 1869, he committed suicide at Fort McHenry, Maryland, at the age of forty-one.[24] After his death, his fellow officers discovered that he owed $325 to the company fund.[25]

Lieutenant Jonas P. Holliday served in the west with the 2nd Dragoons until the start of the Civil War. He was appointed a colonel in the 1st Vermont Cavalry. While serving in the Virginia campaign, he became increasingly depressed and agitated. In March 1862, he killed himself near Harper's Ferry.[26]

Lieutenant William H. C. Whiting, who inspected the fort in 1849, joined the Confederacy and became a major general. He was mortally wounded as a POW. Samuel Cooper, who inspected Fort Worth in 1851 rose to the rank of general in the Confederacy. Brevet Lieutenant Colonel William G. Freeman, who inspected the fort in 1853 just before it closed, resigned in 1856. Colonel Albert Sidney Johnston, who was the secretary of war in Texas during Sam Houston's second term and who was the paymaster for the forts, was selected by Secretary of War Jefferson Davis to head a new cavalry regiment in 1855.* He became a general in the Confederacy and was killed at the Battle of Shiloh.

Lieutenant Charles D. Jordan rose to the rank of major, but was retired as disabled in 1863. Lieutenant Edward D. Blake continued to serve in Texas, and served as a lieutenant colonel in the Confederacy.

Less is known about the enlisted men who served at Fort Worth. Alphonso Freeman lived in Weatherford until 1905. Nicholas Beyer settled in Tarrant County, married a young Swiss woman named Anna Willi, and was living near Handley when he died in 1898. Jacob Dearing settled in Gillespie County, near Fredericksburg, and farmed there until his death in 1896. Louis Wetmore joined the Confederate cavalry, and was killed in Louisiana in 1864.

Simon Gerstring fought at the First Battle of Bull Run, fell from his horse, and was disabled. He was discharged and admitted to the National Military Home, where he lived until at least 1887. Johnston Hughes was married in Hampton, Georgia in 1866, and died in 1879. John Law, who had nearly had his throat cut in Cuernavaca in 1848, served in the 7th U.S. Infantry before the Civil War. He fought against Gen. H. H. Sibley's Texans in New Mexico, and was living in Santa Rosa, California in 1907, one year before his death. First Sergeant Edward Brenner became a first lieutenant in the 4th U.S. Infantry in 1862, but was dismissed from the army a few months later. He died in Philadelphia in January 1899. Henry McCann, the drummer from Capt. Maclay's company, fought as an infantry sergeant in Arkansas in the Civil War, was wounded, and later settled in the state.

Sgt. Abraham Harris of Company F, 8th Infantry was discharged at Fort Worth on January 20, 1852. As a cabinetmaker he built furniture for area citizens, and may have built the famous rocking chair left at the fort. He enlisted on Jan 16, 1862 in the 14th Texas Cavalry, and rose to lieutenant colonel in the regiment. He said he fought in battles of Murfreesboro, Chickamauga, New Hope Church, Lost Mountain, Kennesaw Mountain, Marietta, Cass Station, Chattahoochee, Atlanta, Altoona, Tilton, Dalton, and Spanish Fort opposite Mobile. He was paroled in 1865 at Meridian MS. He stayed in Fort Worth making furniture and telling stories until his death in 1914. He is buried at Pioneers Rest Cemetery.[27]

*It was then the 1st Cavalry, but was renumbered the 4th when the dragoon designation was dropped in 1861.

Hot and Dry

Heat and drought were as much a problem then as now. This view, looking north from behind the officers' quarters, shows the dried-out foliage and the vultures circling in the background. (Copyright William Potter.)

20

An Ideal Meets a Texas Summer

Shortly after Lt. Samuel Star arrived at Fort Worth, he wrote to Eliza that, "There is a French Gentleman here teaching all the officers, Mrs. A, and her two daughters (one 11, the other 6 years old) the French language. I shall begin to take lessons on my return from Dallas. I wish you and Kate were here to join in the study. He teaches the language after a plan very simple, requiring very little effort of the memory. He is a [illegible] genius, teaches music, drawing, dancing—everything."[1]

The Frenchman whom Starr described was Adolphe Gouhenant, who had come to Texas in 1848 as the leader of a group of French socialists to establish a utopian colony in Denton County. The settlement, known as Icaria, existed for three months in the summer of 1848.

The colonists were followers of Etienne Cabet. He was one of the many socialist thinkers who, in the 1830s and 1840s, urged the working classes to band together and live in communes. The example that these communes set would, in theory, persuade others that socialism offered the best hope for the future. In 1841, he published a novel, *Voyage to Icaria*, which depicted his notion of an ideal society. Private property would be abolished, strict equality would prevail, and all would work for the common good. He asserted that Icarianism embodied the spirit of early Christianity.[2] He established a monthly journal, and attracted a wide following.[3]

Most of the Icarians were artisans and skilled craftsmen. The Industrial Revolution was ruining their way of life. Their declining fortunes and the oppression of King Louis Phillippe's regime, made Cabet's ideas especially appealing. One Icarian wrote that he and his comrades hoped to establish "a society where reason and conscience would rule . . . without king or priest. No nobility but that of the heart. No poor, no rich. No tyranny, no oppression. A paradise on earth."[4]

One of Cabet's most devoted followers was Adolphe Gouhenant of Toulouse, who was thirty-six years old in 1841 and was a deeply religious man. He began to correspond with Cabet about Icarianism, and impressed him with his intelligence and sincerity. Cabet sent Gouhenant copies of *Voyage to Icaria* and other Icarian works.[5]

Gouhenant was a painter and art dealer. He supported himself by buying, restoring, and selling old paintings. His business required him to travel in search of paintings and customers. Wherever he went, he talked about Icarianism, distributed pamphlets, and urged people to subscribe to Cabet's journal.[6] The police took notice, and had Gouhenant under surveillance by July 1841.[7] In January 1843, the police arrested him and dozens of other communists in and near Toulouse. He and eleven others were held in prison until August, awaiting trial for sedition.[8]

The police made a clumsy attempt to frame him, claiming that he was organizing a revolutionary army. He wrote to Cabet from prison, asking that he represent him at the trial. Cabet agreed, and published articles defending his disciple.[9] When the twelve communists came to trial, the judge refused to allow Cabet to appear in court. Nevertheless, the jury acquitted the twelve of all charges against them. After the trial, Gouhenant remarked that he cared little what became of him, provided he could be of some service to "the complete triumph of our holy doctrine."[10]

In 1847, Cabet decided to establish Icaria in the United States. He traveled to London and met William S. Peters, the director of the Texas Emigration and Land Company. Peters's contract with the state of Texas would expire on July 1, 1848, and he wanted to settle as many emigrants as possible in the time that remained. On January 3, 1848, Peters and Cabet made a deal to settle thousands of Icarians in the Peters Colony.[11]

The terms of the agreement were similar to those that Peters had offered to earlier settlers. The Texas Emigration and Land Company would award 320 acres of land for every Icarian family that settled in Texas before July 1, 1848. One hundred and sixty acres would be granted for every adult bachelor. The land would be awarded to the Icarian association, rather than to individual settlers.[12]

Cabet sent Charles Sully, a British communist, to prepare the way for the Icarian migration. Sully traveled to Shreveport, Louisiana, and found that the Red River was not suitable to transport the Icarians to the Peters Colony. He determined that the best overland route would be via the Texas towns of Mount Pleasant, Clarksville, Paris, and Bonham. He purchased a farm at Sulphur Prairie, west of Mount Pleasant, to serve as a way station for the Icarians.[13]

One month later, on February 3, 1848, a First Advance Guard of sixty-nine men embarked at Le Havre, France. Cabet and hundreds of supporters came to see them off. The guard wore uniforms: black velvet tunics and gray felt caps. Each man was issued a backpack and a double-barreled shotgun.[14] After listening to speeches and singing the Icarian anthem, the guard sailed for New Orleans.[15]

Cabet made Adolphe Gouhenant the commander of his "Soldiers of Humanity," and designated a secretary, a treasurer, and a governing council. The mission of the First Advance Guard would be to establish the colony, plant vegetables, and collect livestock and poultry. They would also hunt and fish, and prepare quarters and provisions for the Second Advance Guard.[16]

Gouhenant kept a record of the sea voyage:

> 16 February. Winds are favorable, and more gentle. Having determined the need to better know the diverse talents and skills among us, I devise a way to accomplish this. I assemble the council to communicate my plan regarding the organization of labor . . .
>
> 4 March. I make a long speech to the old and new section chiefs. The Leclerc Commission will receive tomorrow the last official reports of the section chiefs. I copy the journal. At five o'clock, the council meets; first official verbal statement of the council: dissatisfaction of the council. I begin to detect a systematic opposition, which disturbs me somewhat . . .
>
> 10 March. Continue the Icarian lessons, and the individual lessons . . .
>
> 21 March. The time to unpack our guns arrives. This is also a good way, by distributing them, to occupy and distract all the brothers . . .[17]

The guard arrived in New Orleans on March 27, 1848. On shore, they learned that Louis Philippe had been overthrown, and a republic proclaimed. Some of the colonists wanted to return to France. Gouhenant made another speech, in which he urged the men to continue their mission. Five men, including one of the guard's two physicians, returned to France.[18]

Gouhenant and the First Advance Guard boarded the river steamer *Monterey* on April 1, and arrived at Shreveport three days later. Cabet planned to use Shreveport as a waystation for the Icarian migration. The

Advance Guard decided to buy a plot of land and construct a building for the colonists and supplies that would follow them.[19]

He set out for Sulphur Prairie with twenty-five men and one supply wagon. The primitive roads made the journey extremely difficult. It rained often. The wagon broke down, and the men had to carry their supplies on their backs. They were hungry and exhausted when they reached Sulphur Prairie.[20] At Sulphur Prairie, Sully advised them to forget the Peters Colony concession. He did not believe that the colony could be established before the July 1 deadline. Sully recommended that they remain at Sulphur Prairie, and develop the 3,000 acres he had already purchased. Gouhenant insisted on pushing on.[21]

After tremendous hardships, he and eight men reached their new home. They settled on the Grand Prairie, near Oliver Creek, about seven miles southwest of the Hickory Creek Ranger Station.* On May 10, 1848, colonist Grillas wrote to his wife in France:

> We arrived at Icaria on May 8. We numbered nine men, because we had to spread out along the route . . . We have a magnificent land, with fine water, abundant trees, a paradise on earth. We suffered terrible difficulties and privations, having to clear roads through the rivers and the forests; I was frequently forced to swim, to find fords for my brothers. I wore out a pair of boots without ever taking them off my feet. We camped out, almost without food, braving all difficulties in order to triumph for our holy cause; and without suffering any illness . . . Have courage, and your happiness is assured . . .[22]

On May 11, the colonists wrote Cabet a collective letter to report their arrival:

> We found the land more and more fertile as we traveled southwest. From Bonham to the headwaters of the Trinity, the countryside is very beautiful and rich, possessing every advantage for our colony. We chose the site of our establishment between Denton and Oliver Creeks, near their intersection, at a site deemed admirable by all accounts. We found there beautiful trees, excellent water, and extremely fertile land. Oliver Creek will allow us to easily establish a grist mill and a sawmill. We are on the edge of the Grand Prairie, and we can extend indefinitely to the south and west, without being blocked by private property.
>
> Gouhenant, after having visited and explored the areas toward the Trinity, took eight brothers with him to choose the site of our first establishment, and to measure some sections of land with

*Today, the town of Justin stands about one mile south of the site of Icaria.

> the agents of the Peters Company . . . During this last exploration, our brothers stayed the night about 20 miles away, in an empty house. Gouhenant bought two oxen and one wagon for 500 francs [$100] to transport supplies and baggage. We expect to commence work in four days. We will start with construction, because we arrived too late to plant crops. We will only manage to plant a small amount of corn and some beans. We will do our best, keeping in mind that we must accomplish as much as possible before July 1st.
>
> Gouhenant returned to our brothers in Shreveport, to smooth out some of the problems they would encounter along the way, and to serve as their guide to Icaria . . .
>
> With money, we will be able to buy everything locally, livestock and provisions, at reasonable prices. It is much better to buy in Paris, only the provisions necessary for the sea voyage; and in New Orleans only for the journey to Icaria. Money is infinitely more valuable here. When, in the midst of our immense prairies, we shall have great herds of cows, horses, pigs, and sheep, our food will cost us nothing. If the Second Advance Guard brings us money, we will use it to this end, and we shall want for nothing.[23]

Twenty-seven men signed the letter. Gouhenant returned to Shreveport to bring up the rest of the Advance Guard. One of these men, Levi, arrived at Icaria on June 1st, 1848 and reported:

> I found there a finished house, two others partially finished; a magnificent countryside, full of hills, crossed by streams of clear, excellent water. The climate must be excellent, for, if we had done in Europe what we have done here, we would all be dead. To walk all day, sleep on the ground, with no tent but a light blanket, drinking from holes in the ground; in short, to suffer all the hardships of a long voyage across an uninhabited and unknown country . . .[24]

Texas is especially beautiful in May and June. The Icarians were thrilled by the beauty of their new home, and by the prospect of creating a new life for themselves. Their letters home expressed great hope for the future. Rousset, one of the colonists, wrote to his wife on May 26, 1848:

> If I were to give advice to my brother, I would tell him to come with you. We will be very happy here, because in this rich country, everything grows marvelously. We have wild grape vines, 100 feet high, filled with grapes; we will have to harvest the grapes among the trees; the fruit are already the size of peas. I think that we will begin harvesting in one month. Everything grows much more quickly than in France; we saw a field of wheat harvested in the first days of May . . .

> We had to do as the old soldiers of Napoleon did, we slept on the ground without becoming discouraged; on the contrary, when it rained, we made, with our songs, more noise than the thunder. You see that the climate of Icaria is healthier than that of France, because not one of us has been sick.
>
> The weather is like the month of July in France, but the breezes are refreshing. We haven't yet seen any dangerous animals; there are lots of deer and game in general, as well as poultry, turkeys, geese, wild ducks, partridges, and larks. It is one of the most beautiful lands in the world.[25]

Hidoux, another colonist, also wrote to his wife about the rich countryside:

> The place at which we halted lies on a prairie, bounded by two small rivers, whose waters are as clear as crystal; on the banks of these two rivers we find the wood necessary for construction.
>
> We can judge today that we will be able to make wine this year, having magnificent wild grapevines, whose fruit are already the size of peas. We have mulberry trees in great quantity, which should be suitable to produce silk. We are assured that every type of wheat thrives perfectly here, and they are of the best quality. We saw them along the way, just at harvest time.
>
> Beside our first point of settlement, we have an immense prairie, 100 miles long and 25 miles wide, which by itself could sustain 50,000 head of cattle, horses, etc., during the summer and the winter.[26]

Colonist Thermes described his new neighbors:

> We have been welcomed warmly by the Americans, who are, I believe, the most hospitable people in the world. They frequently accompanied us a long way, to show us our route. Their customs are very simple, their demonstrations of friendliness are manifested in a handshake. They offer food and drink freely, and it is accepted freely. They are very curious about the objects which they see, and I sincerely believe that we will be able to carry on a brisk trade with them, exchanging the products of our factories for their raw materials, and livestock. They are very sober. They speak little, and very softly. They are generally big and strong; I don't think that they are very lively. The women are very tall and thin. They almost all smoke. Their houses are as simple as possible, all of logs, placed one on top of the other, the space between the logs hardly filled. They have no furniture, their beds are very bad. They have, however, wool, corn leaves, etc., but they don't bother to use them to make mattresses, or they don't know how . . .
>
> One sees no stone houses, but there are quarries, and some day we will have beautiful monuments . . . five of the brothers who

> became lost en route arrived today. We saw them arrive with four horsemen; these horsemen are Texan soldiers Texas rangers, who received them in their camp. The captain had his soldiers guide them here . . .[27]

The Peters Colony agents issued Gouhenant provisions worth 10,000 francs (about $2,000), to be paid for later.[28] Gouhenant waited impatiently for the arrival of the Second Advance Guard. On July 12, he wrote to Cabet, urging the Icarians to come over.

> We arrived in time to construct our cabins on every one of the sections square miles which we were to occupy, and thus took possession. On July 1st, the employees of the Peters' Colony came to visit us, to inspect us, and to take our names and descriptions, in order to make their report to the government. The operation took two days. This formality fulfilled, we gathered again at the site of our first establishment, in order to concentrate our forces, our resources, and our labor.
>
> What a pity, what a loss, what bad luck that the Second Advance Guard didn't arrive before July 1st! We would have obtained an additional ½ section for each family or two bachelors. 200 half-sections make 200 square miles [sic]; it is immense. Two departments, and ten times more fertile than the most fertile land in France: black topsoil 16, 18 feet deep, suitable for agriculture. At any rate, we have 32½ sections; that's already very good, it is very large, it is enough to support 15,000 or 20,000 persons. Moreover, if you wish, or if you send a commission, or send new orders, we can obtain as much land as we want.
>
> Now that the July 1st deadline has passed, we are turning to making our situation more comfortable. Many of the brothers are showing the effects of the fatigues and privations of our long voyage. The change in climate, food, lodging, habits, etc., contributes to a general malaise. We must pay a tribute to Texas in acclimation; but there are no serious illnesses, no danger.
>
> The majority of us are solid, and vying with each other in the zeal and ardor with which we do our work. Some go in the forest to cut down trees, some drive the wagons which transport our supplies. The carpenters are building some wooden houses; our mechanics busy themselves constructing a gristmill, others are building a kiln; the gardeners, the farmers, the terrace-builders, the charcoal-makers, all the brothers are in motion preparing for the Second Advance Guard, which perhaps you Cabet will accompany, all of the things of the first necessity. But when will this Second Advance Guard, so desired by us, arrive? We have no news of you, of them, or of our families; we appear to be abandoned by all . . .

> Come, father . . . come to your new country; it produces enough flowers to make you a crown more great and more beautiful than that of any nation of the world . . . enough space to breathe deeply the pure air of independence, of calm, of virtue; enough Icarian hearts to cherish you; enough intellect to make an eternal monument, which will, for centuries to come, bear witness to our love for you, the savior of humanity . . .[29]

Gouhenant's letter hints at the disaster that would soon befall the settlement. The colonists were beginning to fall ill, probably with malaria. They blamed the fevers on the intense summer heat. In a few weeks, the men were too sick to work. On August 20, the settlers wrote to Cabet again. This letter Cabet declined to publish; two years later, he revealed just two passages:

> The Americans have told us that, in July and August one should, in this climate, abstain from all labor; that this is the most important condition which emigrants should observe, to lessen the illnesses of acclimatization . . . What we regret most is that our pharmacy is most incomplete. We lack many very useful medicines, especially the Raspail pharmacy which, in our view, would be of great assistance.[30]

The Icarians' physician, a Spaniard named Roveira, had left most of the medical supplies in Shreveport. Roveira administered quinine to his patients, with little result. Cabet later wrote that Roveira was mad and incompetent, and had poisoned the settlers with excessive doses of quinine.[31]

Gouhenant was not present to witness the demise of his utopia. Some time after July 12, he was "accused of being a traitor, a police agent, convicted of having offered his services to one of the prefects of Louis-Philippe in some letters signed by him and discovered at the prefecture after the February Revolution."[32] The settlers cut off his long, blond hair and beard, and expelled him from the community.[33]

No record survives of his side of the story. The accusations against him seem odd, in view of his long commitment to the Icarian cause. Cabet had little to say on the subject; he later wrote that revolutionary authorities in Toulouse had accused Gouhenant of committing "a grave political act," and that Gouhenant was "deposed by his comrades." He described it as an internal Icarian matter, and did not say that Gouhenant was guilty of spying. Cabet made the improbable claim that Gouhenant "fled, at first, to live with the savages."[34]

The Second Advance Guard, with twenty-one members, arrived in New Orleans on July 23, 1848.[35] Their leader was a man named Favard. Like Gouhenant's party, they traveled up the Mississippi and

Red Rivers to Shreveport, then overland to Sulphur Prairie. From Sulphur Prairie they made the arduous journey to Icaria, arriving August 29, 1848. Favard wrote to Cabet from Icaria on September 2:

> How can I depict to you the situation in which I found our brothers? Almost all who remain are sick. Four are dead. The first was Guillot; the second, Collet, struck by lightning; the third, Guerin; and the fourth, Sauge!
>
> The least sick prepare the food, and the effort causes them to fall ill again.
>
> The sun is so hot, that if one is exposed to its rays, one is almost certain to develop fever. I didn't hesitate an instant in getting here, because so many were waiting only for our arrival, in order to obtain assistance in leaving.
>
> We were unable to bring the women over these abominable roads. The wagons only made six to nine miles per day. There are no towns, only occasional farms, and none of them have beds for even four people. One can't find any bread, because the country people only make small quantities, with each meal.
>
> When we left Shreveport, we left behind our trunks and mattresses. We loaded our wagons with supplies for ourselves and our brothers. We put the indispensable linens and a blanket in our sacks, and we left. We slept outside all along the route. We had good weather, but this didn't prevent eight of us from falling ill, which people we had to leave along the route. Edouard stayed behind to care for the sick.
>
> I continued the route with the others. We have arrived, and are in good health. All of our concerns are for the most ill, and for our preparations for departure. But the most annoying matter is that there are debts of 7,000 or 8,000 francs [$1400—$1600], and we are hard pressed to pay them off under these circumstances.
>
> We are making arrangements with our creditors, and if these work out, we will hasten to return to Shreveport. We will write you a collective letter and inform you of all these matters . . . I am worried, and would like to have news of you and of our friends.[36]

The *Clarksville Standard* printed another account of the end of Icaria. First printed in the *Caddo Gazette*, the account is from a disgruntled member of Favard's party.

> ICARIA. This is the name of the imaginary Republic which the brain of Mons. Etienne Cabet conceived, and which, as it appears now, he contemplated colonizing by gross misrepresentation. We have before stated the fact, that colonists who passed through this place for Fannin County, Texas, had abandoned the enter-

prise in disgust. Several of them have returned to Shreveport, and are engaged in their different trades. The following is the communication of a previous disciple of the renowned Cabet.

"Honor and glory to Pacha Cabet and his janissaries! Icaria is founded; Icaria exists; it is an Eden, a true Paradise on earth. Oh if you could only see Icaria!" Such are the endearing terms employed in France to entice emigration, and then fleece the poor dupes who listen to them. "Blind and unbounded confidence is required," says the Pacha of Icaria. A modest disciple, like many others, I shut my eyes and took good care not to ask what were the resources of the Icarian treasury. No account was exhibited to us of the receipts or expenditures; nor did the titles of the cession of a million acres of land ever meet our eyes. Poor victims of a misplaced confidence, we handed over our money, and embarked without asking questions.

Scarcely had we put to sea when the agent of Cabet made me acquainted with the fact, that the cession of land did not exist. This was the first deception. At New Orleans, I learned that the watches of the Icarians had been given as security in the sum of one thousand francs! Second deception. I was sick, I enquired for a physician; Favard, the Janissary in chief, replied to me, that the doctors in New Orleans were all quacks; that I was not sick enough to stop there; and that it would be better for me to go to Icaria, and place myself under the care of the physician of the society. But I have learned since that the Janissary Favard had troubled himself but little about a physician; that he had replied, he had no money to pay doctors' bills, and that cash was indispensably necessary to found Icaria. Third deception.

On my arrival at Shreveport I was still more surprised at seeing the accommodations intended for the women, and in which the inhabitants acknowledged they would not be willing to stable a horse. The fourth deception, was the journey across the forests and prairies of Texas. The rapacity of the Janissary in chief having caused us to suffer privations of all sorts. Our arrival in Icaria, however, proved the last and saddest of our many deceptions. We saw, on our arrival, not men but corpses! Not an inch of cultivated ground in this pretended paradise! The first thing that we heard of was a debt of ten thousand francs! The day after our arrival it was unanimously agreed that the society was dissolved; everything abandoned, and every member at liberty to select for himself another paradise on earth.[37]

The Icarians returned to Shreveport. Three more men died en route. Eventually, they joined Cabet and over two hundred new colonists in New Orleans.

After some debate, Cabet decided to establish Icaria in Nauvoo, Illinois, on properties recently vacated by Brigham Young's Mormons. The Mormons had emigrated to Utah, and they wanted to sell off their Nauvoo farms and buildings. The Nauvoo settlement was reasonably successful until 1855, when Cabet took his followers to St. Louis. He died there in 1856.

The Icarians were plagued by bickering, debts, and financial mismanagement, and their numbers dwindled steadily. After numerous splits and relocations, the group established a settlement in Corning, Iowa, which survived for many years. A handful of elderly men and women lived there until 1895.[38]

In the town of Justin, Texas, there is a large bell, which, according to local legend, is all that remains of Icaria. The bell may or may not have any connection with the colony; however, the site of Icaria has survived, undisturbed, as a family farm. One hopes that, in this case, the real history can be preserved along with the legend.

At least three Icarians stayed on in North Texas. When the state legislature settled the Peters Colony claims in 1850, Adolphe Gouhenant, Luc Bourgeois, and Etienne Drouard each received certificates for 320 acres.[39]

Gouhenant undertook many enterprises in North Texas. He opened a saloon in Dallas, where he displayed his oil paintings. He made daguerreotype photographs of local citizens. He married, and had descendants in Dallas at the time of this writing. He is thought to have died in a train accident in Missouri about 1860.[40]

We don't know exactly when he came to Fort Worth, how long he stayed, and how often he traveled back and forth to Dallas. We do know that he was there at Christmas in 1849 because Lt. Samuel Starr wrote about him then. We know he was here in the fall of 1850 because he donated the land for burial of the Arnold children. We know he was there in the summer of 1854, because he was instrumental in getting Maj. Arnold's body returned to Fort Worth. We suspect that he was a Mason, because Arnold's was the first masonic funeral in Fort Worth, and taking care of one's brother Mason is a vow of the order. We know that the street to the south of the cemetery is named Gonouh Street, and that at sometime he changed the spelling of his name so that it would be pronounced correctly in English. We also know that he has relatives still living in the city.[41]

Sick Call

This drawing shows one of the most common occurrences at the fort. The soldiers would assemble when the bugle blew sick call to try to find some relief from their illnesses. From the late spring to the late fall, almost half of the soldiers were sick at one time. This view shows the front of the hospital. Note that some are in white and some in blues. The whites were their fatigues or work uniform. They were made of cotton twill, often called tent cloth. (Copyright William Potter.)

21

Diseases and Medicine At Fort Worth

Pvt. Michael Farrell, a dragoon in Arnold's company, died at Fort Worth of typhoid fever on June 20, 1851. Farrell was the first soldier stationed at Fort Worth who died there of disease.* By the end of the year, eight more soldiers would be buried in the tiny cemetery northeast of the post, next to Bvt. Maj. Arnold's two young children, Sophie and Willis.[1]

The post doctor, Assistant Surgeon Thomas H. Williams, could do little to alleviate Farrell's illness. Physicians in 1850 did not know what caused diseases, nor did they know how to cure them. The practice of medical science was a mixture of tradition, observation, and speculation. Little progress could be made until rigorous, scientific methods of investigation became accepted. Physicians in Dr. Williams's day believed that, in most cases, people became sick when their internal organs received too much or too little stimulation. The excessive or inadequate stimulation caused the organs to operate too quickly or too slowly. These states of organ malfunction were known as "morbid exaltation" and "morbid depression," respectively. When the organs were working too much or too little, the patient felt sick and he or she exhibited signs of illness.[2] To treat a sick patient, the physician sought to restore proper function.[3] He sought to slow down the organs that were working too much, and to stimulate those that

*Pvt. Issac Hollyfield had drowned in the Trinity River a few days before when Company F was moving back to Fort Graham.

were "morbidly depressed." For example, diarrhea was seen as the result of a digestive system that was working too quickly. Something, usually bad food or water, was excessively stimulating the stomach and intestine.[4] To cure the patient, the doctor would remove the offending stimulus from the body by inducing vomiting or giving laxatives. Blood "stimulated" the organs. Removing blood from the patient would decrease stimulation generally, and thus, speed recovery. Fever and rapid heartbeat accompanied many of the common ailments of the day. These symptoms were seen as proof that the heart and circulatory system were excessively stimulated. Bleeding the patient was, therefore, nearly always appropriate.[5]

Assistant Surgeon Williams described Pvt. Farrell's case in his quarterly report to the surgeon general. Farrell had become ill while traveling to Fort Worth with a recruit detachment. The detachment commander left him behind at Fort Croghan. Farrell improved, and finished the journey. On June 1, 1851, he fell ill again, and was brought to Williams's hospital.[6] He diagnosed Farrell's illness as typhoid fever, an intestinal disorder caused by salmonella microbes.[7] He noted that Farrell's symptoms were "chills, followed by fever, epistaxis (nosebleed), diarrhea, great muscular debility, great dullness and confusion of the intellect; headache, passing gradually into delirium, restlessness, vigilance . . . picking at the bedclothes, ringing or buzzing in the ears, and the appearance of the rosy eruption skin rash."[8]

Williams knew that he could do little for Farrell. He noted that "There is no positive treatment for this disease, no antidote; it has a course of its own which it will run, and which cannot be cut short."[9] Nevertheless, he treated Farrell with the standard remedies of the day. Disorders of the digestive system required laxatives in order to purge noxious stimuli. "The bowels were kept gently open, once a day, by means of small doses of Epsom or Rochelle salts; the drastic cathartics were not given as they are apt to produce obstinate, if not fatal, diarrhea."[10] He next treated Farrell's fever. "To allay the febrile symptoms, the surface of the body was sponged with cold water and refrigerant diaphoretics to induce perspiration were freely administered. Cold applications to the head and cups to draw blood from the neck were applied for the intense headache."[11]

As Farrell grew weaker, he saw that it was time to change tactics, and try to stimulate the patient's failing organ systems.

> In the latter stages of the disease, when collapse and sinking came on, stimulants were given; for this purpose I gave brandy, Carb. Ammonia and the oil of turpentine, in the dose of ten to twenty drops every hour . . . The mercurial treatment recom-

> mended by some writers I did not adopt; for the cases in which I have seen it given (both in hospital and in private practice) it was never productive of the slightest benefit to the patient, but was on the contrary injurious. The patient died in a comatose state. No post mortem examination was made, on account of the crowded condition of my hospital.[12]

As Farrell's case shows, the mid-nineteenth century was a discouraging time for American physicians. Any person, with or without training, could practice medicine. Trained physicians were knowledgeable in some areas, such as anatomy and surgery, but the medicines they prescribed were rarely of any value. In many cases, they were harmful. Since most treatments were useless, physicians were apt to prescribe anything they thought might help. For any ailment, three physicians might prescribe three different treatments, none of which were of any value. As a result, much of the American public believed that all physicians were quacks.[13]

Despite this lack of confidence, the medical beliefs of the day influenced how people lived their lives. Army commanders were responsible for the health of their troops, and they listened to the advice of their surgeons. For example, Arnold moved Fort Worth from Live Oak Point to the bluff overlooking the Trinity in order to avoid the miasma thought to arise from the Trinity River bottom. The following passages, taken from a leading medical text of the day, illustrate the prevailing beliefs concerning why people became sick.

The author of the text, Dr. George B. Wood, described five general causes of disease:

> The first group of causes was perversions of those things necessary for life. It is obvious that whatever influences are necessary to sustain the ordinary vital functions, must, if excessive, deficient, or perverted, give rise to disorder . . . These influences include atmospheric air, moisture, light, electricity, food, drink, and clothing . . . The air may prove hurtful by its impurity, its excessive pressure at great depths, or its levity at great elevations. Moisture may be injuriously deficient or abundant. The temperature may be too high or too low, or may produce disease by its sudden changes. Light and electricity may be too intense for health . . . Clothing, under which may be included the covering at night, may be superabundant, and thus produce the effects of excessive heat, or deficient, and thus expose the body to still greater injury from cold, or too tight, so as injuriously to compress the trunk or limbs; or may be composed of materials badly adapted to the season, or the peculiar health of the individual . . . The condition of our external moral relations, so powerfully influential over the mental, and consequently the physical health, is subject

> to constant fluctuations, and either through undue excitement or undue depression, is very often productive of disease.[14]

The second class of causes were processes in any way related to exercise of the will:

> Hence, we must rank in the list of morbid causes, overexertion of body or mind; sedentary habits, and mental inactivity; the wear and tear of the passions; neglect of the intimations of hunger, thirst, or other wholesome want of the system, and over-indulgence of these appetites; inattention to the processes of defecation and micturition; and undue prolongation, or loss of sleep.[15]

Wood's other three causes of disease were worms and parasites; tumors; and drugs of all kinds.[16]

He believed that the causes of disease often acted in concert. He pointed to poor urban populations to prove his point: "A dense population is sometimes exposed to the prostrating influences of meager and unwholesome diet, impure air, contagious effluvia, and the depressing emotions, and are consequently swept off in vast numbers by typhus fever."[17] Doctors recognized that some diseases were contagious, and could be spread by contact, or via contaminated clothing.[18]

The germ theory of disease was still many years in the future. However, some physicians suspected that microorganisms were involved in transmission of plague. One theory held that "animalcules" traveled through the air like swarms of insects, descending on one house or neighborhood while sparing another nearby. The animalcules entered the body and mysteriously stimulated or depressed organ function.[19] This theory was purely hypothetical, and Dr. Wood admitted "epidemic influences . . . are truly occult causes, wholly unintelligible in the present state of our knowledge."[20] Dr. Williams's medical education was based on the teachings of mainstream physicians such as Wood.

Thomas H. Williams was born in Dorchester County, Maryland, on July 13, 1829. He went to school at the Washington Academy at Princess Anne and, like most aspiring physicians of the day, entered medical school instead of a university.[21] He studied at the University of Maryland's medical school from 1846 until 1848, and graduated in March 1848, at the age of eighteen.[22] His medical training was excellent by the standards of the day. The course of study lasted two years, although it included a total of only nine months of instruction. Lecturers taught surgery, pharmacy, therapeutics, anatomy, medical theory, obstetrics, and the diseases of women and children. Students paid $110 per year in tuition, while room and board cost three or four dollars weekly at local boarding houses. He studied cadavers in the anatomy laboratory and observed patients in the Baltimore Infirmary.[23]

He decided to try to join the U. S. Army Medical Corps. Applicants appeared before a board of medical officers, and took a difficult oral and written examination.[24] He passed the examination and was commissioned an assistant surgeon on March 2, 1849.[25] He arrived in Texas in May 1849, and was first assigned to Austin. He left Austin with Bvt. Lt. Col. James Bomford's command when they marched to Buffalo. After Bomford and Maclay's men abandoned the encampment at Buffalo, Williams came to Fort Worth. He remained at Fort Worth, never taking leave, until the post closed in September 1853.[26]

The medical rank of "assistant surgeon" was equal to the rank of captain in the other branches. The pay was equal to that of a first lieutenant of dragoons.[27] They could serve on courts-martial and administrative boards with other officers, but had no command authority, unless they were the only officer present.[28]

Dr. Williams was required to conduct sick call every morning at seven o'clock. A noncommissioned officer formed the sick call men on the parade ground, and marched them to the hospital building. He examined them, and decided who should enter the hospital, and who should return to duty.[29] A hospital steward assisted him in operating the hospital. The steward was chosen from the enlisted men of the garrison.[30] Because of the time and trouble required to train a steward, he was seldom returned to his old duties.[31]

Williams had administrative duties as well. It was thought at the time that climate and weather caused a great deal of disease, so the surgeon general required all post surgeons to compile and submit weather reports.[32] He was responsible for ordering and maintaining medical supplies. The inventory of necessary supplies included twenty-eight types of medical instruments, a stock of 128 drugs and drug ingredients, and twelve reference books.[33]

The Medical Department procured medicines from wholesalers on the East Coast, shipped them to quartermaster warehouses in New Orleans, and then forwarded them to Texas.[34] In November 1851, the steamer *Louisiana* transported five crates of medical supplies to Indianola, which were then hauled by wagon to Dr. Williams at Fort Worth.[35] The army provided hospital tents to shelter the sick where no buildings were available.[36] At Fort Worth, the soldiers built a wooden hospital measuring 34 x 17 feet, with a stone chimney. An adjacent building served as a dispensary.[37] Whereas two soldiers usually shared each bed in the barracks, hospital patients normally slept in individual beds with iron frames.[38]

Fort Worth, like most frontier posts, had an ambulance to transport the sick and wounded.[39] Army ambulances were light wagons, mounted on springs for a smoother ride, and drawn by four or six horses.[40] The army bought these wagons from civilian manufacturers, apparently without special medical features.[41] Ambulances were commonly used as passenger vehicles for officers and their families.[42] Brevet Major General Edward M. Brooke prohibited the private use of ambulances in November 1850, but the practice seems to have continued despite his orders.[43] The army was interested in finding a better type of ambulance. In 1852, the headquarters detachment of the 2nd Dragoons received a new model ambulance from New Orleans. The dragoons sent it back. A board of survey, convened at Fort Croghan on December 21, 1852, submitted the following report:

> In weight it is prodigious, and vastly exceeds that of any ordinary road wagon . . . it seems to have been designed for hauling saw-logs rather than the rapid transportation of the sick and wounded . . . when empty, it is a sufficient load for six of the stoutest mules . . . the board can discover no useful purpose whatever to which this ponderous vehicle can be applied.[44]

The army kept experimenting and, in 1861, began to use ambulances that were designed to carry stretchers.[45]

The medicines that Dr. Williams administered were described in the *United States Pharmacopoeia*.[46] The *Pharmacopoeia* listed the ingredients of those medicines which most mainstream physicians accepted as useful. A companion work, the *United States Dispensary*, described in detail how to prepare those medicines from the medical stores and supplies on the market.[47] Most of the drugs in the pharmacy were preparations of medicinal plants. Others were inorganic chemicals, such as mercury chloride.

The army's table of standard medical equipment indicates that Williams was expected to perform a great number of medical and surgical procedures. The supply table lists one amputation set per post, as well as ball forceps, for removing bullets; spring lancets, to draw blood; and two types of tourniquets. A trepanning set enabled him to repair skull fractures with metal plates. Thermometers and a stethoscope aided in physical examinations. An obstetrical set, a tooth extraction set, and a dissecting set were also authorized.[48]

Ether anesthesia had been used during the Mexican War and, by 1849, army physicians were using both ether and chloroform.[49]*

Malaria was the greatest health problem at Fort Worth. Dr. Standifer and Dr. Williams together reported a total of 1,414 cases of malaria among the approximately four hundred soldiers who served there, with most cases recorded in July, August, and September.[51] Williams blamed the illness on the vapors, or malaria, arising from the river bottom:

> The essential cause of the disease is the malaria arising from the Trinity River bottom. This stream, during the heavy rains of the spring, attains a great height, overflowing all of its bottom, and, upon subsiding, leaves the washings of the soil loaded with vegetable remains reeking in the hot sun; to the miasmatic emanation of which the troops are not only exposed by the close proximity of the post, but have to labor in the bottom every summer and fall, getting out timber for building purposes . . .[52]

The disease which "malaria" caused was known colloquially as fever and ague. Physicians classified it as either intermittent fever or remittent fever. A patient with intermittent fever experienced repeated bouts of fevers and chills, separated by "intermissions," during which time the patient felt relatively well. Intermittent fever was debilitating, but not life-threatening.[53] Remittent fever, in which the patient's temperature remained consistently elevated, could be fatal if left untreated. Williams reported in 1852 that "an unusual number of cases of remittent fever occurred during the third quarter of 1851, attributable to the exposure of the troops on the weekly scouts to Red River during that period . . ."[54]†

The soldiers were fortunate that, in quinine, the doctor had an effective treatment for the disease. Quinine is derived from the bark of the Cinchona tree of South America. The Spanish began using this bark to treat fevers in the seventeenth century.[57] Quinine reduces fever and kills malarial parasites in the blood. Williams gave one large dose initially, followed by three smaller doses each day, until the

---

*Contrary to popular belief, anesthesia was widely available during the Civil War, and the majority of surgical procedures were apparently performed under anesthesia.[50]

†It wasn't until the 1890s that physicians learned the different varieties of malarial illness were caused by three different species within the genus *Plasmodium*.[55] Benign Tertian intermittent fever was caused by *Plasmodium vivax*. Quartan intermittent fever was caused by *Plasmodium malariae*. Aestivo-autumnal malaria, which appears to be equivalent to remittent fever, was caused by *Plasmodium falciparum*.[56]

patient recovered.[58] The drug shortened the course of the illness, and greatly relieved the suffering of the patient. No soldiers stationed at Fort Worth died of malaria.[59] Quinine does not kill all the parasites in a malaria patient's body.[60] Depending on the species, some may survive in the liver, and emerge into the blood months later. This initiates a new bout of illness.[61] Williams observed this phenomenon at Fort Worth. In June 1850, before the malaria season began in earnest, he wrote that the disease was "confined to the same patients that have labored under it during the past winter."[62]*

Since the medicines of the day were usually of little help, physicians often prescribed several drugs. Williams did so in treating malaria. In addition to quinine, "the treatment pursued was, where it was indicated, a purgative dose of calomel, rhubarb and aloes, or compound extract of colocynth, followed by castor oil or Epsom Salts, to cleanse the alimentary canal and excite the functions of the liver."[63] The medicines to which he referred are laxatives. Rhubarb, aloes, colocynth, and castor oil is derived from plants, but calomel is mercury chloride. His treatment followed the recommendations of Dr. George Wood.

If quinine was the best drug in Dr. Williams's pharmacy, calomel was probably the worst. In small doses, it could cause bleeding gums, tooth loss, and destruction of the jawbone. Larger doses could damage the central nervous system and cause death. The toxic effects of calomel were common knowledge, but it remained a popular remedy for digestive disorders until late in the nineteenth century.[67]

The second greatest health problem at Fort Worth was probably digestive disorders, such as diarrhea. Dr. Williams reported that "diseases of the organs of the digestive system have been produced by different causes—as unwholesome food, exposure to extreme heat and moisture, sudden changes in temperature, and dissolute habits."[68] He reported fifty-five such cases in 1850, 103 in 1851, and 35 in 1852.

The second death at Fort Worth occurred one month after Pvt. Farrell died of typhoid fever. On July 24, 1851, Cpl. William McKee

---

*Small doses of quinine taken daily were known to prevent malaria, but the Medical Department did not implement such measures until the Civil War.[64] Malaria was a major problem in Texas until sometime around the Second World War. As late as 1935, the statewide mortality rate from malaria was 10.8 per 100,000 residents. Malaria cases were noted to be increasing in Dallas County in 1936.[65] The disease was finally eradicated from the southern United States through a combination of improved drainage, window and porch screens, increased availability of quinine, and pesticides.[66] It is still a major killer in developing nations around the world, killing millions of people each year.

died of chronic diarrhea, which he had contracted while at Fort Gates. Another man died of dysentery in November.[69] Williams recorded in June 1850 that he treated diarrhea with a dose of castor oil, followed by an opiate . . .[70] Presumably, the castor oil would purge the patient's bowels, and rid them of any noxious stimuli. The opiate would then reduce the diarrhea itself. Acute dysentery required a more aggressive approach:

> The patient was bled to the amount of twelve ounces, and repeated if the pulse continued full and vigorous. Cups to draw blood and warm fermentations were applied over the abdomen to relieve pain. The blood letting was followed by saline cathartics and antimony . . . starch and laudanum injections were given, mucilaginous drinks were freely taken.[71]

Despite the dismal state of medical knowledge, Williams could take pride in some modest successes. Scurvy, a disease caused by a diet deficient in Vitamin C, was always a danger at frontier posts. The regulation army ration contained almost no Vitamin C. Army doctors knew that certain fresh foods would prevent scurvy, and advised commanders accordingly. Only six cases of scurvy appeared at Fort Worth, resulting in one death. He was also responsible for vaccinating the garrison against smallpox. No soldiers at Fort Worth contracted the disease.

Dr. Williams enjoyed a long and successful career. He left the army in 1861 to serve the Confederacy, rising to assistant surgeon general. After the war, he returned to his native Maryland, where he practiced medicine until the 1890s.[72]

Mess Call

The enlisted soldiers would go to the cookhouses to the rear of their barracks to get the food cooked for them. This view is toward the west along the back of the barracks buildings. They have on their great coats to keep out the rain. The officers ate in their own houses. (Copyright William Potter.)

22

Discipline at Fort Worth

The military justice system worked slowly, and Bvt. Maj. Ripley Arnold, like many officers, sometimes imposed unauthorized and illegal punishments. A number of minor offenses, committed at Fort Worth in May and June of 1851 and subsequently tried at Fort Graham, illustrate how Arnold and his sergeants maintained discipline in their companies.

The court-martial met at Fort Graham on July 21, 1851, to try a number of cases from Fort Worth. Dragoon Pvt. William H. Griffin was arrested at Fort Worth on May 8, 1851, for being too drunk to perform guard duty. Griffin was in the guardhouse from May 8 until at least July 21, when he was tried. Griffin pleaded guilty. The court, which included both Maj. Arnold and Lt. Starr, fined him $15.00, and sentenced him to three months confinement.[1]

Another private, Joseph Murphy, got into trouble on the same day as Griffin. At 8:30 am on May 8, 1st Sgt. William Slade ordered Murphy to report for a work detail in two hours. When Murphy failed to report for the detail, Sgt. Nathan Zorkowski went to look for him. He found him at the sutler's store, too drunk to do any duty. Sergeant Zorkowski arrested Murphy. Major Arnold ordered him "bucked" from twelve noon until retreat. "Bucking" a soldier meant having him sit on the ground with his knees drawn up; a stick or rod was placed under his knees, and his hands were tied in front of his legs. Arnold kept Murphy bucked from noon until retreat, and then had him tied up again the next day. He remained in the guardhouse until his trial on July 21. Murphy was found guilty, fined $15.00, and sentenced to four months' confinement.[2] On

December 5, Bvt. Maj. Gen. David Twiggs announced in published orders that long confinement and "other restraints" before trial illegally punished Murphy. However, Twiggs did not name or reprimand Arnold in the order.[3]

Privates could be arrested and tried for the most minor act of disobedience. On May 20, 1851, Pvt. Thomas C. Kelly and two other privates were on stable guard. Company F's horses were turned out to graze on the prairie about two hundred or three hundred yards from the fort. Sgt. John Fritche, in charge of the guard detail, arrested Pvt. Kelly for deserting his post. Pvt. Stephen Decatur, one of the guards, testified that the stable guards' job was:

> to take charge of the horses that were loose, and see that they did not get tangled up with those that were lariated; and that none of the horses strayed away from us on either road, and if they did, we were privileged to go after them, and bring them back to the picket line, stable, or any other place where we could secure them. We reported to the Sergeant whenever we brought in any horses that had strayed off.[4]

Pvt. John Senn, another guard, added, "We were told to watch the roads leading to Dallas, Fort Graham, and to Little's Ford, as those were the directions which the horses would take if they strayed."[5]*

The prisoner, Pvt. Kelly, testified that Sgt. Fritche had arrested him for no reason. While his two comrades ate dinner in the cookhouse, Kelly retrieved two horses that had galloped off on the Dallas road. Kelly secured the horses:

> I passed in front of the Guard House, on my way to get a drink of water, and was accosted by the Sergeant of the Guard, Sergeant J. Fritche, who demanded to know "why I had left my post." I informed him that I had brought to the picket line two runaway horses, and that I wanted to get a drink of water. I procured the water and on my return was confined by the Sergeant of the Guard.[7]

Sergeant Fritche told a different story. At the guardhouse, he observed Kelly heading for the cookhouse, leaving the horses unwatched. Fritche told Kelly to go back to his post. Kelly said that he meant to light his pipe first, and went to the cookhouse to get a light. Fritche arrested him. The court found Kelly guilty and fined him $30.00.[8]

---

*A settler named Little, who served as one of Tarrant County's first commissioners, lived near the post, but it is not known where his ford lay. It probably was north of Live Oak Point about where Samuels Avenue now crosses the river.[6]

On June 9, 1851, Pvt. John Connigland failed to attend guard parade "until brought back from a whiskey shop some three-quarters of a mile distant."[9] Arnold found Connigland, brought him back to the post, and had him tied up. Connigland was in the guardhouse from June 9 until his court-martial in July. He pleaded guilty and was fined $24.00.[10] The whiskey shop may have been Daggett's store.

Boots and Saddles

"Boots and Saddles" was the bugle call to go get the horses, and get ready for the day. This view is looking north in the stable area. (Copyright William Potter.)

23

Horses and Mules

Horses were at the center of the conflict between Indians and whites. Indian raiders wanted horses. Successful raids brought wealth and prestige to the warrior.[1] Army officers quickly learned the Indians' method: "They come on foot in parties of three or four skulk around the settlements and on the first unguarded moment stampede the stock and travel day & night, till they think themselves safe from pursuit."[2] Brevet Brigadier General William S. Harney believed Warren's and Barnard's trading houses bought stolen horses, and thus encouraged raiding. A letter from Charles Barnard to his brother, George, sounds suspicious. Charles wrote George on June 22, 1852, from their trading house opposite Comanche Peak:

> Trade here is good. Jose Maria and his party have brought in two mules of ours but I can see nothing of the young stock. They have two more mules, one marked W, the other I have not seen. I shall get all belonging to us. The Wacos made a haul of nine head of horses on the Leon a short time since—and Towash reports that 10 Wacos have gone down towards the Colorado afoot within three days.[3]

His letter raises questions. If they were paying Jose Maria to bring in mules that they already owned, then why was trade good? Moreover, if they did not buy stolen livestock, why were they so interested in what the Wacos were stealing?

Horses were also at the center of the army's efforts to stop Indian raids. Indians usually fled before the rifles, carbines, and Colt revolvers of the soldiers. Army patrols found themselves chasing their foe through the rugged terrain of South and West Texas. The strength and endurance of their horses determined the success of the pursuit.

Dragoons were equipped to fight a modern army, like that of Mexico or Great Britain. A dragoon's arms and equipment weighed about seventy-eight pounds.[4] To carry this weight, the army bought large, powerful horses that had been raised on grain. Dragoon officers wanted the best possible horses for their troops. Sgt. Percival Lowe served in Company B, 1st Dragoons, from 1849 until 1853.* In his memoirs, he describes the horses his company commander selected. Company B rode sorrel horses.

> Major Chilton wanted sorrels of solid color, chestnut or red sorrels would do, but no light colored ones, no white noses—white feet were not absolutely barred, but unless exceptionally sound would be rejected. Sound feet, flat, sinewy legs, sound hocks and knees, arms and quarters well muscled, short, sinewy back, high withers, rangy walk, bony head, bold eye—no "hog eyes"—fine ear, deep chest, plenty of room to carry his forage, five to seven years old, fifteen to sixteen hands, preferably fifteen and a half, all natural trotters and well broken to saddle . . .[5]

The 2nd Dragoons were just as concerned with the quality of their new horses. On December 13, 1852, Bvt. Lt. Col. Charles A. May wrote from Fort Mason to protest the horses that had been sent to him. He wrote of the horses, "Many of them are very old and have every appearance of having been heavy draught horses."[6] Furthermore, they were invoiced at $153 each. He judged that not one of them was worth $100, and was especially displeased that a quartermaster officer, rather than an officer of the regiment, had selected the mounts.[7]

Dragoon horses performed well on the Great Plains, where wagons could supply grain.[8] In west Texas, where grazing was poor and supplies packed on mules, army horses tended to tire and lose weight. When a dragoon's horse could go no further, he had to walk. Mounted Indians were usually able to outrun dragoons, in part because their horses were not loaded down with extra gear.[9] They often had many horses to ride after a raid; and if their mount tired, they could switch to another. If one of their horses went lame, the Indian might kill it, eat it, and keep riding.

Wild horses, or mustangs, were plentiful in Texas; however, the army never seriously considered using them. They were too different from the traditional notion of a good horse. In the summer of 1854, W. B. Parker, a New Yorker who accompanied an army expedition, saw a herd of mustangs near Preston. He described them as "a poor, miserable, spindle-shanked, puny stock, not one of which I

---

*The same years as at the fort in Fort Worth.

would accept as a gift . . . very vicious, and of no powers of endurance on the road."[10]

Parker was with Capt. Randolph Marcy's expedition to locate an Indian reservation on the upper Brazos. Marcy and Parker met Indian Agent Robert Neighbors near Fort Belknap, from where they set out to find a suitable location for the proposed reservations. After two months of travel in the country west of Fort Belknap, Parker wrote that his party's American horses were a great source of anxiety:

> Accustomed to be cornfed and stabled, they had fallen off lost weight terribly since fed entirely on grass and picketed in the open air . . . The best kind of stock for such service is mules and Indian ponies; they are raised in the country and acclimated, and this fact was clearly proved on our trip, for whilst those we had were fat and in good spirits, our northern horses were drooping and miserably thin.[11]

A court of inquiry in 1851 illustrates the problems, and how it limited army success. Lieutenant Richard Dodge led thirty dragoons into the Bandera Pass region on March 15, 1851. After two weeks in the field, during which he fought one skirmish and killed two Indians, Dodge decided to return to Fort Martin Scott. On the way he discovered an Indian foot trail, but decided that his horses were too weak to pursue it. Instead, he went to the nearest post, Fort Lincoln, and reported the trail. The following testimony comes from a board of inquiry into Dodge's handling of the matter.

> **Corporal John Dunlop** of G. Co. 2d Dragoons, a witness in the case, being duly sworn in, was asked:
> **Question by Lieut. Dodge**: Were you with the scouting party under the command of Lt. Dodge on the 30th of March 1851?
> **Answer**: Yes.
> **Question**: What was the condition of the horses of the command?
> **Answer**: About one half of the horses were entirely broken down, the remainder were in an unfit condition to travel, having sore backs and being lame from the loss of their shoes. Two of the broken down horses did not get into camp until nine o'clock at night.
> **Question**: What was the cause of the horses being broken down and otherwise injured?
> **Answer**: We had pursued a party of Indians from the vicinity of Fort Lincoln until we overtook them on the San Saba, and were returning. We had traveled fast and over bad ground, it was owing to this that the horses were in the condition referred to. Also to the fact that we had no corn and the grazing was very bad.
> **Question**: How many days' rations had the party, when they found the trail of foot Indians?
> **Answer**: We had rations for one day and a half.

> **Question**: To what military post could you have gone quickest from the point where we struck the trail?
> **Answer**: To Fort Lincoln.
> **Question**: What was the condition of the pack mules of the command, at the time this trail was discovered?
> **Answer**: They were very much worn out. Most of them were lame and had bad backs.
> **Question**: How far was the command from Fort Lincoln when the trail was abandoned?
> **Answer**: In a direct line, about thirty or thirty-five miles.
> **Question by the Court**: What was the condition of the horses of the command when they arrived at Fort Lincoln?
> **Answer**: Besides those already spoken of, two or three more gave out entirely, and the whole of them were nearly broken down by the time we got in at Fort Lincoln.[12]

Despite experiences such as those of Lt. Dodge, senior army leaders continued to favor American horses. In 1853, Col. J. K. F. Mansfield, inspecting dragoons in New Mexico, concluded, "the American horse is the only animal able to endure the service required of the dragoon . . ."[13] With experience, other viewpoints emerged. In 1853, 8th Department Headquarters ordered that all express riders in the department should ride mules.[14] This was preceded two years earlier by Harney's suggestion that each infantry company might be issued ten or fifteen mules which they could ride on scouts. When the infantry met the enemy, they could dismount and fight on foot.

In 1856, Capt. Edmund K. Smith, serving with the 2nd U.S. Cavalry in West Texas, reported that his unit was scouting on mules. "Mules we find more intelligent and more enduring than horses. On my last scout with 10 men I rode 75 miles in 26 hours rested my mules 5 or 6 hours let them pick a little grass and started apparently as fresh as ever."[15]

Secretary of War Jefferson Davis acknowledged in 1853 that poor supplies of water and forage killed dragoon horses in the west. He had a novel solution. He proposed camels to replace both horses and mules.[16] He succeeded in bringing a number of camels to Texas in 1857. The camels did well in Texas and elsewhere. The Civil War interrupted the trial, and it was not resumed.[17]

Procuring good horses for the troops in Texas was a subject of considerable discussion. The army purchased horses in Kentucky and Tennessee for about $100 each.[18] They were brought down the Mississippi to quartermaster facilities in New Orleans and shipped to Texas.[19] War Department planners estimated that a horse would be useful for only about four years of service.[20] Buying "American" horses in Texas saved transportation costs. An advertisement in the *Austin Texas State Gazette*, placed by an agent of the Quartermaster Department, offered to buy "for the Dragoon service, Bay, Sorrel, and Grey horses from five to six years old."[21] In San Antonio, Maj. E. B. Babbitt bought 664 horses between June 1849 and June 1851, at about $83 each.[22]

With time, officers came to prefer American horses bought in Texas over those from the Midwest. In 1853, Harney recommended that all horses be bought locally because it took as long as a year for horses to get used to the climate.

> Horses brought hither from the Middle or Western states, have to become acclimated before they are fitted for active service. If they are subjected to hard work before acclimation is completed, great mortality is the consequence. In fact, with all the favor that it is possible to give them, many die under the process of acclimation, and many of those that survive, are so broken in constitution as to be incapable of ever rendering efficient service afterward.[23]

Colonel William G. Freeman, who made an inspection tour of the state in 1853, reiterated this opinion:

> . . . it appeared to be the general opinion of the officers in Texas that the horses of the country are better adapted to the mounted service than those purchased out of the State by the Quartermaster's Department. The latter are twice as expensive, cost more to keep them, and great numbers die in acclimation.[24]

When a mounted regiment acquired new horses, it was customary to assign horses of the same color to the same company.[25] This practice made the unit more uniform on parade, and helped to identify lost or strayed mounts. One source states that new horses were sometimes kicked or abused by older horses in the herd, and that assigning horses by color helped the new ones blend in.[26]

The army ration for horses and mules was eight quarts of grain per day.[27] Corn and oats were the most common feed grain.[28] The grain ration was often supplemented with fourteen pounds of hay.[29] Horses were allowed to graze whenever possible.[30] At Fort Worth, two guards turned out the horses each day to graze on the prairie south of the post.[31] In the field, each dragoon carried a picket pin and a lariat. Horses were picketed to graze each night under guard because stampedes and theft were ever-present dangers.[32]

One account of a scout in Texas in 1849 noted that the guards were mounted in three shifts of three hours each, so that each guard got six hours sleep. Guards were responsible for watering the horses as well.[33] For greater security, the horses could be secured to a rope run between two trees or wagons.[34] This was known as the "picket line."[35] William Drown, who served as a bugler in the 2nd Dragoons during the 1840s and 1850s, kept a diary during part of the 1850s. He wrote that "It gives a dragoon the greatest pleasure imaginable to see his horse thriving on good grass with a fine, sheltery place for him to sleep at night . . ."[36]

Watering the horses was an important matter. It was believed that one could kill a horse by letting it drink water when it was hot, or by letting it drink too much.[37] Lowe described how his company watered their horses at Fort Leavenworth:

> Our horses were ridden to the river for water morning and evening before corn was fed to them which, with the hour's drill, gave them good exercise. They always went to and from water at a walk. I saw other mounted troops go yelping down the hill in outrageous disorder, running races up the hill after watering. B Troop was as orderly and well-behaved going to and from water as if on parade; talk was free but no noise . . . We used the watering bit (snaffle), surcingle and blanket, but no saddle, going to and from water. [A surcingle is a strap, which holds the saddle in place.][38]

Maintaining the horses' health and fitness was especially important in the field. A horse that "broke down" from overwork might be useless for weeks. Marches were usually limited to less than twenty-five miles per day. Horses' backs were especially vulnerable to injury. If the saddle was left in place too long, the blanket became damp with perspiration.[39] A damp blanket could cause the animal's back to become sore or "scalded." The dragoon might have to walk for days, until the horse recovered.[40] To protect his horse's back, dragoons tried to keep it as dry as possible. It was standard procedure to remove the saddles when they halted for the night. Another entry in Bugler Drown's diary describes one way dragoons tried to keep their blankets dry and protect their horses' backs:

> . . . an old campaigner's first objective is to keep his horse blanket dry, and in fact everything else except his own bed blanket. When on a march of this kind we generally take two blankets apiece under our saddles and our overcoat on the pommel of the saddle and two men generally sleep together. Our method of making down the bed in such case is to first spread down one of our bed blankets, with the saddles for a pillow; next spread down the two overcoats, and then the two horse blankets, and then top off with the other bed blanket, and by this means we have dry blankets to put next to the horses' backs the next morning, and the wet one next to the saddle.[41]

While Drown states that dragoons rode with two blankets under the saddle, Harney preferred a different arrangement. In 1851, he ordered his men to lay their bed blankets on top of the saddle, on the seat, during a scout. In 1855, Assistant Surgeon Albert J. Myer wrote that "an old dragoon" showed him a way to keep warm on winter scouts. He unfolded his bed blanket, laid it over the saddle, and draped it over his legs as he rode. Myer found that "the wind blowing against it the blanket holds it in its place and you are perfectly protected . . . the harder it blows the more closely will your blanket enfold you."[42]

A story in the 2nd Dragoons' regimental history illustrates the significance of the equipment. The 2nd Dragoons received new Ringgold saddles in 1845, just before they rode from Fort Jesup, Louisiana to Corpus Christi, Texas. These new saddles made the horses' backs sore and a number were forced to walk most of the way.[43]

Horseshoes protect a horse's hooves from rocks and rough terrain. Each dragoon company was allowed one farrier. Farriers appear to have been enlisted men who had some prior experience with blacksmithing; the army did not begin training farriers until 1869.[44] Pvt. Anthony Kemp, a blacksmith from Germany, was Company F's farrier from February 1847 until his discharge in May 1851.[45] Horseshoes must be fitted individually, and keeping a horse shod cost the government $8 per year.[46]

Farriers apparently acted as veterinarians as well.[47] The Quartermaster Department provided thirteen different medicines. Opodeldoc, a liniment containing camphor, was rubbed on sore joints and muscles. Unfortunately, farriers also used the mercury compound known as calomel, and bleeding animals was a standard remedy.*

Many mounted officers recommended hiring veterinarians for the mounted regiments. Colonel Freeman cited the case of a captain in the Regiment of Mounted Riflemen who inadvertently started an epidemic of the respiratory infection known as glanders. When he selected horses in New Orleans for his men, "He accidentally got one or two that were glandered, and thus, through his instrumentality that destructive disease was introduced into his regiment and a large number of horses swept off. The captain stated that the loss in his own company had been more than sufficient to pay the salary of a Veterinary Surgeon."[49] Freeman added that a veterinary surgeon could train the farriers in horse care.

*Order No. 18, Headquarters, Western Division, dated 8 November 1851, prescribes the following veterinary supply table for 100 animals each year: Aloes, 15 lbs. Ammonia, 6 bottles. British Oil, 12 lbs. Calomel, 10 lbs. Castile Soap, 50 lbs. Horse Syringes, 2. Lard, 50 lbs. Laudanum, 2 qts. Nitre, 10 lbs. Opodeldoc, 4 doz. bottles. Fleams, 2. Salts, Glander, 25 lbs. Sulphur, 15 lbs. Turpentine Spirits, 12 bottles. Vitriol Blue, 4 lbs. No others allowed.[48]

Army horses were branded to show government ownership. Freeman noted in 1853 that:

> . . . there is now but little uniformity in the mode of branding, and the instruments used are often the rudest imaginable. As far as I can learn the only thing regarded as directory on the subject is a plate in the Cavalry tactics, illustrating the "position of the trooper mounted," where the horse is represented with the letters "U.S.D." (a mere fancy of the artist) on his left haunch.[50]

Freeman recommended a uniform system of brands. In the same year, 8th Department Headquarters ordered that all unfit animals be branded on the left haunch with a "C," for "condemned," before they were auctioned off at the posts.[51]

In garrison, dragoons groomed their horses at least once a day. Stable duty was performed in a white, cotton smock, known as a stable frock, which protected the uniform underneath.[52] When a dragoon groomed his mount, he went over the horse's coat with a currycomb to loosen dirt and debris, and then brushed the horse with a soft horse brush. Most units conducted stable call early in the morning. Horses were also groomed at the end of the day if they had been ridden.[53]

To fight effectively on horseback, both horse and rider had to be trained. An Indian fight, which took place in April 1850, illustrates the importance of such training. A Lt. Hudson of the 1st Infantry was returning to Fort MacIntosh in Laredo with a patrol of mounted infantrymen. The infantrymen were not expert horsemen.

> . . . Lieutenant H. commenced his march homeward by a circuitous route, and, on the fourth day out from the post (7th of the month) met another party of fifteen Indians, who commenced running at the first sight of the troops. The Indians retreated to a chaparral thicket, and, as Lieutenant H. and three or four of his men rode up, they fired at them with rifles and arrows. Private M. Leahy was killed, but not till after he had fired at his Indian. Lieutenant H. received a wound in the leg, and Sergeant Ling a very severe one in the chest. O'Donnell and Surbey were slightly wounded. Lieutenant H. then dashed up to an Indian who was on foot, and fired at him three times, and two balls, he thinks, took effect. He now dismounted from the horse, as he found him difficult to manage, to make an attack upon another Indian; but he had hardly got to the ground before this one and three others rushed upon him and shot him with three arrows. Lieutenant H. cut the string of one bow, and caught a second man by the throat and gave him two cuts over the face with his sabre: he was, however, too weak to do him much injury. About this time the rear men came up, and the Indians commenced running . . . Lieuten-

> ant H. lost his horse and six-shooter, and three of the company horses also made their escape.[54]

Many dragoon recruits came from poor or urban backgrounds, and thus had no experience with horses.[55] The army trained all dragoons to ride in the same manner. Ideally, a recruit would spend weeks or months at the Cavalry School of Instruction at Carlisle before he joined his unit. Many recruits, however, joined their regiment from Governor's Island or from a rendezvous, and learned to ride on the job. Contemporary accounts tell of the comic results when recruits rode a horse for the first time. James Bennett enlisted in 1849 and was assigned to the 1st Dragoons. At Fort Leavenworth, Kansas, he and other dragoon recruits began riding lessons; Bennett recounted, "Mounted our horses fully equipped today. It was laughable to see the horses running in all directions, riderless. Some men flying in the air; others came back holding their heads, etc . . ."[56]

Pvt. Bennett joined his company in Santa Fe, New Mexico, and continued learning to ride the army way:

> Nov. 1 1850—Now commences duty. Orders issued for drill and instructions for two hours daily. Mounted our horses. Went on to a circle or ring, riding at all gaits, without stirrups. Rather sore work but occasionally one is interrupted by the attraction of gravity.[57]

Dragoons first learned the basics of riding as individuals. When they were proficient as individual horsemen, they practiced maneuvering as a squad, then as a platoon. They practiced use of the saber, pistol, and carbine as well. How the sergeants and officers conducted such training was spelled out in considerable detail in a three-volume work entitled *Cavalry Tactics*, published in 1841.[58]

The method of teaching horses not to run at the sound of gunfire illustrates the careful training a company needed, to become an effective fighting force:

> A few trained horses accustomed to the firing, are mounted with the young horses; towards the end of the lesson, the troopers who mount the former separate themselves a few paces from the others and fire pistols, while the others continue to march on the track; the troopers taking care to quiet and caress those which are excited or frightened.
>
> This method is continued during some days, the troopers approaching nearer and nearer, and finally firing inside of the square; they fire afterwards when returning to the quarters, at first in rear of the column, then near the centre, and at last at the head, facing it at the distance of a few paces . . .

> When the young horses are somewhat accustomed to the noise of arms, the troopers who ride them having loaded their pistols between the lessons, fire one after another at a signal from the instructor.[59]

The regulation saddle in this period was the Grimsley. The army began buying and issuing Grimsleys at the end of 1846. It had rings and loops to attach a canteen, a rolled-up greatcoat, a nosebag, a picket pin and rope, and a forage sack. Behind the saddle, the dragoon carried his extra clothing and other items in a valise. The valise was a cylindrical case of blue wool. Saddlebags were not generally issued in this period, but equipment receipts show that dragoon companies sometimes had a pair of saddlebags on hand. These were probably for the use of express riders.[60]

Dragoons normally carried a pair of holsters over the pommel of the saddle. Equipment losses noted on muster rolls indicate that holster pairs were far more common than the holster and brush pouch sets, which were also authorized. To guide the horse, dragoons used two types of bridles: a light one for watering, and a heavy one for riding. They secured and led their horses with a seven-foot lead strap, attached to a leather halter, which buckled around the horse's head and neck.[61] The cost of a complete set of horse equipment was estimated at $37.00, and it was expected to last four years.[62]

For minor repairs, each dragoon company had a designated saddler, whom the Quartermaster Department provided with tools, thread, and oil. Major Arnold reported in June 1849 that Private Otto Kaas was "always at work repairing old saddles, etc."[63] Saddles required a major overhaul after two to three years in service.[64] By 1853, the Quartermaster Department operated a saddle shop in Corpus Christi.[65]

Mules hauled the supplies that made military operations possible. The army purchased some mules in the Midwest and South, but many were also purchased locally. A Maj. Babbitt purchased 909 mules at San Antonio between June 1849 and June 1851 for about $50.00 each. Many were driven up from Mexico.[66] Six mule teams hauled supply wagons from the Gulf Coast to the frontier forts. Trains of pack mules accompanied soldiers on scouts. A mule could carry about two hundred pounds. The army usually provided a pack saddle, a neck strap or pack bridle, and, sometimes, a pack cover for each mule.[67] If packsaddles were not available, a pad could be improvised from grain sacks or other materials.[68] Each mule's cargo was secured with a rope. Like horses, mules were normally shod for field operations.[69]

Assistant Surgeon Albert Meyer wrote about his pack mule in 1855. His unit seems to have used some kind of improvised pack saddles:

> A pack saddle looks like a saw-buck fastened upon the animal like a saddle. To the arms of this saw-buck are fastened all those sundry appliances used by "men of war" on their journeys. Imagine—but you can't imagine—a mule buried in tents, blankets, pots, kettles, pans, pork, coffee, Hard Bread, sugar, Jerked Beef, etc. . . .[70]

Civilian teamsters took care of the mules and packed their cargo. Department Headquarters specified in May 1851 that one muleteer could be hired for every forty mounted men.[71] Many of the army muleteers in Texas were of Mexican descent. At Fort Worth, Maj. Arnold employed one white man and one Indian in the spring of 1851 to handle Company F's mules.

Both mules and oxen were commonly used to pull wagons in the American West. There was some debate over which animal was best. Two quartermaster officers, Capts. Samuel French and Alexander Montgomery, favored mules over oxen and reported their observations to Quartermaster General Thomas Jesup. Captain Montgomery, quartermaster officer at Fort Smith, Arkansas, believed mules superior. He planned supply operations for Fort Belknap, and reported that oxen wore out after four years, whereas some army mules had worked for as long as twenty years. Oxen could travel only twelve miles per day; mules could easily cover twice that distance. He bought mules in Arkansas and Missouri for $125.00 each, as well as smaller "Spanish" mules for $50.00 to $75.00.[72]

Captain Samuel French organized and led an expedition to El Paso in the spring of 1849. The expedition's wagon train included 250 wagons, 800 mules and horses, 1100 oxen, and 300 teamsters. French found that mules were hardier than oxen, they could graze on less, they drank one fourth as much water, and they could pull wagons at the rate of 2½ miles per hour, about 900 yards more than oxen. Although oxen cost $20 each versus $50 to $60 for a mule, large numbers of oxen died en route. He reported that:

> . . . mules are more gregarious than oxen and more easily handled at night, though more liable to be "stampeded." I have seen a drove of 300 "stampeded" in the daytime from such a slight cause as one of their number with a saddle on joining the herd at a run. At night an Indian, wolf, or a horse running by is sufficient cause for the loss of a herd, and hence, the great risk in an Indian country. Mules, too, when once in the possession of Indians, cannot be overtaken by the pursuing party, whereas oxen can.[73]

On the whole, French found that:

> . . . the mule is much the more tractable animal and for general service with the troops is much preferable. During a stampede,

when the mules are being led away by a horse, shooting the horse can arrest their flight. Horses should not be permitted to run loose with a herd of mules—for the mules would follow them almost invariably. Such attachment have they for a horse that they will follow him wherever he may be led, being governed by either sight or the sound of a bell.[74]

U.S. Dragoon (on horse) in Uniform. (U.S. Army Center of Military History)

24

Food, Equipment, Weapons, and Uniforms

The army Quartermaster Department faced a financial crisis after the Mexican War. Before the war, most frontier forts sat along the eastern edge of the Great Plains close to navigable rivers. Transporting supplies was simple. However, after the war, Congress continued to fund the Quartermaster Department at pre-war levels, even though costs would increase astronomically. The new forts in Texas, New Mexico, and California had to be garrisoned and supplied. Most were hundreds of miles from a navigable river, and land transportation was much more expensive.

The 8th Military Department drew its supplies from New Orleans. Colonel T. F. Hunt supervised Quartermaster Department operations there. The department rented two storehouses on Poydras Street; the former Merchants Banking building on Camp Street, and a building at #149 Common Street.[1] The Department owned at least two steamers, the *Fashion* and the *Planter*, and two sailing schooners, the *Major Barbour* and the *Aid*, to ferry supplies across the gulf.[2] Each post had an officer designated as quartermaster and in Texas they would sometimes pay for supplies with drafts on New Orleans banks.

Colonel Samuel Cooper inspected and reported on the 8th Military Department in the spring of 1851. Supply arrangements were of prime interest to the War Department. His report provides an overview of the supply system at that time.

He reported that supplies for the posts along the Rio Grande were landed at Brazos Santiago, at the mouth of the river. The

Quartermaster Department maintained a small sailboat, two yachts, and a steamboat, the *Meritorious*, at the small depot. Supplies were forwarded as soon as possible to a larger depot at Fort Brown. Another steamboat, the *Corvette*, carried supplies up the Rio Grande to a depot at Ringgold Barracks where fifty wagons were constantly in service, hauling supplies to Fort McIntosh, near Laredo, and Fort Duncan, at Eagle Pass.[3]

The army did not have a fort at Corpus Christi, but stationed two companies of the 5th Infantry in rented buildings there. Rented buildings also constituted a supply depot for the troops there, and for Fort Merrill, fifty-seven miles inland. Four wagons were available to haul supplies to Fort Merrill.[4]

Most army supplies were brought into Texas via a depot at Indianola. Supplies bound for Austin and Fort Croghan were hauled from Indianola directly there. However, most items were hauled miles to San Antonio, the principal depot of the 8th Military Department.[5] The Quartermaster Department rented the Alamo to serve as a depot.[6]

In San Antonio, Companies A and B of the 8th Infantry were quartered in rented buildings on the military plaza.[7] Department Headquarters was located in the Vance House, where the Gunter Hotel now stands.

At the time of Cooper's visit, the San Antonio depot had 285 wagons, ambulances, and carts, with 1,559 horses and mules. The depot provided all quartermaster stores for Forts Lincoln, Inge, and Martin Scott. It also provided ordnance stores and, occasionally, quartermaster stores for Forts McIntosh, Duncan, Croghan, Merrill, Gates, Graham, and Worth. Supply trains sometimes traveled 700 miles to deliver goods to the troops at El Paso and Doña Ana, New Mexico. Cooper noted that San Antonio had shipped nearly 364 tons of supplies in the previous six months[8].

Forts Gates, Graham, and Worth drew most of their supplies from New Orleans via Houston and the Trinity River.[9] Between November 1850 and June 1851, Forts Worth, Graham, and Gates each received over fifty tons of subsistence supplies from Houston.[10]

To save transportation costs, the Quartermaster Department bought some supplies in the state. Firewood and building materials were purchased locally or cut by the troops themselves. Farmers sold corn, oats, and hay to the army for forage. Fort Duncan at Eagle Pass was in an arid region, and there were no farmers nearby, so the post quartermaster bought grain from farms in Mexico. The quartermaster at Fort Brown hired four men to cut and gather hay for shipment to Fort Duncan.[11]

By 1851, it was clear that the department couldn't afford to continue operations as usual. In General Order #1 for 1851, General in Chief Winfield Scott ordered all western posts to plant gardens and grow their own vegetables. If conditions permitted, soldiers should raise grain crops as well.[12] Brevet Brigadier General William S. Harney was skeptical of the plan—mounted troops were in short supply, and he wanted them to take no part in such manual labor. Instead, he thought that the infantry might try planting crops at Forts Martin Scott and Gates.[13]

Much of the western frontier was too arid for farming. At the end of 1852, Scott admitted that his plan had failed.[14] Fort Worth, however, stood on a fertile, well-watered prairie, and the garrison's garden did well. By 1853, the troops had eight acres under cultivation. Fort Mason's garden was a success as well, and in 1853 produced lettuce, greens, radishes, peas, string beans, squashes, watermelons, okra, cucumbers, corn, and other crops.[15]

The Quartermaster Department employed civilian teamsters, muleteers, mechanics, and carpenters at nearly every post. Civilian labor enabled commanders to keep more soldiers in the field. However, it was also expensive and, unlike most transportation outlays, could be eliminated. On March 20, 1851, Bvt. Maj. Gen. David Twiggs, commander of the Western Division, ordered the immediate discharge of all civilian teamsters and mechanics. Soldiers would become teamsters.[16]

In the spring of 1851, the post quartermaster at Fort Worth employed a wheelwright, a guide, and two muleteers at the post. Fort Worth's guide and interpreter was John Lewis, a Delaware Indian. Little is known of Lewis, except that he served in Black Beaver's company of Delaware Indian scouts during the war with Mexico.[17] The two muleteers were identified only as "an Indian and a white man." The wheelwright was a Frenchman named Maxime Guillot.[18] As a result of Twiggs's order, Lt. Samuel Starr had to fire Guillot. The fort's commanding officer, Maj. Ripley Arnold, appealed for special permission to retain Guillot, but was denied.[19] The chief quartermaster in San Antonio later decided that Guillot should be brought back onto the payroll, and he was hired again in the fall of 1851. On August 10, 1851, Lt. John Bold wrote to 8th Department Headquarters that he had been authorized to hire a carpenter.[20] On August 26, 1851, a Lt. Col. Tompkins recommended the employment of a wheelwright and carpenter at Fort Worth and the erection of a shelter for a large quantity of subsistence stores there.[21]

Letting the civilian laborers go saved money. Colonel Cooper reported that, before the order was issued, the depot at San Antonio employed 295 civilians at a monthly cost of $9,000. After the teamsters and mechanics were discharged, the payroll shrank to only one hundred workers.[22] On the other hand, the economic measures hurt morale, and commanders disliked giving up their troops to serve as laborers. In August, Gen. Twiggs ordered his post commanders to report the savings which his order had generated. Captain Henry H. Sibley, the post commander at Fort Graham, reported that firing the civilians had saved $113 per month. But the extra duty requirements had prompted eight soldiers to desert, taking their horses, saddles, and revolvers with them. The property lost was worth $1,308.[23]

Twiggs's order to have soldiers serve as teamsters was unpopular all along the chain of command. Since every army wagon required a teamster, scores of infantrymen served as teamsters. Colonel Cooper reported from Fort Martin Scott that company and battalion drill had to be canceled because so many soldiers were teamsters.[24]

Infantry officers complained bitterly about losing their troops to the Quartermaster Department. Colonel John Garland, commander of the 8th Infantry, wrote in August 1852, that the arrangement hurt morale. It created the impression: "Nothing new in the infantry, that they are the hewers of wood and drawers of water for more favored corps."[25] Garland also complained that the practice eroded discipline by taking soldiers away from their sergeants and officers: "a soldier employed in driving a mule team for 12 or even 6 months, and detached from his company, becomes little better than a brute."[26] The soldier-teamsters dressed as they pleased, and most wore civilian clothing.[27] In Garland's view, they returned to their companies "ragged, filthy, and almost lawless."[28]

Brevet Major General Persifor Smith was especially opposed to the practice. In March 1852, Smith complained to Quartermaster General Thomas Jesup:

> It is extremely difficult to employ soldiers as teamsters on routes not terminating at the posts to which they belong. They get drunk & disorderly, neglect their animals, & there is no guard to commend them to, nor place of confinement . . .[29]

Smith also reported that "the teamsters (soldiers) sold their forage & starved their animals . . ."[30] According to Smith they also deserted as soon as they reached the Gulf Coast. In April 1852, Gen. Twiggs relented somewhat, and allowed Smith to hire a limited number of civilian teamsters.[31]

Part of the problem may have been that some commanders saw detached service requirements as a way to rid themselves of troublemakers. On September 3, 1850, Col. Garland of the 8th Infantry sent ten of his soldiers to Maj. J. T. Sprague to serve as escorts for a wagon train to El Paso and back. Garland informed Sprague that "some of them have a strong predilection for grog shop and guard house and I wish the whiskey sweated out of them."[32] Garland also noted that one of the men was too large for the cavalry, and suggested that he could walk. Harney acknowledged the problem in February 1853 while he was temporarily in command of the 8th Military Department. He ordered that, in detailing men to serve as teamsters, "commanding officers will be careful to select only such men as are of temperate, reliable & steady habits."[33]

Harney's order did not solve the problem. Five months later, Smith wrote from Corpus Christi that company commanders still picked their worst men to serve as teamsters. The teamsters were still drinking and still stealing from the public stores. "Last night, one of them committed some outrage while drunk and was arrested by the police and imprisoned. Some of the others with axes cut open the jail and released their comrade . . ."[34] He again pointed out that there was no sergeant and no guard house with which to enforce discipline.[35]

Soldiers continued to serve as teamsters until the fall of 1853. At that time, a dispute with Mexico led the War Department to concentrate all available troops on the Rio Grande. On August 24, 1853 Smith ordered all teamsters to return to their companies, draw the proper uniforms and equipment, and serve as infantrymen again.[36]

At Fort Worth, Lt. Samuel Starr acted as both the subsistence officer and the post quartermaster in the spring of 1851. In his role as "acting commissary for subsistence," he was responsible for procuring rations for the command. As "acting assistant quartermaster," he was responsible for all Quartermaster Department activities at the post. The Quartermaster Department had responsibility for transportation, buildings, forage, fuel, tools, and many military supplies.

Not all supplies were Starr's responsibility. Medical supplies were ordered, received, stored, and distributed by Dr. Thomas Williams, the post surgeon. Company commanders requisitioned, stored, and issued their soldiers' uniforms, knapsacks, canteens, haversacks, tents, and mess gear. Swords, firearms, leather accoutrements, and ammunition were supplied by the Ordnance Department directly to company commanders, via the San Antonio and Austin arsenals.[37]

Army rations included beef or pork, flour or "hard bread," beans, vinegar, coffee, sugar, salt, soap, and candles. Rations were calculated per hundred men. When transportation to Fort Worth was included, each man's daily ration cost twenty cents. As part of the effort to reduce supply costs, the War Department ordered all post quartermasters in Texas to report on the supply situation at their post. Headquarters was interested in buying rations locally in order to save transportation costs. If part of the official ration was not obtainable at a post, quartermasters might be able to substitute foods that were available.

Starr reported from Fort Worth on April 22, 1851, that he could buy fresh beef locally, in any quantity, at 3 ¾ cents per pound. There were no flour mills in the region, so flour was almost unobtainable. Beans, vinegar, candles, and hard soap were, likewise, not available locally. Soft soap, small amounts of tallow, and poor quality salt were available from local farmers. Black-eyed peas and corn were abundant. He suggested that these might be substituted for beans and flour, respectively, and went on to discuss the factors which affected the supply situation at Fort Worth:

> Roads: Roads leading from this post are three (viz.) to Austin, Houston, and Shreveport. All good in favorable seasons of the year, and bad in the wet season.
>
> Supplies: Drawn chiefly from N. Orleans and forwarded via the Trinity and Brasos River or via Houston, latterly by the last named place. Transportation done exclusively by hired teams at $3.00 per hundred pounds average.
>
> Building Materials: An abundance of stone and timber, suitable for building purposes, is in the neighborhood of the post. Price of lumber is $30 to $40 per thousand feet.
>
> Water: Plenty of good River and spring water within 1/8 to 1/2 a mile of the post—a well in the garrison furnishes a supply of good water for drinking. For other purposes it is hauled by a public wagon.
>
> Fuel: Abundant and easily obtained and always by the troops. No claim for fuel has been made, nor will any be admitted, until the claimant shall produce a clear title to the land.
>
> Forage: Average price of corn since the establishment of the post is about ninety cents per bushel. Price now paid is $1.15. Hay has been procured by contract. The price last year was $3.19 per ton. Good grass for grazing purposes is plenty in the immediate vicinity of the post—but for hay from one to three miles distant.[38]

The army also considered raising wheat or corn at the frontier forts. Post commanders in Texas wrote Gen. Harney to report whether corn could be grown at the forts. Major Arnold's letter is filed in the National Archives:

> ...I can rent fifty acres of good arable land in the immediate vicinity of my post at $30 per year. This land will have to be fenced and broken up. The fencing will cost about fifty one dollars. And I shall be obliged to pay three dollars per acre for breaking prairie, making in all for first year, without calculating tools, seed, or farming labor, two hundred & thirty one dollars. The seed corn of the first year will yield but little.
>
> Thirty bushels per acre for second year will be about a fair average for the laborers unskilled in agriculture. At this average I might make fifteen hundred bushels of corn second year, which could, at contrast price, delivered at this post amount to $1725.00. I have already my kitchen-gardeners under cultivation. I can increase the size of field to any number of acres at same rates.

The plan to raise grain was later dropped. Many of the frontier posts were in dry areas where farming was not practical. In more fertile areas, such as north Texas, local farmers sold corn to the army at reasonable prices.

The economic measure that the Quartermaster Department initiated in 1851 was moderately successful. Quartermaster Department expenses decreased by $500,000 in 1852 and were expected to decrease by the same amount in 1853.[39]

Whatever the cost of transportation, the army ration was monotonous. A famous story recalled by a Fort Worth pioneer states that one of the soldiers, perhaps looking for some variety in his diet, stole a farmer's pig and butchered it. Arnold punished the soldier by tying the carcass around the soldier's neck and having him march around the parade ground all day.[40]

The period after the Mexican War was a time of transition for U. S. Army arms and equipment. Available reference books often do not give a clear idea of what kind of, and which weapons were in use between 1848 and 1853. Fortunately, company muster rolls itemize the equipment lost or destroyed in the previous two months. And the Benjamin Huger Papers in the National Archives comprise a meticulous record of ordnance supplies issued at Vera Cruz during the Mexican War. By reviewing these sources, it is possible to form a reasonable idea of what was in use during those years.

The 2nd Dragoons carried Hall carbines in Florida, Mexico, and Texas, and brought them with them to Fort Worth. Several versions of the carbine appeared between 1833 and 1843. It appears that the various models were in service simultaneously. Before the Mexican War, some attempts were made to exchange the oldest and least serviceable carbines for better ones. Brevet Lieutenant Colonel William Hardee requested "buck and ball" cartridges for his company at the beginning of the Mexico City campaign, indicating that his company carried the model 1837 Hall.

During the start of the Mexican War, the 2nd Dragoons carried flintlock holster pistols. Beginning in early 1848, model 1842 percussion pistols began replacing the flintlocks. Near the end of 1848, the great majority of the flintlocks were phased out. The 3rd Dragoons, on the other hand, carried percussion pistols throughout the Mexico City campaign. Many officers of all branches purchased a pair of percussion pistols, with holsters, from a Capt. Huger for their private use. There are also rare examples of enlisted dragoons who carried, lost, and were charged for Colt revolvers in Mexico.

Musketoons replaced Halls in late 1850 and proved to be a poor weapon; Harney wanted the army to issue Colt repeating carbines instead. He had been a Colt enthusiast for years, and a Texas Ranger company, under Capt. John Ford, was carrying Colt carbines at about this time.[41] To demonstrate how bad the musketoon was, Harney arranged a trial at Camp Harney on May 12. Brevet Major Hamilton Merrill, who had a lifelong interest in firearms, conducted the trial.

Merrill had eight of the best shots in the regiment fire their musketoons at targets three feet high and 18 inches wide at a range of 50 yards. Only six of sixteen bullets struck the targets. At ninety yards, only one shot in eight hit. Harney sent the results to the adjutant general in Washington.[42]*

Harney also forwarded a letter from Arnold, written at Fort Worth on May 18, 1851. Arnold reported that the swivel, which held the ramrod in place, was prone to break with use, allowing the ramrod to fall out on the ground. Worse yet, the ring that attached the gun to the shoulder sling often broke, and the weapon fell under the horses' feet. One-third of his company's musketoons were already broken in some way. The recoil was also excessive. On horseback, dragoons held the reins with the left hand and fired their musketoon with the right. The recoil could knock the soldier off balance, causing him to fall or lose control of his horse. He closed his letter by noting that "they shoot with no accuracy whatsoever."[43] Many dra-

*The men fired buckshot and ball cartridges, as well as buckshot cartridges. The results described here refer to .69 caliber bullets only.

goon officers shared his views. All agreed that the ramrod-retaining swivel broke off easily.[44]

Colonel Craig of the Ordnance Department reviewed Harney and Arnold's letters and replied with an eight-page discussion of the development of cavalry arms. Craig dismissed the dragoons' criticisms, and suggested that Arnold's men were careless or poorly trained. In any case, dragoons should not expect to be "sharpshooters." Craig quoted an earlier report, which predicted that breech loading weapons would never work.[45]

References to cavalry sabers usually provide no clue as to what kind of sword is involved. However, there are a few references in the Huger Papers to both "American" and "Prussian" cavalry sabers. The American swords were probably model 1833 Ames dragoon sabers, while the Prussian swords were the model 1840 saber, many of which were Prussian imports. No such distinctions appear in the postwar muster rolls.

Most of the 8th Infantry carried flintlock muskets during the Mexican War, however, a few men carried model 1842 percussion muskets. The Huger Papers indicate that this usage was typical for the regular and volunteer infantry regiments. The 2nd, 3rd and 4th Artillery carried chiefly percussion muskets when armed as infantry. It appears that only a limited number of percussion cap pouches were issued in Mexico. The 8th Infantry turned in the last of their flintlock muskets in the spring of 1849. In addition to muskets, infantry sergeants carried a light sword, and musicians carried swords as well.

Privately owned weapons were also in use. Major Arnold owned a Colt Navy revolver at the time of his death. First Sgt. William Slade noted that two or three men in Company F owned pocket pistols in September 1853. Double-barreled percussion shotguns were popular among sportsmen in that era, and many dragoon officers had them on the frontier.

The Texas Rangers of Bell's Regiment used a variety of weapons. Some companies, such as those of Stapp and Fitzhugh, received no government arms or supplies. Most companies received flintlock pistols. Rifles, some of which are identified as flintlocks, also appear in records. B. F. Hill's company drew Hall carbines with slings and cartridge boxes; pairs of flintlock pistols; canteens; haversacks; and forage bags. The Texas Ranger companies raised in the fall of 1849 carried model 1841 percussion rifles. Accoutrements included slings, cartridge boxes, and waist or shoulder belts. Some men drew flask-and-pouch sets rather than cartridge boxes, and a few cap pouches were issued. Each man was authorized a flintlock or percussion holster pistol. Some flintlock pistols were still in service as late as 1850. There is no evidence that the Texas Rangers drew Colt revolvers between 1849 and 1852.

The issue of accoutrements such as infantry cartridge boxes, and dragoon saber belts appears to have followed regulations fairly closely. Cap pouches appear on the muster rolls of the 2nd Dragoons in Florida, but seem to disappear afterward. A few appeared during the Mexican War, with increasing numbers issued in 1848. By 1850, they were standard issue. Pairs of pommel holsters, rather than holster and pouch sets, seem to have been standard dragoon issue.

Canteens of wood, tin, and India rubber were in use simultaneously in Mexico and on the Texas Frontier. In 1851, Maj. Merrill requested India rubber canteens for Company B, 2nd Dragoons; he was issued canteens of wood and of tin. Knapsacks of both painted canvas and gum elastic were also in use.

When a soldier was discharged, his discharge papers included a statement of his clothing account. If the soldier had not received his full allotment of clothing during his enlistment, he received a cash settlement. The paymaster kept a copy of the settlement in order to account for the funds paid out.

Historians are fortunate in that Maj. Albert Sidney Johnston, the paymaster for Fort Worth, preserved his vouchers and receipts. Scores of clothing statements from the frontier forts are found in his papers at Tulane University and provide a precise record of the uniforms issued to a sample of the soldiers at Fort Worth.

The soldiers at Fort Worth wore the wool fatigue uniform on duty. Infantrymen wore sky blue trousers and a matching waist-length blue jacket. Dragoons wore similar trousers with a dark blue jacket. The infantry jacket had white trim on the collars and epaulettes, while the dragoon jacket was trimmed in yellow. These uniforms had been standard issue since about 1833.[46]

All soldiers wore a dark blue forage cap. Members of the 8th Infantry were issued a brass letter, denoting their company, which they wore on their caps. The 2nd Dragoons usually received a brass "2," for their regiment. This practice was not regulation, but it persisted from the Mexican War until at least 1853. During the Mexican War, dragoons sewed yellow bands around the base of their forage caps.[47]

For cold or rainy weather, soldiers were issued a sky blue or blue-gray greatcoat. The greatcoat was his only protection in wet weather, as the army did not issue raincoats until 1855.[48] For winter campaigns, soldiers added gloves, leggings, and other protective clothing to their regulation greatcoat.[49]

Soldiers were issued two white cotton shirts and two flannel shirts each year.[50] Regulations called for soldiers and officers to wear a stock between the shirt collar and the jacket collar. The stock resembled a black leather collar which fastened behind the neck.[51] In addition to shirts and stocks, soldiers received a pair of long flannel drawers and two pairs of wool stockings each year.

Both infantry and dragoons wore heavy black shoes, described as laced boots in official documents, and also known as brogans. These shoes rose to about the ball of the ankle—the high riding boots that most of us associate with the cavalry did not become standard issue until about 1859.[52] However, from 1852 until 1854, many dragoons in Texas received "new pattern" or "cavalry" boots. Many of the men in Bvt. Maj. Hamilton Merrill's company received these boots. They were probably similar to the 1859-style boots.

For summer months, army regulations called for a white cotton version of the fatigue uniform. During the Mexican War, however, the cotton uniforms were evidently stowed away, and men wore the wool uniform year round.[53] The Johnston Papers confirm that summer uniforms were rarely issued to the 2nd Dragoons or 8th Infantry from 1846 until 1849. After the war, the cotton uniforms were dropped from regulations, but large quantities were issued in Texas between 1850 and 1853.[54] It is not clear whether the cotton uniforms were worn for garrison duty; they were issued in a haphazard fashion, and many soldiers never received one. Wool fatigues were evidently the standard uniform in Texas, as in Mexico.[55]

Wearing wool clothing year round was the norm in America at that time. Captain Randolph Marcy explained the thinking of the day in *The Prairie Traveler*:

> A suitable dress for prairie traveling is of great importance. Cotton or linen fabrics do not sufficiently protect the body against the direct rays of the sun at midday, nor against rains or sudden changes of temperature. Wool, being a non-conductor, is the best material for this mode of locomotion, and should always be adopted for the plains.[56]

Army regulations authorized a dark blue dress coat, with tails and wool epaulettes, known as the "uniform coat." It was worn with a plumed shako, called the "uniform cap."[57] Issue of the uniform coats and caps was suspended at about the time the Mexican War broke out.[58] Clothing records in the Johnston Papers confirm that uniform coats were not issued to the 2nd Dragoons or 8th Infantry after early 1846. After the war, the 2nd Dragoons did not resume issue of the old uniform coats, except to musicians of the regimental band. The 5th

Infantry, which served at Fort Belknap and Fort Phantom Hill, drew uniform coats in 1849 and 1850.[59] The 8th Infantry received a large supply of the old uniform coats in 1848. Regimental headquarters prepared to issue them in November 1850.[60] Lieutenant Washington Street wrote to regimental headquarters from Fort Worth in January 1851 that Maj. Arnold had prohibited wear of the uniform coat. Street's men were excused from drawing the coats.[61] It appears that the coats were finally issued to the regiment in 1853.[62]

The army adopted new uniform regulations in 1850 and 1851. The new uniforms, which would be standard issue in the Civil War, were just making their appearance in Texas at the time Fort Worth was abandoned. Old uniforms were issued until the supply ran out. For this reason, many of Maj. Merrill's dragoons were wearing sky blue infantry jackets in the summer of 1853.*

Regulations required men to wear the correct uniform when performing duties in garrison. In the field, men were usually allowed to dress as they pleased. Cotton trousers were sometimes worn in the summer.[63] Tight wool jackets gave way to civilian hunting shirts. A favorite style of shirt on the Texas frontier was the "hickory" shirt, made of heavy cotton, usually of a dark blue, checked material. Theresa Vielé, an officer's wife on the Rio Grande, thought that the shirts were popular because the checked material hid dirt and stains longer.[64] George Barnard sold hickory shirts at his store in Waco, and at the Comanche Peak Trading House.[65] In September 1852, a resident of Belleville wrote that even Indian raiders had been seen wearing "hickory or bed ticking shirts."[66]

Flannel shirts were also popular. Captain Marcy recommended shirts "of red or blue flannel, such as can be found in almost all the shops on the frontier: this, in warm weather, answers for an outside garment."[67] Such hunting shirts were often worn on top of a light cotton shirt, like a loose jacket.[68] Colonel Freeman described the scouting uniforms he saw in Texas in 1853:

> I find the light broad brim Texas hat, of various forms and shades of color, almost universally worn on scouts and about the garrison, when not on duty. The present Pattern of 1851 uniform cap is regarded as entirely unsuited to this hot climate. It is

---

*Freeman's inspection report from the summer of 1853 shows that only Companies D, E, G, H, and I of the Mounted Rifles were wearing the new uniforms. The following units wore the old uniforms: Company A-E & G-K, 1st Infantry; Company A, 3rd Infantry; the 5th Infantry; Company B & K, 4th Artillery, Company A & G, 2nd Dragoons; Company B, C, & F, 2nd Dragoons wore a mix of old pattern infantry and dragoon uniforms.

> suggested whether it might not be expedient to adopt a hat of a proper pattern for the warm seasons.
>
> The Cavalry dragoons and mounted riflemen on scouts invariably wore hunting shirts, generally of dark blue flannel. They are more comfortable than coats or jackets and are a great protection to their clothing. The practice is irregular, but it might be well to sanction it by issuing such shirts, properly made, in lieu of the white cotton fatigue, or stable frocks, now allowed and which from their color are of very little use.[69]

The army issued some broad-brimmed hats to the soldiers in Texas in this period. During the Mexican War, the army procured gray felt hats of this type for the Voltigeur Regiment. The Voltigeurs were disbanded after the war, and the hats remained in a warehouse in Philadelphia. Harney obtained 445 of the hats for the 2nd Dragoons in February 1851. A few of Maj. Merrill's men were issued Voltigeur hats in the spring of 1853.[70]

The authorized clothing issue for a soldier during a five year enlistment found in the Johnston Papers are:

> Woolen jacket—1 per year. Woolen overalls trousers—2 per year. Forage cap—3 per enlistment. Uniform coat—3 per enlistment. Uniform cap—2 per enlistment. Cotton jacket—4 per enlistment. Cotton overalls—3 per year. Greatcoat—1 per enlistment. Blanket—3 per enlistment. Stock—2 per enlistment. Cotton shirt—2 per year. Flannel shirt—2 per year. Wool stockings—2 pairs per year. Laced boots—4 pairs per year. Flannel Drawers—6 per enlistment. Company letter—1 per enlistment. Stable Frock (dragoons only)—2 per enlistment.[71]

Officers were required to buy elaborate, expensive uniforms. Major Arnold or Lt. Col. Bomford, wearing their dress uniforms, would not have looked out of place at a meeting of Napoleon's marshals. For most duties around the post, however, officers wore a dark blue frock coat or jacket, and a dark blue forage cap. Infantry officers wore sky blue trousers, while dragoon officers wore blue-gray trousers. White cotton jackets and trousers were authorized for summer.[72] The 1851 uniform regulations abolished the old, elaborate uniforms, and made the blue frock coat the standard uniform for most duties.[73] Officers dressed as they pleased when they went in the field. Major Merrill, riding across Texas on his way to the Mexican War in 1846, described his field gear as follows:

> Cooking utensils and furniture—1 small frying pan, 2 tin cups, 1 tin canteen, and a knife and fork.
> Utensils—a hatchet and a bowie-knife.

> Outfit—a common tent, 2 blankets, a pair of saddle bags, valise, and carpet-bag, the latter containing my wardrobe for the entire campaign.
> Dress—a wide brimmed straw hat of Texan manufacture, a blue jacket, buckskin tights, and high chaparral boots with large spurs.
> Thus, with a pair of holster pistols, a belt-pistol, a double-barreled gun, and mounted on my finest horse, you have your compagnon de voyager.[74]

The papers of Horace Delano, a lieutenant who served with Company A, 2nd Dragoons at Fort Mason, provide more clues about officers' field uniforms. In March 1852, Lt. T. K. Jackson of the 8th Infantry asked Delano to send his "white blanket overcoat with pearl buttons" to Fort McKavett. Delano's records show that, while visiting Austin in February 1852, he bought "3 linen check shirts, 3 figured shirts, and 1 blue flannel shirt."[75] In October 1851, Lt. Delano received a letter from Lucius M. Walker, another dragoon lieutenant who was encamped at the Indian Villages on the upper Brazos. His company was designated to escort Bvt. Brig. Gen. William Belknap on a reconnaissance. Walker's company relieved Maj. Arnold's Company F who had been encamped at the Caddo Village in September. With winter approaching, Walker asked Delano to send up rations for his company, as well as salt and horseshoes for the horses. He also asked for chewing tobacco, a hunting rifle with ammunition, and warm clothing. He wanted his friend to send up:

> [His] fine shell jacket (lined with red velvet) and a black velvet coat . . . Please get me a pair of soldier's overalls and have them altered to your measure . . . have them made large in the feet to fit over high boots and pockets in the front . . . Get of Evans two colored shirts (not hickory.) I would rather have blue checked. Get also two light colored silk pocket handkerchiefs . . . Oh Lord how bad we want a drink . . .[76]

It is probably safe to assume that Maj. Arnold's camp, unlike that of Lt. Walker, had plenty to drink.

25

The Muster Roll

Of Soldiers Who Served at Fort Worth (1849–53)

Company F, 2nd Dragoons

Stationed at Fort Worth June 1849 to July 1851; and January – August 1852.
(Age = age at enlistment; B = Born; E = Enlisted; D = Discharged)

Muster Roll of Co. F, 2nd Dragoons for June 1849

1st Sgt. Jacob Dearing—E: Fort Jesup, 6-45.—D: Fort Worth, 6-50.

Sgt. Daniel McCauly.—28, B. Antrim, Ire.—E: NY City, 6-46 (Stonecutter)—D: Ft. Worth, 6-51.

Sgt. William Slade. 24. B. England, E: NY City, 10-46. (Laborer)—D: 10-51, Camp near Caddo Valley.

Cpl. James Kepner. 28. B. Pittsburgh, E: NY City, 5-46. (Soldier)—D: Ft. Worth, 5-51.

Cpl. Joseph Schaffer. 19. B. Muenster, Ger., E: NY City, 5-46.—D: Ft. Worth, 5-51.

Cpl. Nathan Zorkowski. 22. B. Poland, Prussia, E: NY City, 5-48. (Machinist) D: Ft. Graham, 1-53.

Bugler Thomas Noland. 12. B. NY City, E: New Orleans, 11-44. D: Ft. Worth, 11-49.

Farrier Anthony Kemp. 23. B, Ger., E: NY City, 5-46. (Blacksmith).—D: Ft. Worth, 5-51.

Philip Anderson. 25. B. Dunbar, Scotland. E: Louisville, 7-48 (Baker)—Deserted, 11-50.

Nicholas Beyer. 30. B. Bavaria, Ger., E: NY City, 5-46. (Soldier)—D: Ft. Worth, 5-51.

Christian Bohrmann. B. Dresden, Ger., E: NY City, 8-48. (Soldier) D: Ft. Graham, 8-53.

Frederick Burlage. 23. B. Ger., E: NY City, 5-46. (Sailor)—D: Ft. Worth, 5-51.

William Dixon. 28. B. Boston, E: Louisville, 7-48. (Clerk) Deserted, August 4, 1850.

Thomas Donnelly. 24. B. Wickford, Ire., E: NY City, 8-48. (Brickmaker) D: Ft. Graham, 9-53.

Hugh Doyle. 25. B. Dublin, Ire., E: Philadelphia, 9-48 (Clerk) Deserted August 4, 1850.

Apprehended and deserted again January 1852, and again June 1852.

George Durfee. 21. B. Jefferson NY. E: NY City, 5-46. (Blacksmith) D: Ft. Worth, 5-51.

Alphonso Freeman. 26.B. Monroe, NY. E: Ft. Monroe, Virginia 6-45. (Soldier)—D: Ft. Worth, 6-50.

Simon Gerstring. 24. B. Bavaria, Ger. E: NY City, 5-46. (Grocer)—D: Ft. Worth, 5-51.

Joseph Gross. 21. B. Ger. E: NY City, 5-46 (Tailor)—D: Ft. Worth, 5-51.

William A. Gwynne. 23. B. Londonderry, Ire. E: Philadelphia, 8-48. (Clerk)

James Hanna. 18, B. Antrim, Ire. E: NY City, 11-46. (Chandler)—D: Ft. Graham, 10-51.

John Hannibal. B. Ire. E: Louisville, 7-48.

Andrew I. Harrison. 23, B. Baltimore. E: Baltimore, 9-48. (Carpenter)—Deserted, August 7, 1850.

Augustus Helmerling. 21. B. Oldenburg, Ger. E: NY City, 5-46. (Boxmaker)—D: Ft. Worth, 5-51.

Johnston Hughes. 21. B. Armagh City, Ire. E: NY City, 6-46. (Clerk)—D: Ft. Graham, 6-51.

Otto Kaas. 28. B. Copenhagen, Denmark. E: NY City, 5-46. (Boxmaker)—D: Ft. Worth, 5-51.

Peter Keough. 30. B. Dublin, Ire. E: NY City, 10-46. (Groom)—D: Ft. Graham, 10-51.

Francis Knaar. 25. B. Ger., E: NY City, 6-46. (Blacksmith)—D: Ft. Worth, 6-51.

John Law. 21. B. Yorkshire, Eng. E: NY City, 5-46. (Machinist)—D: Ft. Worth, 5-51.

Moses McCullough. 24. B. Newburg, NY. E: NY City, 10-47. (Molder)—D: Ft. Worth, 9-49.

Anthony Mendez. 22. B. St. Bernard Par., LA. E: New Orleans, 11-46. (Clerk)—D: Ft. Worth, 11-50.

Blassis Miller. 22. B. Baden, Ger. E: Louisville KY, 8-48. D: Ft. Graham, 8-53.

Stephen Moser. 28. B. Eastern PA. E: NY City, 7-46. (Tailor)—Killed by a soldier of the 8th Infantry at Ft. Graham, June 26, 1851.

Thomas Porthouse. 29. B. Carlisle, Eng. E: NY City, 5-46. (Block Cutter)—D: Ft. Worth, 5-51.

August Poggenpuhl. 27. B. Verter, Ger. E: NY City, 9-48. (Baker)—D: Ft. Graham, 9-53.

Matthew Patterson. 23. B. Cecil, MD. E: Baltimore, 7-48. (Laborer)—D: Ft. Worth, 9-49.

Ferdinand Schultz. 22. B. Prussia. E: NY City, 5-46. (Glazier)—D: Ft. Worth, 5-51.

John Senn. 21. B. Sestal, Switzerland. E: NY City, 7-48. (Painter)—D: Ft. Graham, 7-53.

John Wagner. 21. B. Strasbourg, Ger. E: NY City, 5-46. (Laborer)—D: Ft. Worth, 5-51.

Samuel Weaver. 23. B. Albany, NY. E: NY City, 5-46. (Baker)—D: Ft. Worth, 5-51.

Louis Wetmore. 21. B. Hessian, Ger. E: NY City, 12-47. (Merchant)—D: Ft. Graham, 12-52.

William Wolbel. E: St. Louis, 3-45. D: Ft. Graham, 3-50.

William Zeckler. 26. B. Hessia, Ger. E: NY City, 6-46. (Painter)—D: Ft. Worth, 6-51.

Recruits Who Joined Company F, 2nd Dragoons with Lt. Starr on Christmas Day, 1849

Hugh Brown. 23. B. Halifax, Nova Scotia. E: Boston, 7-49. (Groom)

Thomas Cummings. 21. B. Carlow, Ire. E: Boston, 7-49. (Clerk)—D: Ft. Chadbourne, 7-54.

Charles W. Dennison. 24. B. Boston. E: Baltimore, 7-49. (Machinist)

Stephen Decatur. 24. B. NY. E: NY City, 9-49. (Carpenter)

John Fritche. 24. B. Bremen, Ger. E: Baltimore, 8-49. (Finisher)

James Gray. 28. B. Londonderry, Ire. E: NY City, 8-48. (Laborer)—D: Ft. Worth, 7-50.

Charles Kinsler. 21. B. Stuttgart, Ger. E: Baltimore, 9-48. (Clerk)—D: Ft. Graham, 9-53.

William Lindsay. 22. B. Thompsonville, CN. E: NY City, 5-49. (Laborer)—Deserted, August 7, 1850.

James McDonough. 22. B. Sligo, Ire. E: Boston, 8-49. (Farrier)

Cpl. Levi McWilliams. 26. B. NY City. E: Ft. Jesup, 6-45. (Soldier)—D: Ft. Worth, 6-50.

William Manby. 21. B. Yorkshire, England. E: NY City, 9-49. (Clerk)

James Robinson. 21. B. Rockaway, NY. E: NY City, 7-49.—Deserted, May 30, 1851.

Edward Reardon. 24. B. Kings County, Ire. E: NY City, 8-49. (Laborer)—Deserted November 6, 1850.

Daniel Scanlan. 21. B. Cork, Ire. E: Boston, 7-49. (Farrier)—Deserted January 28, 1850.

Cpl. Samuel Sprague. 22. B. Watertown, MA. E: NY City, 8-49. (Slater)

Cornelius Sullivan. 21. B. Cork, Ire. E: Baltimore, 8-49. (Laborer)—Died, Ft. Graham, July 18, 1851.

Recruits for Company F, 2nd Dragoons Who Arrived November 15, 1850

Bugler Patrick Devine. 21. B. Wexford, Ire., E: Philadelphia, 3-48. (Plasterer)—D: Ft. Graham, 3-53.

James Bennett. 26. B. Brighton, England, E: Newark, 1850. (Laborer)—D: Ft. Graham, 9-51.

Western Buress. 22. B. LaGrange County, TN. E: Richmond, 8-50. (Millwright)

John Coniglandt. 33. B. Donegal, Ire. E: NY City, 7-50. (Laborer)—D: 1-52.

Jacob G. Demarest. 21. B. Patterson, NJ. E: Binghamton, 7-50. (Blacksmith)—Deserted, Ft. Graham, November 15 1851.

John Delaney. 21. B. Armagh, Ire. E: Richmond, 7-50. (Laborer)—Deserted, Ft. Graham, November 15 1851.

Isaac Hollyfield. 25. B. Henrico, VA. E: Richmond, 7-50. (Soldier)—Drowned in Trinity River, June 17, 1851.

Thomas C. Kelly. 22. B. Galway, Ire. E: NY City, 7-50. (Laborer)

James Kennon. 29. B. Caroline County, VA. (Laborer)—Died September 8, 1852, Ft. Graham.

John G. McDermott. 26. B. Seilim, Ire. E: Richmond, 8-50. (Laborer)—D: Ft. Croghan, 11-53.

Bugler John McNamara. 21. B. Limerick, Ire. E: NY City, 5-50. (Laborer)

Edward Riordon. 22. B. Tipperary, Ire. E: Richmond, 6-50. (Laborer)

John F. Terry. 22. B. Amherst County, VA. E: Richmond, 8-50. (Clerk)—D: Fort Worth, 5-51.

Recruits Who Joined Company F, 2nd Dragoons on January 22, 1851.

Richard Barrett. 22. B. County Mayo, Ire. E: NY City, 9-50. (Laborer)—D: Oregon, 1860.

James Doherty. 22. B. Armagh, Ire. E: (Stone Mason)—Deserted, Ft. Graham, November 1853.

William M. Griffin. 22. B. Dublin, Ire. E: Rochester, 4-50. (Shoemaker)

Michael Farrell. 19. B. Galway, Ire. E: Boston, 4-50. (Laborer)—Died at Fort Worth, June 20, 1851.

Patrick Hannigan. 21. B. Cork, Ire. E: Boston, 9-50. (Baker)

Simon Lindsay. 29. B. Kings County, Ire. E: NY City, 9-50. (Shoemaker)—Deserted, June 10, 1851.

Napoleon McLaughlin. 25. B. Orange, VT E: NY City, 5-50. (Clerk)—Deserted August 1852.

William McLane. 27. B. Derry, Ire. E: Newark, 8-50. (Laborer)—D: 8-55.

John McD. Nicholson. 22. B. Longford, Ire. (Baker)—Deserted, June 3, 1851.

Joseph Murphy. 21. B. Derry, Ire. E: Newark, 8-50. (Laborer)—D: Ft. Worth, 5-52.

William Olliver. 23. B. York, PA. E: Carlisle, 9-50. (Laborer)—D: Ft. Chadbourne, 9-55.

Theodore Schittenhelm. 24. B. Wittenberg, Ger. E: Newark, 9-50. (Confectioner)—D: Ft. Chadbourne, 9-55.

John Shirley. 21. B. Kilkenny, Ire. E: Rochester, 9-50. (Clerk)—D: Ft. Chadbourne, 9-55.

Henry W. Simms. 32. B. Henrico, VA. E: Lynchburg, 9-50. (Stonecutter)—D: Ft. Chadbourne, 9-55.

George Siter. 24. B. Steinbach, Ger. E: Rochester, 8-50. (Machinist)—D: Ft. Chadbourne, 8-55.

Other Soldiers who served at Fort Worth in Company F, 2nd Dragoons

Patrick Flannigan. 21. B. Cork, Ire. E: Boston, 9-50. (Brickmaker)—D: Ft. Graham, 5-53.

George Kerr. 26. B. Glasgow, Scotland. E: Baltimore, 8-49. (Soldier)—D: Ft. Chadbourne, 7-54.

Bugler James Moffatt. E: B. NY City, 8-49. Transferred to Co. F June 1852. Deserted at Ft. Graham, 10-53.

Cpl. George Martin. 19. B. Ft. Jesup, LA. E: Austin, 6-51. Joined Co. F 10-51. (Soldier)

Soldiers Who Joined Company F, 2nd Dragoons on July 17, 1852

Joseph Stewart: Charles Green; Wm. M. Bragonier; Andrew Beals; William Barcus; Leopold Burgeaur; John F. Coady; Joseph Conroy; John Crooks; Charles Duncan; Thomas Dundee; Robert Henderson; Michael A. Horgan; Michael Halligan; David Kimball; Patrick King; Andrew McFee; Arthur Monahan; Edward McFarlane; John W. Mulligan; John Mix; Henry Marshall; James O'Brien; John A. O'Neill; Michael Scanlon; John Southward; Lewis F. Talbot; James Tweede; George Waters; Paul Quick; James B. Hughes; John O'Day; Manassus M. Flora.

Company B, 2nd Dragoons

Stationed at Fort Worth August 13, 1852 through September 17, 1853.

Roll of Company B, 2nd Dragoons for August 1852.

1st Sgt. John Black. 27. B. Sligo, Ire. E: Ft. Mason, Texas, 10-51. (Laborer)—D: Ft. Riley, 9-56.

Sgt. Patrick Murphy. B. Kilkenny, Ire. E: NY City, 8-49. (Plumber)—D: Ft. Worth, 8-54.

Sgt. Thomas Marshall. 22. B. Cork, Ire. E: NY City, 7-49. (Shoemaker)—D: Ft. Belknap, 8-54.

Sgt. Charles G. Devine. 22. B. Newark, NJ. E: Richmond, 8-50. (Machinist)—D: Ft. Belknap, 6-55.

Cpl. Joseph S. Clarke. 25. B. Bedford Cty, VA. E: Richmond, 8-50. (Wagonmaker)—D: Ft. Belknap, 8-55.

Cpl. Henry Haugh. B. Woodsborough, MA. E: Baltimore, 7-46. (Soldier)—D: Ft. Riley, 7-51.

Cpl. Frederick Williams. 28. B. Fairfax, VA. E: NY City, 3-52. (Shoemaker)—D: Ft. Riley, 3-57.

Bugler Philip Rivers. 31. B. Champlain, NY. E: San Antonio, 2-49. (Farmer)—D: Ft. Belknap, 2-53.

Bugler John F. Lindahl. 33. B. Sweden. E: Richmond, 7-50. (Musician)—D: Ft. Belknap, 7-55.

Farrier Patterson M. Gaynor. 21. B. Caveen, Ire. E: Rochester, 8-50. (Blacksmith)—Deserted, Ft. Worth, January 9, 1853.

Thomas Adams. 21. B. Monahan, Ire. E: NY City, 3-52. (Farmer)—D: Ft. Riley, 3-57.

Louis Batty. 22. B. Paris, France. E: NY City, 9-48. (Sailor)—D: Ft. Worth, 9-53.

Wilson Buchanan. 19. B. Perry, PA. E: Philadelphia, 8-48. (Farmer)—D: Ft. Worth, 8-53.

John Beatty. 21. B. Tyrone, Ire. E: Boston, 8-49. (Clerk)—D: Ft. Belknap, 8-54.

John Bolger. 23. B. Carlow, Ire. E: N Y City, 8-53. (Laborer)—Died at Ft. Belknap, April 13, 1854.

John Canfield. 27. B. Kilkenny, Ire. E: Augusta, 6-48. (Laborer)—D: Ft. Worth, 6-53.

James Cahill. 25. B. Morgan, OH. E: St. Louis, 10-50. (Soldier)—D: On furlough, Texas, 10-55.

Michael Conroy. 21. B. Petersborough, Canada. E: Rochester, 8-50. (Farmer)—D: Ft. Belknap, 6-55.

Walter Collins. 25. B. Ire. E: Carlisle, 9-49. (Soldier)—D: Ft. Belknap, 9-54.

John Clarey. 21. B. Hartford, CN. E: New York, 10-50. (Painter)—D: On furlough, Texas, 10-55.

Charles Craig. E: Ft. Mason, 5-52. Deserted, Ft. Worth, December 15, 1852.

Michael Cunningham. 23. B. Waterford, Ire. E: Boston, 7-49. (Stonecutter)—D: Ft. Belknap, 7-54.

John Dolan. 22. B. Songford, Ire. E: Pittsburg, 4-52. (Laborer)—D: Ft. Riley, 2-57.

Thomas J. Eely. 25. B. Leitrim, Ire. E: Rochester, 8-50. (Clerk)—D: Ft. Belknap, 8-55.

James Ennis. 23. B. Kilcollan, Ire. E: Richmond, 7-50. (Laborer)—D: Ft. Belknap, 7-55.

Patrick Essip. 20. B. Longford, Ire. E: Boston, 9-50. (Shoemaker)—D: On furlough, Texas, 9-55.

Henry F. Evans. 29. B. Limerick, Ire. E: NY City, 1-52. (Clerk)—Deserted, Ft. Worth, September 28, 1852.

John Franklin. 21. B. Richmond, VA E: Richmond, 8-50. D: Ft. Belknap, 8-55.

Patrick Garvey. 26. B. Sligo, Ire. E: NY City, 8-48. (Laborer)—D: Ft. Worth, 8-53.

John G. Gross. 24. B. Carlisle, PA. E: Baltimore, 11-48. (Tailor)—D: Ft. Belknap, 11-53.

Jacob Haight. 21. B. Wuertemburg, Ger. E: NY City, 8-48. (Soldier)—D: Ft. Worth, 8-53.

William Halloran. 22. B. Coburg, Canada. E: Rochester, 12-50. (Teamster)—Deserted, Ft. Worth, January 1, 1853.

Henry Harding. 21. B. Waterford, Ire. E: NY City, 9-50. (Clerk)—D: On furlough, Texas, 9-55.

George James. E: Fredericksburg, TX, 9-49. D: Ft. Belknap, 7-54.

Edward Kelly. 25. B. Mayo County, Ire. E: Richmond, 8-50. (Laborer)—D: Ft. Belknap, 8-55.

James S. King. 31. B. Renfroshire, Scotland. E: NY City, 7-48. (Muleteer)—D: Ft. Worth, 7-53.

John Kinsley. 21. B. Philadelphia, PA. E: Philadelphia, 9-48. (Baker)—D: Ft. Worth, 9-53.

Martin Leary. E: Boston, 9-50. D: On furlough, Texas, 9-55.

Jeremiah Long. E: Austin, 7-52. Died at Ft. Worth, December 2, 1852.

Thomas Lynch. 22. B. Weymouth, Ire. E: NY City, 3-52. (Laborer)—Deserted, Ft. Worth, September 28, 1852.

William Masterman. 24. B. Yates, NY. E: Baltimore, 3-52. (Farmer)—Deserted, Fort Worth, December 9, 1852.

Charles McCormick. 22. B. Donegal, Ire. E: Philadelphia, 8-48. D: Ft. Worth, 8-53.

Patrick McGrath. 24. B. Wexford, Ire. E: Richmond, 7-50. (Laborer)—D: Ft. Belknap, 6-55.

John McNamara. 21. B. London, England. E: NY City, 2-52. (Laborer)—Deserted, Ft. Worth, December 9, 1852.

Adolph Meyer. E: Austin, 8-51. D: Ft. Riley, 8-56

Edward Miller. 21. B. Poughkeepsie, NY. E: NY City, 3-52. (Carpenter)—Deserted, Ft. Worth, December 9, 1852.

Peter Miltonburger. 21. B. Bern, Ger. E: Baltimore, 8-48. (Butcher)—D: Ft. Worth, 6-53. Re-enlisted; deserted, Ft. Graham, November 11, 1853.

James Moffitt. 28. B. Oswego, NY. E: NY City, 8-48. (Surgeon)—D: Ft. Worth, 8-53.

William Morehead. 23. B. N Y City. E: NY City, 7-50. (Pencil Case Maker)—D: Ft. Belknap, 7-55.

William Murphy. 21. B. Dublin, Ire. E: NY City, 3-52. (Coachmaker)—D: Ft. Riley, 2-57.

John O'Brien. 23. B. Limerick, Ire. E: E: NY City, 2-52. (Shoemaker)—D: Ft. Riley, 2-57.

Raleigh O'Kearney. B. Limerick, Ire. E: NY City, 5-48. (Physician)—D: Ft. Worth, 4-53.

Levi Patterson. E: Boston, 12-48. D Ft. Belknap, 12-53.
George Payne. 22. B. Stafford, VA. E: Fredericksburg, 7-50. (Laborer)—D: Ft. Belknap, 7-55.
William Page. 21. B. Edgecomb, NC. E: Richmond, 7-50. (Carpenter)—D: Ft. Belknap, 7-55.
Auguste Panck. 24. B. Anclarn, Prussia. E: Baltimore, 4-52. (Fur Cleaner)—Deserted near Ft. Croghan, February 2, 1854.
Louis Przyjemski. 33. B. Galicia, Austria. E: Baltimore, 3-52. (Soldier)—Transferred to Company F, December, 1852.
Charles W. Raynor. 21. B. Greenwich, CN. E: NY City, 8-49. (Carpenter)—D: Ft. Belknap, 8-54.
James Reilly. B. Kurmani, India. E: NY City, 2-52. (Tailor)—D: Ft. Riley, 2-57.
Francis Sheridan. E: Austin, 8-51. D: Ft. Riley, 8-56.
Adolph Smith. E: Austin, 8-51. D: Ft. Riley, 8-56.
Patrick Stokes. 24. B. Tipperary, Ire. E: NY City, 3-52. (Laborer)—D: Ft. Riley, 3-57.
Oliver P. Thomas. 24. B. Tipperary, Ire. E: Baltimore, 3-52. (Laborer)—D: Ft. Riley, 3-57.
Patrick Tracey. 27. B. Galway, Ire. E: Louisville, 7-48. (Laborer)—D: Ft. Worth, 6-53.
James W. Walsh. 26. B. Limerick, Ire. E: NY City, 3-52. (Laborer)—D: Ft. Riley, 3-57.

Transferred from Company F to Company B in December, 1852

John O'Day. 21. B. Limerick, Ire. E: Baltimore, 4-52. (Molder)—Deserted Near Ft. Worth, 7-54.

Recruits Who Joined Company B, 2nd Dragoons on April 30, 1853

Nelson Bemis. 21. B. Peekskill, NY. E: NY City, 11-52. (Farmer)—Transferred to Company K, Fort Leavenworth, 9-57.
Bugler Heinrich Brandt. 26. B. Erfurt, Ger. E: Baltimore, 12-52. (Bookbinder)—Transferred to Company D, Fort Leavenworth, 9-57.
Heinrich Braun. 22. B. Hesse-Kassel, Ger. E: NY City, 10-52. (Shoemaker)—Transferred to Company K, Ft. Leavenworth, 9-57.
Henry Bird. 27. B. Bavaria, Germany. E: Philadelphia, 12-52. (Baker)—Deserted, April 1855.
John Cairnes. 21. B. Dublin, Ire. E: NY City, 10-52. (Laborer)—Transferred to Company D, Ft. Leavenworth, 9-57.
James Carr. 29. B. Lincoln, England. E: NY City, 12-52. (Coachman)—Died at Ft. Riley, 6-57.
Ethan Dooley. 30. B. Newark, NJ. E: Baltimore, 10-52. (Shoemaker)—Transferred to Company D, Ft. Leavenworth, 9-57.
John G. Drenning. 24. B. Dublin, Ire. E: NY City, 4-52. (Clerk)—D: Ft. Riley, 3-57.

Byron C. M. Eagan. 24. B. Dublin, Ire. E: NY City, 1-53. (Clerk)—D: Utah Territory, 1-58.

Hugh Gallagher. 22. B. Donegal, Ire. E: Philadelphia, 12-52. (Shoemaker)—Transferred to Company D, 2nd U.S. Cavalry, 2-56. D: Camp Verde, Texas 10-57.

Gottlieb Gehl. 27. B. Baden, Ger. E: Philadelphia, 7-53. (Ropemaker)—Shot and killed by a Texan named Walker, Clear Fork of the Brazos River, August 28, 1854.

Moses Henrick. 22. B. Wexford, Ire. E: Baltimore, 11-52. (Laborer)—Deserted, Ft. Riley, 1-56.

Thomas Johnson. 23. B. Queens County, Long Island. E: NY City, 1-53. (Blacksmith)—D: Utah Territory, 1-58.

Joseph Kerin. 21. B. Claire, Ire. E: NY City, 1-53. (Laborer)—D: Utah Territory, 1-58.

Charles Kohler. 32. B. Berlin, Prussia. E: Philadelphia, 12-52. (Tailor)—D: Utah Territory, 12-57.

John Laird. 22. B. Glasgow, Scotland. E: Baltimore, 11-52. (Groom)—Deserted, Ft. Riley, October 3, 1855.

George Lee. 21. B. Steuben County, NY. E: NY City, 1-53. (Farmer)—D: Ft. Belknap, 6-54.

William Lewis. 21. B. Down, Ire. E: NY City, 12-52. (Laborer)—D: Ft. Laramie, 12-57.

John Montgomery. 22. B. Down, Ire. E: Philadelphia, 11-52. (Miner)—Transferred to regimental band, 7-54.

Wesley Markwood. 26. B. Washington, D.C. E: Baltimore, 11-52. (Soldier)—Transferred to Company A, 5-57.

Frank Pennelli. 25. B. Brugge, Belgium. E: NY City, 11-52. (Carpenter)—Deserted near Ft. Croghan, February 11, 1854.

Lee White. 26. B. Rutland, MA. E: Carlisle, 11-52. (Clerk)—Transferred to Company K, 9-57.

Other Members of Company B, 2nd Dragoons who served at Fort Worth

Peter Haas. 25. B. Holstein, Ger. E: NY City, 4-51. Arrived at Ft. Worth 7-53 or 8-53. (Clerk)—D: Ft. Belknap, 10-54.

Henry H. Jones. E: Ft. Worth, September 10, 1853, by Lt. Holliday. D: Ft. Belknap, 9-54.

Company F, 8th Infantry

Stationed at Fort Worth October 6, 1849 through April 6, 1851; and from June 1851 through January 1852.

Roll of Company F, 8th Infantry for October 1849

1st Sgt. Abraham Harris. 21. B. Montgomery, NY. E: Utica, New York, 1-47. (Cabinetmaker)—D: Ft. Worth, 1-52.

Sgt. Bartholomew Cole. 27. B. Roscannon, Ire. E: NY City, 6-45. (Farmer)—D: Ft. Worth, 6-50.

Sgt. Aaron W. Sprague. 24. B. NY City. E: New Orleans, 11-45. (Mechanic)—Died, San Antonio, Texas, April 9, 1850.

Cpl. Thomas Frisby. 19. B. England. E: Albany, 6-48. (Shoemaker)—D: Ft. McKavett, 3-53.

Cpl. Heronimas Kemmelin. 22. B. Baden, Ger. E: NY City, 5-47. (Blacksmith)—D: Ft. McKavett, 5-52.

Cpl. John McKinney. 21. B. Tyrone, Ire. E: NY City, 5-47. (Laborer)—D: Ft. McKavett, 5-52.

John McCann. 12. B. N Y City. E: NY City, 7-46. (Musician (Drummer))—D: Ft. Worth, 7-51.

Henry F. McCann. 14. B. N Y City. E: NY City, 7-46. (Musician (Fifer))—D: Ft. Worth, 7-51.

Daniel F. Banks. 26. B. Cherokee, GA. E: Philadelphia, 2-48. (Barber)—D: Ft. McKavett, 2-53.

John Barrett. 30. years of age on 1850 Census. B. Ire. E: Poughkeepsie, 7-48. D: Ft. McKavett, 7-53.

John Biggins. 22. B. Edinburgh, Scotland. E: NY City, 4-49. (Farmer)—Deserted, November 7, 1850.

Edward F. Brenner. 30. B. Lancaster, PA. E: Camp Chadbourne, 4-49. (Soldier)—D: Ringgold Barracks, 2-54.

Dennis Coffey. 24 years of age on 1850 Census. B. Ire. E: NY City, 4-49. D: Ringgold Barracks, 2-54.

Timothy Daley. 30. B. Waterford, Ire. E: Boston, 7-49. (Laborer)—D: San Antonio Wells, 7-54.

Frederick Deigleman. 23 years of age on 1850 Census. B. Ger. E: Newport, 7-48. D: Ft. McKavett, 9-53.

Michael Finlan. 22. B. Carlow, Ire E: Buffalo, 3-49. (Laborer)—Deserted, Ft. Worth, January 11, 1851.

Patrick Fitzsimmons. 22. B. Armagh, Ire. E: NY City, 6-49. (Soldier)—Died at Ft. McKavett, January, 1853.

John Ford. 27. B. Mayo, Ire. E: Rochester, 7-49. (Laborer)—D: San Antonio Wells, 7-54.

Thomas Hayden. 31 years of age on 1850 Census. B. Ire. E: St. Louis, 7-48. D: Ft. McKavett, 7-53.

James Higgins. 24 years of age in 1850 Census. B. CT. E: Newport, 8-48. D: Ft. McKavett, 6-53.

John Koch. 28. B. Rassbach, Ger. E: NY City, 5-47. (Soldier)—Died at Ft. Worth, December 28, 1851.

Joseph Langford. 30. B. Kings County, Ire. E: NY City, 3-49. (Wool-comber)—D: Ft. Worth, 5-51.

Anthony Lydon. 31. B. Ire. E: Syracuse, 7-49. (Laborer)—D: San Antonio Wells, 7-54.

James Mason. 22. B. Dublin, Ire. E: Philadelphia, 7-47. (Clerk)—D: San Antonio Wells, Texas 7-54.

Patrick Mahony. 31. B. Waterford, Ire. E: Buffalo, 6-49. (Tailor)—Died, Ft. Martin Scott, July 5, 1852.

Charles McGlenn. 25. B. Ire. E: Wilmington, 3-48. (Laborer)—D: Ft. McKavett, 3-53.

Michael McKennan. 21. B. Tyrone, Ire. E: Harrisburg, 7-49. (Laborer)—Deserted at Corsicana, July 15, 1851.

John Meyer. 36 years of age in 1850 Census. B. Ger. E: Baltimore, 6-48. D: Ft. McKavett, 6-53.

Morris Newman. 22. B. St. Louis, MO. E: Philadelphia, 7-49. (Chairmaker)—D: San Antonio Wells, 7-54.

John O'Brien. 22. B. Cork, Ire. E: Boston, 7-49. (Laborer)—Deserted, Ft. Worth, January 11, 1851.

Patrick O'Callaghan. 21. B. Cork, Ire. E: NY City, 6-49. (Bricklayer)—D: San Antonio Wells, 7-54.

John O'Keefe. 34. B. Cork, Ire. E: Boston, 6-46. (Laborer)—D: Ft. Worth, 1-51.

Joseph Pierpont. 31. B. Catonville, MA. E: Baltimore, 11-48. (Laborer)—Died, Ft. Croghan, March 2, 1851.

James Ryan. 30 years of age on 1850 Census. B. Ire. E: Newport, 8-48. Died at Fort Worth, November 28, 1851.

John Samson. 29 years of age on 1850 Census. B. NY. E: Newport, 10-48. Deserted, Ft. Worth, January 1, 1852.

Frederick Schroder. 40 years of age on 1850 Census. B. Ger. E: Newport, 10-48. D: Ft. McKavett, 8-53.

John Tucker. 19. B. OH. E: Springfield, 3-48. (Laborer)—D: Ft. McKavett, 3-53.

Frederick Young. 28 years of age on 1850 Census. B. Ger. E: Dayton, 8-48. D: Ft. McKavett, 8-53.

Recruits who joined Company F, 8th Infantry in March or April, 1850

Peter Riley. 22. B. Cavan, Ire. E: NY City, 10-49. (Farmer)—Died at Fort Worth, November 29, 1851.

William McConnel. Died at Ft. Worth, December 31, 1851.

Charles W. Child. 18. B. Preston, NY. E: Harrisburg, 9-49. (Farmer)—Deserted, Ft. Worth, January 1, 1852.

James Willett. 19. B. Baltimore, MA. E: NY City, 10-49. (Farmer)

Charles Lohmire. 26 years of age on 1850 Census. B. Ger. E: Syracuse, 10-49. D: Comanche Springs, TX 10-54.

Recruits Who Joined Company F, 8th Infantry on November 18, 1850

John Alcorn. 27. B. Donegal, Ire. E: Burlington, 8-50. (Laborer)—Died at Ft. Croghan, February 19, 1852.

John J. Bond. 28. B. Madison, OH. E: Providence, 8-50. (Stone-cutter)—D: Ft. Worth, 5-51.

John Canton. 28. B. Cork, Ire. E: Boston, 9-50. (Tailor)—D: Ft. Davis, 9-55.

Michael Colter. 23. B. Louth, Ire. E: Poughkeepsie, 8-50. D: Ft. McKavett, 3-53.

Michael Hagerty. 22. B. Clare, Ire. E: Albany, 9-50. (Laborer)—Deserted, Ft. Worth, December 20, 1851.

Peter Garey. 21. B. Tyrone, Ire. E: Buffalo, 12-50. (Laborer)—Deserted, Ft. Worth, August 25, 1851.

Michael Kane. 25. B. Sligo, Ire. E: Buffalo, 7-50. (Farmer)—D: Ft. Worth, 6-51.

Charles Keegan. 22. B. Queens, Ire. E: NY City, 9-50. (Tailor)—D: Ft. Davis, 9-55.

Richard Maloney. 18. B. Athlone, Ire. E: NY City, 12-49. (Carpenter)—D: Ft. Davis, 12-54.

William Morris. E: Boston, 9-50. Died, Ft. McKavett, 7-53.

Patrick McAteer. 21. B. Ire. E: Poughkeepsie, 8-50. (Laborer)—D: Ft. Davis, 8-55.

William McKee. 30. B. Dublin, Ire. E: Boston, 8-50. (Shoemaker)—Died, Ft. Worth, July 24, 1851.

Patrick Roach. 21. B. Wexford, Ire. E: Buffalo, 8-50. (Farmer)—D: Ft. McKavett, 1-53.

James Smith. 22. B. N Y City. E: NY City, 9-50. (Soldier)—D: Ft. Worth, 1-53.

Recruits Who Joined Company F, 8th Infantry on March 4, 1851

Sil Brine. 28. B. Wexford, Ire. E: Newport, 10-50. (Laborer)—D: Ft. Davis, 10-55.

Patrick Dolan. 29. B. Roscannon, Ire. E: Newport, 11-50. (Laborer)—Died, Ft. Worth, November 28, 1851.

Augustus M. Hawkins. 26. B. Genessee County, NY. E: Louisville, 1-50. (Clerk)—Deserted, Laredo, September 1854.

Michael Kelly. 34. B. Carlow, Ire. E: Newport, 10-50. (Laborer)—D: Ft. Davis, 10-55.

William Robinson. 26. B. Union County, PA. E: Newport, 9-50. (Laborer)—Deserted, Ft. Gates, May 1851.

George B. Taylor. 21. B. Pike County, NY. E: Newport, 7-50. (Laborer)

Christian Weaver. 21. B. Minden, Ger. E: Philadelphia, 1-51. (Shoemaker)—Died at Ft. McKavett, March 31, 1851.

Recruits Who Joined Company F, 8th Infantry on April 12, 1851

John Blake. 27. B. Clare, Ire. E: NY City, 1-51. (Farmer)—Deserted, Ft. Worth, December 20, 1851.

Michael Crehan. 22. B. Claire, Ire. E: Buffalo, 1-51. (Laborer)—Died at Ft. Worth, October 25, 1851.

Daniel Fitzpatrick. 21. B. Castleton, Ire. E: Whitehall, NY 12-50. (Laborer)—D: Ft. Davis, 12-55.

George Ingersoll. 21. B. Newton Falls, OH. E: Whitehall, NY 12-50. (Potter)—D: Ft. Davis, 12-55.

John A. Judd. 21. B. Waterbury, CT. E: Syracuse, 12-50. (Laborer)—D: Ft. Davis, 11-55.

Dennis McCarthy. 28. B. Cork, Ire. E: Burlington, 9-50. (Wool Comber)—Deserted, Preston, TX December 5, 1851.

John McInnis. B. Grand River, Prince Edward's Island. E: Boston, 12-50. (Clerk)—D: Ft. Davis, 4-56.

John O'Connor. 23. B. Limerick, Ire. E: NY City, 1-51. (Farmer)—Deserted on furlough, September, 1853.

William Sanders. 21. B. Manchester, England. E: Syracuse, 12-50. (Laborer)—D: Ft. McKavett, 1-53.

John Sullivan. 21. B. Cork, Ire. E: Buffalo, 12-50. (Laborer)—D: Ft. Davis, 12-55.

Andrew P. Sweegles. 22. B. Varick, NY. E: Buffalo, 10-50. (Machinist)—Deserted, Camp Salado, May 2, 1852.

The following men are listed on the roll of Company F, 8th Infantry for January 1852. They may have been new recruits, or recent transfers to the company.

Francis Carver. 34. B. Bavaria, Ger. (Farmer)—D: Ft. McKavett, 3-54.

Peter Cahill. 21. B. Galway, Ire. E: Albany, 12-50. (Laborer)—Died, San Antonio, May 1, 1852.

John V. Palmer. Died, Ft. McKavett, December 2, 1852.

Company H, 8th Infantry

Stationed at Fort Worth June 17, 1851 through January 11, 1852.

Roll of Company H, 8th Infantry for June 1851

1st Sgt. Frederick Greene. E: NY City, 11-49. D: Ft. Davis, 11-54.

Sgt. Christopher McCormick. 35. B. Kildare, Ire. E: NY City, 5-47. (Soldier)—D: Ft. McKavett, 5-52.

Cpl. John Kelly. 31. B. Dunghill, Ire. E: Philadelphia, 7-49. (Seaman)

Cpl. Dewitt McDaniels. 18. B. Newburg, NY. (Farmer)

John Gormley. 15. B. Liverpool, England. E: NY City, 11-48. (Painter)—Deserted, Ft. Worth, 11-51.

Franklin Benedict. 23. B. Berks, Tennessee. E: Harrisburg, 10-48. (Shoemaker)—D: Camp on the Limpia, 10-53.

Christopher Bensinger. 21. B. Wurtemburg, Ger. E: NY City, 1-51. D: Ft. Davis, 1-56.

Thomas H. Bentick. 21. B. Kings County, Ire. E: Pittsburgh, 10-50. (Bricklayer)—D: Ft. McKavett, 1-53.

Michael Bergman. 23. B. Baiern, Ger. E: Philadelphia, 12-50 (Weaver).

Patrick Breen. 21. B. Kenny, Ire. E: NY City, 7-49. (Sailor)—D: Camp Worth, 7-54.

Henry W. Clarke. 23. B. Lorraine, NY. E: Syracuse, 12-50. (Laborer)—D: Ft. Bliss, 12-55.

Michael Cloran. 21. B. Galway, Ire. E: NY City, 8-50. (Baker)—D: Ft. Davis, 8-55.

Samuel Condell. 21. B. Carlow, Ire. E: NY City, 6-49. (Farmer)—D: Camp Worth, 5-54.

Alexander Dubey. 19. B. Quebec, Canada. E: Brooklyn, 11-46. (Clerk)—D: Ft. Worth, 11-51.

Michael Duffy. E: Philadelphia, 10-49. D: Camp on the Limpia, 10-54.

Peter Duffy. 26. B. Donegal, Ire. E: Boston, 9-50. (Laborer)—Deserted, Ft. Worth, July 21, 1851.

Patrick Duffy. 22. B. Monaghan, Ire. E: Providence, 11-51. (Laborer)—Deserted, Ft. Worth, July 31, 1951.

Gordon Dugan. 29. B. Tipperary, Ire. E: Boston, 7-49. (Plasterer)—D: Camp Worth, 7-54.

Thomas Dwyer. 25. B. Tipperary, Ire. E: Boston, 3-49. (Blacksmith)

Charles Faybiszewski. 23. B. Warsaw, Poland. E: Philadelphia, 1-51. (Farmer)—D: Ft. Davis, 1-56.

Stephen Fry. 26. B. Aachen, Ger. E: Philadelphia, 8-50. (Gunsmith)—Deserted, Ft. McKavett, March 29, 1852.

James Finnerty. 19. B. Sligo, Ire. E: St. Louis, 11-47. (Music Student)—D: Ft. McKavett, 11-52.

William Firth. E: St. Louis, 7-48. D: Ft. McKavett, 7-53.

John Fitzgerald. 21. B. Kenny, Ire. E: Buffalo, 12-50. (Laborer)—D: Ft. McKavett, 12-55.

Frederick Fresenius. 24. B. Koln, Prussia. E: Newport, Kentucky, 11-50. (Laborer)—D: Ft. Davis, 11-55.

William Fuller. 21. B. Worcester, VA. E: Providence, 7-50. (Farmer)—D: Ft. Davis, 7-55.

Thomas Griffin. 30. B. Kilkenny, Ire. E: Burlington, 12-50. (Laborer)—Discharged by court-martial, Ft. McKavett, December 1853.

Thomas Halliman. E: Camp Worth, 5-49.

Michael Hartnett. 22. B. Cork, Ire. E: Boston, 8-50. (Laborer)—D: Ft. Davis, 8-55.

Francis I. Heath. 21. B. Petersburg, VA. E: Richmond, 8-46. (Gardener)—D: Ft. Worth, 8-51.

William Henry. 27. B. Southampton, VA. E: Norfolk, 2-49. D: San Antonio, 2-54.

Morris Hefferman. 24. B. Kenny, Ire. E: NY City, 4-49. (Laborer)

Michael Higgins. 28. B. Cork, Ire. E: Providence, 12-51. (Laborer)—D: Ft. Worth, 9-51.

George B. Irwin. 26. B. Derry, Ire. E: Buffalo, 8-50. (Clerk)—D: Ft. Davis, 8-55.

James Johnson. E: Newport, 8-48. D: Ft. McKavett, 7-53.

Martin Johnson. 22. B. Denmark. E: Albany, 7-49. (Laborer)—D: Camp Worth, 7-54.

William Johnson. 25. B. Quebec, Canada. E: Newport, 8-49. (Painter)—D: Camp Worth, 8-54.

Denis Kaloher. E: NY City, 10-49. D: Camp on the Limpia, 10-54.

Charles C. Kane. 21. B. Ellinsburg, NY. E: Whitehall, 12-50. (Laborer)—D: Ft. Davis, 12-55.

Charles Kaneen. 23. B. Isle of Man. E: Newport, 10-54. (Tailor)—D: Ft. Davis, 9-55.

James Lawler. 22. B. Queens, Ire. E: NY City, 9-46. (Laborer)—D: Ft. Worth, 9-51.

John Levice. 22. B. Geneva, Switzerland. E: NY City, 1-49. (Clerk)—D: Ft. McKavett, 1-54.

Thomas Lilcrap. E: Boston, 11-49. Died, Ft. Croghan, March 16, 1852.

Westley Lucas. 28. B. Shenandoah, VA. E: Newport, 9-50. D: Ft. Davis, 7-55.

Edward Lutes. 28. B. Pottssville, PA. E: Harrisburg, 8-50. (Laborer)—D: Ft. Davis, 8-55.

Sylvester Mangan. 26. B. Kings, Ire. E: Poughkeepsie, 10-50. (Laborer)—Deserted, Ft. McKavett, July 7, 1853.

Patrick McBride. 19. B. Letrim, Ire. E: NY City, 10-49. (Laborer)—D: Camp on Comanche Creek, Texas, 10-54.

William H. McDaniels. 19. E: Newburg, 8-46. (Farmer)—D: Ft. Worth, 11-51.

Henry McGladdery. E: NY City, 11-49. D: Ft. Davis, 11-54.

John Marks. 21. B. Galway, Ire. E: NY City, 3-49. (Servant)

Alexander Menoir. 21. B. Montreal, Canada. E: Buffalo, 8-50. (Laborer)—D: Ft. Davis, 8-55.

Henry Menser. 18. B. Huntington, PA. E: Columbia, 5-48. (Laborer)—D: Ft. McKavett, 5-53.

John Murray. 25. B. Kildare, Ire. E: Poughkeepsie, 8-50. (Laborer)—Died, Ft. Croghan, January 1852.

Edward Nugent. 27. B. Tipperary, Ire. E: Providence, 8-50. (Farmer)—Died, Fort Croghan, February 1852.

Peter Paulus. 25. B. Prussia, Ger. E: Albany, 8-50. (Farmer)—D: Ft. Davis, 8-55.

William Rogers. 20. B. Fermanagh, Ire. E: NY City, 11-49. (Farmer)—D: Ft. Davis, 11-54.

Michael Ryan. 21. B. Limerick, Ire. E: Albany, 7-49. (Laborer)—D: Camp Worth, 5-54.

Thomas Scott. 29. B. Dumfries, Scotland. E: Buffalo, 9-50. (Farmer)—Died at Ft. Worth, December 14, 1851.

James Sheedy. 23. B. Limerick, Ire. E: E: NY City, 11-49. (Laborer)—D: Ft. Davis, 11-54.

John Simmons. E: Newport, 11-46. D: Ft. Worth, 12-51.

James Tully. 19. B. Cavan, Ire. E: NY City, 11-49. (Farmer)—D: Ft. Davis, 11-54.

James Trumble. 30. B. Sligo, Ire. E: NY City, 11-49. (Soldier)—D: Ft. Davis, 12-54.

William Walker. 21. B. Letrim, Ire. E: NY City, 1-51. (Farmer)—Deserted, Ft. Worth, November 30, 1851.

John Williams. 27. B. Wales, England. E: NY City, 1-51. (Slater)—D: Ft. Davis, 1-56.

Daniel P. Williams. 30. B. Monmouthshire, Wales. E: Philadelphia, 12-50. (Engineer)—D: Ft. Davis, 3-55.

James G. Wright. 21. B. Paisley, Scotland. E: Whitehall, 12-50. (Farmer)—D: Ft. McKavett, 6-53.

The following men were carried on company rolls at various times, but evidently did not serve at Fort Worth.

Joseph Noland and Charles Fuchs of Company F, 2nd Dragoons. John Munstermann of Company B, 2nd Dragoons. Charles Boland, James Wilson, Alexander Hunter, William Johnston, and James Dickinson of Company F, 8th Infantry. Edward S. Jones and Jacob Stickle of Company H, 8th Infantry. Privates William Dilcher of Company F, 2nd Dragoons, and Herman Meyer of Company F, 8th Infantry both appear on the 1850 census, whereas muster rolls suggest that the men were not actually at the post. I believe that Dilcher and Meyer probably never served at Fort Worth.

Appendix

2–1 Juana Bernard's Recollection of her Capture by Comanches

"I was born in Mexico and raised there until I was 18 years old. I went to visit a friend across the Rio Grande River and stayed several days. I got uneasy and told the woman that I felt like something was going to happen and I wanted to go home, but I didn't get off. So on Thursday, August 15th, at 11 o'clock in the year 1844, the Indians surrounded the house before we knew it."

"There were six of us women at the house, two were washing, the rest were cooking dinner. One woman was combing her hair. They cut her hair off and left her. I ran for my life and hid in some weeds. Another girl was captured. She saw me and told them where I was. So, they took me. Another girl ran out into a pond of water and they went after her. They killed the husband of the woman whose hair they cut off. He was in the woods burning coal. They started with us, and went about five miles down the river, where they made a raid on a house. There they took a little girl, six years old. Her mother had a baby in her arms about one year old. They gave it a sling and threw it in the river. Oh, they were such mean things! Then they tied the mother to a horse's tail and dragged her some little piece, then sent her back home. They tore up everything in the house they could not take with them. They traveled on four days. On Sunday, August 19th in the morning, they came to where a boy about 14 years old and a man were herding sheep. They scalped the boy. He bled to death. Then they stabbed the man. They left him for dead and went to a nearby creek to water the ponies. When they came back by the man, he was gone. They followed him and found him about half a mile from where they first attempted to kill him. He was dying when they found him, but they stabbed him several more times. Then they started on the trail from the Rio Grande into Texas."

"That evening about six o'clock they killed one of the girls they had taken with me. They killed her with the same knife that they killed the man with. She begged dearly for her life but it did no good. They stabbed her in the breast and after they killed her they got clubs and beat her like beating a cow. The old chief came up to me with the knife and asked me if I wanted him to kill me. I told him yes, I wanted to die and he made like he was going to kill me, but I never moved, for I sure did want to die, and I wanted to die with her so when my folks came to hunt for us they would find us together. But he never hit me with the knife. Then he put his hand to my heart to see if I was scared, but I was not. Then he said, 'Brave, brave, you go with us.' So we started from there and met another man herding sheep. I did not see them kill him, but I know they did for they had his clothes and mule. They took knives and just stabbed the sheep and left them. Then they said they were not going to kill me. They said they were going to take me to San Antonio and trade me off for bread and sugar, but they didn't . . . They took me then to the old trading house ten miles sold me to George Barnard for $300.00 in horses and merchandise. His brother Charles E. Barnard came from the north and we married . . ." [1]

#2–2 Cholera and Bvt. Maj. Gen. William Jenkins Worth's Death and Burial

Cholera is an intestinal disorder, caused by the microbe *Vibrio cholerae*, and usually spread by contaminated food or water. The illness causes a sudden onset of vomiting, cramps, and a profuse, watery diarrhea. Without treatment about half of all patients die primarily as a result of dehydration. Survivors usually do well after recovery.[2] Texas and the rest of the United States experienced an epidemic of cholera in 1849. The disease originated in Asia, spread to Europe, and reached New York and New Orleans in December 1848. Travelers bound for the gold fields of California brought the epidemic to San Antonio in April 1849.[3] Between 400 and 700 people died there by the first week of June.[4] Lieutenant Samuel Starr, encamped outside San Antonio in late April, wrote to his wife that 30 had died in a single day.[5]

Another epidemic struck in 1866. Improved sanitation helped prevent epidemics in subsequent decades. No cases of cholera were reported in the U.S. between 1911 and 1973. In that year, a case was reported in, of all places, Port Lavaca, Texas. Medical investigators could not discover the source of the infection.[6]

Brevet Major General William J. Worth was working in his headquarters on the evening of May 6, 1849. He wrote a report to Washington concerning supplies for the 3rd Infantry Regiment, which was preparing to march from San Antonio to El Paso. Worth noted that "the cholera, which had heretofore not been seen in the camps of the 3rd Infantry, has recently appeared in that regiment."[7]

Before he could finish the letter, he experienced the severe diarrhea that characterizes cholera. Dr. J. J. B. Wright, an army surgeon, treated him with the standard remedies of the day. Wright gave his patients calomel, a toxic preparation of mercury, meant to induce vomiting. He also ordered them not to drink any water or other liquids. Wright confessed that none of his treatments were of any use whatever, but he felt obligated to try something. Worth died the next day at one o'clock in the afternoon, and was buried in San Antonio.[8] What Surgeon Wright and most other doctors of the day did in treating Gen. Worth and others was about the worst thing they could have done. Calomel is poisonous and increases dehydration. Wright stumbled across a more reasonable treatment for cholera during the epidemic. A young German fell ill with the disease, and asked Wright to come see him. Wright could not find time to see the German. Dehydrated and desperately thirsty, the patient found and drank a pail of buttermilk. Wright was amazed to learn that, instead of killing the patient, the fluids seemed to help: "From that moment he began to improve; the sickness of stomach subsided; the diarrhea ceased; the cramps . . .

left him, and in his own language he 'got well right off.'" Wright described the case in a medical journal, and suggested that the treatment might prove useful in other cases, but no one seems to have acted on his suggestion.[9] Today, physicians treat cholera by having the patient drink large amounts of water with sugar and electrolytes added. Nearly everyone recovers.[10]

General Worth's remains were moved to New York City in 1850. In 1857, they were interred there in Madison Square, in one of the most lavish state funerals the nation had seen. Today, Worth's grave is marked by an obelisk in the center of Broadway, opposite the Flatiron Building.[11]

#2–3 Dragoons and Drinking

Officers of the 2nd Dragoons had a reputation for heavy drinking and carousing. Lieutenant Saunders drank excessively and, by 1849, was an incorrigible alcoholic, and constantly in trouble with his superior officers. Saunders was a good friend of Assistant Surgeon Josephus M. Steiner, the army doctor at Camp Inge. Steiner and Saunders passed the time by making up comic songs. One of Steiner's songs poked fun at Saunders's red nose, which had resulted from years of heavy drinking.[12] Lieutenant Saunders's drinking probably got him into trouble again at Camp Inge, for on January 29, 1849, he was arrested and charged with dereliction of duty.

When an officer was under arrest, he was relieved of duty, but was usually granted permission to come and go as he pleased. Saunders's drunkenness also bothered Bvt. Brig. Gen. Harney, and he spent much of 1849 trying to force Saunders out of the army.[13]

There seems to be no surviving record of Capt. Arnold's charges against Lt. Saunders;

Harney mentioned the case some months later. At the time of Harney's writing, both Arnold and Saunders had been promoted.

Harney wrote that the situation:

> "...involved charges of so serious a nature that little doubt was entertained before the meeting of the court that Captain Saunders would at least be dismissed from the service, if no more harsh and degrading sentence should be pronounced against him. Unfortunately for the honor of the public service, Maj. Arnold had drawn the charges so loosely that, although every member of the court was morally certain of the guilt of the accused, and of his unworthiness, generally, to hold a commission, it soon became evident that no adequate punishment could be prescribed for his deficiencies."[14]

Arnold's charges against Saunders were dismissed, and Saunders was eventually returned to duty. While both men were at the court-martial, however, Company F would be left with no commander, so Lt. Samuel Starr was ordered to take charge of Company F until Arnold returned.[15]

#5–1 Excerpts from Lt. Viele's Report on Indian Incidents on the Rio Grande in 1849

"On the 21st of July, a flat-boat belonging at this post, which had been sent up the river about twenty miles in charge of some laborers (Mexicans) to procure grass, was cut loose by the Indians while the men were at work on land, the former then concealing themselves for the purpose of a surprise; but being discovered, the Mexicans made a circuit and reached the river at a point where the boat fortunately grounded. They succeeded in getting into it, and reaching the opposite bank before the Indians could get near enough to effect anything, although they were constantly shooting arrows. On the receipt of this information, I sent every man in camp, except a guard of three, to pursue the Indians. This party, which, including soldiers, teamsters, and laborers, amounted to but fourteen, was placed in charge of Lieutenant Johns, who followed the trail of the Indians until it crossed the river into Mexico a few miles above the point at which they attacked the boat. They had crossed the night before, and during the following day attacked a train of pack-mules, killed and scalped one man, and drove off all the animals. The mules were owned in this town."

"On the 12th of this month August 1849 a large party of Indians was seen at the San Juanita, about 20 miles from this place on the Corpus Christi road; and having a large number of horses and mules, it was supposed they were going into the interior: on the contrary, they went down the river, and were pursued by a party of Mexicans whose animals gave out. I was unable to pursue them, as the number of sick and discharges had reduced my command to nine men. I sent, however, an express to the commanding officer at Camp Ringgold; but they traveled so fast as to reach the town of Roma, 17 miles on this side of that post, before the express. On their route they are reported to have taken three children from a rancho opposite Guerrero, to have outraged the persons of three women at a rancho opposite Mier, and to have shot a woman in the town of Roma . . .[16]

#5–2 Quotes from Letter on Citizen Expectations on Setting up a Supply Depot at Buffalo

"The Trinity River is bank-full, as it has been since last November. A boat is expected to land here with Government supplies, for Forts Graham and Worth: the first, you know, is located at the Jose Maria (Anadarko) Village, on the east bank of the Brazos about twenty-six miles below the Comanche Peak, and garrisoned by Company I, 2nd Dragoons, under command of Lieut. Hamilton. The last named post is situated on the west bank of the Clear Fork, where that beautiful stream forms a junction with the west fork of the Trinity. Its gentlemanly commander, Brevet Maj. Arnold, (commanding Company F, 2d Dragoons,) named the post after a man whom old Texans delighted to honor—viz: Major Gen. Worth."

"Our town is honored by the presence of Lieut. Washington P. Street, 8th Infantry, Act. Ass't. Quat'r. Master, who is expecting the arrival of supplies for the use of the several military posts between the Trinity and the Brazos. From him we learn that two companies 8th Infantry under command of Lieut. Col.

Bomford, are en route from San Antonio, and will be stationed in this vicinity. Doctor Steiner, Assistant Surgeon, 2nd Dragoons, accompanied Lieut. Street, and reports favorably of the health of the troops at the above named posts."[17]

#5–3 General Brooke's Rationale for Closing the Buffalo Depot

"In looking on this line from Eagle Pass to the West Fork of the Trinity, each post should have a garrison strong enough to make reconnaissances, and also to pursue any Indian force which may appear to have crossed the border with a view to its capture and punishment, and, at the same time, leave at the post a party strong enough with temporary defenses (until the work is regularly established) to preserve it under any emergency. For this reason, I propose that there should be at all those posts one company of dragoons and one of infantry, where there is now only one company of dragoons, as is now the case at Hamilton Creek Fort Croghan, Fort Graham, and the West Fork of the Trinity . . . "

"There are, under the present disposition of the troops, five companies of the 8th Infantry, entirely out of the line of offence or defense—three at Austin and two at Buffalo. This is too large a part of our weak force to be inactive . . . I am of the opinion that two of the companies at Austin should be ordered to Fredericksburg, and the other to Hamilton Creek—the two companies at Buffalo, one to Fort Graham, and the other to the West Fork of the Trinity. To equalize, and in justice to each corps, I propose to post the officers in such manner as to give them a share in command. For instance, I would send one of the Infantry companies to the West Fork of the Trinity, whose commanding officer would be junior to Captain Arnold. Bvt. Lt. Col. Bomford would go to Fort Graham. At Hamilton Creek a dragoon officer should be the senior, sending one of the infantry companies from Austin, and so on, alternately throughout the chain of forts."[18]

#6–1 Tents of the Time Period

Enlisted men such as Sgt.Harris slept in wedge-shaped "common tents." The common tent was tall enough to stand in, and was about seven feet square. The common tent was seven feet high, six and one half feet deep, and seven and one half feet wide. It used fourteen pins and, with pins and poles, weighed forty-two lpounds.[19] If necessary, as many as six men might share a single common tent.[20]

Officers usually had a wall tent. The wall tent was slightly taller than the common tent, and had a base about ten by twelve feet. Most garrisons also had a hospital tent, which was something like 18 by 24 feet. Quartermaster Department records show that on July 20, 1852, Major Arnold signed for 5 common tents, 1 wall tent, and 1 wall tent fly. On June 20, 1852, the following items were on hand at Fort Worth: 6 common tents with poles; 1 camp kettle; 2 sets of wall tent poles; and 17 knapsacks. On August 27, 1852, as new AAQM of Ft. Graham, Arnold signed for a hospital tent with fly and poles, as well as common and wall tents.[21]

#9–1 Report of Bvt. Capt. William Steele, Leader of the Patrol from Fort Martin Scott (1849)

"I have the honor to report that on the 2nd instant January agreeably to instructions, I proceeded in the direction of the Bandera Pass to look out for the Indians who had been committing depredations in the vicinity of Castroville. I found no tracks in the pass, made since the scout from Seco Fort Lincoln had passed through it in two months previously, proceeding from thence down to the Medina."

"I met Brevet Captain Oaks who had taken the trail from the place where the murders had been committed, but had lost it among the Mustang trails, we then proceeded up the Medina in company and found the trail, followed it up one of the heads of that river, across the heads of the Guadalupe and to a tributary of the Liano where we arrived on the 9th instant. The Indians that far having selected the worst possible country to travel through——taking neither trails nor passes. At the point above mentioned it was necessary to leave the trail and come in to this post Fort Martin Scott to reorganize—- more than half of our horses having lost shoes and became lame and unfit for travel, and our rations exhausted. The trail being seven days old when I left it and my guide (John Connor) telling me that it would be impossible to follow it when it became ten days old."

"I determined to endeavor to strike it at a more advanced point, the guides having decided that the Indians we were following were Wecos and that they would cross the Colorado at a point between Pecan Bayou and the Concho. Leaving this post on the 12th, I went as rapidly as possible to the Colorado striking it a little above the mouth of the Pecan Bayou, thence up that stream examining it carefully but without discovering the trail. The whole country having been burned within two or three days previous, destroying all traces of the small party we were in pursuit of deeming further search useless inasmuch as the trail could not be followed in that condition of the country, if found, I returned by the way of the old Spanish Fort on the San Saba, arriving at this point [Fort Martin Scott] today. My greatest difficulty on the march was to obtain sufficient grass for my horses, the whole face of the country having been burned clear except small spots on the water courses."

"On my return I was informed by a Delaware boy, that he had been informed by some Cadoes, that a party of about twenty Wecos had gone down towards the settlements, in the direction of San Marcos and New Braunfels."[22]

#9–2 Report of Capt. George Blake's Scout in the North

"There I met the principal men of the adjacent villages, comprising deputation's from the Wacos, Keechis, and perhaps Ioins. They professed to have the most amicable dispositions towards the whites, and reprobated the practice of stealing. They acknowledged that some of their young men had been engaged in committing depredations, but reported their inability to prevent the commission of such acts. This was particularly the case with Aquagosh, the chief of the Wacos. He confessed, at the first opportunity, that there was some stolen property at his village, and that he would give it up immediately. One horse was all that was delivered up . . . Notwithstanding the protestations of innocence on the part of the principal men at these villages, I am by no means satisfied of their guiltlessness. If they are not generally active perpetrators in the deeds of plunder, &c, they are raiders and abettors by harboring stolen property, or trafficking for it after it is stolen . . . Their villages are a concentrating and resting depot for the marauders, after they have gone beyond the reach of chastisement or recapture . . ."

"The horses of the entire command returned much jaded and broken down not more, however, than would be expected from a long march (over a rough country), made on grass, immediately after being taken from corn. The condition of my own company horses, as well as those equipped with the same saddle, is to be attributed to the deplorable horse-appointments which are furnished us: most of their backs are sore, and it will require at least six weeks to place them in serviceable condition again."

"I would add here that I have learned from Major Merrill that he passed on the trail, during the first day of his pursuit, the carcasses of a horse and mule -—the horse probably broken down, and the mule killed for food . . ."

"I arrived at this post on the 22nd instant, after an absence of twenty—eight days, having marched upwards of five hundred and fifty miles."[23]

#19–1 Lieutenant Samuel Starr is Court-Martialed Again

In the late summer of 1853, Lt. Samuel Starr was serving at Fort Mason, as the first lieutenant of Company A, 2nd Dragoons. Eliza remained in New York with their three children, Kate, Anne, and Jo. Starr's cantankerous personality got him into trouble with his commander, Bv.t Col. Charles May. This time, Starr's punishment was fairly severe.

On July 17, 1853, Lt. Starr was drilling Company A on the parade ground at Fort Mason. As the company rode forward in a column of fours, Starr ordered the column to turn right. Private James Hennessey started to turn left. Starr corrected Hennessey with a "tap" of his saber. The "tap" cut through Henessey's coat, inflicted a slight wound, and put him in the hospital. Colonel May reluctantly put Starr under arrest, until the incident could be investigated and reported.[24]

The incident probably would have come to nothing, except that Starr became convinced that May was treating him unjustly. Starr apparently had disliked May for some time. May offered to extend the limits of Starr's arrest, so that Starr could leave his quarters. To grant the extension, May would need a written request from Starr.[25]

When May told Starr that he should ask for an extension of limits, he unwittingly touched a raw nerve. Starr disliked asking a favor of anyone. He had once written to Eliza that he would rather have his right arm sawn off than ask a friend or relative for a job: "This is a feeling I cannot overcome . . . It was born with me." Instead of requesting an extension of his limits, Starr sent May the following note: "Sir, I have the honor to request that I may be furnished with a tub for the necessary purposes of nature."[26]

We have no record of May's reaction, except that he pressed charges against Starr for disrespect. When Starr's court-martial convened, Starr made matters worse for himself by mocking and denouncing May from the stand. He declared that his real offense had been that he "habitually declined to sacrifice my dignity on the self-erected altar of May's vanity." Starr also wondered why May should find a request for a tub to be insulting:

> Might the inference be drawn that some unpleasing reminiscence was recalled to the mind of my accuser by the mention of this useful vessel? I assure the court that I have no knowledge of the ancestors of this gentleman, and know very few of the incidents of his private life. I cannot, therefore, be accused of mistaking him for a launderer, or for the son, or the grandson, or the great-grandson of a laundress; or of implying any liaison with a person of this class.[27]

Starr relished this opportunity to insult his commander, but his conduct did not sit well with the jury. Starr was convicted on all counts, and suspended from rank and pay for nine months. He remained in Texas, lonely, idle, and depressed, until about April 1854, at which time he was allowed to go on leave.[28] The following August he was ordered to Jefferson Barracks in Missouri to inspect new dragoon horses.[29]

Publisher's Epilogue

If you see seven things in the city of Fort Worth after you read this book, you will know that my mission is accomplished.

First, if when traveling north on Commerce Street near the courthouse, you see eleven tall trees, framed by a rock wall along the bluff above the river you will be looking at a memorial to the eleven soldiers who died while serving at the fort. The rock wall will include the names of all the soldiers who served here.

Second, if you see people visiting Heritage Park, across Main Street from the memorial above, you will know they are remembering the fort and its soldiers. This beautiful city park, about where the fort's stables were located, is the best-kept secret in the city. It has a stone outline of the fort and a flowing water garden that is smaller but better shaded than the larger one south of the convention center. You can stand on the catwalk and see the same view of the river junction the soldiers saw, and walk down the same trail they used at least twice daily taking their horses to the river for water. The clump of trees to the west was just in front of or behind the stables. There is a rusting metal sign almost grown over with bark marking the location of a business, which occupied the stables when the fort closed.

Third, if you go to Pioneers Rest Cemetery and you see an attractive landscaped area around the graves of Texas Brig. Gen. Edward H. Tarrant, Bvt. Maj. Ripley Allen Arnold, and his two children, Sophie and Willis, and the memorial plaque to the eleven soldiers, you will be looking at a suitable place for their spirits to rest. It should also have a flagpole to use on special occasions.

Fourth, if you go to Pioneers Rest in the early morning of Memorial Day and see a crowd and an appropriate ceremony honoring all the men and women who have served in the armed forces of our country, you will be participating in an event that should always be part of our heritage.

Fifth, if you still find, somewhere near the fort area, a museum featuring the men and women who served at the fort, you will know that the people have not forgotten again.

Sixth, if you see copies of Bill Potters picture of the fort and life in the fort in homes and business around the city, you will know that a few people are saluting those we all need to honor.

Seventh, if you see young men and women visiting the sites above, and other locations in the area, like the site of Camp Bowie, the three World War I airfields, and Carswell Field, you will know that our future is secure. When the young men and women who will serve our country tomorrow see how we honor those who have served in the past, right here at home, they will understand that freedom is not free, and that it always has to be defended.

The author of this book began researching the story of the fort in Fort Worth ten years ago. As a diversion while attending medical school, he went hunting and fishing in archives all over the country. His research is so detailed he could have earned a Ph.D. What he found that really happened here is more interesting and more educational than the few myths about battles and fights that have prevailed until now. The hardships and hard work of these pioneering people is a good story.

The publisher, who, like the men and women at the fort, also served in an unpopular, under-funded and unappreciated war in Vietnam, and who still has an uncle missing in the Pacific from World War II, began his work on this story two years ago. While working on trying to tell the real story of freedom to young men and women in schools, I realized that they needed to be able to see and feel something where they live, not something somewhere else. Most of them don't even remember Desert Storm, much less the Indian Wars in which this area was on the violent front lines. I want them to see how the military served.

Much effort has gone into the publishing of this book. I'd like to thank my wife, Cinda, Clay Perkins, Dr. Doug Harmon, Dr. Donald Worchester, Ms. Susan Pritchett, Ms. Ruby Schmidt, and Charles Berl for their encouragement and input.

Notes

Chapter 1

1 Tyler, Ron. *New Handbook of Texas*. 5 Vols. (Austin: Texas State Historical Association, 1996) Vol. 1: 886–888.

2 Tyler Vol. 3: 1086.

3 Swanton, John R. *The Indian Tribes of North America*. Bulletin 145, American Bureau of Ethnology, Smithsonian Institution. (Washington: Government Printing Office, 1953) 304–5.

4 Tyler, Vol. 3: 1087–88.

5 Lamar, Mirabeau Buonaparte. "Information from Doctor Rowlett on the Red River." Letter, in *The Papers of Mirabeau Buonaparte Lamar*. Ed. Charles A. Gulick, et al. Vol 4, part 1. (Austin: Pemberton Press, 1968) 217–220.

6 Wilkins, Frederick. *The Legend Begins: The Texas Rangers, 1823–1845*. (Austin: State House Press, 1996) 25–58.

7 Benthuysen, A. B. "To M. B. Lamar." 8 December 1837. Letter, *In the Papers of Mirabeau Buonaparte Lamar*. Ed. Charles A. Gulick, et al. Vol. 1. (Austin: Pemberton Press, 1968): 592–595.

8 Dyer, J. H. "To J. S. Mayfield." 21 October 21 1838. Letter, *In the Papers of Mirabeau Buonaparte Lamar*. 256–257.

9 Tyler, Vol. 1: 419.

10 Rusk, T. J. "To M. B. Lamar." 9 January 1939. Letter, *In the Papers of Mirabeau Buonaparte Lamar*. 405.

11 Wilkins 53–6.

12 Proctor, Ben S. *Not Without Honor: The Life of John H. Reagan*. (Austin: U. T. Press, 1962) 30–35.

13 Pierce, Gerald S. "The Military Road Expedition of 1840–1841." *Texas Military History* 6 (Summer. 1967) 115–135.

14 Williams, J. W. "The National Road of the Republic of Texas." *Southwestern Historical Quarterly* 47 (1944) 3:218.

15 Wilkins, 112–3.

16 Petition of Jonathan Bird. 2 November 1842. Deposition of C. R. Johns. 7 October 1843. In Memorials and Petitions, Texas State Archives TSA.

17 Tyler, Vol.5: 167–8.

18 Brown, John Henry. *History of Dallas County, Texas: from 1837 to 1887*. (Dallas: Milligan, Cornett & Farnham, Printers, 1887): 10–13.

19 Muckleroy, Anna. "The Indian Policy of the Republic of Texas." *Southwestern Historical Quarterly* 25 (1922): 200–201.

20 Neighbors, Kenneth F. "Jose Maria, Anadarko Chief." *Chronicles of Oklahoma*. Vol. 44 (Autumn, 1966) 3:254–258.

21 *Old Northwest Texas. Historical, Statistical, Biographical. Volume I-A: Navarro County, 1846–1860*. Compiled by Nancy Timmons and Barbara Knox. (Fort Worth: Genealogical Society, 1980): 143

22 Spence, Issac. "To Thomas G. Western." 9 September 1845. Letter 314 of *Texas Indian Papers*. Ed. Dorman Winfrey. (Austin: Texas State Library, 1960).

23 Armbruster, Henry C. "Torrey's Trading Post." *Texana* 2 (1964): 112–131.

24 Post Returns, Fort Washita.

25 Post Returns, San Antonio.

26 A. C. Horton to James K. Polk, 10 August 1846. In *Records of The Governor* ROG, 301–17 TSA.

27 A. C. Horton to T. J. Fauntleroy, 31 July 31 1846 ROG. The ranger captains were: John H. Conner, Castroville; John J. Grumbles, San Antonio; Shapley Ross, Bryant's Station; Thomas I. Smith, Torrey's Trading House and Andrew Stapp, Trading House on the Trinity.

28 A. C. Horton to A. Stapp 25 July 1846–46 ROG.

29 Muster roll, Captain Stapp's Company of Texas Mounted Volunteers 6 February 1848. Records of the Adjutant General. Record Group RG 94. The National Archives NA.

30 Horton to Fauntleroy.

31 A. C. Horton to G. G. Reynolds, et al 30 July 1846 ROG.

32 Spurlin, Charles D. *Texas Veterans in the Mexican War*. (St. Louis: Ingmire Publications, 1984): 211.

33 Anonymous. "William Fitzhugh, Commander of Frontier Fort, Named Gainesville." *Gainesville Daily Register*. 29 Aug. 1950, C6.

34 A. C. Horton to S. Churchill, 8 January 1846 ROG.

35 J. P. Henderson to Major A. W. Gaines, 12 February 1847 ROG.

36 Barton, Henry W. *Texas Volunteers in the Mexican War*. (Waco: Published by the author, 1970): 75 & 97.

37 Henderson to Gaines, 12 February 1847 ROG.

38 A. C. Horton to Captain Thomas Smith, 31 July 1846 ROG.

39 Faulk, Odie B., Ed. *Early Military Forts & Posts in Oklahoma*. (Oklahoma City: Oklahoma Historical Society, 1978): 54–64.

40 Tyler, Vol.2: 188.

41 Muster roll, Stapp's Company, 6 February 1848. RG 94 NA.

42 Henderson, J. P. to W. L. Marcy 21 July 1847 ROG.

43 Barton 75.

44 J. P. Henderson to Captain William Fitzhugh 15 February 1847 ROG.

45 Tyler Vol. 2: 1101.

46 Muster roll, Captain William Fitzhugh's Company, November 1848. Original in Texas Ranger Hall of Fame Library.

47 Neighbors, R. S. "To W. Medill." 13 April 1847. In Letters Received by the Bureau of Indian Affairs LRBIA, 1824–1880. National Archives Microcopy M-234. Roll 858. Texas Agency, 1847–1852.

48 Neighbors to Medill, 22 June 1847, LRBIA.

49 Neighbors to Medill, 28 November 1847 and 13 December 1847, and J. P. Henderson to Neighbors, 10 December 1847, LRBIA.
50 Neighbors to Medill, 2 March 1848, LRBIA.
51 Farrington, Michael. "Middleton Tate Johnson: Texas' Would be Governor, General, and Railroad Entrepreneur." Master's Thesis. (University of Texas at Arlington, 1980): 1–3.
52 Tyler, Vol. 4; 828 and Vol. 5: 517.
53 Farrington, 5–16.
54 Farrington, 17–28.
55 Muster roll, Johnson's Company of Mounted Volunteers, 5 April 1847, RG 94.
56 Muster roll, Joseph H. Smith's Co. of Texas Mounted Volunteers, 15 December 1848, RG 94.
57 Monthly Returns, Bell's Regiment. August-December 1847. Sleeper & Hutchins: 11. Sleeper, John and Hutchins, J. C. *Waco and McLennan County, Texas*. (Waco: 1876. Reprint 1966 by Texian Press, Waco): 11.
58 Statement of Captain M. T. Johnson. 17 August 1847–7 January 1848. Box 2B1016. Barnard Family Papers. Baylor University.
59 Draft of A. G. Clapton 1 November 1848 Barnard Family Papers
60 Neighbors to Medill, 2 March 1848, LRBIA.
61 Neighbors to Medill, 2 March 1848.
62 The Monthly Return of Officers, Bell's Regiment, 15 January 1848, RG 94.
63 Monthly Return Bell's Regiment, February 1848, RG 94.
64 C. E. Barnard to R. S. Neighbors, 13 April 1847. Enclosed in R. S. Neighbors to W. Medill, 28 April 1846, LRBIA.
65 Neighbors to Medill, 13 September 1848, 26 December 1848, 15 February 1848 and 18 June 1848, LRBIA.
66 Wood to P. R. Bell, 10 May 1848. W. D. Miller Papers, 1878/3–3. TSA.
67 Muster roll, Conner's Co. Texas Mounted Volunteers, 5 May 1848, NA.
68 Barton, 105.
69 Barton, 106.
70 Muster roll, J. M. Smith's Co., 15 December 1848, RG 94.
71 Barton, 108.
72 Return of Texas Volunteers discharged in September, October, November and December 1848 and February 1849. Submitted by G. A. H. Blake 2nd Dragoons 15 February 1849, RG 94

Chapter 2

1 Bauer, K. Jack. *The Mexican War, 1846–1848*. (Lincoln: University of Nebraska Press, 1992): 387.
2 Utley, Robert M. *Frontiersmen in Blue*. (Lincoln: University of Nebraska Press, 1981): 2–5.
3 Utley, 11.
4 Order No. 2, 8th Military Department, 7 November 1848. In Oliver Knight, *Fort Worth: Outpost on the Trinity*. (Norman: University of Oklahoma Press, 1950): 231.

5 Taylor to R. Jones, 3 October 1848. In Letters Sent LS Headquarters Western Division HQWD. NA, 11. RG393e5568.
6 Regimental Returns, 2nd Dragoons, RG 94.
7 Regimental Returns.
8 Pension File, Matthew Patterson. National Archives.
9 Samuel H. Starr to Eliza K. Starr, 12 November 1848. Starr Papers. Barker Center. University of Texas.
10 Orders No. 2, Headquarters, 8th Military Department HQ8MD. 7 November 1848. In Knight 231.
11 Assistant Adjutant General to D. Twiggs 7 November 1848. In Letters Received, Headquarters, 8th Military Department (LRHQ8MD). RG 393, entry70, Part 1.
12 Wallace, Edward S. *General William Jenkins Worth, Monterey's Forgotten Hero*. (Dallas: Southern Methodist University Press, 1953): 3.
13 Muster roll, Co. F 2nd Dragoons, November-December 1848.
14 "Reminiscences of Rev. R. White," in *Memorial and Biographical History of Ellis County, Texas*. (Chicago: Lewis Publishing Co., 1892): 94.
15 Muster roll of Ross's Co., Texas Mounted Volunteers. 10 December 1848. NA.
16 Kelly, Dayton, ed. *Handbook of Waco and McLennan County*. (Waco: Texian Press, 1972): 234.
17 The deed recording the sale of Torrey's Trading Post #2 to George Barnard on 5 July 5 1848 is in the Barnard Family Papers, Box 2B1016, Baylor University.
18 Barnard Family File, Genealogy Collection, Glen Rose Public Library, Glen Rose, Texas.
19 Tyler, vol. 1, p. 385.
20 Sleeper and Hutchins, 11.
21 Order No. 13, 14 February 1849, General Orders and Special Orders G.O. and S.O, HQ8MD. National Archives. In Knight 223–224. RG entry 44 vols. 249–250.
22 G. Deas to R. A. Arnold 25 February 1849 Letters Received LR HQWD. NA. RG 393e5572.
23 W. R. Montgomery to W. J. Worth 30 April 1849 LRHQWD.
24 Orders No. 9 and 13, 8 February 1849, and 14 February 1849, LRHQWD Knight 232–234.
25 Utley, 13.
26 Worth to Wood 15 February 1849, LRHQWD.
27 Orders No. 9, 8 February 1849, HQ8MD.
28 Wood to G. Worth, 12 February 1849. Enclosed in Worth to Bliss, 15 February 1849, LRHQWD.
29 Worth to G. Wood, 15 February 1849, LRHQWD.
30 Worth to Wood, 15 February 1849, LRHQWD.
31 G. Deas to Harney, 15 February 1849, LRHQWD.
32 Muster rolls, Co. I. 2nd Dragoons, NA.
33 M. T. Johnson to H. G. Catlett, 22 March 1849, LRBIA.

34 Orders No. 10, March 1849, Camp Stevens, Towash Village, Texas. Signed by Lt. F. Hamilton, Commander. Starr Papers, Missouri Historical Society (MHS), St. Louis, Missouri.
35 Knight, 239.
36 S. H. Starr to Eliza Starr, 6 April 1849, Starr Papers Barker Center.
37 Post Return, Ft. Graham, April 1849. RG 393. National Archives.
38 Regimental Returns.
39 Post Return, Fort Graham, May 1849.
40 See Petition of John C. Brice, May 1849. Box 401–1153. Ranger Records. Adjutant General's Office. Texas State Archives.
41 Muster roll, Co. F May-June 1849. NA.
42 Tarrant County Census, 1850.
43 Harney to Deas, 1 May 1849 in Knight 235–238.
44 Order No. 16, 10 May 1849. Return of the 2nd Dragoon detachment at Austin, Texas, May-June, 1849. NA. Order No. 16, issued at Austin (Harney's headquarters) on May 10, 1849, and received at Fort Graham on May 15, 1849, ordered Arnold and Company F to the West Fork of the Trinity. Post Return, Fort Graham, May 1849. Harney officially assumed command of the 8th Military Department on May 14, 1849, according to the Return of the 2nd Dragoon detachment at Austin, Texas May-June 1849. The regimental return of May 31, 1849, shows that Co. F had "1 Sgt., 1 Corporal & 13 Pvts on detached service at Camp Worth on the West Fork of the Trinity River since 15 May 1849."
45 Spurlin, 129.
46 Spurlin, 41.
47 S. Farrar to C. C. Cummings, September 1893. Typescript in Vertical Files, Tarrant County Historical Commission TCHC.
48 *Fort Worth Register*, 19 January 1902.
49 Regimental Return.
50 Post Return, Ft. Graham May 1849.
51 Company F monthly returns.
52 Report of Lt. Samuel Starr, 22 April 1851. In Knight, 244.
53 R S Neighbors to F. Hamilton, 23 June 1849. LRHQWD.
54 R A Arnold to G. Deas, 13 July 1849. LRHQWD.

Chapter 3

1 From Arnold's application file in the USMA Archives. Courtesy of Susan P. Walker, USMA archivist.
2 R A Arnold to Henry Clay, 1/22/51. Correspondence file, R A Arnold, OQMG.
3 Letter from Susan Walker, USMA archivist.
4 Corder, Jim W. *Hunting Lieutenant Chadbourne*. (Athens: University of Georgia Press, 1993): 94.
5 U.S. Army Court-martial Records. Record CC-243. NA.
6 Court-martial Record CC.-225.
7 CC 225.

8 CC-275.
9 CC-270.
10 Battalion Order No. 36. U.S. Military Academy. 17 March 1838. USMA Archives.
11 CC- 270.
12 Battalion Orders No. 50. U.S. Military Academy. 5 May 1838. USMA Archives.
13 Tarrant County Census, 1850.
14 Garrett, Julia K. *Fort Worth: A Frontier Triumph.* (Austin: Encino Press, 1972): 76.
15 Regimental Returns.
16 Hamilton Merrill to Nathaniel Merrill 3 April 1840. Letter In Hamilton Merrill Papers. Huntington Library. San Marino, CA.
17 Rodenbough, Theo F. *From Everglade to Canon with the Second Dragoons.* (New York: D. Van Nostrand, 1875): 59.
18 Regimental Returns.
19 McCall, George A. *Letters From The Frontiers.* (Philadelphia: Lippincott, 1868). Reprint by the University Presses of Florida, 1974: 402–3.
20 Garrett, 76.
21 McCall, 403.
22 Regimental Returns.
23 Court-martial of R. A. Arnold. 2 December 1844. Court-martial Record EE-16. NA.
24 EE-16.
25 Rodenbough 93.
26 Arnold to Henry Foote, 16 December 1848. Letters Received, Secretary of War. NA.
27 Bauer, K. Jack. *The Mexican War 1846–1848.* (Lincoln: University of Nebraska Press, 1992): 101.
28 Voucher for back pay. R. A. Arnold. 31 March 1852. A. S. Johnston Papers. Tulane University.
29 Curtis, Samuel Ryan. *Mexico Under Fire.* (Fort Worth: TCU Press, 1994): 146.
30 Curtis 154.
31 Voucher Arnold 31 March 1852.
32 Regimental Returns.
33 Erving, Lt. Col. J., Superintendant. "To R. A. Arnold 7 July 1848." In Records of the Office of the Quartermaster General, File Box e33, #80. R. Arnold, 11 June 1849. NA.

Chapter 4

1 Muster rolls, Co. F.
2 Muster rolls, Co. F.
3 Enlistment records, U.S. Army. Microfilm 223. NA.
4 Regimental returns.

5 H. H. Sibley to P. Jones, 31 May 1846, Adjutant General's Office (AGO) LR. RG 94. In Jerry Thompson. *Henry Hopkins Sibley: Confederate General of the West* (Natchitoches: Northwestern State University Press, 1987): 51.
6 Thompson, 51–52.
7 Muster rolls. Co. F.
8 Rodenbough, 451.
9 Smith, Franklin. *The Mexican War Journal of Captain Franklin Smith*. Ed. Joseph E. Chance. (Jackson: University Press of Mississippi, 1991): 154.
10 Bauer 232–252.
11 Ewell, R. S. *The Making of a Soldier*. Ed. Percy G. Hamlin. (Richmond: Whittet Shepperson, 1935): 60–61.
12 Rodenbough, 135.
13 Bauer, 259–268.
14 Gleim, Albert F. *The Certificate of Merit*. (Arlington, VA: Published by the author, 1979): 33–37.
15 Rodenbough, 148.
16 Kirkham, Ralph W. *The Mexican War Journal and Letters of Ralph W. Kirkham*. Ed. Robert R. Miller. (College Station: Texas A & M University Press, 1991): 47.
17 Rodenbough 151.
18 Rodenbough 152–3.
19 Miller, Robert R. *Sword and Shamrock*. (Norman: University of Oklahoma Press, 1989): 95, 107, 159–165.
20 Court-martial Record of Henri Langenhammer Records Relating to the San Patricio Battalion. AGO Document file number 27932. RG 94 and 153.
21 Bauer, 308–311.
22 Rodenbough, 523.
23 Bauer, 326–351.
24 Mexican War Pension File of John Law NA.
25 Miller, 107.
26 Mexican War Pension File of John Law NA.
27 Mexican War pension file, Alphonso Freeman. NA.
28 Pension file of Alphonso Freeman. Muster rolls, Co. F. Regimental Returns.
29 Tarrant County Archives.
30 Regimental Returns.

Chapter 5

1 Crawford to Brooke, 4 June 1849. House Executive Document #5, 31st Congress, 1st Session HE #5, 31–1: 138–139.
2 Brooke to Crawford, 14 July 1849, HE #5, 31–1: 138–140.
3 Brooke to Scott, 19 July 1849, LRHQWD.
4 Brooke to Scott, 19 July 1849.
5 G. Brooke to R. Jones, 11 August 1849, HE #5, 31–1: 140–141.
6 Hardee to George Deas, 26 August 1849, HE #5, 31–1: 146.

7 Harney to Brooke, 26 August 1849, HE #5, 31–1: 144.
8 HE #5, 31–1: 142.
9 Brooke to R. Jones, 31 August 1849, HE #5, 31–1: 143.
10 Tyler, Vol. 2: 1101.
11 Brooke to R. Jones, 24 August 1849 and 31 August 1849, HE #5, 31–1: 141—143.
12 Report of W. S. Harney, 1 May 1849. In Knight, 236.
13 Tyler, Vol. 1: 810–811 & Vol. 5: 277.
14 "From the Upper Trinity." *The Texas Republican*, Marshall, Texas 23 August 1849. Col. 4, Page 2. In the collection of the Amon Carter Museum.
15 Thomas Wilhelm. *History of the Eighth U.S. Infantry, from its Organization in 1838*. 2 vols. (New York: Headquarters, Eighth Infantry, 1873): 27.
16 Brooke to Harney 4 August 1849 LRHQWD.
17 Post Return Ft. Graham October 1849.
18 Post Return.
19 Allardice, Bruce S. *More Generals in Gray*. (Baton Rouge: L.S.U. Press, 1995): 148–9.
20 Regimental Returns.
21 Company Returns; also: P. Morrison to R. Jones 26 March 1849; T. G. Pitcher to R. P. Maclay, 20 January 1850 in Letters Sent 8th U.S. Infantry. RG 391. Series 1279. Vol. 2 LS8IR.
22 Registers of Enlistment U. S. Army. Microfilm 223. NA.
23 Company muster rolls.
24 Company rolls.
25 Discharge statement, A. S. Johnston Papers.
26 Morrison to W. J. Worth, 30 December 1848, LS8IR.
27 Morrison to Worth, 30 December 1848, 13 January 1849, and 18 February 1849, LS8IR.
28 Morrison to Worth, 30 December 1848, and Morrison to R. Jones, 5 January 1849, LS8IR.
29 Regimental Returns.
30 Morrison to G. Deas, 2 February 1849. LS8IR.
31 Regimental Returns.
32 Post Returns.
33 J. Garland to G. Deas, 1 August 1852, LS8IR.

Chapter 6

1 "Colonel Abraham Harris." *Fort Worth Mail Telegram*, 17 November 1901. Typescript in Abraham Harris file, Series IV, Box 2, Mary Daggett Lake Papers. FW Public Library.
2 Bold, John. Report of the Condition of the Public Buildings at Fort Worth, Texas. 5 October 1851. Records of the Office of the Quartermaster General. Consolidated File, Fort Worth, Texas. RG 92. NA.
3 Quarterly Medical Returns Fort Worth. RG 94 entry 634 NA.
4 Bold's report, 5 October 1851.

5 Reports of the Secretary of War. Senate Executive Document No. 64 in the 1st Session of the 31st Congress on 24 July 1850.
6 W. J. Hardee to G. Deas, 26 August 1849, HE#5,33–1: 146.
7 Reports of the Secretary of War, SED #64.
8 Reports of the Secretary of War, SED #64.
9 Swasey, Charles and W. M. Melton. *Directory of the City of Fort Worth*. (Fort Worth: Morrison & Fourney Directory Co., 1877): 3.
10 Inspection Report of Samuel Cooper to Adjutant General, 26 June 1851. Microfilm in Confederate Research Center, Hill County College: 42–3.
11 "W. G. Freeman's Report on the Eighth Military Department." Edited by M. L. Crimmins. Southwestern Historical Quarterly 53 (April, 1950) 4:459–462.
12 "Medical Diseases and Topography of Fort Worth." By Assistant Surgeon Thomas H. Williams. In Senate Executive Document No. 96, 34th Congress, 1st Session: 373–4.
13. Ms. Dee Barker of the TCHC states that abstracts in the Tarrant County Courthouse establish that the land on which Ft. Worth stood was first patented that is, claimed by M. T. Johnston on August 15, 1854. See also Abstract of All Original Texas Land Titles. (Austin: General Land Office, 1941): 764.
14. R A Arnold to R Jones, AG, 20 August 1851, with enclosed court records. LR Adjutant General's Office. NA.

Chapter 7

1 Camp Leona was re-named Fort Inge at the end of 1849, in honor of Major Arnold's West Point classmate. Smith, Thomas T. *Fort Inge*. (Austin: Eakin Press, 1993): 29.
2 Tyler Vol. 2: 1108.
3 Tyler Vol. 2: 1110.
4 Ft. Croghan is in today's Burnet. Tyler Vol. 2: 1096.
5 Tyler Vol. 2: 1114.
6 Order No. 13 HQ8MD 14 February 1849. See Knight 233. See also Helen Chapman, *The News From Brownsville*. Ed. Caleb Coker. (Austin: Texas State Historical Association, 1992).
7 Tyler Vol. 2: 1116.
8 Tyler Vol. 2: 1098–99.
9 Returns of the Detachment of 2nd Dragoons at Austin, Texas. 1850–1852. RG 94.
10 Order No. 20, 20 March 1849 HQ8MD.
11 Order No. 13, 14 February 1849. G.O. & S.O. HQ8MD. In Knight 233–34.
12 See R. T. Huntington. *Hall's Breechloaders*. (York, Pennsylvania: Shumway, 1972).
13 See Robert Whittington, *The Colt Whitneyville-Walker Pistol*. (Hooks, Texas: Brownlee Books, 1984): 71–74.
14 See Knight 237.
15 Harney to Starr 15 June 1849 Starr Papers Barker Center.
16 S.O. No. 9 HQ8MD noted on Ft. Graham post return of July 1849.
17 Order No. 28, 25 May 1849 General Orders HQ8MD.

18 Harney to Asst. Adjutant General HQWD 5 July 1849 LRHQWD.

19 R. Jones to G. M. Brooke, 20 August 1849. In *Texas Indian Papers*. Ed. Dorman Winfrey. (Austin: Texas State Library, 1960). 5:48–9.

20 Orders No. 24, 14 May 1849 and No. 33, 18 June 1849, General Orders HQ8MD.

21 Tyler Vol. 1: 748.

22 Order No. 41, 13 July 1849, G.O. HQ8MD.

23 Order No. 42, 18 July 1849, G.O. HQ8MD.

24 Special Order No. 42 9 July 1949 G.O. HQWD.

25 R. P. Maclay to W. W. J. Bliss, 20 August 1851, LRHQWD. Maclay's report of 27 April 1851 states that "John Lewis, Delaware Indian" was Fort Worth's guide & interpreter.

26 Special Order No. 42, 9 July 1849 G.O. HQ8MD.

27 4,339 lbs. of ordnance stores were shipped to Ft. Worth from San Antonio in the 4th quarter of 1849. House Executive Document #2, 32nd Congress, 1st Session: 264.

28 R. A. Arnold to R. Jones 18 June 1849. In Knight 239.

29 George Deas to George T. Wood, 23 July 1849. In Winfrey, *Texas Indian Papers,* 5: 41.

30 Annual Report of the Secretary of War 1849. Senate Executive Document #1. 31st Congress 1st Session: 188 Table A.

31 Roll call of Company F, 2nd Dragoons 19 June 1849. In Knight 240–2.

32 R. A. Arnold to R. Jones 15 June 1849 and 19 June 1849. In Knight 240–2.

33 J. P. Henderson to James K. Polk 23 November 1846. ROG: 301–17. TSA.

34 Muster roll, Fitzhugh's Co., November 1848. Texas Ranger Hall of Fame Library.

35 Post Return Ft. Worth June 1849.

36 Malaria was known as "Intermittent Fever" in 1849. Standifer, J. M. "Quarterly report of the Sick and Wounded at Fort Worth, Texas, for the Quarter ending 30th September, 1849." Filed by J. M. Standifer. RG 94 NA.

37 Post Return.

38 Standifer was paid $100.00 per month from September 1 to December 31, 1847 at Waco Village. Executive Document #17, 30th Congress 2nd Session: 20. Standifer is named as a member of Johnson's company in a statement of account prepared by George Barnard on 10 April 1848 and again on 28 August 1848. Barnard Papers, Box 2B1O16, Folders 7 & 9. Standifer does not appear on the company muster roll. Spurlin 142–4.

39 "Reminiscences of Julia Standifer Walker," cited in F. W. Hatchett "To M. D. Lake 9 March 1927. In Standifer Family file, M. D. Lake Papers. Fort Worth Public Library.

40 *Malaria*. Ed. W. H. Weisdorfer and Sir I. MacGregor. (New York: Church-Livingstone, 1988): 8–10.

41 Report of Lt. Samuel Starr, AAQM Fort Worth, Texas. 22 April 1851. In Knight 244.

42 Post Returns and Quarterly Medical Returns Ft. Worth.

43 Quarterly Medical Returns Ft. Worth.

Chapter 8

1 R. A. Arnold to R. Jones, 27 December 1849, Records of the AGO Letters Received, RG 94.
2 Obituary, Samuel H. Starr. *Philadelphia Public Ledger* 25 November 1891. In Starr Papers. MHS.
3 Records of Enlistment U.S. Army.
4 S. H. Starr to E. K. Starr 14 March 1847 Starr Papers MHS.
5 Register of Regular Army Enlistments.
6 Obituary, Starr, *Philadelphia Public Ledger.*
7 S. H. Starr to E. K. Starr 8 December 1847 Starr Papers MHS.
8 H. B. Yeager to J. C. Yeager, 9 September 1846. In Yeager Papers. Daughters of the Republic of Texas Library. The Alamo. San Antonio, Texas.
9 Record of Regular Army Enlistments.
10 Muster roll, Company A Corps of Engineers. RG 94 NA.
11 Muster roll, Company A.
12 Smith, G. A. *Company A, Corps of Engineers, 1846–1848 in the Mexican War.* (Battalion Press, 1896): 16.
13 S. H. Starr to E. K. Starr, 23 October 1846 Starr Papers MHS.
14 S. H. Starr to E. K. Starr, 12 November 1847 Starr Papers MHS.
15 George W. Cullum. *Register of the Officers and Graduates of the US Military Academy, at West Point NY, from March 16, 1802 to January 1, 1850.* (New York: Trow, 1850): 271.
16 S. H. Starr to E. K. Starr, 14 March 1847, Starr Papers MHS.
17 S. H. Starr to E. K. Starr, 30 March 1847, Starr Papers MHS.
18 S. H. Starr to E. K. Starr, 5 April 1847, Starr Papers MHS.
19 S. H. Starr to E. K. Starr, 8 December 1847, Starr Papers MHS.
20 Undated message. Yeager Papers.
21 S. H. Starr to E. K. Starr, 23 April 1847, Starr Papers MHS.
22 H. B. Yeager to J. C. Yeager, 20 April 1847, Yeager Papers.
23 G. A. Smith 40.
24 S. H. Starr to E. K. Starr, 9 June 1847, Starr Papers MHS.
25 S. H. Starr to E. K. Starr, 9 June 1847.
26 Muster rolls.
27 S. H. Starr to E. K. Starr, 30 August 1847, Starr Papers MHS.
28 S. H. Starr to E. K. Starr, 30 August 1847.
29 S. H. Starr to E. K. Starr, 30 August 1847.
30 S. H. Starr to E. K. Starr, 23 September 1847 Starr Papers MHS.
31 S. H. Starr to E. K. Starr, 23 September 1847.
32 Cullum, 271.
33 S. H. Starr to E. K. Starr, 23 September 1847.
34 S. H. Starr to E. K. Starr, 18 February 1848 Starr Papers MHS.
35 H. B. Yeager to J. C. Yeager, 21 March 1848 Yeager Papers.
36 S. H. Starr to E. K. Starr, 8 December 1847 & 28 February 1848 Starr Papers MHS.

37 S. H. Starr to E. K. Starr, 8 December 1847.
38 S. H. Starr to E. K. Starr, 28 February 1848 Starr Papers MHS.
39 Hiram Yeager's letters from Mexico City discuss these efforts in the spring of 1848, and discuss Yeager's attempts to be discharged, or commissioned as an officer. (Yeager papers.)
40 S. H. Starr to E. K. Starr, 8 December 1847.
41 S. H. Starr to E. K. Starr, 8 December 1847.
42 S. H. Starr to E. K. Starr, 8 December 1847.
43 S. H. Starr to E. K. Starr, 13 July 1848, Starr Papers MHS.
44 Coffman, Edward M. *The Old Army*. (New York: Oxford University Press, 1986): 202.
45 S. H. Starr to E. K. Starr, 13 September, Starr Papers Barker Center.
46 S. H. Starr to E. K. Starr, 27 November 1848 and 6 May 1849, Starr Papers Barker Center.
47 Regimental Returns.
48 S. H. Starr to E. K. Starr, 6 May 1849, Starr Papers Barker Center.
49 Coffman 203.
50 S. H. Starr to E. K. Starr, 6 May 1849.
51 S. H. Starr to E. K. Starr, 6 May 1849.
52 King, Grace, et al, *From Muskets to Mohair*. (Waco: Texian Press, 1992): 45–6.
53 Myer, Albert J. "I Am Quite a Texan Already." SWHQ 82 (July 1978): 34.
54 S. H. Starr to E. K. Starr 29 June 1949. Margin note by E. K. Starr. Starr Papers Barker Center.
55 Record of Court of Inquiry held at Camp Worth, July 21, 1849. CG-82 NA.
56 Court-martial of Private Dennis Oates CG-80 NA.
57 Report of Board of Inquiry, Camp Worth, Texas, July 21, 1849. CG-82 NA.
58 Trial of Lieutenant Samuel Starr. CG-83 NA.
59 Trial of Starr
60 S. H. Starr to G. Deas, 4 August 1849. Trial of Lieutenant Samuel Starr. CG-83 NA.
61 Court-martial of Samuel H. Starr CG-83 NA. Also Order #2 HQ8MD 15 January 1850 GO & SO HQ8MD.
62 S. H. Starr to E. K. Starr, 6 January 1850, Starr Papers Barker Center.
63 S. H. Starr to E. K. Starr, 15 January 1850, Starr Papers Barker Center.

Chapter 9

1 G. Wood to G. Crawford, 14 December 1849. House Executive Document #5 31st Congress 1st Session HE#5, 31–1: 13–15.
2 G. Crawford to G. Wood, 19 January 1850, HE#5, 31–1: 15.
3 G. Brooke to R. Jones, 3 January 1850, LRHQWD. In Ft. Martin Scott Papers NA.
4 Brooke to R. Jones, 3 January 1850.
5 Brooke to R. Jones, 20 January 1850. House Executive Document #1, 31st Congress, 2nd Session, Part II HE #1, 31–2/2: 23–4.

6 G. Brooke to P. Jones ,7 March 1850, HE #1, 31–2/2: 26–7. G. Brooke to W. Scott 28 May 1850 HE #1, 31–2/2: 35–6. G. Brooke to W. G. Freeman 28 July 1850 HE #1, 31–2/2: 51–2.
7 G. Brooke to R. Jones, 20 January 1859 and 31 January 1850, HE #1, 31–2/2: 23–5.
8 G. Brooke to P. Jones, 7 March 1850, HE #1, 31–2/2: 28–30.
9 Brooke to Bell, 6 March 1850, HE #1, 31–2/2: 31.
10 Muster rolls, Wallace's Co. Tex. Mounted Volunteers RG 94 Box 4714 NA.
11 G. Brooke to R. Jones 7 March 1850 HE #1, 31–2/2: 26–27.
12 G. Brooke to W. G. Freeman 6 November 1849 LRHQWD In Ft. M. S. Papers NA. Also Tyler Vol. 2: 1114.
13 Tyler, Vol. 2: 1111.
14 Post Order #3, Fort Worth, Texas 9 January 1850 Starr Papers MHS.
15 Receipts 8 February 1850 and 12 March 1850. Starr Papers MHS.
16 Post Returns.
17 Cullum, 338.
18 Post Returns.
19 "Genealogy and Other Information about the Family of General Joseph Montfort Street." W. C. Trimbly Unpublished essay in Street Family Papers. Ca. 1976. State Archives Des Moines, Iowa.
20 Pay voucher, W. P. Street, December 1850, Johnston Papers Tulane.
21 A page in the Street Family Bible notes that James M. Street had two black servants named James and Patsy Triplett in 1827. Another entry shows a black servant named London, age 19 in April 1821. Street Family Papers Des Moines.
22 Special Order No. 22, 30 April 1850 HQ8MD. Noted on Post Return Ft. Graham. May 1850.
23 Whittington, 78–79.
24 Inspection Report of Samuel Cooper 3.
25 Harney to Starr, 15 June 1849. Starr Papers MHS.
26 Company Return.
27 HE #1, 31–2/2: 411.
28 HE #1, 31–2/2: 56–9.
29 HE #1, 31–2/2: 58–9.
30 HE #1, 31–2/2: 59.
31 G. Brooke to G. Deas 15 August 1850 HE #1, 31–2/2: 54. See HE #1, 31–2/2: 56, 62–3. Also Order No. 42 HQ8MD.
32 HE #1, 31–2/2: 59–61
33 Rollins to Brooke, 25 September 1850, LRHQWD. In Ft. M. S. Papers.
34 G. Brooke to P. R. Bell, 6 October 1850. ROG TSA.
35 Post Returns.
36 Carl P. Russell. *Guns on the Early Frontier*. (New York: Bonanza Books, 1957): 172.
37 Circular of 11 November 1850, noted on Ft. Graham Post Return of November 1850.

38 Hardee to Deas 20 November 1850. LRHQ8MD.
39 Report of Col. G. Talcott, 13 November 1850. In James E. Serven. *Colt Firearms from 1836*. (Harrisburg: Stackpole Boosk, 1979): 307.
40 Post returns.
41 S. H. Starr to E. K. Starr, 4 July 1850, Starr Papers Barker Center.
42 S. H. Starr to E. K. Starr, 20 July 1850, Starr Papers Barker Center.
43 Correspondence files in the A. S. Johnston Papers Tulane.
44 Tyler Vol. 3: 970. See also Roland, Charles P. *Albert Sidney Johnson, Soldier of Three Republics*. (Austin: Univ. of Texas Press, 1964): 154.
45 A. S. Johnston Papers Tulane.
46 Roland, 156–8.
47 A. S. Johnston Papers, Tulane.
48 Pay Vouchers of R. A. Arnold, 2 February 1851 and 14 July 1851. NA.
49 Pay Vouchers of R. A. Arnold, 1 November 1850, 2 February 1851, 11 October 1852, etc. See also Slave Schedule for Tarrant County Texas, 1850. Tarrant County Archives.
50 Pay Voucher of John Bold, 4 February 1852. NA.
51 Lt. Horace Haldeman of the 8th Infantry, stationed at Fort Gates, took this arrangement a step further and began to deal in slaves himself. On June 20, 1851, Haldeman bought two slaves, Howard and Lydia, from General Harney for $600 each. He hired Lydia to his commander, Colonel C. A. Waite, at $12 per month. Haldeman hired out Howard at $10 per month, and sold him five months later, for a net gain of $250. Haldeman's cash book shows that he bought at least nine slaves while stationed at Fort Gates. "Cash Book, 1850–1852." Haldeman Papers, Texas State Archives.
52 Coffman, 152–4.
53 Coffman, 154.
54 Coffman, 154–5.
55 Pay voucher of Nicholas Beyer, 18 May 1851. A. S. Johnston Papers, Tulane University.
56 Pay voucher of Frederick Burlage, 13 May 1851. A. S. Johnston Papers, Tulane University.
57 Coffman ,155–6.
58 Pay voucher of Nicholas Beyer, 15 November 1851; Beyers settlement was paid to the post sutler, Alex Young.
59 James Bennet. *Forts and Forays* (Albuquerque: University of New Mexico Press, 1948): 22–3.
60 R. A. Arnold to A. S. Johnston, 31 October 1850, Johnston Papers.
61 Order No. 48, 11/7/50. Fort Worth, Texas Starr Papers. MHS.
62 Post Returns.
63 President Zachary Taylor died on July 9, 1850 after only 16 months in office. Taylor's vice president, Millard Fillmore, became the 13th president of the United States. Fillmore replaced Secretary of War George Crawford with George Conrad. President Fillmore and Secretary Conrad initially made few changes in the War Department's policies regarding Texas.
64 Conrad, C. M. "Annual Report of the Secretary of War." HE #1, 31–2/2: 3–5.
65 Order No. 69, 6 January 1851, HQ8MD GO & SO HQ8MD.

66 G. Brooke to R. Jones 25 December 1850 LRHQWD. In Ft. M. S. Papers.
67 G. Brooke to P. H. Bell 26 December 1850 ROG TSA.

Chapter 10

1 Brooke to R. Jones, 7 January 1851, LRHQWD.
2 Brooke to R. Jones, 7 January 1851, LRHQWD.
3 Brooke to R. Jones, 15 February 1851, LRHQWD.
4 Brooke to R. Jones, 5 February 1851, LRHQWD.
5 Brooke to R. Jone,s 5 February 1851, Also Brooke to Harney, 7 February 1851, LRHQWD.
6 Order No. 13, 14 February 1849, HQ8MD.
7 Order No. 42, 18 July 1849, HQ8MD.
8 Brooke to Harney, 7 February 1851, LRHQWD.
9 Brooke to R. Jones, 5 February 1851, LRHQWD.
10 Circular 8 February 1851. Noted on Ft. Graham post return February 1851. It is not apparent if the order came from the headquarters of General Harney or General Brooke.
11 Harney to Commander, Co. A, 2nd Dragoons, 12 February 1851. In Delano Papers. Duke University Special Collections.
12 Harney to Commander Co A, 12 February 1851, Delano Papers. Duke University.
13 Frantz, Joe B. *Gail Borden, Dairyman to a Nation*. (Norman: University of Oklahoma Press, 1951): 201–211.
14 Report of Hamilton Merrill et al. on the meat biscuit. 21 June 1851. In Box 2G223. Ashbel Smith Papers. Barker Center. University of Texas.
15 Report of Hamilton Merrill, 21 June 1851.
16 Deas to Bliss, 9 March 1851, LRHQWD.
17 Order No. 32, March 1851, HQ8MD.
18 Order No. 34, 22 April 1851, HQ8MD.
19 Post Returns May 1851.
20 Order No. 21, 20 April 1851, HQ8MD.
21 Marchman, Watt P and Robert C. Conner. "Indian Agent Jesse Stem: a Manuscript Revelation." *West Texas Historical Association Year Book*. Vol. 39 Oct. 1963: 125. See also Harney to Jones, 17 May 1851, LRHQWD.
22 *The New York Herald*, 14 May 1851. In the Hamilton Merrill Papers. See also Marchman 134.
23 Harney to R. Jones, 29 August 1851, LRHQWD.
24 Harney to R. Jones, 17 May 1851, LRHQWD.
25 Harney to Bliss, 22 September 1851, LRHWD. See also Marchman, 126.
26 Harney to R. Jones, 17 May 1851, LRHQWD.
27 Order No. 46, 15 May 1851, HQ8MD.
28 Harney to R. Jones, 17 May 1851. In Letters Received, HQ Western Division LRHQWD.

Chapter 11

1 A. D. Lee to H. F. DeLano, 19 February 1851. In DeLano Papers.
2 J. Garland to G. Deas, 1 August 1852. LS8IR Vol. 2.
3 "Register of Letters Received, Department of Texas and 8th Military Department, Volume 2." RG 393e4776. W. Street, 7 January 1851, LRHQ8MD. RLR HQ8MD.
4 "Register of Letters Received, Department of Texas and 8th Military Department, Volume 2." RG 393e4776. S. Starr, 19 May 1851, LRHQ8MD. RLR HQ8MD.
5 Harney to R. Jones 2 April 1851 LRHQWD. Also Order No. 23, 18 March 1851, HQ8MD.
6 Post Returns.
7 *Washington, Arkansas Telegraph* 11 June 1851. Photocopy provided by Stan Hoig. The story was reprinted in the *Clarksville Northern Standard* on 26 July 1851.
8 Todd to Arnold 9 April 1851 Starr Papers MHS.
9 *Washington, Arkansas Telegraph* 11 June 1851.
10 Order No. 23 Fort Worth, Texas 10 April 1851. In Starr Papers MHS.
11 *Washington, Arkansas Telegraph* 11 June 1851.
12 *Proceedings of the 7th Annual Reunion of the Texas Association of Mexican War Veterans in the City of Fort Worth, Texas, May 20–21, 1902.* (Austin: Gammel-Statesman Publishing Company, 1903). In Box 2–22/669. Texas State Archives.
13 *Fort Worth Register* 1 June 1902.
14 Post Returns.
15 "Tales of Early Days Here are Recalled by Women Pioneers." Mae Biddison Benson. Unidentified Ft. Worth newspaper, circa 1921. Vertical files, Tarrant County Historical Commission.
16 Arnold 20 April 1851. RLR HQ8MD.
17 Post Returns.
18 Peak, Howard. *A Ranger of Commerce or 52 Years on the Road.* (San Antonio: Naylor Printing Co., 1929): 163–9.
19. Peak 166

Chapter 12

1 Harney to Bliss 17 May 1851 LRHQWD.
2 Inspection Report of Samuel Cooper to Adjutant General, 26 June 1851. Microfilm in Confederate Research Center, Hill College. 37–39.
3 Post Returns.
4 Post Return, June 1851.
5 Lt. Col. T. Staniford to Lt. J. C. Pemberton, 23 October 1846, LS8IR Vol. 2 RG 391 e1279.
6 Post Returns, June 1851-July 1851.
7 L. Staniford to R. Jones 3 November 1851 and 4 January 1852 LS8IR.
8 Post Returns.

9 Unpublished autobiographical essay, Frederick Follett (Sr.,). Minnesota Historical Society. Page 6 of typescript.
10 Taylor to Adjutant General 30 October 1848, LSHQWD RG 393.
11 Brooke to D. Twiggs 25 August 1850, LRHQWD.
12 Order No. 20, 20 March 1849, HQ8MD.
13 Crawford to Twiggs, 22 June 1849, LRHQWD.
14 W. W. Markell to Brooke, 5 July 1849, LSHQWD. RG 393.
15 Vielé, Teresa G. *Following the Drum.* (New York: Rudd and Carlcton, 1858). Reprint by University of Nebraska Press, 1984: 223.
16 Twiggs to Scott, 5 July 1849, LSHQWD.
17 Cochran, Thomas C. (ed.) *New American State Papers*. Scholarly Resources: 1973. Vol. 4: 101.
18 NASP Vol. 4: 101.
19 NASP Vol. 2: 214.
20 NASP Vol. 2: 217
21 NASP Vol. 2: 217.
22 Brooke to R. Jones, 7 March 1850, LRHQWD.
23 The infantrymen were from Company E, 8th Infantry. C. G. Merchant to W. J. Hardee, 20 May 1850, LRHQWD.
24 Brooke to D. Twiggs, 25 August 1850, LRHQWD.
25 Inspection Report of Samuel Cooper, 1–2.
26 Harney to R. Jones, 24 June 1852, LRHQWD.
27 E. K. Smith to mother, 1 June 1853. E. K. Smith Papers, Southern Historical Collection. University of North Carolina.
28 Orders No. 57, 11 May 1853, HQ8MD.
29 Orders No. 92, 6 October 1853, HQ8MD.
30 Orders No. 94, 27 October 1853, HQ8MD.
31 Crimmins, M. L. (ed.). "W. G. Freeman's Report of the Eighth Military Department." SWHQ 53 (January, 1950): 312.

Chapter 13

1 General Order No. 10, 10 March 1851. Discussed by Ben G. O'Neal in "The Beginnings of Fort Belknap." SWHQ Vol. 61 No. 4. April 1958: 510–11.
2 O'Neal, 512–13. Also Post Returns, Ft. Belknap.
3 Post Returns.
4 Tyler Vol. 5: 335.
5 Bearss, Edwin C. and Arrell Gibson. *Fort Smith: Little Gibraltar on the Arkansas*. 2nd ed. (Norman: University of Oklahoma Press, 1979): 223–30. Early letters from the post appear in George H. Shirk, "Mail Call at Fort Washita," *Chronicles of Oklahoma* Vol. 33 Spring 1955: 14–35.
6 Special Order No. 28, 14 July 1851, HQ8MD. Post Return Ft. Graham July 1851.
7 Letter, R. Arnold 18 August 1851. Register of Letters Received Department of Texas & 8MD. Vol. 2.
8 Letter to A. K. Starr, 22 September 1851, Starr Papers Barker Center.

9. Special Order No.39, 17 September 1851, HQ8MD. Noted on Ft. Graham Return September 1851.
10 Inspection Report of Samuel Cooper 40–42.
11 "Report of Colonel Samuel Cooper, Assistant Adjutant General of the United States, of Inspection Trip from Fort Graham to the Indian Villages on the Upper Brazos Made in June, 1851." Ed. E. B. Ritchie. SWHQ 42 (April, 1939) 4:327–333.
12 Ritchie, "Report of Col. Cooper," 333.
13 Inspection Report of Samuel Cooper, 42–43.

Chapter 14

1 General Order No. 11, 10 October 1851 GO & SO HQWD RG 393 e5579.
2 Shearer, Ernest C. "The Carvajal Disturbances." SWHQ 55 (July, 1951): 200–230.
3 P. F. Smith to W. W. J. Bliss, 6 October 1851, LRHQWD.
4 Letter, P. F. Smith, 9/28/51, LRHQWD.
5 Letter, P. F. Smith, 9/28/51.
6 Letter, P. F. Smith, 9/28/51.
7 Letter, P. F. Smith, 9/28/51.
8 O'Neal 515–18.
9 Order No. 91, GO & SO, HQ8MD.
10 O'Neal 516–17. See also Foreman, C. T. "General W. G. Belknap." *Chronicles of Oklahoma* 20 (1941): 124–142.
11 Early letters from Phantom Hill appear in George H. Shirk, "Mail Call at Fort Washita," Chronicles of Oklahoma Vol. 33 Spring 1955: 27–34.
12 L. Staniford to G. Deas 30 January 1852 and 31 January 1852 Letter Book, LS8IR RG 391 e1279.
13 Muster rolls, Co. F & H.
14 W. P. Street to J. H. D. Street, 18 August 1852. Street Family Papers Des Moines. Copy provided courtesy of Jerry M. Sullivan, Texas Department of Parks and Wildlife.
15 Quarterly Report of The Sick and Wounded at Camp McKavett, Texas for The Quarter Ending 30 September 1852 NA.
16 J. H. D. Street to Rev. Lin, 24 October 1852. Street Family Papers Des Moines.
17 Tyler Vol. 2: 1111 and Vol. 1: 940. An entry in the Register of LRHQ8MD records that Fort Gates was not completely abandoned until 26 February 1853. Lt. Col. D. D. Tompkins to Adjutant, 8th Military Department 9 March 1853. NA.
18 Tyler Vol. 1: 947 and Vol. 2: 1092. Ft. Clark was first named Fort Riley.
19 Tyler Vol. 2: 1100.
20 Tyler Vol. 2: 1108.
21 Tyler Vol. 5: 335.
22 E. K. Starr to Catherine Arnold, 27 November 1852. Starr describes Jo as being a year old in November 1852.

Chapter 15

1 Muster rolls, Co. F and Co. H 8th Infantry.
2 Post Returns.
3 S. H. Starr to E. K. Starr, 18 January 1852, Starr Papers MHS.
4 C. B. Arnold to E. K. Starr, 27 February 1852, Starr Papers Barker Center.
5 E. K. Starr to C. B. Arnold, 12 March 1852, Starr Papers Barker Center.
6 E. K. Starr to C. B. Arnold, 27 November 1852, Starr Papers Barker Center.
7 Extra duty payroll for the quarter ending 31 March 1852.
8 RG 391. Records of U.S. Army Mobile Units. Records of the 2nd Cavalry. Miscellaneous Records, 1845–1912. Papers of R. Arnold. NA.
9 "Abstract of purchases paid for at the post of Fort Worth, Texas, by Bvt. Maj. R. A. Arnold, 2nd Drag. a.a.Q.M. in the Quarter ending on the 31st March 1852." Papers of R. Arnold. NA.
10 "Monthly Report of Horses, Mules, & Oxen for which Forage has been issued at Fort Worth, Texas, by Capt. & Bvt. Major R. A. Arnold 2nd Drags. a.a.Q.M. during the month of March 1852." R. Arnold Papers NA.
11 "Abstract of Disbursements, etc. for the quarter ending 31 March 1852." R. Arnold Papers.
12 "Statement of Account of Capt. & Bvt. Maj. R. A. Arnold, a.a.Q.M., for the quarter ending 31 March 31 1852." R. Arnold Papers.
13 William Slade, Record of auction of public property at Fort Worth, Texas, 26 July 1852.
14 R. Arnold Papers.
Note: References 7–14 above are from photocopies in the author's files. These papers were copied at The National Archives (NA) by Mrs. Mary Curtis, who subsequently gave them to the author. Originals were not found in later visits to the Archives.
15 Post Return Fort Belknap December 1851.
16 Williams, J. W. *Old Texas Trails*. Ed. Kenneth Neighbours. (Austin: Eakin Press, 1979): 276–7.
17 Williams 279–80 and Post Return. See also Fred R. Cotten, "A Note on Lawrie's Trip to Northeast Texas, 1854–1855." SWHQ 56 (July, 1952): 102–105 and Bennett L. Smith. *Bethesda*. (Ft. Worth: Published by the author, 1969): 1–7 & 83. The Texas General Land Office map of Young County also shows segments of the old Fort Belknap Road.
18 Company Returns.
19 R. A. Arnold to Adjutant, 8th Military Department 25 April 1852 and 27 July 1852. "Register of Letters Received, Department of Texas and 8th Military Department, Vol. 2," NA.
20 Letter book of Bvt. Maj. Gen. Persifor Smith, August 1852. Pennsylvania Historical Society, Philadelphia, PA.

Chapter 16

1 Obituary of James D. Merrill. *Waukesha Wisconsin Democrat*. 9 August 1879. In Merrill Papers. Huntington Library. San Marino, CA.
2 *Batavia Progressive American*, 19 October 1883. Clipping in Merrill Papers.

3 H. W. Merrill to A. Hewitt 19 December 1838. Merrill Papers.
4 "Old Whitey Has a Rival." Unattributed newspaper clipping. Merrill Papers.
5 Diary of Hamilton Merrill. 13 November 1841. Merrill Papers.
6 Merrill Diaries, 14 November 1841.
7 Merrill Diaries, 18 December 1841.
8 Merrill Diaries, 15 December 1841.
9 Merrill Diaries, 22 December 1841.
10 Merrill Diaries, 12 January 1842.
11 Merrill Diaries, 10 January 1842.
12 Merrill Diaries, 10 January 1842.
13 Merrill Diaries, 24 January 1842.
14 Merrill Diaries, 4 February 1842.
15 Post Returns, Ft. Washita.
16 Merrill Diaries, 22 January 1844.
17 Merrill Diaries.
18 H. W. Merrill to Nelson or James Merrill 10 December 1844. Merrill Papers.
19 Merrill Papers.
20 Merrill's letters from Mexico are found in the Merrill Papers.
21 H. W. Merrill to H. Ames, 7 June 1848, Merrill Papers.
22 "Captain H. W. Merrill." Unidentified Rochester newspaper. October 1848. Merrill Papers.
23 *Batavia Advocate, 23 November 1847. Merrill Papers.*
24 Unidentified newspaper clipping, Merrill Papers. Also "Captain H. W. Merrill," in unnamed Rochester newspaper. October 1848. Merrill Papers.
25 Muster rolls, Co. B, 2nd Drg. Also, unattributed newspaper clipping January 1850 in Merrill Papers.
26 *Batavia Republican-Advocate* 20 October 1848. Merrill Papers.
27 "Old Whitey Has a Rival." Unattributed newspaper clipping. Merrill Papers.
28 The Merrill Papers include numerous newspaper clippings describing Black Warrior's career. His obituary appeared in the *New York Herald* about 14 November 1857.
29 Report of Board of Inquiry, Record HH49. NA
30 Obituary of James D. Merrill. *Waukesha, Wisconsin Democrat*, 9 August 1879. Merrill Papers.
31 The farm was on Section No. 16, East Troy Township. "A Wisconsin Farm-for a residence." Circa 1850. Author & publication not given. Merrill Papers.
32 Post Returns, Ft. Martin Scott and Ft. Mason.
33 These transactions are recorded in the deed records of the Mason County Courthouse. Book H, p. 94; H-96; P-628; S-149; T-341; V-191; Z-1O; X-556; 1–8; 1–119. See also C. H. Holmes to H. W. Merrill 5 April 1884 & 8 October 1884. Letter Book, H. M. Holmes. Box 1976/191–1, Charles Biershwale Papers; and C. H. Holmes to H. W. Merrill 19 June 1886. Box 1976/1–11, Charles Biershwale Papers, Texas State Archives.
34 Merrill to T. J. Wood, 30 May 1852; 4 July 1852; and 25 July 1852. RLRHQ8MD. NA.
35 Post Returns.

36 Special Order No. 46, 8th Military Department. HQ8MD. NA. Text of the order is found in Corder: 142. See also Tyler Vol. 2: 1091.

37 Tyler Vol. 1: 940.

38 P. F. Smith requested on 26 September 1852 that he be allowed to move his headquarters to Corpus Christi. E. Canby to P. F. Smith 16 October 1852. LRHQWD. NA.

39 General Order No. No. 7, 11 June 185 GO & SO HQ8MD, states that the General Depot of the Quartermaster Department would remain at San Antonio, supervised by Bvt. Maj. J. Belger. Bvt. Maj. E. B. Babbitt would serve at Indianola as Chief Q.M. of the Department. Captain W. B. Blair was Chief of the Commissary Department.

Chapter 17

1 Order No. 3, 13 January 1853, GO & SO HQ8MD NA.

2 Special Order No. 30, 19 April 1853 GO & SO HQ8MD NA. Also Tyler Vol. 2: 1111.

3 H. W. Merrill to Adjutant, 8th Military Department, 18 January 1853 RLRHQ8MD.

4 H. W. Merrill to Adjutant, 8th Military Department ,15 May 1853 & 23 May 1853 RLRHQ8MD.

5 H. W. Merrill to Adjutant, 8th Military Department, 15 May 1853.

6 Cates, Clifford D. *Pioneer History of Wise County*. (Decatur: 1907). Reprint by Wise County Historical Collection, 1975: 51–53.

7 Brisbane & Considerant's journey is described by R. V. Davidson in the introduction to Victor Considerant's *Au Texas*. (Paris: Librairie Phalansterienne, 1854). Reprint, with additions by R. V. Davidson. (Philadelphia: Porcupine Press, 1975): 9–11.

8 Considerant, Victor. *The Great West*. (New York: Dewitt & Davenport, 1854). Reprinted in the Porcupine Press's edition of *Au Texas*: 9–11.

9 Considerant, 14.

10 Affidavit of H. W. Merrill 16 August 1854 on microfilm at the University of Missouri at Columbia.

11 Considerant, 10.

12 Considerant, 20.

13 Considerant, 20.

14 Considerant, 11.

15 Considerant, 45.

16 Considerant, 17.

17 Considerant, 18.

18 Post Medical Returns.

19 Tyler Vol. 2: 281. R. Davidson discusses La Reunion in the introduction to the Porcupine Press's edition of *Au Texas*.

20 Consolidated Correspondence File, Fort Worth. Records of the Quartermaster General. NA.

21 Consolidated Correspondence File, Fort Worth. Also George Wilson to Adjutant, 8th Military Department 20 July 1853 LRHQ8MD.

22 H. W. Merrill to T. S. Jesup, 15 August 1853, Consolidated Correspondence File, Fort Worth.

23 H. W. Merrill to T. S. Jesup, 20 August 1853, Consolidated File, Fort Worth.

24 H. W. Merrill to T. S. Jesup, 20 August 1853.

25 E. K. Smith to his mother, 1 June 1853, E. K. Smith Papers, Southern Historical Collection.

26 G. R. Paul to Adjutant, 8th Military Department, 18 June 1853, RLRHQ8MD.

27 L. B. Webster to Adjutant, 8th Military Department, LRHQWD NA. Captain G. W. Phelps reported Mexican hostility on July 13 and 14, 1853. Phelps to Adjutant, 8th Military Department. LRHQ8MD?

28 Reports of the disturbances in El Paso are found in file A.141 September 1853 LRHQWD NA.

29 Order No. 50, 20 August 1853, GO&SO HQ8MD NA.

30 Order No. 54, 20 August 1853, GO & SO HQ8MD.

31 Order No. 50, 20 August 1853.

32 Orders No. 50 & No. 54.

33 J. LaMotte to Mrs. LaMotte, 15 September 1853. LaMotte-Copinger Papers. Missouri Historical Society.

34 Crimmins, SWHQ 53 (April, 1950) 4:459–463.

35 H. W. Merrill to S. Cooper. RG 94, AGO. 21 September 1853. On Microfilm 516.

36 Special Order No. 95, 31 October 1853 GO & SO HQ8MD NA.

37 Letter, H. W. Merrill to Colonel S. Cooper, AG, USA. RG 94. AGO. 9 December 1853. M516.

38 Interview with Ms. Ruby Schmidt. June 6, 2001.

39 P. F. Smith to AAG, Western Division 7 September 1853 and 15 September 1853 LRHQWD NA.

40 Special Orders No. 87, 8 October 1853 and No. 84, 4 October 1853 GO & SO HQ8MD NA.

41 In November, the War Department changed the name of the 8th Military Department to "the Department of Texas." Order No. 67, 23 November 1853 GO & SO HQ8MD. In accordance with War Department General Order 25.

42 Special Order No. 125, 15 December 1853 GO & SO HQ8MD NA. These orders made the following assignments: Ft. Belknap: Co. B & I, 2nd Drg. Ft. Chadbourne: Co. C & F, 2nd Drg. Ft. McKavett: Co. A & G, 2nd Drg.

43 King, Grace, et al. *From Muskets to Mohair*. (Waco: Texian Press, 1992): 92.

44 Tyler, Vol. 2: 1110.

45 Tyler, Vol. 2: 1113.

46 Tyler, Vol. 2: 1110.

Chapter 18

1 Crimmins, "W. G. Freeman's Report of the Eighth Military Department." SWHQ 53 (January, 1950): 463.

2 Post Return Ft. Graham.

3 W. J. Hardee to Adjutant, 8th Military Department, RLRHQ8MD NA.

4 S. H. Starr to E. K. Starr, 19 May 1853, Starr Papers Barker Center.
5 Simpson, Harold B. *Hill County (Texas) Trilogy*. (Hillsboro: Hill College Press, 1986): 4–5.
6 Diary of J. M. Steiner, 3 May 1849. Steiner Papers Barker Center.
7 Post Returns.
8 J. M. Hawes to Adjutant, 8th Military Department 9 August 1853 RLRHQ8MD NA.
9 Report of R. H. Anderson, 7 September 1853. Senate Document. 33rd Congress, 2d Session. Report of Committee #395: 2–3.
10 Testimony of William Slade, 10 September 1853. Recorded by C. Brooks, Justice of the Peace, Hill County, Texas. NA. Microfilm in Confederate Research Center, Hill College.
11 Report of R. H. Anderson.
12 Testimony of Cpl. J. Stewart, 10 September 1853. Recorded by C. Brooks.
13 Testimony of J. Stewart, E. P. Dolan, and J. Donnelly, 10 September 1853. Recorded by C. Brooks. See also Report of R. H. Anderson, 7 September 1853. Senate Document. 33d Congress, 2d Session. Report of Committee #395: 2–3.
14 Simpson, 9.
15 Ida Steiner's papers are found in the Burleson Papers in the Barker Center, UT.
16 Simpson, 13.
17 W. Patton to K. A. Parker, 24 April 1902. In Pension Record of Catherine B. Arnold NA.

Chapter 19

1. W. B. Parker's *Through Unexplored Texas* describes the expedition. (Reprint—Austin: Texas State Historical Association, 1990).
2 Tyler, Vol. 1: 714–15.
3 Tyler, Vol. 2: 242–3.
4 Tyler, Vol. 5: 1107–8.
5 Tyler, Vol. 6: 602–3.
6 Tyler, Vol. 5: 498–9.
7 Pension file, Catherine B. Arnold NA.
8 Pension file, Catherine B. Arnold NA.
9 Thomas Manlove died June 26, 1880, aged 38. Dorman, John F. ed. *Genealogies of Virginia Families* (Baltimore: Genealogical Publishing Co, 1982) Vol. 1: 506.
10 Marriage certificate of Kate Arnold and Samuel J. Parker. 10 October 1865. Falls County Courthouse. Texas.
11 Records of U.S. Army Mobile Units, 1821–1942. RG 391. 8th U.S. Infantry. Military Histories of Officers, 1838–1869. Captain Robert P. Maclay, 62. NA
12 *Register of Graduates and Former Cadets 1802–1990*. Ed. Paul W. Child. (West Point: Association of Graduates USMA, 1990): 265.
13 *23rd Annual Reunion of the Association of the Graduates of the United States Military Academy at West Point, New York, June 9th, 1892*. (Saginaw, Michigan: Sebmann & Peters, 1892): 74–5. A photo of an elderly Bomford appears in

Roger Hunt and Jack R. Brown's *Brevet Brigadier Generals in Blue*. (Gaithersburg, Maryland: Olde Soldier Books, 1990). Bomford is buried in Evergreen Cemetery in Hillside, New Jersey.

14 Obituary of Hamilton Merrill. *New York Times*, 14 July 1892. In Merrill Papers.

15 Crimmins, M. L. "Major Hamilton Wilcox Merrill in Texas." *West Texas Historical Association Year Book*, 1937: 96–97.

16 Cordell, Eugene F., M.D. *Medical Annals of Maryland, 1799–1899*. (Baltimore: Medical and Chirurgical Faculty of the State of Maryland, 1903): 623. (Williams and his wife, Bettie, are buried in Christ Church Graveyard in Cambridge. Marshall, Nellie. *Tombstone Records of Dorchester County, Maryland, 1678–1964*. (Dorchester County Historical Society, 1965): 92. Williams's obituary appears in the *Dorchester County Democrat and News* 26 September 1904.)

17 Starr's career is outlined in his obituary, which appeared 25 November 1891 in the *Philadelphia Public Ledger*; a copy is filed with the Starr Papers, MHS. His reports from Seven Pines are printed in John Y. Foster's *New Jersey and the Rebellion*. (Newark: Martin R. Dennis & Co., 1868): 138–42.

18 Mueller, Heinrich G. "Glimpse of Trooper Life." (no page, no date). In Starr Papers MHS.

19 Longacre, Edward G. *The Cavalry at Gettysburg*. (Lincoln: University of Nebraska Press, 1993): 235–6.

20 Longacre, 236.

21 Obituary of Samuel Starr, 25 November 1891, Starr Papers MHS.

22 McConnel, H. H. *Five Years a Cavalryman*. (Jacksboro: J. N. Rogers & Co., 1889). Reprint by Jack County Historical Society, 1963: 49–50.

23 Starr Papers Barker Center and MHS. A son, Samuel Benjamin Starr, was living in 1891.

24 Ben F. Follett to Frederick Follett, 14 April 1869.Follett Papers. Minnesota Historical Society.

25 Frank Beach to Ben F. Follett, 15 April 1869, Follett Papers.

26 Lowery, Thomas P. *Tarnished Eagles*. (Mechanicsburg, PA: Stackpole Books, 1997): 194–6.

27 Pioneers Rest Cemetery, 2001, Tarrant County Genealogical Society.

Chapter 20

1 S. H. Starr to E. K. Starr, 6 January 1850, Starr Papers Barker Center.

2 Cabet, Etienne. *Proces du Communisme a Toulouse*. (Paris: Bureau du Populaire, 1843): 1. DeGolyer Library, SMU.

3 Sutton, Robert P. *Les Icariens: The Utopian Dream in Europe and America*. (Urbana: University of Illinois Press, 1994).

4 Sutton, 40.

5 Cabet, *Proces*, 3.

6 Cabet, *Proces*, 42–3.

7 Cabet, *Proces*, 68.

8 Cabet, *Proces*, 45–9.

9 Cabet, *Proces*, 12 & 54.

10 Cabet, *Proces*, 80, 84, & 96.

11 Begos, Jane Dupree. "Icaria: A Footnote to the Peters Colony." *Communal Societies* (1986): 84–92.

12 Begos, 86–87.

13 Cabet, Etienne. *Defense du Citoyen Cabet devant la Court d'Appel de Paris, 11 Decembre, 1850*. (Paris: Bureau du Populaire, 1851): 7, 13.

14 Cabet, *Defense* 37.

15 Sutton, 50.

16 *Le Populaire,* 20 August 1848.

17 *Le Populaire,* 20 August 1848.

18 *Le Populaire,* 20 August 1848.

19 *Le Populaire,* 20 August 1848.

20 *Le Populaire,* 20 August 1848.

21 Sutton, 57.

22 *Le Populaire,* 11 July 1848.

23 *Le Populaire,* 11 July 1848.

24 *Le Populaire,* 20 August 1848.

25 *Le Populaire,* 20 August 1848.

26 *Le Populaire,* 20 August 1848.

27 *Le Populaire,* 20 August 1848.

28 Cabet, *Defense,* 9.

29 *Le Populaire,* 1 October 1848.

30 Cabet, *Defense,* 40–1.

31 Cabet, *Defense,* 15, 41.

32 Cabet, *Defense,* 16.

33 Begos, 90.

34 "Colonie Icarienne," Nauvoo, Illinois, 2 August 1854.

35 Cabet, *Defense,* 15.

36 *L'Observateur,* January 1881.

37 *Clarksville Northern Standard,* 20 January 1849.

38 Sutton, 142–144.

39 Begos, 89.

40 Information provided by Mrs. Caroline Selzer of Dallas, a direct descendant of Gouhenant.

41 The members of the First Advance Guard were as follows:
Abandoned their brothers, March 27, 1848: Dr. Leclerc; Myet; Piquenard; Pasquier; Boissier. Abandoned them later: Cochard; Petit; Sieyes; Vocquefen; Maurice; Paquot. Expelled: Gouhenant. Struck by lighting: Collet. Died in Texas: Guillot; Guerin; Chauvin; Sauge; Levy; Barroux; Berson. Died of cholera at New Orleans: Ludwig; Uker-Pelagius. Stayed in Texas, or Shreveport, to work: Bourgeois; Drouard; Hedouix; Hidou; Piquee; Thorel. Hostile Dissidents: Roveira (went mad, committed suicide in New Orleans); Moity; Rousset; Dargelas; Paut; Blitz aine; Caudron jeune. Left without hostility: Blitz jeune; Boue; Buisson, de Nantes; Cardot; Crombez; Douzin; Jacob; Lafosse; Layoux; Lucas; Sacreste; Teyssier; Van den Eden; Viardot. Faithfully persevered, and entered the communal house in New Orleans: Bellets; Berthet; Bira; Boissonet;

Buisson, de Lyon; Champeau pere; Chainpeau fils; Conefray; Damours; Esnault; Grillas; Labrunerie; Larbalestier; Marchand (Alexis); Marchand (Louis); Marinelli; Mazoir; Meslier; Rougier; Therme.

Chapter 21

1 Post medical reports, 1851.

2 Wood, George B. MD. *A Treatise on the Practice of Medicine*. (Philadelphia: Grigg, Elliott, & Co., 1847): 2–14. Dr. Wood was a prominent "regular" physician of the day; his textbook was part of the curriculum at Dr. T. H. Williams's medical school. See the *Forty-first Annual Circular of the Faculty of Physic of the University of Maryland. Session of 1848–1849*. No author. (Baltimore: James F. Woods, Printer, 1848): 9. Dr. Williams acknowledges Wood's influence on page 1 of his dissertation, "An Inaugural Dissertation on Enteric Fever." Special Collections, Health Sciences Library, the University of Maryland at Baltimore.

3 Wood, *Treatise,* 203–17.

4 Wood, *Treatise,* 129 & 131.

5 Wood, *Treatise* ,156.

6 Post medical return, 2nd quarter 1851.

7 *Harrison's Principles of Internal Medicine*. Ed. Kurt J. Isselbacher. 13th Edition. (New York: McGraw-Hill, 1994): 672–674.

8 Post medical return 2nd quarter, 1851.

9 Ibid.

10 Ibid.

11 Ibid.

12 Ibid.

13 See Rosenberg, Charles E. *The Cholera Years*. 2nd edition. (Chicago: University of Chicago Press, 1987): 151–72.

14 Wood, *Treatise,* 129.

15 Wood, *Treatise,* 129.

16 Wood, *Treatise,* 129–30.

17 Wood, *Treatise,* 130.

18 Wood, *Treatise,* 153.

19 Wood, *Treatise,* 139.

20 Wood, *Treatise,* 130.

21 Cordell, Eugene F. MD. *The Medical Annals of Maryland*. (Baltimore: Medical and Chirurgical Faculty of the State of Maryland, 1903): 623.

22 *Forty-first Annual Circular of the Faculty of Physic of the University of Maryland* 10.

23 *Forty-first Annual* 1–12.

24 Gillett, Mary C. *The Army Medical Department, 1818–1865*. (Washington, D.C.: The Center for Military History, 1987): 78–79.

25 Cordell, 623.

26 Post Returns.

27 Gillett, 79 & 97.

28 Gillett, 97.

29 Utley, Robert M. *Frontiersmen in Blue*. (Lincoln: University of Nebraska Press, 1981): 44.

30 Crimmins, SWHQ 53 (October, 1949) 2:207.
31 Gillett, 129–30.
32 Gillett, 76–8.
33 *Regulations for the Medical Department of the Army*. (Washington, D.C.: War Department, 1850): 30–33.
34 Gillett 130–32. Also, T. F. Hunt to W. W. J. Bliss 17 March 1851. LRHQWD.
35 Letter H.72, LRHQWD.
36 Major Arnold signed for a hospital tent in early 1852 at Fort Graham. "Return of Clothing, Camp and Garrison Equipage Received & Issued at Fort Worth & Fort Graham, Texas, by Captain and Brevet Major Ripley A. Arnold, AAQMI in the Quarter Ending 30 April 1852." Records of the Office of the Quartermaster General, Consolidated Correspondence File, 1794–1890. RG 92. Fort Worth. NA.
37 Knight, 245.
38 Crimmins, Vol. 53: 73.
39 "Monthly Return of the Public Animals, Wagons, Harness, and Horse Equipment in Possession of Capt. & Bvt. Maj. R. A. Arnold 2nd Drag. AAQM at Fort Worth, Texas, during the Month of March, 1852." RG 92. Ft. Worth. NA.
40 McSherry, Richard MD, USN. *El Puchero, or, A Mixed Dish From Mexico*. (Philadelphia: Lippincott, Grambo & Co., 1850): 29. Paymaster A. S. Johnston signed for a four-horse ambulance in August, 1851. Receipt in Johnston Papers Tulane University.
41 Gillett, 115–116. See also House Executive Document #17, 30th Congress, 2nd Session. 12.
42 Lane, Lydia S. *I Married a Soldier*. (Albuquerque: Horn & Wallace, 1964): 33.
43 Order No. 64, 29 November 1850, GO & SO HQ8MD.
44 Report of board of survey, Fort Croghan, Texas, 21 December 1852, LRHQWD.
45 Gillett, 157.
46 National Medical Convention. *The Pharmacopoeia of the United States of America*. (Philadelphia: Lippincott, Grambo & Co., 1850).
47 Wood, George B. MD, and Franklin Bache, MD. *The Dispensatory of the United States*. 9th Edition. (Philadelphia: Lippincott, Grambo & Co., 1850).
48 *Regulations for the Medical Department of the Army* 31.
49 Gillett, 17–19.
50 Gillett, 286–7.
51 Compiled from post medical reports, 1849–1853.
52 T. H. Williams, 374.
53 Wood, *Treatise*, 225–9.
54 T. H. Williams, 374.
55 *Malaria*. Ed. W. H. Weisdorfer and I. MacGregor. (New York: Church-Livingstone, 1988): 23–25.
56 Wilcox, Aimee. *Manual for the Microscopical Diagnosis of Malaria in Man*. (Washington, D.C.: U.S. Public Health Service, 1942): 7–11.
57 Wilcox, *Malaria*, 13–14.

58 T. H. Williams, 374.
59 Post medical returns.
60 Wilcox, *Malaria,* 46.
61 Harrison's, 887.
62 Post medical report, 2nd quarter 1850.
63 Wood, *Treatise,* 242–48.
64 Wood, *Treatise,* 253; Gillett ,171.
65 E. C. Faust, Ph.D. "Malaria, Mortality in the Southern United States for the Year 1936." Southern Medical Journal. July 1938. Vol. 3: 816.
66 Wilcox, *Malaria,* 34–48.
67 Wood & Bache, 394 & 1034.
68 T. H. Williams, 374.
69 Post medical reports.
70 Post medical report, 2nd quarter 1850.
71 Post medical report, 2nd quarter 1850.
72 See note 21 above.

Chapter 22

1 Court-martial of William H. Griffin, Co. F, 2nd Dragoons. Court-martial Record HH-23. NA.
2 Court-martial of Pvt. Joseph Murphy, Co. F, 2nd Dragoons. Court-martial Record HH-93. NA.
3 Twiggs's order gives 25 July 1851 as the date of Murphy's trial, whereas the court-martial record shows July 21. Order No. 19, HQWD. RG 393, entry 5579. NA.
4 Testimony of Private Stephen Decatur. Court-martial of Pvt. Thomas Kelly. Court-martial Record HH-23. NA.
5 Testimony of Private John Senn, Page 20, Court-martial Record HH-93. NA. Howard Peak identified the Dallas Road as Houston Street. Peak 177.
6 See M. B. Benson, "Tales of Early Days Here are Recalled by Women Pioneers." See also *Laws of the Third Legislature of the State of Texas*. (Austin: W. H. Cushman, 1850): Vol 3, part 1, p. 15.
7 Testimony of Pvt. Thomas C. Kelly. Trial of T. C. Kelly. Court-martial Record HH-93. NA.
8 Testimony of Sgt. J. Fritche. Trial of Pvt. T. C. Kelly. Court-martial Record HH-93. NA.
9 Trial of Pvt. John Connigland, Co. F, 2nd Drg. Court-martial Record HH-93. NA.
10 Trial of Pvt. John Connigland.

Chapter 23

1 Richardson, Rupert N. *The Comanche Barrier to South Plains Settlement.* Arthur H. Clark Co, 1933. (Reprint, Austin: Eakin Press, 1996): 7.
2 E. K. Smith to his mother, 1 September 1856 from Ft. Mason, Texas. E. K. Smith Papers. Southern Historical Collection. University of North Carolina.

3 C. Barnard to G. Barnard 22 June 1852. Box 2B1016, Barnard Family Papers, Baylor University.

4 House Executive Document #2, 32nd Congress, 1st Session. 253.

5 Lowe, Percival G. *Five Years a Dragoon*. (Reprint. Norman: University of Oklahoma Press, 1991): 118–19.

6 C. A. May to G. Deas 13, December 1852 ,LRHQWD.

7 C. A. May to G. Deas, 13 December.

8 See Percival Lowe, *Five Years a Dragoon*. (Kansas City: Hudson Publishing Co., 1906). Reprint.

9 Richardson, 8–9.

10 Parker, 76.

11 Parker ,129.

12 The transcript in the Dodge inquiry is found in LRHQWD with Harney's letters for 1851; box 6.

13 Mansfield, 66.

14 Order No. 53, 8 March 1853 GO & SO HQ8MD NA.

15 E. K. Smith to mother 1 September 1856. Smith Papers SHC. Cited in Joseph H. Parks, *General Edmund Kirby Smith, C.S.A.* (Baton Rouge: LSU Press, 1954): 91.

16 House Executive Document #1, Part II. 33rd Congress, 1st Session. 24–25.

17 See Eva J. Boyd, *Noble Brutes: Camels on the American Frontier*. (Plano, Texas: Republic of Texas Press, 1995.)

18 New American State Papers NASP, Military Affairs, Vol. 13, 252–57.

19 T. L. Hunt to T. S. Jesup, 4 September 1852, LRHQWD NA

20 NASP Vol. 13: 252–57.

21 *Texas State Gazette* 15 June 1850. The ad was placed by "T. F. Chapman, Agent, QM Dept." Cited by Thomas Lemmons in "Fort Gates and the Central Texas Frontier, 1849–1852." M.A. Thesis, (Abilene Christian College, 1967): 87.

22 House Executive Document #2, Vol. II, Pt. 1. 32nd Congress, 1st Session. 259.

23 Harney to Assistant Adjutant General, HQ, Western Division, 22 February 1853, LRHQWD.

24 Crimmins, 205.

25 For example, Company B, 1st Dragoons, rode sorrel horses. Lowe 83 & 118.

26 Steffen, Randy. *The Horse Soldier, 1776–1943*. 4 Vols. (Norman: University of Oklahoma Press). Vol. 1: 174.

27 Forage return, 30 April 1851, Delano Papers.

28 House Executive Document #2, Vol. II, Pt. 1. 32nd Congress, 1st Session. 257.

29 Forage return, 1 December 1851, Delano Papers.

30 Lowe 128.

31 Court-martial Record of Pvt. T. C. Kelly NA.

32 Lowe, 86 & 130–1.

33 Lowe, 130–1.

34 Lowe, 86; 288–9 & 294.

35 Trial of Pvt. James Davis. Co. C, 8th Infantry. Court-martial Record CG 80. NA. 46–51.

36 Rodenbough, 219.

37 A. McRae to D. Twiggs, 16 March 1852, LRHQWD.
38 Lowe, 76.
39 Lowe, 61–2.
40 Trial of Pvt. J. Davis, 46.
41 Rodenbough, 195–6.
42 Myer, Albert J. "I Am Already Quite a Texan." Ed. David A. Clary. SWHQ, 82 July, 1978) 1:54.
43 Lambert, Joseph I. *One Hundred Years with the Second Cavalry*. (Fort Riley: Capper Printing, 1939): 26.
44 Steffen, Vol. 2: 106.
45 Company muster rolls.
46 New American State Papers, Vol. 13: 252–7.
47 Crimmins, SWHQ 54 (July, 1950) 1:209–10.
48 Orders, Headquarters, Western Division. RG 393, e5579. An undated requisition in the Delano Papers from Cpt. Hamilton W. Merrill requests these listed supplies for Co. B, 2nd Drg for the first half of 1852.
49 Criminins, SWHQ 54 (July, 1950) 1:210.
50 Crimmins, SWHQ 54 (July, 1950) 1:206. See plate 51, Vol. 2 in *Cavalry Tactics*. 3 Volumes. No author. (Philadelphia: Lippincott, Grambo, and Co., 1855). Edition of 1841 not available.
51 Special Order No. 18, 17 March 1853, HQ8MD. Noted on Ft. Graham post return March, 1853.
52 Steffen, 109.
53 Averell, William W. *Ten Years in the Saddle*. Ed. E. K. Eckert & N. J. Amato. (San Rafael, California: Presidio Press, 1978): 57.
54 H.Ex.Doc. #1, 31/2. 33–4.
55 Coffman, 157.
56 Bennett, James. *Forts and Forays*. Ed. Frank D. Reeve. (Albuquerque: University of New Mexico Press, 1948): 11.
57 Bennett, 17.
58 *Cavalry Tactics*, Vol. 2, 65–66.
59 *Cavalry Tactics*, Vol. 2. 65–66.
60 Steffen discusses the Grimsley saddle in considerable detail in Volume 1 of *The Horse Soldier*. 161–174.
61 Steffen, Vol. 1: 168.
62 NASP Vol. 13: 252–57.
63 Knight, 242.
64 W. L. Elliott to W. W. J. Bliss, 12 February 1852, LRHQWD.
65 Crimmins, SWHQ 51 (April, 1948) 4:355.
66 House Executive Document #2, Vol. 2, Pt. I. 32nd Congress, 1st Session. 259.
67 Equipment Receipts, 30 April 1851; 14 August 1851; and 1 October 1851. Delano Papers. A Grimsley pack saddle is shown in Steffen Vol. 1: 173.
68 Franklin Smith. *The Mexican War Journal of Captain Franklin Smith*, 76.
69 Mansfield 66. Lt. H. F. Delano signed for 500 mules shoes at Ft. Mason on October 18, 1851.

70 Myer, Albert S. "I am already quite a Texan." Ed. David A. Clary. SWHQ Vol. 82, #1: 63.
71 Order No. 46, 15 May 1851, GO & SO HQ8MD.
72 Bearss, Edwin C. and Arrell M. Gibson. *Fort Smith: Little Gibraltar on The Arkansas*. 2nd ed. (Norman: University of Oklahoma Press, 1988): 219–220.
73 French, Samuel G. *Two Wars: An Autobiography*. (Nashville: Confederate Veteran, 1901): 115–16.
74 French, 115–16. Lowe also mentions using a horse with a bell to lead mules 215 & 295.

Chapter 24

1 T. F. Hunt to W. Bliss, February 1851, LRHQWD.
2 T. F. Hunt to W. W. J. Bliss, 7 March 1851, LRHQWD.
3 Inspection Report of Samuel Cooper, 14–24.
4 Inspection Report of Samuel Cooper, 25.
5 Inspection Report of Samuel Cooper, 4.
6 Tyler, Vol. 2: 1117.
7 Inspection Report of Samuel Cooper, 1–3.
8 Inspection Report of Samuel Cooper, 4–5.
9 Inspection Report of Samuel Cooper, 4–5.
10 House Executive Document #2, Vol. 2, Part 1. 32nd Congress, 1st Session. 268.
11 Inspection Report of Samuel Cooper, 11 & 24.
12 House Executive Document #2, Vol. 2, Part 1. 32/2. 164–5.
13 W. S. Harney to R. Jones, 23 April 1851, LRHQWD.
14 House Executive Document #1, Vol. 1, Part 2, 32nd Congress, 2nd Session. 35.
15 S. H. Starr to E. K. Starr, 19 May 1853, Starr Papers Barker Center.
16 Order No. 3, HQWD 20 March 1851, GO & SO HQWD. RG 393. Entry 5579.
17 Muster roll, Black Beaver's Company. RG 94. NA.
18 R. P. Maclay to W. W. S. Bliss, 20 August 1851, LRHQWD.
19 W. W. J. Bliss to W. S. Harney, 3 June 1851, LSHQWD PG 393 Entry 5568. Vol. 11: 12.
20 J. Bold to Adjutant, 8MD 10 August 1851. RLRHQDT & 8MD NA.
21 Tompkins to Adjutant, 8MD. RLRHQ8MD. NA.
22 Inspection Report of Samuel Cooper, 5.
23 H. H. Sibley to W. W. S. Bliss, 31 August 1851, LRHQWD NA.
24 Inspection Report of Samuel Cooper, 33.
25 J. Garland to G. Deas, 1 August 1852. LS8IR. RG 391. Entry 1279. Vol. 2.
26 J. Garland to G. Deas, 1 August 1852.
27 Statement of James Belger, A.Q.M. 15 March 1853. In File H.16. LRHQWD. NA.
28 J. Garland to T. J. Wood, 6 March 1853. LS8IR. RG 391. Entry 1279. Vol. 2.
29 P. F. Smith to T. Jesup, 22 March 1852, LRHQWD.
30 P. F. Smith to T. Jesup, 22 March 1852.
31 Special Order No. 27, 3 April 1852, GO & SO HQWD. RG 393, Entry 5579.

32 J. T. Garland to Sprague 3 June 1850. LS8IR. RG 391. Entry 1279. Vol. 2.
33 Order No. 11, HQ8MD, 9 February 1853, GO & SO HQ8MD.
34 P. F. Smith to W. W. J. Bliss, 17 July 1853, LRHQWD.
35 P. F. Smith to W. W. J. Bliss, 17 July 1853.
36 Order No. 54, HQ8MD, 24 August 1853, GO & SO HQ8MD.
37 File H.72, November 1851, LRHQWD.
38 Knight, 244–246.
39 House Executive Document #1, Part 2. 33/1: 4–6.
40 Knight, 58.
41 Muster roll John Ford's Company Texas Mounted Volunteers, 23 September 1851. RG 94.
42 W. S. Harney to R. Jones, 12 June 1851, LR Adjutant General's Office (AGO).
43 R. A. Arnold to T. J. Woods 18 May 1851 LRAGO.
44 See *Mansfield on the Condition of the Western Forts*, 66. See also Crimmins, SWHQ 54 (July, 1950) 1:208.
45 A. K. Craig to R. Jones, 12 July 1851, LRAGO.
46 Kimmel, Ross M. "American Forces in the War with Mexico, 1846–1848." Military Illustrated, Past & Present. Part 2. November 1991: 39–41. See Also *Regulations and Notes for the Uniform of the Army of the United States, 1847*. Compiled and edited by Jacques N. Jacobsen, Jr.(Staten Island: Manor Publishing Co., 1977).
47 Nevin 88, 182–3, & 200. See also Kimmel Pt. 2: 14.
48 Steffen, Vol. 2: 37. See also Time-Life Books, *Arms and Equipment of the Union*. (Alexandria, Virginia: Time Life Books, 1991): 215. Also, Kimmel 39–40.
49 Rodenbough, 212 & 216.
50 These shirts were issued for many years in the mid-nineteenth century, according to Mr. Thomas Shaw, curator of the Fort Snelling Museum. Two are pictured in *Arms and Equipment of the Union*. 126.
51 See *Arms and Equipment of the Union*, 126.
52 Steffen, Vol. 1: 111.
53 Kimmel ,Pt 2: 37.
54 Steffen, Vol. 2: 5–6. Also, Clothing Records, Johnston Papers Tulane.
55 The post surgeon at Camp Joseph E. Johnson reported that the 8th Infantry was wearing wool fatigues in the summer of 1852. Senate Executive Document #96. 34th Congress, 1st Session. 380.
56 Marcy, Randolph. *The Prairie Traveler*. Harper & Brothers, 1859. Facsimile edition by West Virginia Pulp & Paper Company, 1961. 40.
57 Kimmel, Pt 2: 39–40.
58 Kimmel, Pt 2: 37.
59 Clothing Records, Johnston Papers.
60 Lt. A. Crozet to company commanders, 8th Infantry 18 November 1850. Letter Book 8th U.S. Infantry Vol. 2. RG 391. E1279.
61 T. G. Pitcher to W. P. Street, 3 January 1951. Letter Book 8th U.S. Infantry.
62 The uniform coats do not appear in the Johnston Papers, but when Col. Freeman inspected the 8th Infantry in late 1853, seven companies were wearing them.

63 Urwin, Gregory J. *The United States Infantry: An Illustrated History, 1775–1918.* (New York: Sterling Publishing Co., 1991): 82

64 Vielé, Teresa G. *Following the Drum.* (New York: Rudd and Carleton, 1858). Reprint by University of Nebraska Press, 1984: 225.

65 Invoice Book, Barnard's Trading House. 1 August 1849. Box 2B1016. Barnard Family Papers Baylor University.

66 "Late News From Texas." *The New York Herald*, 6 October 1852. Mattress ticks were commonly made from blue-and-white checked material in the mid-19th century. See J. R. Weissman & W. Lavitt, *Labors of Love.* (New York: Random House, 1987): 5.

67 Marcy, 40.

68 Joseph H. Parks. *General Edmund Kirby Smith, CSA.* (Baton Rouge: Louisiana State University Press, 1954): 90. A group of California miners, dressed in this manner, appear in a Daugerreotype made about 1852 in Beaumont Newhall's *The Daugerreotype in America.* 3rd Edition. (New York: Dover Publications, 1976): Plate 85. See also the hunting shirt of the Mexican War volunteer in Nevin 224.

69 Crimmins, SWHQ 54 (July, 1950) 1:210.

70 Steffen, Vol. 2: 15. The Delano Papers include a shipping receipt for 70 voltigeur hats, sent from the Watervliet Arsenal to Co. A, 2nd Drg in February 1851.

71 Johnston Papers

72 See Steffen, Vol. 1; Uniform Regulations, 1847; and Urwin.

73 Steffen, Vol. 2: 5–15.

74 H. W. Merrill to N. Merrill, 25 August 1846, Merrill Papers.

75 Delano Papers, 27 March 1852 and 14 February 1852.

76 M. Walker to Delano, 15 October 1851, Delano Papers.

Appendix

1 Statement of Juana Barnard, transcribed by Vernie B. Allison. Typescript in the Barnard Family File, Glen Rose Public Library.

2 *Harrison's Principles of Internal Medicine.* Ed. Kurt J. Isselbacher. 13th Edition. (New York: McGraw-Hill, 1994): 681–3.

3 Wright, J. J. E. "Report on the Topography of San Antonio, and the Epidemic Cholera that Prevailed There in 1849." Southern Medical Reports, Vol. 1: 415–35.

4 Wright, 429.

5 S. H. Starr to E. K. Starr, 6 May 1849, Starr Papers Barker Center.

6 *Cholera.* Ed. Dhiman Barun and William B. Greenough III. (New York: Plenum Books, 1992): 23.

7 Worth to R. Jones, 7 May 1849, LRHQWD.

8 G. Deas to AAG, Western Division, 7 May 1849, LRHQWD.

9 Wright, 428–9.

10 *Harrison's*, 681–3.

11 Wallace, Edward S. *General William Jenkins Worth, Monterey's Forgotten Hero.* (Dallas: Southern Methodist University Press, 1953): 3–9.

12 Diary of J. M. Steiner, 4 March 1849, Steiner Papers Barker Center.
13 B. J. Fisher. "Military Justice on the Texas Frontier." *West Texas Historical Association Year Book, 1988*. Vol. 64.
14 Trial of William H. Saunders, Record CG-75: 56, NA.
15 S. H. Starr to E. K. Starr 27 February 1849 Starr Papers Barker Center. Arnold signed over $100.00 in public funds to Samuel Starr at Camp Thornton on March 6, 1849. The receipt is in the Starr Papers, Missouri Historical Society, St. Louis. Arnold probably left for the court-martial soon afterward.
16 House Executive Doc. #5: 31–1: 142.
17 "From the Upper Trinity," *The Texas Republican* Marshall, Texas. 23 August 1849. Col 4, p. 2. In the collection of the Amon Carter Museum.
18 Brooke to Harney, 4 August 1849, LRHQWD.
19 *Mansfield on the Condition of the Western Forts, 1853–1854*. Ed. R. W. Frazier. Norman: University of Oklahoma Press, 1960): 60.
20 Myer, Albert S. "I am already quite a Texan." Ed. David A. Clary. SWHQ Vol. 82, #1: 27.
21 "Return of Clothing, Camp & Garrison Equippage received & issued at Ft. Worth & Fort Graham, Texas, by Captain & Bvt. Maj. R. A. Arnold, 2nd Drg, AAQM, in the Quarter Ending 30 Sept. 1852." Records of the Office of the QM General. Consolidated Correspondence File, 1794–1890. Fort Worth. RG 92. NA.
22 W. Steele to Staniford, 26 January 1850, LRHQWD.
23 G. A. H. Blake to G. Deas, 2 August 1850. House Executive Doc. #1, 31–2/II 59–61. Lt. Washington P. Street and twelve mounted infantrymen rode with Merrill and Blake.
24 Court-martial of Samuel Starr, September 1853. Record HH328: 99–134. NA. A transcript of Samuel Starr's testimony is in the Starr Papers MHS.
25 Court-martial of Samuel Starr, HH 328: 125–6 NA.
26 Court-martial of Samuel Starr, HH 328 NA.
27 Testimony of Samuel Starr, Starr Papers MHS.
28 T. J. Wood to S. H. Starr, 4 April 1854, Starr Papers MHS.
29 T. J. Wood to S. H. Starr, 5 August 1854, Starr Papers MHS.

The Final Retreat.

The last retreat at the Fort of Fort Worth was on December 7, 1853. The sun is low in the southwestern sky, and the soldiers are lowering the flag. The officer of the day is to the left, and the 12-pound mountain howitzer is at the flagpole ready to fire the final salute. (Copyright William Potter.)